COME
TOGETHER
LENNON & McCARTNEY
IN THE SEVENTIES

COME
TOGETHER

LENNON & McCARTNEY
IN THE SEVENTIES

RICHARD WHITE

This edition published by Omnibus Press and distributed in the United States and Canada by The Overlook Press, Peter Mayer Publishers Inc, 141 Wooster Street, New York, NY 10012.

For bulk and special sales requests, please contact sales@overlookny.com or write to us at the above address.

Copyright © 2016 Omnibus Press
(A Division of Music Sales Limited)
14/15 Berners Street,
London, W1T 3LJ, UK.

Cover designed by Fresh Lemon
Picture research by Sarah Datblygu

ISBN 978-1-4683-1384-0

Every effort has been made to trace the copyright holders of the photographs in this book but one or two were unreachable. We would be grateful if the photographers concerned would contact us.

Printed in EU.

A catalogue record for this book is available from the British Library.

Cataloguing-in-Publication data is available from the Library of Congress.

Visit Omnibus Press on the web at www.omnibuspress.com

CONTENTS

ACKNOWLEDGEMENTS

Come Together has been completed following detailed planning, research and writing work during the last three years. After 15 years spent enjoying and studying The Beatles' classic body of work, my book also draws on contemporary sources and new interviews with both musicians and producers.

In December 2011 I met Olivia Harrison, George's widow, who was in Liverpool to promote Martin Scorsese's lauded biopic of her late husband's life, and discussed with her my plans for a Beatles-themed book which subsequently evolved into *Come Together*. Having wished me well with my work, Olivia read an early extract, and offered comments on the interpretation of George's music.

In September 2013 I conducted a lengthy and wide-ranging interview with vastly experienced and well-respected session drummer Jim Keltner, a close friend and long-time studio colleague of Lennon and Harrison who worked with both men on their finest seventies material in London, New York and Los Angeles. Keltner also generously discussed his enduring friendship with Lennon and, in particular, with Harrison, and we co-operated closely on early draft material during four months of subsequent discussions.

Jim and Olivia were also due to discuss my project during their attendance at the Grammy Awards ceremony dinner in Los Angeles in February 2014, where Paul McCartney and Ringo Starr performed after receiving Lifetime Achievement Awards. Keltner also met with John Lennon's former partner, May Pang, in New York shortly before Christmas 2013, where they discussed my project. Pang and her secretary, Pat Jennings, also read early extracts from the book. Pang's relationship with Lennon facilitated a gradual change in his outlook on The Beatles' legacy (and an encouraging *rapprochement* with McCartney) as both men broached thoughts of a musical reconciliation.

Come Together also benefits from the memories of maestro American arranger and producer Allen Toussaint, specifically his work on McCartney's *Venus And Mars* album, and recollections of New Orleans' rich musical heritage. "Paul treated everybody with a wonderful respect," enthused Toussaint from his Deep South office during our mid-summer interview. "It had a lasting effect on everyone here. You couldn't have picked a better subject to write about." Toussaint's sudden passing, in November 2015, came during the final stages of the book's preparation, and the writer is indebted to Allen for his enthusiasm about McCartney's work and his contribution to this project. I have also revisited the period of the *Venus And Mars* recording experience in the Crescent City with studio engineer Alan O'Duffy, veteran musician Tom Scott, private McCartney photographer Sidney Smith and then-fledgling photographer Sylvia de Swaan.

Former *Melody Maker* writer Chris Charlesworth, who during his term as their US Editor based in New York became acquainted with Lennon, has also contributed personal insights and unpublished diary recollections of his social and professional experiences with Lennon during the mid-seventies. Chris was an interviewee for the critically acclaimed *The US v John Lennon* documentary, and the film's co-director, John Scheinfeld, was interviewed for my book in February 2014 about Lennon's music and politics, his love of New York, his American dream and his battle to become a US citizen.

Gary Van Scyoc, Lennon's bassist in his New York band, Elephant's Memory, has discussed his time onstage, in the studio and in the city with Lennon, even performing a few bars of 'Imagine' on Lennon's Wurlitzer piano down the phone line for me from his New Jersey home. I have also explored Lennon's affinity with New York with radio broadcast DJ Dennis Elsas, who interviewed Lennon in September 1974. A huge Beatles fan, Elsas provided recollections of the occasion and his own insights into the man he met shortly before Lennon became an American *Billboard* chart-topper, the celebrated artist that his contemporaries sought to collaborate with in 1974–75.

Elsas appears in the Michael Epstein-directed *LENNONYC* documentary alongside world-renowned rock photographer Bob Gruen, who also appeared as an interviewee in Scheinfeld and David Leaf's documentary film. Gruen has shared memories of his close friendship with John, and of Lennon's musical and cultural experiences of New York City. I have also interviewed *Walls And Bridges* and *Rock 'N' Roll* engineer Greg Calbi about working with John's music during the mid-seventies in New York.

ACKNOWLEDGEMENTS

Musician, engineer and former roadie Ed Freeman, present on The Beatles' controversial 1966 US tour and the rumoured bassist during Lennon and McCartney's Burbank reunion session in 1974, has also shared his thoughts on the group.

The book includes either opinion or interview-based contributions from a number of respected Beatles authors including McCartney biographer Chris Welch, Alan Clayson, Peter Doggett, Keith Badman, Paul Du Noyer and Steve Turner. Lennon's Liverpool art college contemporary, Beatles friend and author Bill Harry has graciously discussed his time with The Beatles during their nascent years in Liverpool and beyond. *That'll Be The Day* screenwriter and Beatles biographer Ray Connolly proved an entertaining and insightful interviewee, full of anecdotes and enthusiasm for the subject. I was also interviewed by BBC Radio Merseyside DJ Spencer Leigh in order to discuss my Beatles book project.

Aside from his earlier contributions, I extend special gratitude to Omnibus editor Chris Charlesworth for his diligent manuscript work, his skill and expertise in toning some of the book's weighty or overly-enthusiastic passages of musical analysis, his knowledgeable suggestions and his prompt, reliable professionalism in bringing the book to fruition during the summer.

Special thanks to Annabelle Curran for her help, encouragement and devotion during the course of writing this book: for her tea-making, her crucial printing assistance, for our journeys to The Beatles' home city and the visits to John and Paul's family homes, for her belief in me . . . and for her love. Without her, this book would not have been possible.

Richard White
September 2015

INTRODUCTION

THE journey begins at Heathrow Airport, where American session drummer Jim Keltner is a recent arrival from the United States. Keltner awaits the appearance of his famous friend, a former Fab and his temporary chauffeur for the day. With the motorway lights stretching out before them into the distance, Keltner's camera begins to roll in order to capture the unfolding journey. "I've got something to play you," George Harrison tells his passenger, a keen Beatles fan.

Travelling in Harrison's Mercedes to his huge Friar Park estate at Henley in Oxfordshire, they listen to a rare set of recordings which would eventually see the light of day in 1994 as The Beatles' *Live At The BBC* collection. What Keltner heard that day *en route* to George's stately spread left him suitably impressed. The drummer learnt that they had recorded live at the BBC with just a few microphones. Despite the limitations of mono recording in the radio studio, where two takes might be edited onto one track or some basic overdubbing may occur, the group often performed directly onto tape or live on air. "The singing was perfect of course," he admitted, "and the tuning was spot-on." "We used the Beeb like a giant loudspeaker," McCartney would later reflect on The Beatles' early spirit and energy coursing across the airwaves. "We were there often, and they would put out our music to all the country, then it would get on the *World Service*, so you knew you were getting round the world with it. So it was a great machine to plug into."

Having transmitted something of the group's nascent *joi de vivre* and the rush of musical energy as it traversed the airwaves, the radio arena had allowed an increasingly comfortable and confident young group to be themselves. "When I listen to the BBC recordings, there's a lot of energy. I think spirit and energy are the main words I'd use to describe them. We are going for it, not holding back at all, trying to put in the best performance of our lifetimes. By the way, of course," McCartney added with no little modesty, "we were brilliant."

1

Thrilled to hear the group's live radio performances through Harrison's enthusiasm for his old group, Keltner was stunned by what he heard. As they drove at some speed back to Harrison's home, Keltner naturally honed in on the rhythmic accompaniment. "The drumming was like that of a black, middle-aged R&B guy," he told me. "I just kept commenting on that. I couldn't get over it."

Ringo Starr, Keltner generously insisted, revolutionised rock drumming. "You may have to be a rock drummer to understand what I'm saying, but Ringo played differently from the norm." And as Keltner's seventies studio colleague, John Lennon was frequently fond of reminding everyone within earshot, Ringo was his favourite drummer too. "He'd say it with a little gleam in his eye. I remember thinking: 'I love it when he says that, because Ringo is my favourite too.' I was always talking about him, and there were times when I would say: 'Well, Ringo would do it like *this*,' and John would say: 'Yeah, but I want you to do it the way *you* want to do it.'"

When the time came to select cover material for their radio recording commitments and their earliest album sessions, The Beatles could draw on a rich source of fifties and early sixties work following their apprenticeships in Liverpool and Hamburg. This included an assortment of cover versions of the likes of Chuck Berry, Ray Charles, Little Richard and Buddy Holly, and contemporary material from the Leiber & Stoller songwriting team. "John used to tell me: 'We didn't just used to *listen*, Jim, we *ate* it up. Every American record that came through the port there in Liverpool.' In many ways, they took the American art form, and did more with it than the Americans," Keltner enthused. "Man, the English have always *loved* the blues."

The Beatles, as *Rolling Stone* critic Jon Landau would insist, weren't intimidated by their idols. "They never interpreted old rock; they simply played it as well and as joyfully as they knew how. The Beatles didn't care whether they got the music right, so long as they got the feeling." Having inspired them as teenagers, Little Richard's 'Lucille', the song on which Lennon took the lead during his fabled spring 1974 'reunion' with McCartney at Los Angeles' Burbank studios, was part of his subsequent revival of the classic American fifties material that resulted in the *Rock 'N' Roll* album of 1975.

"John always used to talk about how hard it had been for Elvis, and how the four of them had each other. I remember George and Ringo talking about being lucky because of that. Only those four guys knew what it was like to be The Beatles. They were the ultimate game changers," Keltner generously insisted, particularly on the other side of the Atlantic. "They were so unusually gifted and brilliant. It's amazing that they had that body of work, and that they lasted as long as they did. They went through this amazing thing together, and they're still bonded."

An intrigued Keltner had often asked both Harrison and Lennon about the strength of the group's fabled rapport. "The bond the group shared was probably stronger than most. They really loved each other, and what I took away was that they were brothers, and they interacted in the same way that brothers do. They had great moments, but then they had moments of real division, the way a family does. In any group of people, it is inevitable. There's no perfect situation. Especially when you have brilliance like they had." "The combination of those four guys was pretty interesting," McCartney asserted, later to describe their combined presence as "four corners of a square. There was something very special about The Beatles."

"We usually hung together somehow," Lennon later explained. "There'd always be someone to lean on when there's four of you. There'd always be someone that would be together enough to pull you through the difficult phases." Starr, meanwhile, insisted that they reined in each others' excesses, providing a counterbalance that ultimately saved them. They may have been four individuals, but as Beatles they were one. "We're all really the same person," McCartney explained in the mid-to-late sixties. "We're just four parts of the one. We're individual, but we make up one person. We all add something different to the whole."

Honesty between each other, and about the music they were producing, was a key facet of their combined presence. Producer George Martin has noted the incredible inspiration and strength they drew from each other's presence. Importantly, there was a mutual and unanimous desire to achieve. "What I think about The Beatles is that if there had been even Paul and John and two other people, we'd never have been The Beatles," Lennon opined. "It had to be that combination of Paul, John, George and Ringo to make The Beatles. There's no such thing as, 'Well, John and Paul wrote all the songs, therefore they contributed more.'"

For Martin, the whole was greater than the sum of the parts. As author Ian MacDonald has noted, The Beatles represented a "quartet of seemingly telepathic minds".

Naturally, it wasn't just a swathe of satisfying musical moments that Keltner enjoyed with Harrison. "It was the other moments and if I think about them, I just laugh out loud," the drummer chuckles. "George was a funny guy, and he had a great way of being sarcastic. And he had a way of saying stuff about one of his brothers with a grin, so you knew it wasn't mean-spirited. But he would do it so often that I would start joining in. And one day I said something similar about one of them, and he said: 'You know, the thing is Jim, *I* can do this, but you can't.' He and John were both like that."

For the drummer, John was a total explorer in the studio, always looking for a new way to make something happen. He was also an influential and amazingly convincing guy. Keltner had been told that, in the early sixties before coming to America, Lennon could be somewhat intimidating. Guys wouldn't want to talk in his presence, for fear of appearing to be not so bright. "John *could* be quite intimidating to people, and you really had to stand up to John and tell him where to get off," Liverpudlian writer and Lennon's art school friend Bill Harry insists. "Then he was okay, and he wouldn't mess with you again, and you could be friends."

During conversation one day with Apple Records PR Tony King, Keltner also learned that Lennon had begun to change when he began his relationship with Yoko Ono. In addition Lennon had grown increasingly attracted to the ideals of the radical underground as the seventies dawned. Having relocated to America, Lennon started Primal Scream therapy in California in 1970. "I was told that he kind of cooled out," Keltner recalls, "and got to be a little nicer."

"I think most analysis is just symptomatic, where you just talk about yourself," Lennon would later confide. "I don't need to do that because I've done a lot of it with reporters. I still think the therapy is great, but I just don't want to make it into a Maharishi thing. If people know what I've been through there, and if they want to find out, they can find out. But then of course I'm not through with it. It's a process that is going on. We primal almost daily and the only difference . . . I don't really want to get this big primal thing going, because it gets so embarrassing. The thing in a nutshell: Primal Therapy allows us to feel feelings continually, that's all. Because before I wasn't feeling things."

The creative result of Lennon's therapy was 1970's seminal and critically acclaimed (if commercially overlooked) *Plastic Ono Band* album, partly

produced in the company of legendary American Wall of Sound helms-
man Phil Spector. "You can hear Spector on the album . . . [but] I did
quite a lot of it before Phil came. But we'd done quite a few tracks
together, Yoko and I, and she'd be encouraging me in the other room and
all that, and . . . at one point in the middle we were just lagging, and Phil
moved in and brought in a new lease of life, because we were getting
heavy and we had done a few things, and the thrill of recording had worn
off a little. You can hear Spector here and there . . . there are no specifics,
you can just hear him."

"I have no real memory of Phil producing this record at all. He came in,
later," Starr has recalled, "but I have no real feeling that: 'Oh, Phil produced this record.' The engineer took down what we did, and John would
mix it." "Let's not take away from what he did do, which was bring a lot
of energy and he taught me a lot and I would use him again," Lennon
would enthuse to *Rolling Stone* editor Jann Wenner. "When I say to Phil,
'I want this,' he gets it for me."

The atmosphere of the album sessions, bassist Klaus Voormann argued,
was of Lennon openly sharing his experiences with the musicians, who felt
these experiences for themselves, and which they subsequently strove to
relate on tape in their own way. "The atmosphere of those people being
together in the studio comes on the record. You can feel it, and there is a
difference."

"The sparseness of the band and the force of John, that's why he is one
of the greats. That's how it is," Starr admits. "It's so incredible, the
emotion on this record is just mind-blowing." "John is so special because
he writes, right away, what he feels. With John, he has to measure up to a
level," Voormann recalled. "With the *Plastic Ono Band*, he knew that this
was not going to be a hit record – 'This is what I wanna do.' It's a milestone people are never gonna forget."

With just Voormann, Starr and Lennon in the studio to perform rhythm
section duties on what became a classic cadre of new material, the bassist
has insisted there was no concern about the quality of the songs being
recorded by a three-piece group. Moreover, it was the power of simplicity
in what the bassist and drummer played that, Starr insists, gave Lennon "an
opportunity to really use his voice and his emotion how he could. He
would just sit there and sing them, and we would sit there and jam, and we
found out how they would go, and it was very loose. And with it being a
trio, it was a lot of fun."

Starr revelled in his role as a timekeeper, insisting that his playing was straight and relatively fill-free, holding down the song to enable Lennon to take it wherever he so wished. "For me, I play drums, and if he wants to search, I'll play with you." Starr was particularly impressed with his own performance on 'I Found Out', raising his game as he introduced more tom-tom work to the track. "I think it's nice. It drives along. I don't know . . . ask Eric Clapton, he thinks I can play," Lennon admitted. "I'm a *cinema verite* guitarist. I'm a musician, and you have to break down your barriers to be able to hear what I'm playing."

Meanwhile, engineer Phil McDonald highlighted Voormann's ingenious bass playing on 'Hold On', which found Lennon offering a note of reassurance through being in the moment. "That's how we're living now, but really living like that and cherishing each day," Lennon later admitted. "I'm really beginning to cherish it when I'm cherishing it. Yeah, just hold on, day to day." "It's very important to him [Lennon] that he puts what he's writing in the song into the way that he's singing it," Voormann would later enthuse, "that's what makes him a good singer, that's the way he has to sing."

Keen to capture and convey feeling above all else in his voice, many of Lennon's vocal tracks were first takes while playing rhythm at the same time on either guitar or piano. John was always keen to communicate everything he wanted to say in his voice, something he achieved with startling conviction. "You can hear on *Plastic Ono Band* the quality of his singing," critic Richard Williams opined. "It's very exposed, and it withstands that exposure."

"It's [my singing] probably better because I had the whole time to myself. I mean, I'm pretty good at home with me tapes. This time it was my album . . . it used to get a bit embarrassing in front of George and Paul because we know each other so well: 'Oh, he's trying to be Elvis, oh he's doing this now.' We were a bit super-critical of each other, so we inhibited each other a lot, so I can perform better; and I relaxed, you know." The songs for the album were written both in England and California, where the Lennons were undergoing Primal Scream therapy. "All these songs just came out of me. I didn't sit down to think: 'I'm going to write about my mother' or I didn't sit down to think: 'I'm going to write about this, that or the other.' They all came out, like all the best work anybody ever does."

Lennon considered 'Mother' to be commercial, at least during its composition, due to its stately and memorable emotion. He had already envisaged the track as the album's opening cut and the lyrics, of course, were unduly unforgiving. "Many would not like 'Mother' because it hurts them," said John. "The first thing that happens to you when you get the album is you can't take it, everybody's reacted exactly the same. They think: 'That's how everybody is.'"

"It was a big thing which John was going through: a hard, heavy time of finding himself," Starr later noted of the primal period, "dispelling his childhood, and putting it into a real space. He was brave, and he always put it out there, and sometimes the consequences were harsh, but he always put it out there, and that's why you can't help but love him."

"I had a few ideas to do this and that with 'Mother', but when you just listen, the piano does it all for you, your mind can do the rest of it," said Lennon. "I think the backings on mine are as complicated as the backings on any record you've ever heard: if you've got an ear, you can hear. Anybody knows, any musicians will tell you, just play a note on the piano, it's got all the harmonics in it. So it got to that. I didn't need anything else."

"I would have to drop in the tape so he could do the screaming on 'Mother'," session tape-op John Leckie recalled. "It's one of the highlights of the record, and no one had ever really sung like this before, especially a Beatle, to let rip like that." By stark contrast, the tender piano ballad 'Love' proffers a beautiful melody and an uplifting, heartfelt and poetic lyric, and as Williams argued, gave great attention to texture and phrasing in a song of heartfelt devotion. "The thing is, 'Love' would attract more people because of the message," said John. "I like the song 'Love', you know, I like the melody, and the words, and everything, I think it's beautiful . . . but I'm more of a rocker." Lennon also considered 'Isolation' as a commercially viable single. "I'm just going to go where my mood takes me," he said, as he prepared himself at the piano before cutting the song.

"John just learnt to play the piano and he picks these three notes — there's a leading note on the left hand," Voormann recalled, "and it's just beautiful the way he does it. And this is the way to write songs — if he can do this, he can do anything." 'Remember', meanwhile, was an eight-minute extended ad lib which, Lennon later joked, morphed into a song that sounded not unlike Frankie Laine.

"I think it's the best thing I've ever done," a satisfied Lennon admitted of his new album in late 1970. "I think it's realistic and it's true to me, and has been developing over the years from 'In My Life', 'Help' and 'Strawberry Fields'. They're all personal records. I always wrote about me when I could. I like first person music. But because of my hang ups, and many other things, I would only now and then specifically write about me. Now I wrote all about me and that's why I like it, it's me. And nobody else."

A Primal Scream therapy-influenced Lennon opened up with remarkable candour about his feelings towards the band, informing Jann Wenner during his legendary *Rolling Stone* magazine interview that not only had McCartney taken over the band and led them round in circles, but he and George and Ringo had effectively become his sidemen. "I can't imagine what George thinks to [*Plastic Ono Band*]. Well, I suppose he thinks I've lost the way or something like that. But to me I'm like home. I'll never change much from this."

"I think we didn't really realise the extent to which John was screwed up," Harrison insisted. "For instance, you wouldn't think he could get bitter, because he was so friendly and loving, but he could also be really nasty and scathing. As a kid, I didn't think, 'Oh well, it's because his dad left home and his mother died,' which probably did leave an incredible scar. It wasn't until he made the album about Janov, primal screaming, that I realised he was even more screwed up than I thought."

However, Harrison later defended Lennon's memorable, yet momentary, denouncement of The Beatles on his *Plastic Ono Band* album track 'God'. As a reactionary comment, Lennon claimed that he didn't believe in the group in terms of what they represented to themselves. Assuming the role of DJ for Los Angeles' KHJ station in September 1974, a snatch of Lennon's '*I don't believe in Beatles*' lyric circulated over the airwaves, prompting him to insist that, yes, he *does* believe in them. A newly matured Lennon insisted he no longer believed "in father figures any more, like God, Kennedy. I'm no longer searching for a guru. I'm no longer searching for anything."

George remained a little aggrieved that Lennon had been denied the right to change his mind on the matter. Characteristically, a refocused, happier John had retracted statements such as these some two years later. Less agreeable to Harrison was Lennon's rejection of mantra meditation and the *Bhagavad Gita* in the same song. 'God' had been constructed from three separate songs, and Lennon had built it around the central pretext of its opening line: that God was a concept by which we measured our own pain.

The song, in Janov's estimation, demonstrated that Lennon could simplify a profound philosophical concept and make it easy for his audience to grasp. Billy Preston contributed stately gospel accompaniment on Steinway piano to this incredible track, having been invited to bring his church roots to the song. "So when you have a word like that [God], you just sit down and sing the first tune that comes into your head and the tune is simple, 'cos I like that kind of music and then I just rolled into it. And it was just going on in my head, and *I Ching* and Bible and the first three or four [lyrics] just came out, whatever came out, you know. I don't know when I realised I was putting down all these things I didn't believe in, I could have gone on. I thought: 'Where do I end?' and 'Who have I missed out?' It got like that, you know, and I thought I had to stop."

Lennon would later enthuse over 'God' and 'Working Class Hero' as the album's other key enduring moment. "You see I don't believe in Dylan. Zimmerman is his name. Anybody that sings with a guitar and sings about something heavy would tend to sound like Dylan. I'm bound to be influenced by those because that is the only kind of real folk music I ever listen to. So in that way I've been influenced, but ['Working Class Hero'] doesn't sound like Dylan to me," he informed Wenner. 'Look At Me', meanwhile, was a previously unfinished Beatles-sounding acoustic piece penned circa *The White Album* and which received steady airplay on the album's release.

And while The Beatles' eponymous double album had been full of Lennon's post-LSD-influenced lyrical surrealism and humour, this new work contained no allusive imagery. "But the poetry on this album is superior to anything I've done because it's not self-conscious in that way. I had least trouble writing the songs of all time. I always liked simple rock and nothing else. I was influenced by acid and got psychedelic, like the whole generation, but really, I liked rock'n'roll. And I express myself best in rock."

Meanwhile, the diminutive Phil Spector duly returned to England to take the helm for Lennon's subsequent album, *Imagine*. "Lennon might be a trailblazer in all kinds of ways, but he was at heart a populist – an artist but also an entertainer," wrote Paul Du Noyer. "The task was to frame his ideas in music that listeners loved and took inside their hearts."

Keltner had initially been invited by Spector to participate in the sessions while staying with Eric Clapton. American sax player Bobby Keys was on board too. "We [Keltner and Clapton] had been driving into

Olympic [Studios, Barnes] every day to meet Stevie Winwood. We were in writing mode. Unfortunately, my main thrust at the time was staying in an altered state. And I later never forgave myself for that."

The phone rang one morning at Eric Clapton's house at Ewhurst in Surrey. Keltner picked up the receiver in an otherwise empty house. "I answered the phone and it was Phil Spector, and he wanted to speak to Eric, and I said: 'I can't wake him up 'cos he's asleep.' He said: 'Well, I want him to come and play on John's record.' I said: 'Well, I'll take the message.' And he said: 'How about you? Would you like to come and play on the record?' So I said: 'I think I'd like to do that, yeah.'"

Keltner had met Yoko before he'd met John, having been called to Lennon's Tittenhurst estate in Ascot to participate in Ono's *Fly* album. Driven to Ascot by musician friend Colin Allen, Keltner's first recording experience with Lennon was incredible. "John was really funny, and he was very much in command. We set up the drums, and the first thing I remember was hearing this song with John singing in my headphones, and looking at him across the room. It was awesome. When you're hearing a great and distinctive voice singing these wonderfully evocative lyrics and playing so strong and confidently, you could think that you wouldn't necessarily even *need* drums."

Hearing Lennon's voice proved powerful and calming. Keltner knew that when he participated, it would all come together. A beautiful song which later boasted lush strings and florid Nicky Hopkins piano, the experience of working on 'Jealous Guy', the initial choice as the album's lead single, left an indelible impression on Keltner. "It was a dreamlike state that I was in. Every time I hear it, I always tend to well up."

A candid and apologetic self-portrait of Lennon's emotional foibles and possessiveness, 'Jealous Guy' is lifted by the song's sweet, persuasive melody. "If John felt that his last album – forbiddingly stark to some ears – had not found the mass audience its songs deserved," writer Paul Du Noyer commented in his album liner notes, "he was not about to make the same mistake with *Imagine*. 'Jealous Guy', in its finished form, was a key song of John's maturing outlook, expressing his rejection of the macho values he had grown up with."

As a touching confessional, *Rolling Stone* noted 'Jealous Guy''s brilliantly tortured vocal and the eloquent string arrangement. "John was singing the song," bassist Klaus Voormann recalled, "right there in front of you. You're closing your eyes, and you just play, and I'd feel everything, and

I'd see John sitting there, and I didn't even know what key it was in. I'd just play, and it goes by itself. It's like a dream. It's like meditation. He gave me those moments, and that's what I'm going to take with me."

Meanwhile, Voormann's first experience of playing with his drummer friend on this *Imagine* track remains an equally memorable one. "People like Jim Keltner, they *listen*. There's no, 'Oh, what do you want me to play?'" From there, each time the two men played together, it would prove a magical experience. "Klaus has played on some really big records because his feel is so great," Keltner reciprocates. "And he is just *so* musical."

While Voormann would note the early drum-free appeal of 'Imagine' while listening to a playback in the control room, drummer Alan White's contributions to the anthemic title track were taped just a day or two prior to the recording of 'Jealous Guy'. Documentary film of the in-development song shows Lennon and Hopkins playing side by side on a white grand piano. The song, as critic Paul Du Noyer maintains, soon became a standard, and one of which Lennon would remain proud. "'Imagine' was a sincere statement. It was 'Working Class Hero' with chocolate on. I was trying to think of it in terms of children."

"It's such a classic. I still love looking at footage of him singing it," McCartney later admitted when he was asked about the song. "It's an anthem everyone can relate to, and it's got to be one of John's best songs." A little ungraciously, Lennon would fire back with unnecessary vitriol soon after its release: "So you think 'Imagine' ain't political? It's 'Working Class Hero' with sugar on for conservatives like yourself."

"'Imagine'," *Rolling Stone* reviewer Ben Gerson insisted, "is simply the consolidation of primal awareness into a world movement. It asks that we imagine a world without religions or nations, and that such a world would mean brotherhood and peace." A positive, collective visualisation of a better future was, one critic argued, a key facet of the song's spiritual appeal. Moreover, the solemn-sounding introduction was composed on piano, hence its church-like, hymnal tones. Critic Chris Ingham rightly stated that the classic piano motif running through this utopian peace tract "hints at how close we are to realising the possibilities of Lennon's dreaming, if only we would imagine with him."

"John, early on, shaped my thinking about a lot of stuff," claims Keltner. "I believe and think certain things that I would never have thought without John, a great powerful force of a guy. The way that I think about a lot of ordinary things in life are because of John. He was hugely influential."

The session would prove a memorable occasion for Keltner. Having arrived in heavy fog (much like the mist shrouding Lennon in the 'Imagine' video) he pulled up in his friend Colin Allen's Mini Cooper. Keltner anticipated an amazing day, hoping to produce the goods for the benefit of Lennon's new set of songs. Asked to play on 'Jealous Guy', it was a surreal experience to be using a borrowed set of drums in a small bedroom of Lennon's Ascot mansion.

Keltner recalls that drummer Alan White had just recorded instrumental vibes in the same room for what became the stately title track. Keltner also has a strong recollection of working on the album's heaviest, most search-ing cut, the fevered pacifist rant of 'I Don't Wanna Be A Soldier (Mama)'. Keltner had heard Lennon and Spector's comments on the song whilst he sat in the control room. "John had recorded it earlier, and Jimmy [Gordon, drummer] was out there working hard to get it right. I could see that they wanted a quirkier approach which I was able to pull off. John really liked it, and I knew *why* he liked it. It forged a bond right there."

While one reviewer compared the song's melodic barrage to The Kinks' 'You Really Got Me', Lennon liked the song's long, loose two-chord feel and its peculiar rhythm. Free of musical constraint, he would also compliment both Keltner and Voormann's work in keeping pace with him as he adjusted lyrics and sang simultaneously in different keys. For Keltner, the session was brief yet intense, and he would later recount some of this experience to *Rolling Stone*. Having started work on the album, John would often be found messing with the faders on the recording console. "He was always looking for happy accidents with the sound," Keltner recalled. Where 'It's So Hard' was concerned, it was unclear if the track had been recorded before or after John's Primal Therapy experience. The song seemed to represent, in the eyes of critic Paul Du Noyer, "more of a boastful swagger than a self-pitying whinge," despite being "magically uplifted by Spector's added strings."

This eight-bar blues shuffle offered basic yet effective rhythm guitar, courtesy of Lennon and some rousing sax work from the legendary King Curtis. As *Imagine* photographer Kieron Murphy recalls, Lennon was exu-berant about his presence on the record. "He was really proud. It was: 'We managed to get King Curtis!'" Curtis recorded his contributions for 'It's So Hard' and 'I Don't Wanna Be A Soldier' in less than an hour.

Recording for *Imagine* was completed in early July 1971, with the addition of saxophone and string overdubs in New York City's Record Plant East studio.

Having recorded the album during early summer at Lennon's Ascot studio, the tapes travelled to New York for overdub work at the Record Plant, Lennon's first recording experience in the States. "I remember when we were recording all of the violins for the *Imagine* album," engineer Roy Cicala recalls. "[Phil]'d want to stop the tape and stop the musicians to make a change, even though he didn't even know what the change should be." The strings were performed by members of the New York Philharmonic Orchestra, whom Lennon dubbed The Flux Fiddlers. Lush arrangements for 'Imagine', 'Jealous Guy', 'It's So Hard', 'How Do You Sleep?' and 'How?' were scored by veteran Broadway arranger Torrie Zito.

Keltner is also quick to commend the maestro session pianist Nicky Hopkins for his contributions to the album. "He was one of the greatest musicians I ever met in my life. He could get a sound out of the piano that was like no one else," the drummer graciously insists. "I played keyboards throughout much of *Imagine*, but on the title track I only played a bit of electric piano," Hopkins later recalled, "which sounded like a synthesiser and wasn't prominent."

In footage later screened in the *Gimme Some Truth* documentary, the musicians in the studio discuss the most suitable piano treatment for the track. Lennon teaches a suitably impressed Hopkins the piano-based ballad before Voormann suggests running a microphone through to the main room to allow Lennon to play the iconic white grand piano. According to an enthusiastic Hopkins, John was adamant about playing it himself, despite Yoko's suggestion that Hopkins should play piano instead. The album, Nicky would later recall, was recorded in about nine days. "John had a real high energy level, and he liked to get things done fast."

Having conceived of the song's initial melody late in 1970, and finished it quickly with Ono's assistance late one night, the delicate 'Oh My Love' was a joy for Lennon to sing and record. His senses awoken to true love for the first time, John's oriental-sounding note in the song's '*heart*' refrain had been tried out on organ the night before the cameras captured Harrison rehearsing this "post-primal testimonial", as *Rolling Stone*'s Ben Gerson described it in his thoughtful review. During a second run-through of this tender song in front of the documentary cameras,

Lennon discusses George's electric guitar playing during their rehearsal of this paean to loving self-awareness. The soft, lilting song is then interrupted by the engineer switching reels. "A brief, gentle song of awakening tenderness," as Du Noyer wrote of a song that sat between two of the album's more unsettling moments.

With Harrison standing intently at his shoulder, viewers then witnessed Lennon's gleeful expression during a rough piano run-through of the chiding 'How Do You Sleep?'. George later proffered some sterling slide licks which John considered amongst his former partner's finest playing. Surrounded by a group of assembled musicians that included a relaxed Voormann and studious Hopkins, the song's malicious swing was slowly honed as the song came together in one of Lennon's more considered production efforts.

Commencing work on 'How Do You Sleep?' as early as 1969 according to its creator, Lennon would always maintain this 'angry letter' song was as much an assault on himself as his former songwriting partner. He'd also lament the critics and record-buying public's lack of humour. "Every element," noted critic Chris Ingham, "serves as vivid, compelling expression of Lennon's disenchantment with his former partner and friend."

Meanwhile *Rolling Stone* found Lennon's "character assassination" of McCartney "horrifying and indefensible, [but which] nevertheless has an immediacy which makes it more compelling than most of the rest of the album. When they were both Beatles, their rivalry was channelled towards the betterment of The Beatles as a totality." With the song's heavy rhythm softened by the track's arid orchestral work, the "Eastern-sounding" strings, Lennon pointed out, were the result of violins playing guitar parts. Although Lennon was unhappy with his vocal performance, his rhythm work compensated for this in a strong live production. "There is something almost endearing in the way that the *Imagine* album can range from the highest aspirations of global consciousness-raising," wrote Du Noyer, "to the tiny-minded bickering of the school playground."

"I think it's silly," McCartney later responded. "So what if I live with straights? I like straights. It doesn't affect him. He says the only thing I did was 'Yesterday'. He knows that's wrong. He knows and I know that's not true." Much to Lennon's probable competitive envy, 'Yesterday' was a song that had famously arrived, almost fully formed, in an inspired early morning, dreamlike state. "I liked the melody a lot, but because I'd dreamed it, I couldn't believe I'd written it. I thought, 'No, I've never

14

written like this before.' But I had the tune, which was the most magic thing. And you have to ask yourself, 'Where did it come from?' But you don't ask yourself too much or it might go away. For something that just emerged in a dream, even I have to acknowledge that it was a phenomenal stroke of luck."

Lennon later revealed that the album boasted three recently-written songs including 'Crippled Inside' and the plaintive, sweeping plea of 'How?' Lennon is seen self-consciously reciting the former song's humorous lyrics, later wedded to a Nashville-driven rhythm, for the cameras while entertaining guests at his Tittenhurst mansion.

According to Lennon, 'How?' was Harrison's favourite song, with the guitarist particularly drawn to the track's soothing and serene strings. With verses penned the previous year, the song's middle eight, a real 'moment' for Lennon due to the newness of its creation, was written during the recording session. Lennon believed that his vocal, set against an appealing melody, had let the song down. As film footage ably demonstrates, this wasn't the case. Apart from its ornate orchestration, Du Noyer surmised that the track "would sit logically inside the previous album, given the themes of fear of the future and emotional incapacity." Another critic noted its resemblance to the suspended chords found in McCartney's 'The Long And Winding Road'.

The remainder of the existing material was polished off during the recording sessions in Lennon's home studio. One of these songs, 'Gimme Some Truth', was an old *Get Back*-era number whose lyrics were refined later in the recording process. Lennon even claimed that McCartney had made a lyrical contribution to the song's middle eight. Meanwhile, Harrison contributed a commendably seething solo to the track. "He's not too proud of it," Lennon insisted in the wake of the album's release, "but I like it."

In the footage Spector looks on from the control room at Lennon who, after a jokey Eddie Cochran imitation, screams his way through the song's often vitriolic yet rhythmic attack with articulate disgust. "I like the overall sound on this track, though I'm not sure I'd go out and buy it," he later mused. Offering up a series of stinging denunciations, Lennon later played 'Gimme Some Truth' and 'Imagine' at Tittenhurst to gauge journalist Ray Connolly's opinion. Should he go with his angered diatribe against conservative society or opt instead for what became a global anthem and commercial milestone? "I said: 'Gimme Some Truth' is okay, and yeah, I like it," Connolly recalls, "but surely 'Imagine' is the single, isn't it?!' John turned to Yoko, and said, 'see, Ray likes 'Imagine' . . ."

"An accomplished mid-paced *tour de force* in the main, 'Imagine' veered off at an acute angle when John's anti-authoritarian streak flared up," wrote critic Paul Moody. Meanwhile, Paul Du Noyer argued the song "looks out with an idealist's impatience to the political world". Voormann believed this sense of restlessness meant the song did not receive due care and attention. "John was always impatient, very impatient. He always needed quick answers. John just wanted to get out of the studio, that's the main reason. He wanted to get the songs out as quick as possible, and get them out of his system."

"Whatever John did was simple, which I think was part of his genius," Keltner claims. Lennon's musical instinct for what worked in the studio also impressed the drummer. "John worked very quickly," Jim continues, "but he was impatient in the right way. And he could *feel* when something was about to happen. When you're making records with people, a real trust factor is involved." Lennon later reasoned that *Imagine*'s commercial success had given him the artistic leeway to produce something more musically challenging. *Rolling Stone*, meanwhile, believed Lennon now faced the most extraordinary challenge of his career. "But then, great artists, of whom John is one," Gerson enthused, "are nothing if not resourceful."

Lennon's growing radical focus had emerged during the making of *Imagine*, with songs like 'I Don't Wanna Be A Soldier (Mama)' and 'Gimme Some Truth' grounding the album's often airy tranquillity. While fraternising with left-wingers Tariq Ali and Robin Blackburn, Lennon discussed the making of his new album and briefly previewed one of his latest compositions. "While the radicals could clearly see the potential of having a world-renowned ex-Beatle in their corner," wrote Paul Moody, "Lennon benefitted too, pouring his newly-found leftist enthusiasms into his music with the relentless zeal of Dylan and Phil Ochs."

Ali would later find it laughable that America, as the world's most powerful nation, could feel so intimidated, even threatened, by Lennon's populist influence as a Beatle. *The US v John Lennon* documentary producer David Leaf believed a courageous Lennon scored a memorable victory in fearlessly speaking truth to the highest powers in America. Lennon was a man keen on individual empowerment in order to make a difference to the world. Lennon fought to do what he believed was right, as a musician, an artist and anti-war activist.

Having sincerely promoted pacifism ('Give Peace A Chance'), encouraged communal hope and unity ('Imagine') and opposed violent conflict 'Happy Xmas (War Is Over)', his songs would gain greater significance in the political landscape of the United States. Leaf claims that Lennon's 'American adventure story' illustrates a world-famous musical figure's attempts to utilise his celebrity to launch a campaign for world peace. The early part of the film concerns Lennon's anti-war sentiments during the sixties; the 'All You Need Is Love' global broadcast; the social backlash following his controversial 'bigger than Jesus' comments; and his peace protest efforts upon the release of the anti-war movement anthem, 'Give Peace A Chance'.

"The peace idea and thought was planted in people's minds," claims Lennon photographer and friend Bob Gruen. "Every newspaper would have the word peace on the front page. John wanted to use humour to capture people's attention to promote peace."

The Lennons had cleverly utilised the attention of an obsessive media to promote their peace campaign. Lennon never lost hope of the dream that the people of the world could live together in peace. He also believed there was still time for peace to transpire in our lifetime. Holding onto hope and praying for it to come to fruition, Lennon became a vociferous, evangelical spokesman for the peace cause.

With pride in his work, Lennon derived a great sense of emotional satisfaction from hearing the capital's masses perform a mantra-like recitation of 'Give Peace A Chance'. The idea of peace had always been with The Beatles, with a sense of appeasement in the name of love being apparent in their early songs. Lennon's desire for world peace would be an outward manifestation of the meditation-based search for inner peace propounded by Harrison. McCartney, meanwhile, later took great pleasure in the fact that the majority of The Beatles' songs dealt with peace, love and understanding, totems of optimism, self-empowerment and hope.

Upon the release of 'Happy Xmas (War Is Over)', Lennon marked the occasion with a worldwide billboard advertising campaign to promote his peaceful sentiment. The anti-war message was also marked by the growing need for heightened political awareness. It was something that, he insisted, had become unavoidable. Following the release of rebel-rousing single 'Power To The People' and having relocated to America, Lennon's cultural cache had been targeted to help mobilise popular activism during anti-Nixon crusades ahead of the 1972 presidential elections. Lennon's musical presence was envisaged by Abbie Hoffman and Jerry Rubin on a 'political Woodstock' campaign tour that summer.

During a radical and unforgettable era, Lennon and Ono flew to New York on August 31, 1971 and – although it probably wasn't his intention at the time – never returned to the UK. He could scarcely have entered America at a more tumultuous and difficult time. "There's no question that the America to which John and Yoko came in the early seventies was a turbulent and divisive place," John Scheinfeld asserts, co-director of the acclaimed *The US v John Lennon* documentary on the political upheavals of Lennon's American life against a backdrop of Government agency intimidation. The film is a thrilling, myth-dispelling journey and addresses pertinent reasons for the US government's targeting of Lennon, and why he was perceived as such a threat. The film also explores the turbulence characterising the social, political and cultural landscape of Vietnam War-era America.

Yoko Ono was later quoted in complimentary form on the project. "Of all the documentaries that have been made about John, this is the one he would have loved because it speaks the truth." But what is the most important truth about this film of John through the seventies? "As some historians have observed, America was at war with itself – the older generation versus the young, women versus men, liberal versus conservative, black versus white," Scheinfeld emphasises. "All of this and more was fodder for John's songwriting and album-making."

PART 1

NEW YORK & LONDON

CHAPTER ONE

Que Pasa, New York!

JOHN Lennon must have felt some kind of pressure in following *Imagine*, a classic album that was still doing good business on both sides of the Atlantic. His subsequent work, *Some Time In New York City*, was an immediate, newspaper-style statement on American society in 1972. "They were living in [Greenwich] Village then, and their apartment had two rooms; a front room for secretaries and a bedroom," Keltner told *Rolling Stone* after the album's creation. "They had a huge bed, and that's where they did everything. They lived the same way they worked – very simply – and I was always impressed by that."

"John really liked his TV," Gruen recalls. "He had it on all the time. John and Yoko would meet people on the bed, take interviews on the bed. And I asked him one time: 'Why do you do that? We can't talk while you have the TV on.' He said: 'Well, you can talk if the window is open, right? Well, that's my window to the world.' And that's the way he felt about it."

Handed to him by political activist Jerry Rubin in late 1971, Lennon heard a tape of politicised hard rock band Elephant's Memory. The group were, for their pianist Adam Ippolito, a radical New York protest band playing energetic new wave rock at local demonstrations, rallies or benefits on a regular basis. "We heard he was in New York through Jerry," the group's bassist Gary Van Scyoc recalled. "We heard that Jerry had been hanging out with John. They'd had a couple of meetings. We thought: 'Hmm, how do we get a tape to this guy?' We gave a performance on Radio WLIR in Long Island one day and that live performance, that's the tape that made it to John."

Van Scyoc believes their combined energies produced complementary ingredients similar to those of the Plastic Ono Band. "He [John] just loved it. He freaked out, and thought the band had a lot of soul. John knew we were studio musicians, and we had what he was looking for: a band that was equipped to back up the studio players he had been using." Seemingly well-suited to following in Eric Clapton's footsteps, 21-year-old Wayne 'Tex' Gabriel was a tremendously capable and prominent Les Paul guitar player from Detroit. "Having a strong guitar player [like Lennon] added to Tex was like adding another strong piece to the puzzle. It was awesome."

Van Scyoc's big fat bass sound ably replicated that of Voormann, while the powerful vintage sax work of Stan Bronstein marked him as a more than able successor to Bobby Keys. "Stan was a little older than anyone else. His inspiration came from Arthur Prysoc, the older bop kind of stuff," Van Scyoc insists. "Stan wore a Zoot suit tailor-made for him. He was in his glory wearing that onstage [at Madison Square Garden in 1972]. That was him in a nutshell right there."

Van Scyoc also believes that Lennon had tired of trying to reconvene the Plastic Ono Band, and was hungry to play. Lennon soon realised the group were rehearsing just a block from his apartment on Broom Street, and one night he decided to pay them a visit, totally uninvited. He was eager to meet them, but was told they weren't keen on being interrupted, and could appear intimidating with their buck knives and leather jackets. The group kept Lennon waiting in the studio vestibule for an hour-and-a-half, refusing to believe a Beatle had arrived to see them at their modest Magne Graphics rehearsal space. "We had a road manager with a sense of humour, and he kept telling us he was out there and really wanted to meet us," Van Scyoc insists. "He finally came in, and my jaw just *dropped*. He was wearing a white suit – whether it was *the* white suit he had on the *Abbey Road* cover, I don't know, but it looked like it to me. And my knees buckled. You can imagine how exciting it was for us."

Ippolito, meanwhile, recalls being introduced to Lennon by Rubin. A fervent Stones and Animals fan, he eventually grew to love The Beatles. He also recalls drummer Rick Frank phoning from the Hit Factory to announce he was with Rubin and Lennon. With the band impatiently waiting to rehearse in the Village, no one would believe Frank. Lennon was clearly voracious about playing live, running through every rock'n'roll song in his extensive repertoire. Eight hours later, Elephant's Memory were exhausted but satisfied, unable to play any further due to sore hands and endless laughter. Ippolito was amazed to feel the power (and hear the sound) of John's edgy, unique rock'n'roll voice.

Van Scyoc still smiles when he recalls that first, all-night rehearsal room jam session. "It was just so magical that night. We ran through all those rock'n'roll songs. 'Dizzy Miss Lizzy' was the first song we played. 'Roll Over Beethoven', a lot of Chuck Berry songs. And he was a Bo Diddley fan. That's when I realised how strong a guitar player he was. He had a Latin *clave* kind of thing. I thought, 'Wow. This guy can *play*.' He was wailing live, and so strong. We were all so impressed. He was like a rock. His sense of time. You might think that he hadn't done a lot of touring, and hadn't got his chops strong. That he might have laid off too long and he might be weak? He was *so* solid, and had a sense of time that never wavered. We didn't really chat a lot; we kind of dove into it. It couldn't have taken more than two or three songs before we all started looking at each other and saying: 'Oh my God, this guy can *play*.' It was so impressive."

According to Van Scyoc, no pressure about following the commercial and critical acclaim for *Imagine* was articulated as sessions got underway at New York's Record Plant studios in March. "It was just like that had never really happened. We didn't really get to thinking about *Imagine* until we thought: 'This guy has written a hit record, and we're going to be on the *Mike Douglas Show* to promote it with him.' That's when it hit us, that John was promoting a hit song, and we'd better be serious about being good."

"We could have sat on *Imagine* for a year-and-a-half, but the things were coming out of our minds," Lennon later reasoned, "and we just wanted to share our thoughts with anybody who wanted to listen."

It was widely believed that Lennon's relationship with McCartney was at its lowest point at this time, but Van Scyoc saw ample evidence that this simply wasn't the case. "You would read in the *New York Post* that they were at each other's throats. I had a copy of the paper in my kit bag, and as I walk into the session, John is on the phone with Paul in Scotland for an hour-and-a-half and they're yakking it up. That doesn't really sound like two people who are at each other's throats, does it?"

Back in December 1970, despite being at the height of the fractious tensions with the rest of the group just prior to taking legal action to dissolve The Beatles, McCartney admitted to the press that he still loved his former bandmates. He believed them to be "the most honest, sincere men I have ever met. I don't mind being bound to them as a friend. I don't mind being bound to them musically, because I like the others as musical partners," he enthused, "but we must change the business arrangements we have."

Lennon, Harrison and Starr were opposed to McCartney's suggestion that they become managed by New York lawyer John Eastmann, his father-in-law, siding instead with Allen Klein, whom they had appointed as their manager in 1969. Paul's response was seen as an act of pique over minor tensions caused by the release date of The Beatles' *Let It Be* album, which threatened to delay the release of his debut eponymous solo album. McCartney had, in effect, been forced to sue his friends in order to win his creative freedom as an artist and, more importantly, to rescue the accumulated Beatles fortunes from Klein, who had managed to secure a large advance for the group's new contract. It was a horrific experience for McCartney to endure and a shock to the system for his bandmates, but Paul won the case in March 1971. It would be some time before they thanked him for what he was forced to do.

With Apple affairs continuing to dominate their dealings as 1971 turned into 1972, McCartney and Lennon conversed regularly down a transatlantic line from the Record Plant to Paul's remote Scottish hideaway during the fortnight-long *Some Time . . .* sessions. "I think it was mostly Apple talk, you know? They would be talking, and I wasn't in on the conversation," Van Scyoc admits, "but right at the initial part of the call, there'd be some business for like, ten minutes. And then it was family stuff."

However, there *were* instances of less amicable discussions, as Lennon's biographer Philip Norman later recounted. "When Paul was in New York, he would usually telephone John, sometimes to be greeted in friendly though distant fashion, other times by: 'Yeah, what do you want, man?' in an accent sounding more and more American." In early 1972 McCartney had even visited Lennon's two-room apartment at 105 Bank Street to discuss their frayed friendship. According to Philip Norman, a brief guarded chat ensued, with both parties agreeing "not to dump on each other anymore, either in song or through the media. But that slight thaw did not develop."

The ongoing matter of a semi-fractious musical dialogue wasn't pleasant listening for millions of adoring Beatles fans. The front cover of McCartney's *Ram*, written and recorded in the summer and autumn of 1970, featured a rugged-looking McCartney holding a sheep, and was notoriously lampooned by Lennon on the reverse of his *Imagine* sleeve. "John held a pig instead of the ram," said Paul. "Me and Linda decided to catalogue all our sheep, so there's a photograph of me holding every sheep in the flock; over 100 of them. I was supposed to be cropped out."

Not only was Lennon mocking his former bandmate on his *Imagine* album sleeve, but he also aimed some insinuated lyrical jibes at the clean-cut, conservative McCartney image on 'Crippled Inside'. Meanwhile, Lennon would taunt McCartney for taking his critiques on 'How Do You Sleep?' too personally and too seriously. In the song, he had intimated that, as part of this McCartney character assassination, he hadn't grasped the full force of *Sergeant Pepper*. Perhaps his producer, Phil Spector, had partly encouraged Lennon's semi-vitriolic attitude by goading him about the supposed mediocre quality of McCartney's *Ram* album.

However, Lennon seemed more depressed than satisfied as the impressive and accomplished *Imagine* assumed commercial pole position while McCartney appeared to flounder, despite his ambition to make a more professional sophomore album in the States.

With a succinct title that also reflected McCartney's urge to forge ahead with strong resolve, *Ram* contained 'Too Many People', a clear message to Lennon "across the airwaves", as Paul would later remember. "As it was, the whole thing just escalated nastily. I'd taken a few mild digs at John in some of my early solo songs like 'Too Many People'. I was trying to tell John something with that. I wasn't really addressing the world. We were digging at each other in the press. I did feel like he was preaching a little bit, about what everyone should do, how they should live their lives. I felt that some of it was a bit hypocritical. I remember there was one little reference to John in the whole thing. He'd been doing a lot of preaching, and it got up my nose a little bit. I wrote: '*Too many people preaching practices*' I think is the line. I mean, that was a little dig at John and Yoko. There wasn't anything else on it that was about them."

"And there were all the bits at the beginning of *Ram* like: '*Too many people going underground.*' Well that was us, Yoko and me," Lennon argued. "And '*You took your lucky break,*' that was considering we had a lucky break to be with him." Lennon's assistant Dan Richter later recalled: "I said, 'You guys have had your divorce, you did so much stuff together . . . you should be talking.' But John still felt that Paul's attitude to Yoko created an unbridgeable gulf and that, anyway, Lennon and McCartney had both been changed too much by their respective spouses ever to find common ground again. John used to say: 'Paul will always be a performer. I've been a rock'n'roll star. I've done it. I want to move on.'"

The following year's *Wild Life* album would include the dramatic and haunting stand-out track 'Dear Friend', a private and thoughtful 'letter' song that saw McCartney extending the hand of comradeship in a song which "was very much 'let's be friends' to John. 'Let's have a glass of wine and forget about it.' A making-up song." The album represented a fresh start for McCartney and the newly assembled group Wings who began recording in London on leftover material from the Los Angeles sessions for *Ram*.

Wild Life took its name from what McCartney biographer Howard Sounes describes as an "inchoate title track about animal welfare", and featured songs that may not have passed the quality control test on previous recorded outings. This time, McCartney had no producer who might have reined in his excesses. However, five of the eight tracks were apparently first takes, including the *laissez-faire* studio jam 'Mumbo', the minimalist ditty 'Bip Bop' and the album's other stand out track, 'Tomorrow'.

While new guitarist Denny Laine had envisaged something of a rough, blues rock sound for McCartney's new group, Seiwell recognised the problems that the newly-christened Wings would face in musical comparisons to McCartney's famous former group. "Whatever we did as a band was going to be compared to the last thing they heard from The Beatles, so what we were trying to do was give an honest representation of this new band, and we didn't want to use every studio trick in the world . . . it's gonna be a little raggedy, but that is what we are. The record was done in a heartbeat."

Any discussions of McCartney's former group were also off the agenda too, it seemed, unless it was with regard to Apple business matters. "I just want the four of us to get together somewhere and sign a piece of paper saying that we want to divide the money four ways," Paul argued, while Lennon had apparently wanted McCartney to sell his share of the Maclen company to the rest of the group. "John had already commented publicly on the physical similarities between Wings and his own Plastic Ono Band convolutions," mused critic Dave Thompson. "Was it so bizarre that musically both should follow a similar course? Paul opted for a roughshod acoustic ambience, John took the same course electrically."

Meanwhile, with no little trepidation, Linda had tentatively agreed to be part of her husband's new post-Beatles musical enterprise when they eventually took the stage. Later guitar recruit Henry McCullough would suggest hiring a session keyboardist to compensate for Linda's musical shortcomings. Taking their time to bring the album to fruition in the studio, Paul encouraged his wife to relax before performing the daunting task of recording her vocals. Paul was also impressed by the tone of her voice, and would relish the challenge of singing with a female counterpart for the first time. It was comforting for Paul to have Linda, his wife and best friend, at his side on this transitional album. "When we were doing *Ram*," Linda later recalled, "the headlines were: 'Who does Linda McCartney think she is?'"

"As she went on, she learned a lot, and became an integral part of the band," Paul admits. "God, I tell you, I worked her on the album. Because she hadn't done a lot, so it was a little bit out of tune. She understood that it had to be good and I gave her a hard time, I must say, but we were pleased with the results. It just meant we really forced it. [We] worked on all the harmonies even if they were hard harmonies – just stuck on it."

On his farm in Scotland, a place they both loved, McCartney began to compose ideas for new material during what he recalled was a golden summer, a world away from the feelings of the previous year. "Just to keep myself amused, I'd sit around making stuff up on the guitar. So we thought: 'Maybe that's the way to go. See what forms out of the bare elements. Rather than think we've got to have super musicians, let's just find ourselves.' Linda was there while I'd be writing things, so if I got stuck I'd ask her for suggestions," Paul would later recall. "We ended up co-writing them. We didn't write them bit for bit; she wasn't a writer like John. It wasn't that kind of collaboration. It was good to have a sounding board. We enjoyed writing those things together."

Having travelled to Linda's home town of New York, they found a warehouse space in which to search for a different slant on the record. Asking a number of prominent drummers to audition for Paul's new band, McCartney duly recruited session man Denny Seiwell, beginning the album with him as the need for musical professionalism inevitably arose. "A lot of the boys were really put out at being asked to audition. Paul just asked me to play, he didn't have a guitar, so I just sat and played. He had a certain look in his eyes . . . he was looking for more than a drummer. He was looking for a certain attitude too. I just played . . . I always say that if you can't get it on by yourself, you can't get it on with anyone."

McCartney also drafted in guitarist Hugh McCracken, who in 1980 would appear on Lennon's *Double Fantasy,* to play on a few of the album tracks. (Lennon would joke with McCracken that his duties on *Ram* had been a mere rehearsal for his work on Lennon's comeback album.) "He [Hugh] came to Scotland to rehearse, but he was such a New York guy that he didn't really like to be away from America, and I can see that," McCartney admitted later. "New York is such a satisfying town, you can walk one block and get anything."

Studio whiz kid David Spinoza was also hired to add his finesse to the *Ram* sessions. Working at CBS studios in Manhattan, Paul, Linda, drummer Seiwell and accomplished session guitarists Spinoza and McCracken made varied contributions. By November, they had produced the bulk of the new album, in co-operation with producer Jim Guercio. A pressurised Guercio, however, felt that McCartney had no need of his services, and was an artist whose ideas required support rather than collaboration.

The producer eventually left the sessions, handing care to studio engineers of around 20 songs, some of which dealt with McCartney's feeling about the group. "I really think that *Ram* was all the angst coming out. A lot of these tunes were written at the end of The Beatles period, and there was a lot of emotion in all the writing," Seiwell claimed, "and the preparation for the tunes." McCartney also recorded 'Another Day', his first post-Beatles single. "I like to collaborate on songs if I can have Linda working with me, then it becomes like a game," McCartney insisted. "It's fun. So we wrote about 10 songs."

Linda wasn't a musician, and her vocal or instrumental prowess was far from noteworthy at this point. The album's resulting material sounded more polished and commercial than its predecessor, albeit a little undisciplined without a band to focus his efforts in the studio. McCartney clearly needed someone to edit his whimsical tendencies or a strong musical contributor to work with at this point, hence his decision to form a new band.

While rehearsing in Scotland, Denny Seiwell was agreeable to McCartney's offer of a place in his as-yet-unnamed group. However, homesick New Yorker McCracken politely declined. Former Moody Blues pianist and guitarist Denny Laine was recruited after Paul recalled his friendly and agreeable presence as the support act on Beatles tours in the early-to-mid-sixties and an occasional visitor at the *Sergeant Pepper* sessions. Paul's new band, Wings, were christened after the birth of Paul's second daughter, Stella, in September 1971, following McCartney's 'vision' of an angelic presence while the new father and mother were ensconced at the London hospital, a symbol of the Holy Spirit.

Feeling suitably liberated from the musical conventions he had experienced during the sixties, Paul asked his wife if she was prepared to join him onstage to play Wings' earliest original material, alongside a smattering of rock'n'roll classics. "I said: 'Do you want to go on the road? A little bunch of friends going out and making music?' In Linda's case, she hadn't really played much keyboard. She was a quick learner. And then, the other element was that I knew I couldn't just try and make a carbon copy of The Beatles – I knew that was impossible. Without John, George and Ringo, there was no way I could do that. So I knew I had to try and make something new. So each of the albums was to try and establish an identity for Wings that would then be recognised in time as Wings music – the Wings sound."

Yet as Howard Sounes notes, the *Ram* album, one of Paul's finest works in retrospect, also commemorated a sense of the happy family life they had experienced on their Scottish farm in songs such as 'Heart Of The Country'. "Both of us had been city dwellers for so long, but both of us loved nature so much. The idea of getting out into the country was very attractive. We were lucky 'cos each of us was free to go where we liked. She was a photographer and didn't have a nine-to-five desk job, so she was flexible that way. And I could work anywhere. We were both free to go where we wanted."

As a pun on his early sixties stage moniker, 'Ram On' was "a cute little thing on a ukulele, 'cos I used to carry one around with me in the back of New York taxis just to always have music with me. They thought I was a freak, those taxi-drivers." 'Uncle Albert'/'Admiral Halsey' was an epic, tempo-changing song suite of effects, voices and strings made in the vein of *Abbey Road*, "a number one in America, surprisingly enough," Paul proudly reflected years later. "It's a bit surreal, but I was in a very free mood. I like all of that."

'Dear Boy', meanwhile, was originally a message to Linda's former husband, reminding him how much he may have missed about his wife. Elsewhere, 'Back Seat Of My Car' was a romantic ode to Paul's burgeoning new relationship. "'We can make it to Mexico City'. That's a real teenage song, with the stereotypical parent who doesn't agree, and the two lovers are going to take on the world."

It was after hearing 'Too Many People' that Lennon would direct his derogatory song 'message' to McCartney in 'How Do You Sleep?' "When I heard *Ram*, I immediately sat down and wrote my song, which is an answer. It's a moment's anger, but when I sang it wasn't quite as angry, because it was four weeks later. It was like a joke – we didn't take it all that seriously. I wasn't really feeling that vicious at the time. But I was using my resentment towards Paul to create a song. He saw that it pointedly refers to him, and people kept hounding him about it. But there were a few digs on his album. He's so obscure other people didn't notice them, but I heard them. I thought, 'I'm not obscure, I just get right down to the nitty-gritty.'"

"He came out with 'How Do You Sleep?' where he suggested that the only thing I ever did was 'Yesterday' and so on," Paul would recall. "John later said that the song was about himself. Well, it didn't sound like that." Lennon later recalled sitting in a Spanish restaurant and being serenaded by a violinist playing this classic McCartney staple. "Then he asked me to sign the violin. I didn't know what to say, so I said: 'Okay,' and I signed it. One day, he's going to find out that Paul wrote it."

When friction with John began to escalate in the press, McCartney insisted it precipitated an intense period of self-doubt. "But then I'd think to myself: 'Wait a minute, he wasn't a mug. He wouldn't work with me all that time if it didn't mean something to him.'" This brief spate of war in song didn't last long before normal service was resumed. "John had sung '*How do you sleep?*', and I nearly did a song that said: '*Quite well, thank you.*' But it settled down, the Beatle mess got sorted out, and we were able to talk to each other like human beings and friends. We'd been through too much to let business arguments blow up our whole relationship." However, McCartney was also suffering with a sense of low musical self-confidence during his early solo career. "I assumed that a lot of stuff I did then was no good. But now, when I go back to it, I sort of think, 'I remember why I did that.' It wasn't just some flippant, off-my-head gesture."

Looking back at *Ram* today, McCartney insists the album appears more accomplished than it did on release. "It was nice enough," producer George Martin added, "but very much a home-made affair, and very much a little family affair. I don't think he ever really rated it as being as important as the stuff he'd done before. I don't think Linda is a substitute for John Lennon, any more than Yoko is a substitute for Paul McCartney."

"I think the truth, as a lot of people have said, is that we were missing each other. We missed the collaborative thing of John saying: 'Don't do that', or 'Do that,'" McCartney conceded in a 2001 Fab retrospective. "Sparking each other off. For a while I was certainly very conscious of it.

The only good thing was that I had been writing without John for a while, towards the end of The Beatles, so it wasn't as bad as it could have been. It was still a pretty big shock just not to be hanging out with these guys."

Starr, working on a film set in Spain shortly after *Ram*'s release, was a little more forthright. "I feel sad with Paul's albums because I believe he's a great artist, incredibly creative, incredibly clever but he disappoints me on his albums. I don't think there's one tune on the last one, *Ram* . . . I just feel he's wasted his time, it's just the way I feel . . . he seems to be going strange."

"*McCartney* was better because at least there were some tunes on it, like 'Junk'. I liked the beginning of 'Ram On', the beginning of 'Uncle Albert . . .' and I liked some of 'Three Legs'," a slightly more generous Lennon recalled soon after the album's release. "I liked the little bit about '*Hands across the water*', but it just tripped off all the time. I didn't like that a bit! That's what he was getting into on the back of *Abbey Road*. I never went into that opera bit. I like three-minute records like adverts."

It's of little surprise, then, that Lennon's *Some Time In New York City* would be an album which, Ono insisted, went against the expectations of rock'n'roll convention. McCartney later acknowledged that Lennon was in love and wanted to create something new, something of his own making. "It was to do with intensity of feeling. And looking back on it, he was absolutely right," he'd later state in defence of his old partner. "Everything they did, I think, was good," McCartney later admitted. "John had proved himself a master in conventional terms, and in joining up with Yoko, he was about to prove himself in unconventional terms. In a way, that was in both our thinking."

"Throughout their artistic careers, separately and together, the Lennons have been committed *avant-gardists*. Such commitment takes guts," wrote *Rolling Stone*'s Stephen Holden, who was critical of the wealthy couple's 'right on' mentality, "who think they can patronise all whom they would call sisters and brothers."

On the other side of the Atlantic, at almost the same moment that John was composing 'Sunday Bloody Sunday', Paul was in London recording 'Give Ireland Back To The Irish'. "It would be interesting to know," Du Noyer stated in his *We All Shine On* Lennon study, "if the two rivals were aware of each other's efforts at the time." As Lennon biographer Philip Norman noted, "Paul's post-Lennon & McCartney songs were increasingly criticised for being bland and cutesy, yet if he attempted to step out of character – as with his own comment on the Ulster Troubles, 'Give Ireland Back To The Irish' – people threw up their hands in horror."

While McCartney's February 1972 single release was ultimately a slow, stylised and somewhat incongruous piece given the seriousness of the incident, Lennon's journalistic reaction to the violent events in Derry, Northern Ireland was captured in the tautly composed and menacing vocalese of 'Sunday Bloody Sunday'. "I hear about 13 people shot dead in Ireland and I react immediately. And being what I am, I react in four-to-the-bar with a guitar break in the middle. I don't say: 'My God, what's happening, we should do something.' I go: '*It was Sunday Bloody Sunday/and they shot the people down . . .*'"

'Give Ireland Back . . .' was the maiden Wings project for Ulster Protestant guitarist McCullough, who, as Sounes opined, "must have found it difficult to remain indifferent to a song that commented directly on the delicate politics of his homeland." The song was unsurprisingly banned by the BBC for its political message and criticised for its simple narrative, while Paul suggested the public should decide for themselves.

"Before I did ['Give Ireland . . .'], I always used to think, 'God, John's crackers, doing all these political songs,'" McCartney reflected in *Rolling Stone*'s company two years later. "I understand he feels deeply, you know. So do I." He also told the music press that he had no intentions of becoming a politically motivated singer. The single's release also coincided with Wings' first UK tour of small unadvertised provincial shows and University gigs, opening at Nottingham on February 9, 1972 and thereafter visiting York, Hull, Lancaster, Leeds, Sheffield, Manchester, Birmingham and Swansea, performing their controversial new song amongst original material and the odd rock'n'roll cover – but no Beatles material.

Indeed, politics was also heavy in the air in New York at the time, and it coursed through John's lyrics. One interviewee for this book insisted Lennon was keen to be known as an Irishman during the early period of his residence in the Big Apple. "Still more extreme sentiments permeated a companion ballad, 'The Luck Of The Irish'," wrote biographer Philip Norman, "this time expressed with the same bitter sarcasm as 'Working Class Hero'." However, its lyrically clichéd folk protest form could not quite convey the same sense of authenticity.

Back on the other side of the Atlantic, I asked Van Scyoc about the reactions within the band to the lyrical content of songs such as 'Sunday Bloody Sunday'. "It wasn't too long, maybe a week-and-a-half of rehearsing before there was word of a new song, 'Woman Is The Nigger Of The World', and then I heard something about 'Sunday Bloody Sunday'. Pretty heavy topics. '. . . Bloody Sunday' was the first track we did, and I thought that would have made a pretty good single too. Not so much with a few of the other tracks."

Naturally, the old sense of competitive one-upmanship between Lennon and McCartney persisted. As pianist Adam Ippolito recalled in his *LENNONYC* documentary interview: "Whenever we did something, he [John] was thinking, 'Well, Paul did 'Give Ireland Back To The Irish', and we've done '. . . Bloody Sunday'. But now we've done 'Woman Is The Nigger Of The World', we're gonna beat Paul to the women's issue.' There were a lot of dynamics involved in the writing and performing of the songs like that."

"But with 'Woman Is The Nigger Of The World', I just looked at Adam, and we knew that this was going to be a big problem," Van Scyoc recalls. This was a crucial reminder of John's pioneering and proto-feminist mindset, a song imbued by its fantastic production value. "Unfortunately, it wasn't a hit. He was trying to say that women were as put down as African-American women," Ippolito concedes. "People heard it as a racist lyric. But with respect to John, a lot of the other lyrical things were political, but not nearly as provocative as that. I didn't really know that that was going to be the single at the time, quite honestly."

"I know it was political with a capital 'P', but that was what I had in my bag at the time and I wasn't just going to throw them away because they were political," Lennon reasoned in a staunch defence of his work. "I still like the song 'Woman Is The Nigger Of The World'. I like the sound of it and it gets me off, but it just happened that it didn't please people." The song, as critic Philip Norman later noted, earned "a bravura performance rivalled only by 'Twist and Shout'".

It is also worth remembering that Lennon, the voice of his generation, was attempting to escape The Beatles' shadow as he and his former colleagues struck out on their own. The Beatles had been such an emphatic influence and presence that Lennon had begun to resent comparisons to his solo work, deliberately sidestepping these criticisms over the years. Furthermore, he was in competition with his own incredible creative legacy. "Perhaps after working with The Beatles for 10 years with George Martin, and building really epic records, it was a nice approach to do it raw and do it right the first time," Ippolito maintains. "And if not, go with it anyway, because that's as fresh as it's gonna be."

With a need to really establish themselves as solo artists, Lennon was still going through the process of shedding his old Fab Four skin. But he and Paul would always be Beatles, and McCartney's musical presence, however remote, re-appeared when Lennon and Elephant's Memory waited to appear on the *Mike Douglas Show*. The moment proved that Lennon had a thinner skin about his old partner than Van Scyoc imagined. "We were late getting there because we'd been down to a music store. We were standing in the wings about to go on national television. No pressure, right? We hear Mike Douglas start singing 'Michelle', and John looked at me. I'll *never* forget the look on his face. He looked so angry and frustrated! It just showed me a whole other side of him."

"John had his style, Paul had his style, and they were different," Ippolito insists. "When Paul and John were together, it was magic, let's face it. As a songwriting team, just amazing."

The *Some Time . . .* sessions would prove as far removed as possible from the disciplined Beatles recording environment of the early-to-mid sixties, when the group gradually became the architects of increasingly polished aural pictures. "It was: 'Let's get a sound, and let's go,'" the Elephants' bassist recalls. "Roy Cicala, the engineer, was tremendous." The ever-astute Cicala insisted that McCartney's studio ethic involved a cleaner approach in his search for a sound that captured what he heard in his head. By contrast, John's earthier, music-making approach involved taking the feel for a song arrangement from either Frank, Keltner or Van Scyoc's playing, rather than having a set idea when developing the songs in the studio. The group had added Keltner on drums, feeling completely comfortable with his presence. Being the first opportunity he'd had to work with the drummer, Van Scyoc was really on his game.

While Voormann insisted that John's impatience meant he was keen to record as fast as possible, Van Scyoc felt it was Lennon's intensity which was the key to the Record Plant sessions. "He did not want to fool around. Honestly, he might get to take a break once in 12 hours. He was totally involved in the track, and taking care of business the whole time. Seeing how intense he was, and how seriously he took it, helped me as a studio musician later on." Lennon had prepped his new and enthusiastic movement band of street musicians for a provocative, political work. Keen to record fast in the spirit of the moment, John wanted to produce a tabloid-style album full of 'front-page' songs delivered in a *reportage* style.

34

"He had pictures of people who he was singing about. For him, it was a journal of what was going through his mind at the time," Ippolito asserts, "and what he felt needed fixing, and what he wanted to let the world know about."

"He was learning, every day of his life," Pang has since recalled. "He would sit up with his first cup of coffee, and he would read *The New York Times*, and he would just absorb. He absorbed info constantly. But he realised he couldn't change a lot of things. He realised that after he did *Some Time In New York City*, which was a very heavy, activist type protest album."

"I think he learned his lesson," Van Scyoc laughs. "He would come in with a new song every night, and sit down and play it on an acoustic guitar, and within half an hour we'd be laying down the first track. You'd go in every night, from seven at night, not knowing the song. And at seven the next morning, we'd be there knowing that we'd put down a fabulous song. And it was mixed and ready for the radio. And we did that for two weeks straight."

"When you're live, you're playing with all your emotion," Ippolito insists. "The basic rhythm track, he wanted that to be fresh. The perfectionist of someone wanting to get it right is not rock'n'roll." The pianist also recalls Lennon entering the studio and taking him into a room, where he would sing and play guitar when presenting a new song. "We worked as editors and arrangers with him, that's what we did. We wrote the chords down where they belonged. We would figure out where they fell rhythmically, and I would write out a chord chart. But basically, the songs were not that difficult, so we could play them after learning them." Many of the songs were first or second takes, the bassist recalls, with maybe an hour spent on Jim Keltner's drum sound.

The Elephant's Memory band's live aesthetic provided a strong injection of energy into the room. With McCartney's prospective collaborative input at this point, the often acerbic side of Lennon's work of the 1970–72 period may have been mollified or tempered. "I tried to make my songs uncomplicated so that people could understand them," Lennon would reflect on this tumultuous creative period. "Now they're openly attacking me for writing simplistic lyrics. It almost ruined it. It became journalism and not poetry. And I basically feel that I'm a poet. Then I began to take it seriously on another level, saying: 'Well, I am reflecting what is going on, right?'"

"Not everyone was political-minded like we were at the time," Van Scyoc confirms. "I can see how it might go over people's heads in the Midwest. But if they can write all those songs in a week, there must be a lot of other great songs." The bassist recalls a different political topic being tackled every night as the group enjoyed the challenge of finding an appropriate musical style for each subject they approached. "On a couple of the tracks, it was just Jim Keltner, John and I. For instance, on the track 'John Sinclair'," a highly effective protest song which made use of Lennon's agit-rock intentions in a slide guitar stomp.

"So I got to be in the Plastic Ono Band for a couple of nights. I cherish those nights. It was just John, and Jim and Yoko and I, with Roy." Meanwhile 'Angela', a dour musical excursion into political chic, had been aroused by the plight of radical activist Dr. Angela Davis, who featured in Leaf and Scheinfeld's *The US v John Lennon*. Davis was satisfied that Lennon would devote his art to her cause, and was impressed by his ability to understand the linkages and connections between various social movements. "Dr. Davis absolutely respected his solidarity with these movements," says Scheinfeld, "and was willing to use his skills and talents in service of a larger cause for justice, peace and equality."

"Though the message to Ms. Davis was heartfelt enough, its lyrical content left a little to be desired," groused critic Peter Doggett. Lennon and Ono's vocal pairing was also far from convincing. However, Davis had seemed impressed with The Beatles' political statement, 'Revolution'. As the first new composition to be recorded during the *White Album* sessions in 1968, it was an impressive start with a song that Lennon was keen to promote as a potential Beatles single.

A brusque and direct anti-destruction song, this transitional moment in Lennon's musical development demonstrated the growth in his counter-cultural interests. Having pondered the 'in'–'out' conundrum over violent revolution while in India, by the time he'd re-recorded this exhilarating song at a faster tempo in July, he had become an ardent peacenik, attracting criticism of his stance from both left- and right-wing observers. As MacDonald noted, "Lennon sang *'everything's gonna be alright'* – God would take care of the human race, despite political ructions."

Having opposed the release of a political statement parcelled in a Beatles single, McCartney had unsurprisingly feared a certain element of controversy (thanks to a post-LSD, radicalised Lennon) over its release. The song became the subject of heated debate. (An extended, six-minute coda formed from vocal and feedback effects created by Lennon and Ono, working on the credo of intuitive creativity and meaningful random experiment, formed the basis of the controversial 'Revolution #9'.) This intense, pretence-shedding blues-rock song, replete with loud, fuzz-toned guitars pre-empted Lennon's imminent move towards expressive lyrical simplicity. It was, MacDonald rightly insisted, "raw, direct and minimal in the style of *Plastic Ono Band*".

Four years on from 'Revolution', Lennon set his topical politico views to music across a full album with a New York protest band. Lennon principally liked Elephant's Memory for three reasons: they were fiercely political, they played hard rock and they wrote their own material. "He wouldn't have hired us if he didn't think it was a good match," Van Scyoc admits. "You just *know*."

"The Elephants were great, and they were a political band. They had a similar kind of background, sixties R&B, and Bo Diddley," Gruen confirmed. "They had a solid rock'n'roll background and they were basically the kind of R&B musicians, and the kind of band, that John was looking for at the time. He liked them very much."

Even though Lennon had a classic approach to producing his songs, he didn't want his records to sound like everyone else's product on the radio at the time. "He wanted them to sound something like old Sun records. 'Give me the stuff they used to use back then, what they gave to those guys in the old days,'" claims Keltner. "He always wanted to make his records sound as unique as Elvis Presley." According to Van Scyoc, Lennon would eulogise over Presley all the time, something he feels has been written out of history. "The first thing I asked John was: 'Are you an Elvis fan?' We did a couple of Elvis tunes, because that was my inspiration as a child. When I started out in the music business, everyone was into those R&B artists, like Chuck Berry." John idolised Elvis, openly telling pianist Adam Ippolito as much. "He told us, and yelled it out in concert. '*I love you Elvis!*' We did 'Hound Dog'. We'd played it before."

Lennon was definitely attracted to both the band's political and musical energy, one of the key reasons for their strong connection. "He obviously knew our politics, and he'd been told about it from when we'd done benefits. He knew we were right on the money in terms of that. I think what he needed to do was to scope us out musically," Van Scyoc insists, "and how we could relate to different kinds of situations in the studio. Jamming: was it productive? How easy were we to work with?"

On the first night, Lennon presented a couple of new songs to his colleagues, even though they had yet to play together. Van Scyoc claims they didn't record anything that night. According to engineer Cicala, Van Scyoc and co were a frenetic bunch of Village musicians who loved to play. "They should have been in a garage recording with two microphones. We tried to do it in the studio, but when we did make it clean, no one liked it. We had to catch them in the first two hours of the recording, 'cos they were in Neverland after that . . . I think you understand. John was almost there. Yeah, he was there too, why not?"

Elephant's Memory had only been playing with Lennon for around a month, something overlooked in criticisms of the record. The pace and energy of the group's sound matched the in-the-moment urgency of the messages he attempted to broadcast to his record-buying public. "It was just a question of getting it down, putting it out and the next one's coming up soon," Lennon would later emphasise. "We needn't have done it." Writing a new song almost every day in late 1971 and early 1972, pressure from both Lennon's musical impulses and record company agendas took their toll.

"Capitol would call us up in the middle of the album," Cicala reflects, "and say, 'We need it next week, we've got our schedule,' and we used to tell them to 'eff off sometimes, 'cos what you gonna do? Change the creative part of John? In some cases, we did get it ready, but we would go three days straight mixing it, and then at the end of those three days, we would sleep for a week. No matter what you took, it didn't help, because you lose your power of being creative after the second day." While Lennon would admit to his disappointment about the often severe reaction to the album, Cicala maintains that this was never fiercely articulated. "He never showed it. It was out, he'd be on to the next one already. If he did, I never knew about it. He'd just go on and on and on, because he loved to write and perform."

Despite its flaws, *Some Time In New York City* was a fascinating concept, chock full of topical stories and pressing issues. Lennon had never produced anything remotely like this, and the live feel and fast-paced aesthetic of the city informed the writing of the album, and was intrinsic to its content. While a great concept, the journalistic approach to his politicised minstrel music inevitably needed an editor's input. Lennon carried on regardless. "There were mistakes, a little harmony wasn't perfect. We didn't go back and perfect every note. But we just printed it out to make a statement on society, right now, right away. Just say it: 'I think this is wrong, and this is my opinion.'"

"He [Lennon] once described rock'n'roll as the folk music of the age," declared critic Dave Thompson, "and, with *Some Time In New York City* as a cogent example, he was right." As a fan of the subsequent album, Keltner found its rough sound appealing, with Lennon's musical attitude on the record taking the drummer back to his earliest days as a fan when he'd set out on his own path. "I think John was the one who would be concerned with having everything not sounding like a regular record. John was always concerned that his record would sound too normal. I have him on tape saying, 'I don't want that clean sound on my record.' What I did gather was that he was extremely adventurous – he was never happy or satisfied, and he never wanted his guitar to sound like a guitar. But he had a classic approach to making records."

Lennon was very much an equal with his new street band colleagues. Van Scyoc soon realised that John was only too happy to lower his guard. "He was one of the guys when we played together. And that was one of the fun things about it: he didn't make it a big deal, and that's what he loved. He hadn't played live very much with a band that could keep up with him. It was perfect for him to have some guys on call that he could rock with anytime he wanted." Van Scyoc remembers 3 a.m. phone calls from Lennon, inviting him to the Dakota to work out a feel for an upcoming new song. "That was a beautiful thing," the bassist wistfully recalls.

Work on the *Some Time In New York City* album was followed by the recording of a double Elephant's Memory album before Ono's *Approximately Infinite Universe* was committed to tape. "I came into the studio at the end of the recording sessions for the *Some Time In New York City* album," Gruen recalls of his photographic role, "but they were in there for almost a year recording the Elephants and Yoko's album." As Gruen remembers, a considerable amount of tequila was enjoyed during protracted recording sessions. "There were months and months of nights in the studio, so there was a lot of drinking." He also told Philip Norman: "There'd be maybe 10 bottles of tequila between eight people – and that was every night. Then after working in the studio, we'd go out drinking, we'd have more shots of tequila."

Cicala claims a huge quantity of "that mirror stuff" was consumed too. "To hear Roy talk, you'd think we were drunk and stoned the whole night," Van Scyoc laughs. "That's not the way we were. We were a party band, but we couldn't have been that out there and produced that kind of stuff. If you'd already laid down a track, then you smoked a joint or had a couple of extra shots of tequila. But not before you took care of business: it was *after* you had your parts done." Van Scyoc insists that Lennon's notorious drunken weaknesses presented more of a problem than any group indulgences did. "John didn't hold his liquor well, that was his problem. But it was blown out of proportion because he was a Beatle."

There was also a procession of famous visitors too. Jackie Kennedy would often appear during the sessions, sometimes bringing her two children with her. On one occasion, she appeared during the recording of 'Sunday Bloody Sunday'. Rudolf Nureyev also stopped by to socialise. Carly Simon, who fronted the Memory band for around six months in the late sixties, suddenly began appearing at the Record Plant when she learned her former bandmates were working with Lennon. Appearances from such notable visitors at the Record Plant studio reminded Elephant's Memory of Lennon's incredible connections.

Despite these auguries, *Some Time In New York City* was widely panned by the critics, the first time that one of Lennon's commercial album releases faced a negative press. "People were shocked," recalls Gruen. "They didn't like Yoko on the album, or that a Beatle was singing about such serious things. They didn't want that. They wanted The Beatles. They were shocked to see what he had become." When Lennon's new album emerged, Gruen recalls the audience's bemusement at its content and the concept of a fifties-style rock band accompanying him onstage and on record. "People really didn't like the album," he insists. "The album sold very little and he was not as on top as he'd been as a Beatle."

Lennon's immigration problems, Beatles lawsuits, marital stress, Nixon's re-election and frozen Apple funds also didn't ease matters. "So you see the kind of pressure Yoko and I were getting," Lennon would reflect in 1980. "Not only on a personal level, and the public level, and the court case, and the government, and this, that, and the other, but every time we tried to *express* ourselves, they would ban it, would cover it up, would censor it."

The spirited and earnestly delivered *Some Time In New York City* received decidedly lukewarm critical reviews upon its respective June and September releases. "I understood what John was saying, but I was kind of naïve about the way the media would show it. And it was 1972, don't forget," Van Scyoc recalls. "I think he was disappointed. He wasn't disappointed in us, but I think he was disappointed in the reaction. I realised that the political issues held the album back, in terms of sales."

"One way or another," wrote Paul Du Noyer, "while John was making *Some Time In New York City*, the future was being made without him. His overtly political music had brought him very little reward, either creatively or commercially." Paul Moody later argued that the album resembled a political pamphlet, "focusing on every significant movement of the day with the humour-free tone necessary for radical politics". Reassuringly, if somewhat surprisingly, engineer Jack Douglas insisted that if Lennon had pursued this path of socio-political commentary a little further, he may have found the right musical direction for his 'radical' *modus operandi*: a fired-up arrival in New York with something compelling to articulate to his musical readership. "The mood of almost every track may be angry," biographer Philip Norman noted, "but an artful range of commercial pop effects sweetens the harangue."

McCartney, meanwhile, took his inexperienced band out on tour for the first time in Europe in the summer of 1972. With the group having accepted his wife as nothing more than a token member, Paul seemed breezily nonplussed about subsequent audience reaction to his songs due to the ceaseless public acclaim for his Beatle work. With family life becoming pre-eminent over his musical output, the release of 'Mary Had A Little Lamb' was seen as an ironic riposte, a musical nose-thumb to the group's detractors over the controversy stirred by the release of 'Give Ireland Back To The Irish'. Travelling the continent on a brightly painted double-decker bus, the *Wings Over Europe* tour took in small, remote venues in France, Germany and Switzerland while his musicians began to grumble about their meagre pay and the increasingly high living expenses. While playing Sweden, McCartney encountered drug possession problems with the authorities, leading to the potentially career-threatening ban from entering the States, where his former partner was preparing to take the stage again.

In late August 1972, Lennon and Elephant's Memory performed at the One To One concert, a raucously received occasion and arguably one of the loudest gigs ever staged at Madison Square Garden. With around 20,000 fans enjoying each of the two performances, the amps onstage were, in true heavy rock tradition, ratcheted all the way up to 11. With Lennon eager to play live, the Garden performance arose as an ideal opportunity for John and his group to take the stage in a prestigious setting. "The only way to get around the legal loophole was to play a benefit gig," Van Scyoc recalls. "I guess if they'd got paid, they would have donated the proceeds. He enjoyed New York, but he couldn't go out and play because he didn't have a work visa. He kept hanging on from one extension to the next. The whole time I was with John and Yoko, that was the case."

From the beginning of their musical relationship, the bassist claims it was their intention to put a set together for a concert tour, one which was intended to promote peace. "We started buying equipment every day. 'Let's do it.' John had to put it off. I think he thought it would be rectified soon. He wanted to go and play." Yet critical reaction to the *One To One* concert led to the postponement of the proposed tour.

Ahead of the huge concert performance that summer, Lennon rehearsed the band twice a day for two weeks at the Fillmore East. He clearly wanted to have a tight band that was well prepared. "John was like a slave driver," Van Scyoc laughs. "He was amazing. He was taking care of business." The group tried gently coercing John into playing a selection of Beatles material onstage at Madison Square Garden, to no avail. After two weeks, he finally acquiesced into performing a defining live version of 'Come Together'. It didn't prevent him, however, from forgetting part of the song's enigmatic lyrics. "I sang something else instead of what it should have been, and it was never noticed."

Elephant's Memory had a number of songs they'd have happily performed, but Lennon would not relent. "We wanted to do 'Day Tripper', and we'd have done a whole set of Beatle songs, but he wasn't keen on it. He wanted to do 'Imagine', and he did 'It's So Hard' and 'Cold Turkey'. He wanted to keep it to solo stuff. He was very aware of trying to build a solo career: 'I wanna make sure people realise this is me.'"

"That's another thing that puts me off playing live – the fact that you've got to do the same thing over and over again every night, and the audience wants to hear the songs you're associated with," Lennon told *Melody Maker* the following year. "I remember I sang 'Imagine' twice in one day when I was rehearsing it, and that bored me. I've nothing against the song, in fact I'm quite proud of it, but I just can't go on every night singing it. I'd try and vary it, but then I don't like to see that myself. If I go to watch an artist I'd expect to hear the things I know. I understand it from both points of view."

When Gruen heard Lennon sing 'Imagine', he immediately realised that this was the voice of the former Beatle onstage, the voice of his generation, and not the New York friend he had come to know in the last year. In the music room of his New Jersey home, Van Scyoc proceeds to play a few bars of 'Imagine' down the phone line, sitting at the Wurlitzer piano on which Lennon performed his classic anthem at the Madison Square Garden concert. Or, at least he *thinks* it's the same instrument. "I'm not sure if it's the *exact* one John played on," he chuckles. "There were two onstage, side by side, and there's no way to know which it is. But in *my* mind, it's his."

Lennon proved a sterling frontman, guiding his group through a momentous night. Who was to know that it would be one of his final, definitive performances? "We thought, 'That was good, we'll get it better next time.' It was all about things that were going to go down in the future when we played again," Van Scyoc remembers. "I was shocked when he consented to do 'Hound Dog'," Ippolito recalls after the group had run through the song, along with other favourite Elvis tunes, in rehearsal. "That was really stepping out for him," Van Scyoc admits. "I think the pressure was off by that point and he felt, 'Let's just *do* it.'"

"John did a great job," claims Keltner. "The band were great, but I don't think the audience saw them the way they imagined John and Yoko. Musically, it came off really good. I don't know exactly what they expected." Gruen insists Lennon suffered stage-fright because of his lack of live work in recent years. "I think they did 'Imagine', Jerry Rubin was playing a bongo. There were a lot of people with instamatic cameras – John said, 'People take all these pictures, we never get to see them.'"

For Gruen, the Madison Square Garden performance was one of the most exciting shows he'd ever witnessed. "They were really into it, and it was good; loud, fast and loose rock'n'roll. Everybody was on a high," the photographer enthuses. "The audience seemed to have a good time, but the critics didn't seem to enjoy it. I don't think it was the kind of music that they expected. I think it was a little depressing for John, because he likes to be liked, like most people. He seemed a little upset that they didn't understand the statements that they were making, and that kind of threw him. At the same time, they were breaking up with Allen Klein, their manager, his money was being held in escrow, and it was kind of a down time."

In a nostalgic mood, during early 1973 Lennon spent considerable time with Ringo Starr, then enjoying surprising chart success compared to his old Beatles colleagues. Keltner had first met Ringo when Harrison invited him to Trident studio to work on Starkey's 'It Don't Come Easy' single, and was introduced to the Beatles drummer. "I was just knocked out to meet the man, and he was really cool. He handed me a pair of these huge maracas and asked me to play them on his song. I was telling him how much of a huge fan I was. I was all over him, I was really gushing. I felt at the time that he wasn't comfortable hearing that. He really didn't feel that he was that good, as crazy as that sounds."

On March 13, three former Beatles convened in Los Angeles to work on a brief session of new material for Ringo's eponymous (and finest) solo album. Harrison and Lennon's work on the latter's song, 'I'm The Greatest', acted as a promising precedent to thoughts of a more formal get-together. It would ultimately prove the closest the four men would get to a full studio reunion. "We're all friends, even if we had split up," Starkey recalled. "So I said: 'Have you got any songs, boys?' and John said: 'Yeah, I've got a song,' so I said: 'Well, come and play.'"

"It seemed the natural thing to do," Lennon recalled after he'd begun writing the song after watching *A Hard Day's Night* more than two years earlier. 'I'm The Greatest' was given a commercial makeover with Starkey in mind. "For the track, I was on piano, Billy Preston was on organ, Ringo was on drums, George was on guitar and Klaus Voormann was on bass." As Starr recalled, this was a session that became an unplanned Beatles convention. The three men, Preston recalled, clearly enjoyed the experience of playing together. On hearing of this studio rendezvous, one Los Angeles station took it upon themselves to circulate regular updates on this promising news story. Starkey told McCartney that Harrison had also written him a song, 'Photograph'. Paul wasn't about to be left out, and donated a new song, 'Six O' Clock', having already played on 'You're Sixteen'.

With friendships seemingly restored, John, Paul and George's individual songwriting efforts all contributed to the *Ringo* album. After Harrison and Lennon had worked on new material with Starkey in Los Angeles, the new work was brought to England for Paul to play on. McCartney also hoped that this form of collaboration might set a precedent for future work. "I think that kind of thing might happen more often. I'm happy to play with the other three and I'm sure they are too, if it is physically possible."

This early musical gathering and partial studio collaboration also appeared to bring the group closer to a point of reconciliation. "I think that's a beginning," McCartney declared some months after the studio gathering. "I think that shows what someone can do if he just asks. That's all he [Ringo] did. So if it's that easy, then lots of things could be done in the future. And I'd like to see some *great* things done."

McCartney had apparently been amenable to making a contribution to 'I'm The Greatest' too, but had been unable to participate due to visa restrictions. Although neither former Beatle had played simultaneously on any of the other album material, writer Alan Clayson believed the juxtaposition of 'John', 'Lennon', 'Paul' and 'McCartney' on the album's closing monologue could only have been a deliberate act on Starkey's part.

"Ringo had that song ['Early 1970'], where he went through all the band members' names and who would play with him," Ray Connolly recalls. "'*I think George will play with me, I think John will play with me, I hope Paul will play with me . . .*' I think by that time, had they gotten together again, I don't know if it would have been The Beatles, it would have been John Lennon and Paul McCartney. There would have been some sort of collaboration, or helping each other on solo albums, and I think they needed it. I think that could have happened. I thought it was always possible for them to have gotten together now and then, and helped each other out."

Ringo sang 'I'm The Greatest', a tongue-in-cheek Lennon song which, according to producer Richard Perry, was a chronological outline of their shared careers. "The night we were going to record it, Ringo, John, Klaus and myself grouped around a piano in the studio to put the finishing touches to the song." Having witnessed John's live guitar acumen on countless occasions in Hamburg, Voormann was still impressed by Lennon's abilities as a vocalist and rhythm guitarist in the studio in the early seventies. "John's playing was very simple. He didn't play long runs. He didn't know many chords either. He'd find something and say, 'That sounds nice.'"

Voormann also believed that Lennon had a complementary, and well-developed, musical bond with Starkey. "Rhythm guitar is very important. It's the feel of the song, but it can't be rock'n'roll without the drums. That rhythm guitar really lays down where you're going. What-ever he did, he did it well. It was nothing to do with technique, it was all feeling." As a drummer, Keltner also rated Starr as one of the greatest studio players he ever had the pleasure to work with. "It's like that thing John said about Ringo not being the best drummer in The Beatles, and people took that as a big put-down of Ringo. It was a humorous joke," insists Bill Harry. "But people tend to take it seriously. Ringo was generally thought of as a drummer for hire initially, and he wasn't even regarded as part of the group. Basically it was George who wanted Ringo there. He got on well with Ringo right from the start."

Having arrived in Los Angeles a day or two earlier and learnt news of the session, Harrison was keen to join his friends. Perry was duly called out of the studio to take an important phone call. "I said to John, 'George is on the phone and wants to come down to record with us. Is it OK?' 'Yes,' John said. 'Tell him to get down here right away and help me finish this bridge.'" "It was the first time the three ex-Beauties had played together since – well, since they last played together," Lennon joked in a mock press release in early 1973.

"George arrived," Perry remembered, "and without saying a word, he joined in on the same wavelength we were on. He played guitar and John played piano, and they complemented each other perfectly. There was The Beatles' magic unfolding right before my eyes. Everyone in the room was gleaming," Perry purrs. "It's such a universal gleam with The Beatles."

"They knew how to compartmentalise their feelings, setting business differences aside in favour of deeper emotional connections," Du Noyer informed me. "And as artists I suspect that curiosity would have impelled them, sooner or later, to see what magic might be re-ignited." Perry's work on the *Ringo* album helped it to achieve best-selling status for Starkey. Asked about the Starkey/Perry union in the studio, Lennon insisted their collaboration was an unqualified success.

"Perry's great, Ringo's great, I think the combination was great and look how well they did together. There's no complaints if you're number one." In a mock press release the same month, Lennon joked about the producer, and the surfeit of rumours inevitably arising from the news of the session. "Richard Perry, who planned to take the tapes along to sell them to Paul McCartney, told a friend: 'I'll take the tapes to Paul McCartney.'" Paul would most probably have joined in, Lennon suggested after the session, but he wasn't around to do so. "The extreme humility that existed between John and Paul seems to have evaporated," Lennon joked in the same mock press release. "'They've spoken to each other on the telephone – and in English, that's a change,' said a McCartney associate.'"

Having worked successfully with Ringo, Perry's studio experience with Lennon remains firmly imprinted in his memory. "It was probably the greatest thrill of my career. He had amazing energy and electricity. He worked at a fast pace, and it spread to everyone else. He loved the record-making process as much as anyone in the business, and whenever he was in the studio, he was smiling." Despite the contractual wrangles which rendered reunion speculation somewhat premature, the question remained: just how valid were these songwriting contributions to *Ringo* in prompting a more formal studio collaboration? It seems an enduring mutual affection for the drummer had persuaded the remaining Beatles to contribute in the first place. "All three of them could relax when they were working for Ringo, in a way they couldn't have done if they were being 'The Beatles' again. I think that one didn't necessarily act as a stepping-stone towards the other, though it didn't hurt, either," Peter Doggett claims. "It was a case of three old friends helping a mate out," Keith Badman insists. "They all knew Ringo could suffer on his own, so they chipped in with compositions."

Perhaps due to Starkey's limited songwriting abilities, he accepted a number of acting roles during the seventies. His commendable part in Ray Connolly and David Puttnam's *That'll Be The Day*, which also featured David Essex and Keith Moon, earned the drummer welcome plaudits in the same year as his *Ringo* hit. Connolly takes up the story of Starkey's part in a defining film on late fifties society. "Me and David Puttnam went to ask Ringo what it had been like to be at Butlin's, because Ringo used to play there with Rory Storm. So I rang Derek Taylor at Apple, and we went along one lunchtime. We sat there with Neil Aspinall, Derek and Ringo. They amused us, and Ringo told a few funny stories. And on the way out, I suggested to David Puttnam that we should offer him the part of Mike. And David said: 'Do you think he can do it?' And I said: 'Well, he was good in *A Hard Day's Night*!'

"So we went down to the Isle Of Wight, and he only had a 10-day window to shoot it in. When the film was in the projection room, people were laughing when Ringo said his lines, and this is always a good sign. He was extremely easy to get on with, he was no trouble and he did the job. He also brought his own wardrobe. He'd worn some of the clothes at The Beatles fancy dress party for the *Magical Mystery Tour*. He worked well with David Essex, and it was a great experience. He brought a common touch to it, and he added great presence. And when the reviews came out, he stole the reviews from David. I think he should have gone on and done more films." In retrospect, Starr's acting roles appeared to be a valid move, one which duly helped to enrich his sense of a post-Beatles identity.

CHAPTER TWO

Four Fab *Freres*

FOLLOWING the 1973 release of The Beatles' commendable career-spanning *Red* and *Blue* double albums, time was spent reflecting on the highlights of their back catalogue, no doubt raising some issues surrounding The Beatles' unfinished musical legacy. McCartney, however, took little interest in the gold-record earning collection. "I still haven't heard them," he admitted. "I know what's on them because I've heard it all before, you know."

As Lennon reminded one interviewer, the albums succeeded in helping to bring back the spirit of the sixties. "I think the official reissue albums came out around the right time. Maybe we'd have sold more if we'd got them out before the bootleggers, but they didn't do too badly at all. They got gold records each. They brought back the sixties. When I first received a copy of the compilation albums, I was too nervous to play them in case they were mixed badly. I thought the sound was a bit rough."

Lennon would memorably insist that 'Revolution' had, to his ears, been sanitised through the stereo treatment of their work. One thing they *did* illustrate was the fact that each Beatle now appeared to be moving in different directions towards the end of their career. "Those guys were brilliant, those guys really knew what they were doing," Keltner enthuses, "and they produced themselves. This is what I was told by George and John: that he [George Martin] showed them the way, in a lot of ways, and his arrangements helped them see the possibilities. But we all know one thing. We love those records as much as we love anything by any master of music from our time. By the virtue of Beatle records, I heard all these great sounds. That was a very momentous thing for me."

As the group's producer (and having increasingly assumed the role of mediator, orchestral arranger and collaborator over time), Martin admitted that he did not have much input in terms of the lyrical refinement of the group's work. "I would tell them if I didn't think a lyric sounded good, or suggest they ought to write another eight bars or so, but they tended to give me the finished songs. My work was mainly a question of contributing arrangement ideas."

Lennon and George Martin had recently enjoyed a drunken evening of musical reminiscences at the Beverly Hills Hotel in California. The producer was considering selling his AIR London studio set-up and buying a boat in the Caribbean from which to run his recording operations. "Give me a call when you have the tapes balanced so they don't fall in the water and I'll be there!" he quipped. Martin, meanwhile, had exercised more control than the former group members over the choice of material set for inclusion on the *Red* and *Blue* compilation albums. These twin double albums were intended to accompany what was initially conceived as the *Long And Winding Road* documentary film.

Following Starr's session for 'I'm The Greatest', Perry's conversation with George Harrison would prove equally memorable for the producer as the two men discussed the merits of The Beatles' four-disc compilation set in late March. The *Red* record, covering the years between 1962 and 1966, featured classic singles and choice album tracks captured during the Beatlemania years.

Debut single 'Love Me Do', recorded in June and September 1962, was an intriguing introduction to their public. Written mainly by McCartney as a 16-year-old schoolboy, the song was fresh, original and epochal in miniature, with a lyrical simplicity married to an unusual sound. "It was the first one we dared do of our own because we were doing such great numbers of other people's," said Paul. "It was quite hard to come in singing 'Love Me Do'. But we gradually broke that down and decided to try them. The Lennon/McCartney songwriting collaboration was forming during that period. We went on from 'Love Me Do' to writing deeper, much more intense things." McCartney was clearly concerned at the likely reaction if they had gone along with Martin's proposal to record Mitch Murray's 'How Do You Do It?'

According to Martin, the best Beatles original was this slow and rather moody blues number. Somewhat ponderous, 'Love Me Do' sounded as if the group were singing directly to the listener. Lennon contributed the song's middle eight and passionate harmonica wail. But it was its unusual sound and open harmonies that produced a "freshness that suited the group and seemed intriguingly hard to categorise", as one critic noted. Paul later stated that 'Love Me Do' was, in its succinctness, one of the most philosophically perfect songs they ever recorded.

Released in October, press officer Tony Barrow claimed that EMI effectively downgraded promotion (at least in terms of Radio Luxembourg's playlist) for 'Love Me Do'. Harrison claimed that when he first heard it on the radio, "it sent me shivery all over. It was the best buzz of all time. That was great, but after having got to number 17, I don't recall what happened to it . . . what it meant was, the next time we went to EMI, they were more friendly. 'Oh, hello lads. Come on in.'" By the end of the year, the single had sold 100,000 copies, mostly in their home city. "Even though 'Love Me Do' didn't make number one, it was exciting. All we had wanted was a piece of vinyl – my God, a record that you hadn't made in a booth somewhere!" Starr later enthused. "And now we wanted to be number one. They were both as important."

"We made number 17 in the *NME* chart, and I remember wanting to wind the window down and shout, 'We're number 17, wah-hey!' The thrill of our first chart position," McCartney later gleefully recalled, "all of that was pretty incredible." "It suddenly hit me, right between the eyes," Martin later recalled of the group's early impact. "This was a *group* I was listening to. That distinctive harmony, that unique blend of sound – *that* was the selling point. It was that 'something' I had dimly recognised from the demo . . . I could not think of any other group or sound in pop music like it . . ."

Partly influenced by the mid-tempo, big ballad vocal style of the Big O, Roy Orbison, in striving for an effective air of simplicity, Lennon claimed that the group's second single, 'Please Please Me', was directed straight at the Hit Parade. "It was a slow, Roy Orbison kind of thing. . . .'*Come on (dum-dum), come on (dum-dum), please pleeeeeease me . . .*' Big note at the end," McCartney recalled, "just like Orbison." "But what made it more exciting," Lennon concurred, "was that we almost abandoned it as the B-side of 'Love Me Do'. We were getting very tired, and we just couldn't seem to get it right. We are conscientious about our work, and we don't like to rush things."

Martin would describe it as "a very slow rocker" with a high vocal part before making the suggestion of raising the song's tempo. 'Please Please Me''s "octave leaping chains" and the "exciting musical tensions of the syncopated bridge of call and response" were thrilling, Ian MacDonald maintained. Lennon also acknowledged the alliterative influence of the repetitive '*ease*' sound of the '*please lend a little ear to my pleas*' lyric found in Bing Crosby's thirties single, 'Please'.

"'Please Please Me' was only arrived at after much doubt on my part as to whether they could actually write a hit song," Martin later admitted. Asked to review and revise the song between sessions in the following weeks, they did their homework and returned with a successful faster tempo reading. "We altered the words slightly and went over the idea of featuring the harmonica," Lennon recalled, "just as we'd done on 'Love Me Do'." The group persuaded Martin to listen to the re-vamped number. "I said: 'OK, we'll give it a whirl, let's try your song and see if it works.'" After 18 takes, Martin informed them that they had just recorded their first chart-topper, and 'Please Please Me' duly reached number one in February. From this point, Lennon and McCartney gradually began their development into accomplished songwriters.

McCartney claimed that 'Please Please Me' was the first instance of Martin seeing beyond what the group were offering him. But it was the success of 'From Me To You' which followed that bestowed on Lennon and McCartney's songwriting the stamp of critical success on their road to fame. "You could be big headed and say: 'Yeah, we're going to last 10 years,'" Lennon intimated at the time, "but as soon as you've said that, you think, 'You know, we're lucky if we last three months.'" "That is the main problem with fame – that people forget how to act normally," Harrison concurred. "They are not in awe of you, but in awe of the thing that they think you've become."

'From Me To You' was instinctively recognised by the group as an obvious single candidate. Steering clear of complicated wordplay in favour of lyrical simplicity, another letter-style song emerged. 'From Me To You', featuring a melody line that carried the title phrase, had been written on a journey between York and Shrewsbury on tour in early 1963. McCartney declared that the song's middle eight (and its attendant "strange chord") had been a big compositional departure. "Say you're in C, then go to A minor, fairly ordinary, C, change it to G, and then F, but then it goes '*I got arms . . .*' and that's a G minor. Going to a G minor and a C takes you to a whole new world."

Of equal significance was that, from 'From Me To You' onwards, the group's songwriting credits would now read 'Lennon/McCartney' instead of 'McCartney/Lennon', a galling development that would continue to irritate McCartney in the years that followed, given the number of largely self-composed songs that were credited to both men. While Orbison had provided Lennon with crucial inspiration for their previous single, McCartney recalled that this sense of healthy songwriting competition with their American counterpart after hearing 'Pretty Woman' encouraged them to compose 'From Me To You'. They had subconsciously drawn their inspiration from the *From You To Us* letters column in the *New Musical Express*.

" 'From Me To You' was both of us: very much together. I remember being very pleased with the middle eight because there was a strange chord in it, and it went into a minor [chord]. *'I've got arms that long . . .'* We thought that was a very big step," McCartney also recalled. 'From Me To You' was a pivotal, co-penned song which, according to McCartney, constituted their real start as professional pop songwriters. Lennon's distinctive voice and wailing harmonica were pointers to the defining sound of Beatlemania, alongside their audience-enlivening harmonies.

'From Me To You''s successor, 'She Loves You', testified to unconditional love: an anthem of faith that encouraged loving each other through the personalisation of lyrics in a direct fashion. "There was a little trick we developed early on and got bored with later," McCartney admitted, "which was to put I, me or you in it, so it was very direct and personal. I suppose the most interesting thing was that it was a message song, it was someone bringing a message. It wasn't us anymore, it was a third person, which was a shift away."

In 'Love Me Do', 'Please Please Me', 'From Me To You' and 'She Loves You', the emphasis is placed on either an unconditional love or in spreading this love. 'She Loves You' was a classic 'custom-built' new single which enjoyed huge success as a number one in England, a fully co-written composition inspired by Bobby Rydell that was written on tour in a hotel room. "I'd planned an answering song where a couple of us would sing *'She loves you . . .'* and the other one answers, *'Yeah, yeah'*," McCartney later claimed. "It was Paul's idea: instead of singing *'I love you'* again, we'd have a third party," Lennon also recalled. "That kind of little detail is still in his work. He will write a story about someone. I'm more inclined to write about myself."

The song featured irresistible three-part harmonies, although Martin warned that Harrison's idea for a sixth chord harmonic cluster for its exuberant ending sounded too much like a corny musical cliché to his experienced ears. "But we said: 'It's such a great sound it doesn't matter, we've got to have it, it's the greatest harmony sound *ever*, We'd say: 'We like it man, it's bluesy'," McCartney insisted.

"I said [to myself]: 'I wonder if they are doing the right thing here?'" said Martin. "'Isn't this a bit unhip?' They looked at me as though I was mad. And Paul said: 'It's great! It's great!'"

Engineer Norman Smith was not overly impressed after reading the lyrics prior to recording the song. He soon reversed his opinion when he heard the urgently-delivered, conversational vocal and infectious hook. McCartney's father Jim, meanwhile, objected to the song's Americanisms when the group chanted '*yeah, yeah, yeah!*' instead of the more acceptable 'Yes, yes, yes!' Paul patiently explained that the grammatically precise phrase wouldn't work in a Beatles song. Released in August, 'She Loves You' became their third consecutive number one. Having been instructed in what to say as messengers, the song's reportage style conveyed a clear loving *communique*. The song's electrifying boldness and confidence was, as one critic described it, "the perfect synthesis of everything that made The Beatles great". Having opened the door in England and precipitated Beatlemania, Martin believed that 'She Loves You' would be the song to establish them in America.

Lennon and McCartney sang almost continuously in unison throughout 'She Loves You', swapping phrases before entering into glorious (and irresistible) harmonised territory, completed by Harrison's climactic G6th chord. "There were a lot of harmony songs around. Harmony in Western music is natural," Harrison would later opine. Lennon had the confidence that this motif would work well with their audience, and with echoes of Elvis' vocal mannerisms in its contagious '*yeah, yeah, yeah!*' refrain, their audience immediately felt the song's musical might. Alongside what Lennon classed as powerful and effective sound words, the song's opening drum roll also proved intrinsic to the track's dynamic momentum. The familiar signature details of The Beatles' energising stage presence coalesced into an unforgettable musical soundtrack to the outbreak of Beatlemania that simmered during the summer of 1963.

McCartney correctly stated that he and Lennon knew the '*yeah, yeah, yeah*' phrase would be effective, and they were proved right once it became synonymous with (and virtually defined) Beatlemania. "From then we were hooked on the recording drug," McCartney later enthused, "and when John and I sat down to write the next batch, it was with this in mind: 'Remember how exciting it was? Let's see if we can come up with something better.'"

The solemn album cover of their sophomore LP, *With The Beatles*, was in stark contrast to the musical and cultural maelstrom now surrounding them. If their early stage material was often little more than a marriage of musical expression of sound and words with rudimentary lyrics, then these early, electrifying love songs, culminating in 'She Loves You' and, a few months later, 'I Want To Hold Your Hand', proved to be a perfect magnet for America, the land of milk and honey where, traditionally, British acts had failed to prosper.

The group had resolved not to visit America until they had secured a number one, perhaps with an intuitive sense of the fortuitous circumstances that would surround their arrival. "We waited, and I think that was one of the best moves we ever made," insisted McCartney. "We were very cheeky. So we said: 'We're not going until we get a number one and we're headlining.'"

Released in November 1963, it's difficult to overestimate the impact and importance of a song like 'I Want To Hold Your Hand', their first US chart-topper in January of 1964. It remains a critical song in their early canon of work, and marked a new phase in the burgeoning Lennon-McCartney partnership. As the two men sat side-by-side at the piano, John turned to Paul as he found what became the song-defining chords, exclaiming: 'That's it! Do that again!' "In those days we really used to absolutely write like that," Lennon enthused, "both playing into each other's noses."

George Martin identified its importance, while claiming that no concessions were made to the American market. Yet it's difficult to envisage a more appropriate vehicle than this for the group's introduction to a new audience. As music broadcaster Paul Gambaccini noted, the country had been in deep mourning over the death of President Kennedy, and the American populace wanted a lift. 'I Want To Hold Your Hand', literally and figuratively, enabled the healing to begin.

From a group who subsequently became the soundtrack to a generation of young lives, 'I Want To Hold Your Hand' was a sincere and climactic Lennon-McCartney collaboration pitched at a new and inspiring creative level in which the group was able to strengthen their work into a tight, idiosyncratic structure.

Lennon admired (and had enjoyed singing) the song's beautiful co-written melody, claiming in 1970, somewhat surprisingly, that he would be keen to revisit the song again. This unique song seems to have every-thing, also combining the influence of contemporary French experimental music with a repeated, stuck-record style '*I can't hide*' phrase.

Written at Jane Asher's house, 'I Want To Hold Your Hand' was a charismatic marriage of melody, harmony and sound that offered unique – for its time – lyrical allusions and vocal phrasing. The song represents a creative high watermark in their early work and, given the song's lyrical inferences, exemplifies what Harrison believed was The Beatles' calming presence in troubled situations: an ability to transform a negative situation with positive energy. Lennon, meanwhile, soon realised that The Beatles were being looked upon as nothing less than faith healers – four spectral figures in the public eye – and, as the most intelligent of the four, was quick to recognise its potential dangers.

"I think that, particularly in the old days, the spirit of The Beatles seemed to suggest something very hopeful and youthful," McCartney would later reflect. "So, often, someone would ask us to say 'hello' to handicapped kids; to give them some kind of hope." The intensity of belief in The Beatles' aura of healing power through their musical presence prompted Martin to describe the frequent scenario of variously afflicted children being taken backstage to be 'healed'. Despite its enig-matic expression ('*I'll tell you something, I think you'll understand*'), the song's candid, tactile words have a genuine poignancy: '*When I touch you*', '*it's such a feeling*', '*I feel happy inside*' and the plea to '*hold your hand*' suggest the need for a responsive, healing connection.

The song's harmonies suggest an imminent sense of cathartic release, and when millions of Americans sang this song for themselves, it assuaged a stunned nation's pain during one of its darker hours. Replete with rousing handclaps and joyous harmonies, Hunter Davies claims the song was originally intended to be a modern take on the American gospel song. This was a potent record that enacted nothing less than a cultural revolu-tion. "The thing is, in America, it just seemed ridiculous – I mean, the idea of having a hit record over there," Lennon later marvelled. "It was just something you could never do."

Prior to their first trip to America in February 1964, The Beatles had performed a bill-topping, three-week residency at the Olympia Theatre in Paris in January. The Beatles learnt news of their Stateside success via a Capitol Records telegram. "He [Epstein] came running into the room, saying: 'Hey, look. You are number one in America!' 'I Want To Hold

Your Hand' had gone to number one," McCartney recalled. "It was such a buzz," Harrison reflected. "It was a great feeling because we were booked to go to America directly after the Paris trip."

"America was probably the definitive big flash, the real clincher," Paul confirmed. "But we had no idea how big we were out there. So we stepped off the plane and the crowd was enormous. The noise was deafening. On a scale of one to 10, that was a hundred in terms of the shock of it." The joy and energy of 'I Want To Hold Your Hand' effectively lifted a grateful America out of its wave of depression and forever changed the substance of the group's fame and career.

There was clearly something unique and exciting about the time of The Beatles' first flight to America. Assured of a safe passage and free to be themselves, The Beatles were still unsure what to expect. Starr was clearly enthralled. "America was the best. It was a dream, coming from Liverpool. I loved it." Following their fabled arrival in America on February 7, 1964, the reverence and affection they received proved a glorious moment. If there was a turning point in their career, Epstein mooted, a date on which "the breadth and scope of their future was to be altered, then it was the day their Pan Am jet touched down at Kennedy International Airport to a welcome that has seldom been equalled anywhere in history".

Before their arrival, American TV host Ed Sullivan had witnessed Beatlemania at first hand at Heathrow Airport when The Beatles returned to England from a brief tour of Sweden the previous July. References to Beatlemania had begun appearing in the British newspapers in late October, conferring on them a level of stardom that, with media coverage on their activities now emerging on an almost daily basis, was similar to that of the Royal Family. "He [Sullivan] didn't know us and we didn't know him," Lennon recalled. "All these forces started working so that when we landed in the US, the record was number one." "We'd already been hired by Ed Sullivan," Harrison added, "so if it had been a number two or number 10, we'd have gone anyway, but it was nice to have a number one."

Their five-song performance in front of 72 million viewers on *The Ed Sullivan Show* two days later, February 9, proved a zeitgeist-defining moment and a pivotal, epoch-making event in American post-war culture: a watershed day on which The Beatles and America came together. "It is still supposed to be one of the largest viewing audiences ever in the

States," Paul enthused. "It was very important."

"We were aware that Ed Sullivan was the big one, because we got a telegram from Elvis and the Colonel," Harrison later recalled.

"I didn't think beyond the moment during that US trip," Harrison reflected. "I wasn't really aware of any change-over in our fame. I don't think I looked to the future much. I thought: 'Well, we'll enjoy what's happening and go out there and do our thing.'"

Having landed in New York, their lively, irreverent press conference proved almost as memorable as their music. "I think people from Liverpool do have an affinity with Americans," McCartney would later insist, "with the GIs and the war and that. It is almost as if Liverpool and New York are twin towns." From the airport, the group travelled by Cadillac into Manhattan, where they stayed at the Plaza Hotel. "I remember, for instance, the great moment of getting into the limo and putting on the radio, and hearing a running commentary on us. 'They have just left the airport and are coming towards New York City' . . . it was like a dream. The greatest fantasy ever."

The city's music business impresario, Sid Bernstein, watched the group pull up on Fifth Avenue with McCartney revelling in the adoration of crowds of female fans. "We went into Central Park in a horse-drawn carriage. We had this huge suite of rooms in the Plaza hotel," Starr recalled, "with a TV on in each room, and we had radios with earpieces. This was all so fascinating to me."

While on air in the company of so-called 'Fifth Beatle' Murray The K, a bold New York broadcaster, Lennon also recalled: "We phoned every radio in town, saying: 'Will you play The Ronettes doing this?' We wanted to hear the music. We didn't ask for our own records, we asked for other people's."

"In 1964, The Beatles merely had to be themselves," writer David Fricke recounted. "Sullivan had the eyes of America. Together, they made it possible for rock'n'roll to change an entire nation – overnight." McCartney would later speak of the princely experience of travelling to New York in their first flush of Stateside success. The group had been convinced that they didn't stand a chance of succeeding in the States, but media articles soon began to generate interest and Stateside DJs began to play the group's records. "We did have three records ['Please Please Me,' 'From Me To You' and 'She Loves You'] out in America before this one. The others were on two different labels," Harrison recalled of the limited push behind their Swan and Veejay-licensed material. "It was only after all the publicity and the Beatlemania in Europe that Capitol Records decided: 'Oh, we will have them.' They put out 'I Want To Hold Your Hand' as our first single, but in fact it was our fifth."

Having refused previous requests from EMI and a frustrated Martin to promote The Beatles' early singles, Capitol – EMI's US outlet – was clearly astonished by The Beatles' gathering momentum and took an immediate interest in promoting their back catalogue. "I would send each one to my friends at Capitol Records in America and say: 'This group is fantastic. You've got to issue them, you've got to sell them in the States,'" recalled Martin. "And each time, the head of Capitol would turn it down. Of course, they had to accede to public demand. It took a whole year before they really conquered the world."

Given '. . . Hold Your Hand''s undeniable commercial appeal and European magazine coverage on The Beatles' rise to prominence, with Capitol now behind the group, Harrison knew success was assured.

Perhaps their refusal to go to America until they'd achieved a number one single was a subliminal leap of synchronicity; of being in the right place at the right time in order to coincide with (and facilitate) the lifting of America's spirits after the assassination of John F. Kennedy. Performed for their US audience, the song became a life-affirming antidote for a grieving American populace. America was crying out for their vibrancy and The Beatles were clearly happy to provide. Nothing, it seemed, could have stopped them now. As a positive force at a tumultuous time, The Beatles' arrival was clearly an epic moment, soundtracked by a song of healing imbued with an undisguisable inner joy.

American listeners (as well as countless future musicians and song-writers) sensed a powerful, precedent-setting moment courtesy of this potent-sounding song. 'I Want To Hold Your Hand' precipitated a new era and "perpetrated an act of cultural revolution" which ultimately changed millions of lives. "As the decade advanced and they continued to bring off variations on this trick," noted Ian MacDonald, "a sense grew among their audience that the group 'knew what was going on' and were poised above events, guiding them through their music."

Meanwhile, McCartney's songwriting flair was developing fast. 'All My Loving', from the group's second LP and the first track on the *Red* album not to have been issued as single, was another of his 'letter'-style songs, and may also have represented a sense of distance healing, sending love from afar. "Sometimes I've got a guitar in my hands, sometimes I'm sitting at a piano. It depends, whatever instrument I'm on, I write with. Every time it's different. 'All My Loving' I wrote like a bit of poetry, and put a song to it later."

A simultaneous UK and US number one, 'Can't Buy Me Love' owed some of its appeal to Martin's decision to open the song with its chorus refrain. "I thought we really needed a tag for the song's ending," the producer insisted, "so I took the first few lines of the chorus, changed the ending, and said, 'Let's just have these lines, and by altering the end of the second phrase, we can get back into the verse pretty quickly.'"

For the title song of their first film, *A Hard Day's Night*, producer Walter Shenson had asked John and Paul if they'd write a song especially for the opening and closing credits. "We thought about it and it seemed a bit ridiculous writing a song called 'A Hard Day's Night' – it sounded funny at the time, but after we got the idea of saying it had been a hard day's night and we'd been working all these days, and get back to a girl and everything is fine – and we turned it into one of those songs."

"I was going home in the car, and Dick Lester suggested the title from something Ringo had said," Lennon later recalled. "I had used it in *In His Own Write*, but it was an off the cuff remark by Ringo, one of those malapropisms – a Ringoism – said not to be funny, just said. So Dick Lester said, 'We are going to use that title,' and the next morning I brought in the song.

"The only reason Paul sang on 'A Hard Day's Night' was because I couldn't reach the notes: '*When I'm home, everything seems to be right . . . when I'm home . . .*' which is what we'd do sometimes. If one of us couldn't reach a note but he wanted a different sound, he'd get the other to do the harmony."

'A Hard Day's Night' strove to make impressive musical advances. Replete with huge, resonant, chiming chords, the song gave the listener a powerful sense of the group's growing musical ambition. Its blues-driven sound and Lennonian melody, too, set the stage for their forthcoming sense of sonic adventure and expressive confidence.

Furthermore, the song's striking opening chord represented a move into a progressive period, when The Beatles could be relied upon to produce something that was different, unusual and original.

Lennon was at his most dominant as a writer on *A Hard Day's Night*, explicitly so: creating 10 new compositions while McCartney supplied just three songs, albeit classics in their own right. Critic Mark Hertsgaard makes clear the significance of Lennon's pre-eminence as a rapidly growing original talent: breathtakingly creative and demonstrating an emotional depth that relied on far more than merely rock'n'roll, cynicism and his occasionally caustic wit.

Amidst the album's darker moods, there was always beauty by contrast. '*A love like ours, could never die, as long as I have you near me,*' McCartney sang on 'And I Love Her', his sublime romantic paean to girlfriend Jane Asher, a beautiful young stage and screen actress he'd met in April 1963. Four years Paul's junior, she became his most significant and enduring romantic partner during the turbulent years of Beatlemania.

Asher's father, Richard, was a doctor while her mother Margaret was a music teacher and oboeist who'd instructed George Martin. Jane's younger sister, Claire, was a violinist, and her elder brother Peter became half of the pop duo Peter & Gordon and, later, a successful record producer. This sophisticated, cultured and energetic upper middle-class family would all perform together in their 18th century Wimpole Street townhouse, where McCartney would reside for the next two years. A piano was installed for him in the basement music room, and the environment of the household unquestionably influenced Paul's growth as a musician and cultural explorer.

Asher was more interested in Beethoven than The Beatles, and she encouraged Paul to attend classical concerts at the local Wigmore Hall, marking the beginning of his passage towards a more refined outlook as he became an increasingly intellectual equal to the Asher brood. "He felt it was important to be at the centre of things," insisted press officer Tony Barrow. "And that's where Jane Asher came in, being not just the girlfriend, but somebody who could lift him up that social ladder."

The *Red* album continued with 'Eight Days A Week' from the *Beatles For Sale* LP, a US number one that was never released as a UK single. It proved a tough proposition. "We struggled to record it and struggled to make it into a song," Lennon admitted. "It was his [Paul's] initial effort, but I think we both worked on it."

"I remember writing that with John, at his place in Weybridge," McCartney confirmed, "from something said by the chauffeur who drove me out there. John had moved out of London, to the suburbs. I said, 'Hey, this fella just said, "'Eight days week,'"' John said, 'Right – *ooh, I need your love*' and we wrote it. We were always quite quick to write."

More appropriately, however, the song may be better interpreted in the original guise of *Eight Arms To Hold You*, '*hold me, love me, hold me*' as a potential title for their second film. It was not until mid-to-late 1965 onwards, when The Beatles resumed their more important work, that the music and the lyrics began working together once again. However, they were now focusing on new means and methods of expression in sound, as 'A Hard Day's Night', 'I Feel Fine' and 'Ticket To Ride' proved.

'I Feel Fine' was strongly influenced by the guitar riff in Bobby Parker's 'Watch Your Step', a particular favourite of Lennon's. "George and I play the same bit on guitar together," thus creating a double-tracked effect. "I suppose it has a bit of a country and western feel about it, but then so have a lot of our songs. The middle eight is the most tuneful part," Lennon later told the music press.

Lennon would remain proud of the song's precedent-setting feedback introduction, the first deliberate use of this effect on a pop record and one of their first sonic experiments to appear on record. "John got a bit of feedback unintentionally, and liked the sound and thought it would be good at the start of the song," Harrison remembered. 'I Feel Fine' went on to top both the UK and US charts that Christmas.

By 1966, Lennon was rumoured to be taking LSD on a daily basis, immersing himself in an endlessly introspective state, self-absorbed and experiencing an extreme negation of ego. Through dissolving his sense of self, he became a softer, mellower personality, all of which would have a profound effect on the songs he wrote.

As the latest instalment in a series of intriguing and innovative compositions, *Help!* highlight 'Ticket To Ride' was advertised as a new (even uncommercial) musical adventure, the start of what one critic coined their "weightless, ageless legend". It constituted arguably the group's earliest response to the creative effects of LSD, insofar as the drug could reveal to its user previously unknown layers of awareness.

'Ticket To Ride''s dissonance and unusual emotional depth bore the distinctive hallmark of a heartfelt Lennon composition. Coloured by an adventurous intensity which distinguished it from anything else they recorded in 1965, 'Ticket To Ride' was not an immediate choice as a Beatles single. "'Ticket To Ride' was slightly a new sound at the time. I'll show you what it is really, but you can hear it there," Lennon later enthused. "It's a heavy record and the drums are heavy too. That's why I like it."

'Ticket To Ride' was also a song full of newness: a melancholy wall of noise boasting huge chiming electric guitars, replete with a 12-string drone that gave way to gorgeous chord changes. Commercialised for release in a dense, driving production, its vibrant sound ambitiously pre-dated 'Tomorrow Never Knows' and 'Rain' by more than a year: an "extraordinary sheer sound event as one of the earliest heavy metal records", noted MacDonald.

Meanwhile, Lennon's patent admiration for Bob Dylan during the period of *Beatles For Sale* and *Help!* was best exemplified by 'You've Got To Hide Your Love Away'. "I'd started thinking about my emotions. Instead of projecting myself into a situation, I would try to express what I felt about myself, which I'd done in my books. I think it was Dylan who helped me realise that – not by any discussion or anything, but by hearing his work."

As we shall see, the song found the group singing, in part, about a feature of their subsequent musical direction, a point when few people were truly *listening* to their loving message or generous spirit on record. While this started becoming clear on *Rubber Soul*, after striving to find new, more artful ways of replicating their original optimistic, loving message, this effectively led to the largely forlorn, loveless-sounding *Revolver*.

"John was already doing it in his own right. He was writing before he'd heard of Bob Dylan. I'm sure this kind of thing found its way into our music, and into our lyrics," said McCartney. "Occasionally, we'd have an idea for some new kind of instrumentation, particularly for solos. On 'You've Got To Hide Your Love Away', John had wanted a flute. George Martin was very understanding, even though we were going to change style and get more psychedelic and surreal."

Marijuana had come to increasingly dominate their lives, something made patently clear during the making of their second feature film, *Help!* "Most people think it ['Help!'] is just a fast rock'n'roll song," said John. "I didn't realise it at the time – but later, I knew I was crying out for help. 'Help!' was about me, although it was a bit poetic. I was fat and depressed and I was crying out for help. It's real."

In striving to describe his own emotions and state of mind, Lennon's subsequent reaction to the song found him secure in his own state of self-awareness and lyrical acuity. "I remember I got very emotional at the time singing the lyrics. Whatever I'm singing, I really mean it. I don't mess about. And then there's always that very emotional music going on at the same time." "John never said that when he wrote it, he said it retrospectively," Harrison recalled. "He just didn't feel right."

While Lennon was experiencing a changing physical demeanour and an intellectual malaise, he was still the dominant force in terms of the group's output. In the studio, Martin would keep the tape running to capture everything The Beatles wanted to document. "It took us three or four records before we really got our sound," Lennon recalled. "I suppose it will be the same with films." However, Lennon ultimately remained unhappy with the film product and single release, believing neither were representative of what they wanted or who they were as a group.

McCartney recalled sitting down with Lennon and co-writing a fair proportion of the song once John had conceived the idea for the title track. "I helped with the structure of it and the little counter melodies. When we'd finished, we went downstairs and played it to Cynthia and [journalist] Maureen Cleave, and they thought it was good." The journalist's approval was ironic considering her earlier aspersions on Lennon's lyrical stylings. "I remember Maureen Cleave said to me: 'Why don't you ever write songs with more than one syllable in the words?' I never considered it before, so after that I put a few three syllable words in . . . I was insecure then, and things like that happened more than once."

Lennon defended 'Help!' as one of the few emotionally authentic Beatles compositions. The song found him exhibiting a somewhat startling means of self-expression, growing emotional in the studio while singing these stark, candid lyrics. "If you analyse our songs, John's are often on one note, whereas mine are often much more melodic," McCartney later enthused. "I enjoy going places with melodies. I like what John did too, but his are more rhythmic. So to take away from the solo note a little bit, I wrote a descant to it. That's what I was there for, to complete it."

Lennon always bemoaned the musical compromises made in order to ensure its commerciality, although the import placed on a forthright melody remains a key element to almost all recording activity. Nevertheless, it is now perceived that the *ennui* behind this watershed song was a 'cry for help' during what he described as his 'fat Elvis' phase: overindulgent and underwhelmed by fame's lack of fulfilment. His emotional vocal was imbued with authority, reverting time and again to a sense of tension and anxiety.

Side two of the *Red* album closes with 'Yesterday', perhaps the most successful song by any contemporary writer of McCartney's generation. Paul claimed to have awoken in the night with what became the melody for 'Yesterday' in his head, and had simply assumed he had remembered one of the many jazz standards played to him by his father. A hesitant McCartney was convinced that the virtually fully-formed song had been unconsciously drawn from his vast memory bank of musical compositions.

McCartney duly fell out of his bed in the small garret at the top of the Asher home in Wimpole Street, and headed straight for his bedside piano to search for the appropriate chords, beginning with G. "I said to myself, 'I wonder what it is?' I just couldn't figure it, because I'd just woken up. And I got a couple of chords to it. I got the G, then I got the nice F sharp minor seventh, that led very naturally to the B, which led to the E minor. It just sort of kept tumbling out with these chords. I thought, 'Well, this is very nice,' there was no logic to it at all. And I'd never had that. It was fairly mystical when I think about it, because of the circumstances. It was the only song I ever dreamed! That's why I don't profess to know anything. I think music is all very mystical. You hear people saying: 'I'm a vehicle, it just passes through me.' Well, you're lucky if something like that passes through you."

Having ensured he remembered the song, McCartney canvassed his friends at every opportunity in an attempt to place the song's origin, convinced that he had not knowingly written it due to its dreamlike genesis. He even played it for Yardbird Eric Clapton, who didn't recognise it either. "I took it round to Alma Cogan, a friend of ours and she said: 'I don't know it, but it is rather nice.'" Her mother even suggested a provisional lyrical focus for the song. "It didn't have any words at first, so I blocked it out with 'scrambled eggs'. Over the next couple of weeks I started to put in the words. I liked the tune, and I thought I'd like to take some time over the words," Paul later admitted. *En route* to a holiday in Portugal in the spring of 1965, McCartney began penning surprisingly mature lyrics based around the nostalgic theme of yesterday and his mother's passing.

Harrison would famously quip that his bandmate now believed himself to be in the same compositional class as Beethoven, having written what he considered his most complete song. This lachrymose ballad, more suited to Frank Sinatra or Ray Charles, was orchestrated to give the song a classical elegance. As a track which essentially comprised of Paul's solo vocal performance against his acoustic guitar, it sounded unlike anything else they'd thus far recorded. Martin's work on the arrangement marked a significant moment in terms of his creative contributions to the group's music.

The *Help!* soundtrack album's most illustrious and timeless offering, 'Yesterday' led one critic to claim it offered sterling proof of the group's genius. "The song's understated quartet arrangement, with its suggestive associations with the past," reasoned critic Walter Everett, "is a fit colouring for a retrospective and sentimental song." Often the recipient of fans' praise for Paul's classic composition, Lennon seemed to be unaffected by, and certainly not envious of, its incredible success. "The song was around for months and months before we finally completed it. Every time we got together to write songs for a recording session, this would come up. We almost had it finished. Paul wrote nearly all of it, but we just couldn't find the right title. We called it 'Scrambled Egg' and it became a joke between us."

Though not strictly a Beatles record, McCartney claimed he wouldn't have agreed to its release as a solo single. "We never entertained those ideas. It was sometimes tempting; people would flatter us: 'Oh, you know, you should get out front' or 'You should put out a solo record.' But we always said 'No.'"

"Then I said, 'Well, what can I do with it?'" Martin later recalled. "The only thing I can think of is adding strings. I said: 'What about a quartet?' He thought that was interesting. And I went and worked on it with him. He had ideas too, and we booked a string quartet and overdubbed the strings – and that was the record." 'Yesterday' boasted yearning suspended chords and, with McCartney's supervisory input, Martin's first string arrangement for the group was one of austere clarity. In contrary fashion, McCartney's subsequent love songs during this period began to sound progressively sombre, an ominous portent for his relationship with Asher. The knowledge that 'Yesterday' had arrived almost fully formed served to reinforce The Beatles' trust in their own musical instincts as they became progressively more experimental in the months to come.

Looking beneath the surface of the material produced during their 1965 *Rubber Soul* album sessions, a number of the songs reveal a sense of disillusionment with a lack of illumination, strained communication and impatience with the limits of perception among their audience. Striving to clarify themselves on record in the mid-sixties, songs of the calibre of 'We Can Work It Out' called for people to take on board their message. While they weren't necessarily providing 'answers', there was a sense of their need to remind people about their musical purpose.

Attempting to promote a mood of mutual conciliation, McCartney wrote the song's chorus and Lennon penned the middle section, although whether Paul's 'we can work it out' entreaty was as selflessly optimistic as John believed remained to be seen. As biographer Howard Sounes correctly notes, it suggests more of a 'my way or else' mentality (*try to see it my way*) in opposition to Lennon's genuine determination to beseech peace (*life is very short, and there's no time for fussing and fighting, my friend*). The song demonstrates truly complementary attributes in one of their most articulate creations. Due in part to the element of serendipity, the song was partly composed on a Salvation Army harmonium, and duly carried a gospel-like percussive warmth and an intriguing, Mediterranean flavoured waltz-like drone effect.

During their controversy-ravaged US tour in 1966, Lennon was asked whether the group planned to record any anti-war messages. "All our songs are anti-war!" he defiantly stated. "On our first tour [August 1964], there was an unspoken thing that Mr. Epstein was preventing us talking about the Vietnam War. Before we came back for the second, George and I said to him: 'We don't go unless we answer what we feel about the war.'" "We were always saying we should speak out about Vietnam, and I think we did at times," Harrison would concur. "I think about it every day, and it's wrong. Anything to do with war is wrong."

'We Can Work It Out' is an unusually urgent yet peaceable entreaty towards resolution and equanimity, an early forerunner to 'All You Need Is Love' and, in the name of peace, was their attempt to foster a spirit of loving harmony amongst their audience. Moreover, McCartney may also have been singing to his bandmates as much as his partner and the world at large, as initial creative or personal differences began to intervene in the group's songwriting partnership.

Again, Asher and McCartney's blustery relationship helped inspire the lyric. "Something of a breakthrough for Paul, his part of the lyric displays a dramatic instinct which would soon begin to dominate his work," MacDonald surmised. During the next two years, McCartney began moving into the ascendancy as a writer, arranger and group motivator. Elsewhere on the album, the likes of 'Nowhere Man' and 'Michelle' were permeated by lyrical themes such as: *Why won't you listen?*, *Why can't you see?* and *Why can't you understand?*

With a vaguely tongue-in-cheek, comedic air, 'Michelle' was a Chet Atkins-like, folk-tinged acoustic number. Paul sought translation assistance from Ivan Vaughan's French tutor wife, Jan, who was asked to think of a French girl's name and a descriptive rhyming adjective. The song found McCartney spreading a transparent message of love, with assistance on the middle eight from Lennon's *'I love you, I love you, I love you'* line. But behind the gentle, beautiful song's otherwise amorous lyricism, the themes of perception, awareness and understanding were reiterated when McCartney sings *'the only words I know that you will understand . . . I need to make you see . . . I'm hoping you will know what I mean.'*

"My contribution to Paul's songs was always to add a little blues edge to them," Lennon insisted. "Otherwise 'Michelle' is a straight ballad. He provided a lightness, an optimism, while I would always go for the sadness, the discords, the bluesy notes." McCartney remembered being present at the Ad Lib nightclub and hearing the song in the company of David Bailey. Startled into defending the song's authenticity, Paul later concluded that its left-field qualities added to its attraction.

Lennon's philosophical 'answer' to 'Michelle' came in the form of the sighing, wistful 'Girl' and its devout anti-Papal sentiment (*'Was she taught when she was young that pain would lead to pleasure'*). With a world-weary air, it was artfully constructed around his feminine bohemian ideal and boasted a Greco-Mediterranean, mandolin-like two-step rhythm. "I was trying to say something or other about Christianity, which I was opposed to at the time because I was brought up in the church. I was talking about Christianity, in that you have to be tortured to attain heaven. That was the catholic Christian concept." Meanwhile, 'Nowhere Man' (*'He's as blind as he can be/ just sees what he wants to see . . . knows not where he's going to/ Can you see me at all?'*) bore the most direct reflection of Biblical influence, at least in terms of its writer searching for the light as he sought for a new direction. Others have concluded that it expressed Lennon's boredom as he wiled time away in his Surrey mansion.

These were weary reflections of a privately insecure, wealthy musician in one of his more introspective periods, and the song's repetitive and predictable harmony was equally unusual of its author. However, the dense vocal textures and the gleaming treble of Lennon and Harrison's unison solo gave the song a bright, autumnal warmth. It was received in suitably mediumistic fashion at dawn after Lennon had spent five hours attempting to write a strong and meaningful song. Once he had allowed his conscious mind to 'let go', the requisite inspiration arrived: some form of prophetic or divine assistance with the temporary quandary surrounding his artistic expression.

"'Nowhere Man' was one of John's, coming from a big night the night before and getting to bed about five in the morning," claimed McCartney. "That was a great one. He said: 'I started one last night.' It turned out later that it was about me: '*He's a real nowhere man.*' I maybe helped him with a word here or there. But he'd already got most of it. Part of the secret [of] collaboration was that we like each other. We liked singing at each other. He'd sing something and I'd say, 'Yeah,' and trade off on that. He'd say, '*nowhere land,*' and I'd say, '*for nobody*': it was a two-way thing."

Easing his temporary writer's block during the autumn 1965 album sessions, Lennon was in a relaxed, switched-off state when the lyrical inspiration for the song arrived. "I was just sitting, trying to think, and I thought of myself sitting there, doing nothing and going nowhere. Once I thought of that, it was easy, it all came out. I'd actually stopped trying to think of something. Nothing would come. I was cheesed off and went for a lie down, having given up. Then I thought of myself as nowhere man – sitting in this nowhere land. 'Nowhere Man' came, words and music, the whole thing."

A similar approach also paid dividends on 'In My Life'. "I'd struggled for days and hours, trying to write clever lyrics. Then I gave up, and the song came to me – letting it go is the whole game." This remains a wonderful piece of work of which Lennon rightly remained proud. A wise, heartfelt song which he considered his first 'serious' composition, it's one he always sought to emulate. "I had one mind that wrote books, and another mind that churned out things about '*I love you*' and '*you love me*', because that's how Paul and I did it. I'd always tried to make sense of the words, but I never really cared. It was the first song that I wrote that was really, consciously about my life. It was sparked by a remark a journalist and writer [Kenneth Tynan] in England made after *In His Own Write* came out."

Lennon's *In His Own Write* was published in March 1964. Some of the book originated from Lennon's schooldays and his *Daily Howl* digest, a comic full of jokes and *avant-garde* poetry. Other sections were freshly written, and duly appeared in the *A Hard Day's Night* film. "He [Tynan] said to me: 'Why don't you put some of the way you write in the book in the songs? Or why don't you put something about your childhood into the songs?'"

Understandably enough, Lennon derived great satisfaction from seeing his published effort acclaimed by the writing fraternity. "I like writing books. It's just my style of humour. And the reason is that it's part of a different world. What success really does for you is to give you a feeling of confidence in yourself. It's an indescribable feeling, but once you've had it, you never want it to stop." Initially a teenage fan of Chaucer, Lennon would gravitate towards Lewis Carroll, James Thurber and Ronnie Searle.

McCartney recalled visiting a teenage Lennon working away at his humorous, surreal verse while seated at the typewriter at home in Liverpool. "An awful lot of the material was written while we were on tour. A friend, an American who shall remain nameless called Michael Braun [author of *Love Me Do: The Beatles' Progress*], took all the remaining material to the publishers and the man there said: 'This is brilliant. I'd like to do this.' And that was before he even knew who I was."

Having been reminded about his lyrical gift for novelistic word play, Lennon utilised this agility in 'In My Life', a mature song that not only recalls the past, but implores others to tell people, here and now, what they mean to us. "Most of my good songs are in the first person. They're all personal records. I always wrote about me when I could. I like first-person music. But because of my hang ups, and many other things, I would only now and then specifically write about me. I wrote the lyrics first and then sang it. That was usually the case with things like 'In My Life' and 'Across The Universe' and some of the ones that stand out a bit. I wrote it in Kenwood, upstairs, where I had about ten tape recorders, all linked up. I'd mastered them over the period of a year or two."

"He wrote some beautiful ballads," an admiring Paul would later recall. "The interesting thing is we actually come out rather equal. The more you analyse it, the more you get to the feeling that both of us always had, which was one of equality." 'In My Life' was also a favourite of their producer, who admired its charming Lennonian touch. "John couldn't decide what to do in the middle and, while they were having their tea-break, I put down a baroque piano solo which John didn't hear until he came back," Martin later reflected. "What I wanted was too intricate for me to do live, so I did it with a half-speed piano, then sped it up, and he liked it."

'In My Life' was also a reminder to its author that we must acknowledge what our heart says about love. "I'd struggled for days and hours, trying to write clever lyrics," he recalled. Giving up the fight duly produced the goods. Having attempted to incorporate suitable references, as soon as his conscious mind let go, the lyric took shape and the song 'came through'. The song originated from a poetic document, *Places I Remember*, an account of an adolescent journey through familiar Liverpool landmarks. "It started out as a bus journey from my house on 251 Menlove Avenue to town. I had a complete set of lyrics naming every sight. It became 'In My Life,' a remembrance of friends and lovers of the past. Paul helped with the middle eight musically."

As McCartney recalled, the song was one of very few instances where its original source caused disagreement with Lennon. "I remember writing the melody on a Mellotron that was parked on his half landing. John might have half an idea, something like '*There are places I remember . . .*' I think he had that first as a lyric – like a poem, and we'd work out the extra melody needed, and the main theme. When we strung them together in a composition they sounded contrived."

'Norwegian Wood', meanwhile, was a poeticised Lennon account of a clandestine liaison. "I'd always had some kind of affairs going, so I was trying to be sophisticated in writing about an affair, but in such a smoke-screen way that you couldn't tell. I was writing from my experiences, girls' flats, things like that. We went through many different versions of the song. It was never right and I was very angry about it; it wasn't coming out like I said. They said, 'just do it how you want'. And I did the guitar very loudly into the mike and sang it at the same time."

Acoustic bass and 12-string guitar had been recorded and, as Harrison recalled, it needed some additional colour. With The Beatles growing increasingly fascinated with their search for interesting new sounds and broader musical horizons, it was down to Martin to help accommodate this in the studio. "They were always waiting to try new instruments even when they didn't know much about them."

George's interest in Indian music had been sparked during the filming of *Help!* when he experimented on the Indian musician's instruments during a restaurant scene. As the year progressed, Harrison would be made aware of the maestro Indian musician Ravi Shankar during conversations with friends. Encouraged to explore his music, George duly bought one of Shankar's albums. The incredible sounds he heard precipitated a lifelong love affair with Indian music. "When I first heard Indian music, it was as if I already knew it. There was something about it that was very familiar, but at the same time, intellectually, I didn't know what was happening at all." Harrison duly felt that a meeting with Shankar would be inevitable under the proper circumstances, already aware of press attempts to put the two men together after his recording work on 'Norwegian Wood'.

Having purchased a rudimentary sitar from the Indiacraft store in London, Harrison had precious little knowledge of the instrument, and was yet to figure out what to do with it. "George had the sitar and I asked him: 'Could you play the piece that I'd written?' He was not sure whether he could play it yet, because he hadn't done much on the sitar, but he was willing to have a go, as is his wont," Lennon recalled, "and he learnt the bit, and dubbed it on after." "It was quite spontaneous," George remembered. "I found the notes that played the lick. It fitted and it worked."

"It was such a mind-blower that we had this strange instrument on a record. We were all open to anything when George introduced the sitar," Starr admitted. "Anything was viable. Our whole attitude was changing. We'd grown up a little I think."

The album's accompanying single, 'Day Tripper', was, according to its author, a somewhat forced and pressurised affair. "It was very hard going that, and it sounds it. It wasn't a serious message song," Lennon insisted. "It was a drug song – in a way, it was a day tripper – I just liked the word." 'Day Tripper' was a salute to their appropriation of the 'Respect' lick on the equally ironic 'Drive My Car'. "In the early days they were very influenced by American rhythm and blues," Martin insisted, "I think the so-called Beatles sound had something to do with Liverpool being a port. Maybe they heard the records before we did. They certainly knew much more about Motown and black music than anybody else did, and that was a tremendous influence on them." The album definitely showed the group now moving in a fresh musical direction.

With a comedic undertone coursing through its rhythmic groove, album opener 'Drive My Car''s contemporary black American R&B feel had been partly infused by Memphis' then-fashionable Stax house sound, while Harrison's bassline was a clear copy of Otis Redding's 'Respect' riff. "The sort of people we were listening to then were on Stax and Motown," McCartney recalled. "George used to have a great collection of Stax records on his jukebox. The Miracles were a big influence on us, where Little Richard had been earlier."

McCartney, like Lennon, remembered that 'Drive My Car' was one of the most difficult songs they had ever brought to fruition, striving to get past the early lyrical hook of '*You can buy me golden rings*'. "We struggled for hours. I think we struggled for too long. Then we had a break, and suddenly it came. 'Wait a minute! Drive my car!' Then we got into the fun of that scenario. 'Oh, you can drive my car.' Golden rings became '*Beep, beep, yeah.*' We both came up with that."

The songs to be found on *Rubber Soul* formed a natural preamble to the work that accompanied the consciousness-raising drug experiences of the mid-to-late sixties. McCartney has since admitted that, through their 'breakthrough' experiences on LSD, many moments occurred of looking at each other and recognising themselves. "After I took it, it opened my eyes. Just think what we could all accomplish if we could only tap that hidden part. It would mean a whole new world . . ."

While The Beatles clearly had no real interest in replicating or writing with their live sound in mind in the studio, sessions for the subsequent *Revolver* album produced the heavily amplified sound experiment 'Paperback Writer', an exciting one-chord manifesto parcelled as a letter concerning the virtues of a lightweight novel. In truth, the double-tracked song was Paul's attempt to engage us with our hearts' desire. Someone who has the ability to write can follow the path of their choosing, he insists, and succeed by listening to their heart. It also features a cryptic '*frere Jacques*' reference to 'brother John', either for his bandmate or a possible, if tenuous, Biblical reference.

"I remember showing up at John's house with the idea for 'Paperback Writer'. I had a long drive to get out there," recalled McCartney, "and I would often start thinking and writing on my way out, and I developed the whole idea in the car. I came in, and said: 'How about if we write a letter: Dear Sir or Madam, next line, paragraph etc. I wrote it all out, and John said: 'Yeah, that's good,' it just flowed."

Lennon characteristically described the song as being the "son of 'Day Tripper'" – a "rock'n'roll song with a guitar lick on a fuzzy loud guitar." Martin noted the song's heavier sound, and the emphasis now being placed on rhythm in their compositional approach. In retrospect, 'Paperback Writer' is a partly satirical, effect-driven song, although the vocal arrangements, suggestive of The Beach Boys, perhaps inspired the subsequent '*brother John*' reference in their 1967 song, 'Surf's Up'.

McCartney's fluid, pounding bass work showed him evolving further as an actively melodic and innovative player. However, in his attempt to define a new sound and direction for the group in the wake of the transitional *Rubber Soul*, McCartney's enthusiasm for new production techniques, growing self-confidence and his 'persistent' attitude towards the more patient Harrison's guitar-playing probably didn't promote much warmth and unity. Yet, this was not essential for the *Red* album's two concluding songs, McCartney's string-driven *Revolver* landmark 'Eleanor Rigby' and children's singalong, 'Yellow Submarine'.

Given the controversy that surrounded Lennon's comments on religion, it's somewhat ironic that McCartney's stark portrayal of a fading lack of faith should have been overlooked. McCartney later referred to the church's failure to account for the world's suffering as part of their subsequent interest in meditation. Now making increasingly sophisticated music, there came this powerfully original and evocative song. 'Eleanor Rigby', a poignant tale and a dramatic slice of timeless commentary partly consisted of what McCartney described as "almost Asian, Indian rhythms".

"It was the first inklings of what I'm starting to get into now, writing a solo piano piece, writing a piece for classical orchestra or the Oratorio." Playing the piano in Jane Asher's basement, Paul found a simple, two-chord / E minor Dorian melody for this melancholic parable. "I used to disappear there, and while I was fiddling on a chord some words came out. '*Dazzie-de-da-zu, picks up the rice in a church where a wedding has been . . .*' the idea of someone picking up rice after a wedding took it in that poignant direction. That came out of the blue. I didn't know where that came from. I was very keen to get a real-sounding name for that tune and that whole idea. We were working with Eleanor Bron on *Help!* and I liked the name Eleanor; I saw Rigby in a shop in Bristol one evening. I thought, 'Oh great name, Rigby. It's real, and yet a bit exotic.' Eleanor Rigby."

Paul had sought a wintry string octet arrangement, and Martin provided a sublime Herrmann-style orchestration. Displaying his growing skill at fitting rhyming words to a melody as an increasingly novelistic writer, McCartney created this tense episode of Beckett-influenced drama. Through Margaret Asher, McCartney had attempted formal piano lessons with a Guildhall School of Music tutor. "I showed him 'Eleanor Rigby' because I thought he'd be interested, but he wasn't." Immersed in London's theatrical and cultural heartland, Jane had apparently introduced Paul to the wonders of Vivaldi's music.

Meanwhile, the surreal idea of children's song 'Yellow Submarine' had arrived for McCartney through inner hearing during a pre-sleep period. "I remember lying in bed one night, in that moment before you're falling asleep, that little twilight moment when the silly ideas come into your head," he recalled. "I quite like children's songs, I like children's minds and imagination. So it didn't seem uncool to me to have a pretty surreal idea that was also a children's idea."

"I don't actually know where they got the idea for it, I just felt it was a really interesting track to do. I'd been doing a lot of covers, at that time, I did either covers or something they wrote specifically for me," Starr remembered. Singer-songwriter Donovan offered assistance with the song's '*Sky of blue, sea of green*' lyrics, while the group further enlivened the track based on McCartney's initial nautical inspiration.

"They had a great time in the studio, and in the main, they were enormously happy times," their producer recalled. "They would fool around a lot and have a laugh, particularly when overdubbing voices. John was funny, they all were. My memory is of a very joyful time," said Martin, whose comedic production and record-making experience with The Goons proved invaluable in creating a chaotic subterranean haven of noise effects. "As soon as The Beatles began kicking over the traces of popular musical conventions," Martin later insisted, "it gave me the freedom to do more of what I enjoyed; experimenting, building sound pictures, creating a whole atmosphere for a song, all the things I'd always loved doing . . . creating atmosphere and sound pictures." With its proto-'All You Need Is Love' sentiment of '*Every one of us has all we need*', the subsequent *Yellow Submarine* animation film of the same name found all four Beatles depicted atop a 'YES' sign, an affirmation of the song's loving message.

Meanwhile, during the summer of 1966 the group (and their huge popularity) became the target for a vitriolic, controversy-inflamed backlash in America and the Far East. This hostility towards The Beatles, coupled with the partial intimidation they faced, not to mention the musical limitations in performing their adventurous new work onstage, would ultimately prove a decisive factor in their abandoning the stage for good.

Revolver had proved a last full gasp of old-fashioned Beatles unity. The previously strong bond in Lennon and McCartney's songwriting relationship was now showing signs of tension. The *Revolver* sessions had begun with one eye clearly on the future with 'Tomorrow Never Knows' and ended with Lennon's partly nostalgic 'She Said, She Said', which recounted actor Peter Fonda's unnerving words during an acid trip with the group at a Los Angeles mansion in the summer of 1965.

While neither song was included on the *Blue* compilation, Lennon's lyrics were, with hindsight, a partial admission of spiritual disorientation and a reflection of childhood memories that he'd eventually fully acknowledge during Primal Scream therapy in 1970. "I was at his house one day, and he was struggling with some tunes," Harrison later recalled. "He had loads of bits, maybe three songs that were unfinished, and I made suggestions and helped him to work them together so that they became one finished song."

'She Said, She Said' also illustrated the energy Lennon was still pouring into his music, confronting or drawing on his pain for the good of his art.

CHAPTER THREE

Rhythm Of The Saints

RICHARD Perry and Harrison then began to consider the merits of the group's post-*Revolver* achievements as found on The Beatles' *Blue* album. The producer singled out for particular praise one of Lennon's most wondrous creations, the 1967 single 'Strawberry Fields Forever'. For Lennon, language in song was like trying to describe a dream. The result was an often startling yet inspiring verification of his own experiences. The creative journey undertaken by The Beatles between 'Love Me Do' and 'Strawberry Fields . . .' not only illustrated the rapid development in their songwriting art and evolution of musical expression, but indicated that this was the work of two very different and vastly distinguishable Beatles.

While it may have taken time for The Beatles to make 'Strawberry Fields . . .' into what it was always intended to be, they were now looking towards new musical horizons, articulating greater emotional sensations in their songs; opening a new vista through which a free flow of musical light entered their creative world.

"Way ahead of its time, strong and complicated both in concept and execution, highly original and quickly labelled 'psychedelic', 'Strawberry Fields Forever' was the work of an undoubted genius," Martin insisted in his *Sergeant Pepper* memoir, *The Summer Of Love*. "He [John] had broken through into different territory to a place I did not really recognise," the producer recalled. "It was completely unlike anything we had done before. We could not have produced a better prototype for the future. For my money, it was the most original and inventive track to date in pop music."

An articulate and musically compelling work, 'Strawberry Fields . . .' was indeed well ahead of its time. "The care and attention we lavished on the track," commented Martin, "its technical and musical excellence – these things set the pattern for what was to become *Pepper*. John's other world, the one in his mind, was always and forever the world he preferred to live in. It was a far more comfortable place to be."

"I was trying to describe myself, how I felt, but I wasn't *sure* how I felt," Lennon would later admit. "The second line goes, '*No one I think is in my tree.*' Well, what I was trying to say in that line is: 'Nobody seems to be as hip as me, therefore I must be crazy or a genius.' It's the same problem as I had when I was five. 'Strawberry Fields . . .' was psychoanalysis set to music, really."

Having ceased touring and unsure of The Beatles' next creative move, Lennon had begun composing this halting, exploratory track whilst filming *How I Won The War* with director Dick Lester in Almeria, Spain in early autumn 1966. The song's prophetic lyrical tone ('*Living is easy with eyes closed/misunderstanding all you see*') Lennon later insisted, was not a personal sentiment but a worldly observation. Lennon's evocation of a sense of illusion ('*Nothing is real*') would be shared by Harrison in 'Within You, Without You'. Once Lennon had found his voice, the song effectively proved the literal starting point in preparing the way for what became *Sergeant Pepper*.

Arguably Lennon's greatest composition, 'Strawberry Fields . . .' was, as Martin later noted, 'a sweet, gentle song' prior to the introduction of heavy instrumentation, swooping cellos and blaring brass. Having recorded an acoustic, pre-psychedelic version of the song, Martin happily recalled his first exposure to Lennon's masterpiece in waiting. "It was magic," the producer insisted. "It was absolutely lovely. I love John's voice anyway, and it was a great privilege listening to it." Lennon's halting expression and uncertain struggle for emotional articulacy was evident on this unique and thrilling song.

Famously unsatisfied with the original, ethereal sounding version of the song, Lennon decided to re-make 'Strawberry Fields . . .' before editing the two distinct renditions together. "He could hear what he wanted, in his head, but he couldn't make it real," recalled Martin, who was as determined as Lennon to fully realise (and artfully manage) the emotional expression, inventive instrumentation and captivating sound of this enigmatic song. However, The Beatles never worried about something seeming impossible in the studio.

Based initially on the old Salvation Army home for kids that John lived in close proximity to in Liverpool, 'Strawberry Fields . . .' had been envisaged by its author as an idealised image, a dream garden or secret hideaway in the group's attempt to create a suitably vivid sound picture. Establishing its own place in the psychology of pop music thanks to its articulation of ambiguous, intense or confusing emotions, this was "a magical, all-beautiful, all-loving vision in which opposites are peacefully reconciled," one critic observed.

The song's setting was not only a childhood fantasy retreat but a visionary location accessible via Lennon's imaginative powers. "'Strawberry Fields Forever' was a magical childhood place for [John], and we transformed it into the sort of psychedelic dream; it was like *everybody*'s magic place instead of ours," claimed Paul in 1992. "We took them from being little localised things, to making them more global." Meanwhile, the song's classical moods and textures encouraged Martin to describe the song as a 'complete tone poem'. Through an essentially economical songwriting approach, The Beatles managed to avoid self-indulgence and creative frippery, producing powerful musical art in the process.

'Strawberry Fields . . .' marked a turning point in Lennon's writing, wherein he began looking to the past for lyrical inspiration. This may have begun as early as 'In My Life', an incredibly mature and knowing song for a 25-year-old. 'Strawberry Fields . . .' also exhibits a similar sentiment to that of 'Rain', with regards to its sense of perception: '*You can't tune in*' followed the earlier song's exclamation of '*Can you hear me?*'

Critic Walter Everett reasoned that Lennon's grasp of his own higher awareness compared to others did not create a sense of superiority, but instilled a sense of the outsider. '*No-one is on my wavelength*' ran one of the song's early lyrics: part of an enigmatic work which develops and refines the lyrical threads of the *Rubber Soul* and *Revolver* era, and reflected the band's newly experimental music-making approach.

As a complement to the powerful, idiosyncratic strings, flugelhorn and trumpets, the song featured a magical series of random Mellotron notes, while cellos wove around Paul's guitar fills and the brass fanfare. With a divine, flute-like figure during the song's introduction and Harrison's swordmandal *glissando* providing an exotic, charming element to the song, this was a deeply colourful, purposeful and emotional work.

When Lennon sought to merge the first half of the original airy version with the dark urgency of a faster and denser second recording, his producer had insisted that the different versions were virtually irreconcilable. Lennon knew it was feasible and was proved right, thanks to masterful editing work. "The key change was in the right way, and John could sing in almost any key," Martin would later recall. "It was a section brimming with energy, and I was determined to keep it." However, Lennon later considered re-recording the song once again. Both 'Strawberry Fields . . .' and McCartney's response, 'Penny Lane', represented two thrilling complementary sides of a single, classic Lennon-McCartney statement, inspiring an awakening of the imagination and the senses in their audience. McCartney recalled their intentions of transforming both sides of The Beatles single into a place of universal awareness for the listener.

Both songs should have featured on the subsequent *Sergeant Pepper* album, and the joint decision reached with manager Brian Epstein over their omission still rankles with their producer. Feeling that the group had relinquished something of their popular appeal, Epstein requested a classic single for the New Year. Having just produced arguably their finest ever tracks, Martin resolved to release a Beatles double-A-side in early 1967. Not only did they fail to reach the top of the charts, these wondrous pieces of modern musical art were then kept off the subsequent Beatles album. "That was a crazy idea, and I'm afraid I was partly responsible. It's nonsense these days," Martin later admitted.

Having pulled The Beatles back together, McCartney effectively took the lead in bringing their garlanded, transitional 1967 album, *Sergeant Pepper*, to fruition. Paul's 'Penny Lane', an equally colourful song of heightened perception and understanding, represents a greater sense of higher awareness and a veritable awakening to divine sound, replete with brazen trumpets.

The song, as Martin recalled, had partly been inspired by a musical epiphany of sorts for its composer. "Paul came to me one day and said: 'I've been listening to Beethoven, George. I've just sussed it out. You know the beginning of the Fifth? It's only unison. There are no chords. Everybody's playing the same notes! It's a great sound! The whole orchestra speaks with one voice – that's genius. Most people probably don't even realise that it is the whole lot of them all playing single notes at once.'"

McCartney had also seen the English Chamber Orchestra play Bach's second Brandenburg Concerto in F major and requested a high, quasi-baroque piccolo trumpet solo from David Mason. As one music critic noted, the song moves between two different keys, a back and forth transition between the current and the past. The listener duly moves between two different worlds before the song finds a modicum of resolution. It's little wonder that The Beatles were being treated as heralds of a bright new era, energised by their restless musical and artistic exploration.

Like Lennon's interior world, McCartney was, in effect, writing about a location he knew intimately and viewed wistfully. "I suppose the way things did go was that each of us would say, mine's 'Strawberry Fields . . .' yours is 'Penny Lane'. That did start to happen. It's part fact, part nostalgia for a great place – '*blue suburban skies*', as we remember it, and it's still there."

"John would tell me what kind of mood he wanted on a song, whereas Paul would ask for a cello, or a trumpet at a certain point," Martin insisted. "Then, at the end, John would be unhappy that he had not got the final result he wanted." 'Penny Lane', McCartney maintained, was just as surreal, albeit in a cleaner fashion. "I remember saying to George Martin: 'I want a very clean recording – I was into clean sounds – with maybe a Beach Boy influence at that point. The '*fireman with his hourglass*' and all that imagery was us trying to get into a bit of art. The lyrics were all based on real things.

"There was a barber called Bioletti who, like all barbers, had pictures of the haircuts you could choose. It was changed around to '*Every head he's had the pleasure to have known.*' A barber showing photographs – like an exhibition. It was twisting it to a slightly more artsy angle, more like a play. These were all the little trippy ideas we were trying to get in."

The complementary natural flipside to the darker psychedelia and lazily horizontal movement of 'Strawberry Fields . . .', McCartney's bounding and confident 'Penny Lane' was breezily vertical both in melody and harmony. 'Penny Lane' successfully distills the bright, vivid optimism of its period, and this subversive song, with its multi-focal lyrics and semi-hallucinatory quality was just as accomplished as 'Strawberry Fields'. Triumphant achievements for their respective authors, how interesting it would have been had this sense of spiritual awakening infused and inspired the rest of the album.

In his discussion with Harrison, Richard Perry highlighted the significance of the *Sergeant Pepper* album, which saw The Beatles becoming a new band. Changing at speed and leaving their old identities behind, they still looked to each other as part of a new group consciousness. Reflecting something of the earliest tracks' air of nostalgic surrealism, the original intention for the *Sergeant Pepper* album had involved an element of autobiography concerning the group's childhood lives in Liverpool.

It duly included cultural, geographical and musical reference points from their Northern upbringing: brass bands, music hall, light-hearted comedy and local events. McCartney had been inspired by the psychedelic fad for elaborate, Victorian-sounding monikers amongst emergent American rock acts, hence the decision to submerge their collective personae in a new group identity. "I took an idea back home to the guys in London: 'As we're trying to get away from ourselves – to get away from touring and into a more surreal thing – how about if we become an alter-ego band, something like, say, 'Sergeant Pepper's Lonely Hearts Club Band?'"

"*Sergeant Pepper* is Paul, after a trip to America," Lennon recalled. "The whole West Coast long name group thing was coming in, when people were suddenly Fred and His Incredible Shrinking Grateful Airplanes. He was trying to put some distance between The Beatles and the public – and so there was this identity of *Sergeant Pepper*. Intellectually, that's the same thing he did by writing '*she loves you*' instead of '*I love you.*'" As biographer Howard Sounes noted, many elements now came together to enable the group to make the next leap forward in their musical journey.

According to Starr, the album was always intended to open with 'Sergeant Pepper . . .', while his own cameo, 'With A Little Help From My Friends', helped to create the effect of a stage album. "It was going to run like a rock opera. It had started out with a feeling that it was going to be something totally different, but we only got as far as Sergeant Pepper and Billy Shears singing 'With A Little Help From My Friends'. It still kept the title and the feel that it's all connected, although in the end we didn't actually connect all the songs up."

The all-inclusive song 'With A Little Help . . .' was written specifically for Starr. Paul concocted the line that became the song's title, before he and Lennon proceeded to write the remainder on a 50/50 basis. Lennon considered his subsequent album contributions to have little or nothing to do with the concept of *Sergeant Pepper*. "Every other song could have been on any other album. But it works, because we said it worked, and that's how the album appeared."

More significantly, the songs on *Sergeant Pepper* dared to dream, pushing forward in their conscientiously artistic approach. The album demonstrated the vast possibilities of the group's new enthusiasm for music-making. The Beatles were fully aware they were making something very special, as Starr insisted. For Lennon, the album would still come to represent a part of their own psychedelic evolution. "*Sergeant Pepper* is one of the most important steps in our career. It had to be just right. We tried, and I think, succeeded in achieving what we set out to do."

At this point, The Beatles were far ahead of their music-making con-temporaries, as critic Walter Everett argued. "No object in its entire history can match the immediacy and power with which a collection of songs exemplifies all of these aspects so intensely above and beyond its fellows as *Sergeant Pepper* . . . all of this seems possible because of the seren-dipitous peakings of McCartney's leadership, Lennon's imagination and Harrison's confidence."

After George had been allowed to grow and explore outside the confines of the group, his return to the studio hierarchy of this particular creative environment proved challenging. "It was difficult for me to come back into the sessions. Everybody else thought that *Sergeant Pepper* was a revolutionary record – but I had gone through so many trips of my own and I was growing out of that kind of thing." As far as McCartney was concerned, *Pepper's* creative *modus operandi* was akin to writing a novel, rather than sustaining their rich pantheon of classic album-supporting singles.

Sergeant Pepper embraced the sense of a bygone theatrical/music hall past, but would somehow prove an ideal mirror of its times. The album also epitomised the height of their growing relationship with Martin, and marked the point at which the boundaries between producer and musician became much less distinguishable. The resulting work contained a diverse series of what one critic coined "polished and scintillating tunes" hung together in the same musical universe, "the soundtrack to the movie of a time when anything is possible." As Hunter Davies opined, the group's combined musical energy encouraged them towards more accomplished musical heights.

The album's vibrant title track, acting as a prologue to the main pro-gramme, was a shrewd blend of psychedelia, mid-weight rock, orchestra and vaudeville replete with audience atmospherics from a comedy revue. 'Sergeant Pepper . . .' also featured a superb, Hendrix-like guitar solo and sandpapered vocal from McCartney. A mere two days after the album's release in June 1967, Hendrix opened his Saville Theatre concert in London with a rendition of the title track, one of the highest compliments that McCartney, a huge fan of Jimi, could have received.

Meanwhile, Lennon's son Julian arrived home from school one day with a piece of interesting artwork. This curious-looking painting intrigued his father and provided a thrilling source of inspiration. "He showed me his drawing with this strange-looking woman flying around. I said: 'What is it?' And he said: 'It's Lucy in the sky with diamonds' and I thought, 'That's beautiful.' I immediately wrote a song about it." When Paul arrived, they adjourned to Lennon's music room and swapped suggestive psychedelic imagery in the process of composing the song's lyrics. "They [Julian's pastel-drawn 'diamonds'] were child's stars, but he said diamonds because they can be interpreted as diamonds or stars," McCartney recalled. "And we loved it, and she was in the sky, and it was very trippy."

The title of Julian's painting duly provided the song's hook and chorus, and the imagery-laden lyrics strove to recreate the psychedelic experience. "The images were from *Alice In Wonderland*. It was Alice in the boat. There was also the image of the female who would someday come save me – '*a girl with kaleidoscope eyes*' who would come out the sky," Lennon admitted in retrospect. "I remember coming up with '*cellophane flowers*' and '*newspaper taxis*'," McCartney would later recall, "and John answered with things like '*kaleidoscope eyes*' and '*looking glass ties*'. We never noticed the LSD initial[s] until it was pointed out later – by which point people didn't believe us."

Lennon would later insist: "I swear I had no idea it spelt that. The whole album had been published. And somebody noticed the letters spelt out LSD, and of course after that, I was checking all the songs to see what the letters spelt out. They didn't spell out anything, none of the others. It wasn't about that at all." Harrison, meanwhile, remained a clear advocate of the song's musical edge. "I particularly liked the sounds on it, where I managed to superimpose some Indian instruments onto the Western music. But under normal circumstances that wouldn't work on a Western song like 'Lucy . . .', which has chord changes and modulations (whereas sitars and tambouras stay in the same key forever). I liked the way the drone of the tamboura could be fitted in there.

"There was another thing: during a vocal in Indian music, they have an instrument called a sarangi, which sounds like the human voice, and the vocalist and sarangi player are more or less in unison in a performance. I thought of trying that idea," with Harrison perhaps seeking to feel a sense of proximity within the group, "but because I'm not a sarangi player, I played it on the guitar. In the middle eight of the song, you can hear the guitar playing along with John's voice. I was trying to copy Indian music."

When the group came to record 'Lucy . . .', Martin opined that the song's simple, gentle organ melody was one Beethoven may well have envied. As critic Ian MacDonald suggested, this was a stream-of-consciousness work with slow melodic circles of sensory sound against which Lennon sang this most dreamy-sounding song. In a curious vocal manner, he deliberately separated each syllable in very distinct fashion.

However, the song's carefully crafted introspection and poetic gentility was supplanted by Paul's countermelody and stomping, three-chord rock chorus. Coming after 'With A Little Help From My Friends', Martin reasoned that the song represented a "complete change of musical colour – it was like saying: 'Here's a green show, with the first two tracks, then the lights changed and there was a red show . . .' you wanted a change there, you wanted something different."

Having involved a form of unconscious inspiration or intuitive rationale on John and Paul's part to vary their writing formula and keep things interesting, it formed part of the then-current countercultural spirit. Unfortunately, they soon began to lose the ability to discern between creativity and self-indulgence. At this time, Lennon's LSD-soaked mentality found him increasingly dependent upon the others to stop him drifting away for good.

Recorded early in the *Sergeant Pepper* sessions, and with Lennon and McCartney's collaborative powers of creativity now at their height, they produced arguably their finest ever piece of work, 'A Day In The Life'. The song constituted their most ambitious composition, but was one of comparative simplicity in its original studio guise. Lennon began writing it just a few days before recording work commenced at Abbey Road on January 19. 'A Day In The Life' was first played by Lennon in serene fashion on acoustic rhythm guitar in front of their producer.

Having expressed his reticence about learning the piano in case it inhibited his technique, Paul's evocative grand piano work boasted roaming, authoritative chords, acting as a sedentary, gospel-like accompaniment to Lennon's other-worldly vocal. Starr's thrilling drum fills acted as a commentary to accompany Lennon's lyrics.

The dramatic instrumental introduction to 'A Day In The Life' demonstrated Starr's subtler abilities, as his bandmates inspired and coached him through his stateliest drumming performance to date. It was later re-recorded at the same time as Paul's bass in order to save track space. "Paul would be aware that if he made a mistake with his bass playing, he might be ruining a great take from Ringo," recalled Martin, "and Ringo would be thinking the same thing about his own performance. It was an added spur for them to play well."

The song allowed Lennon to realise a new lyrical wisdom that he was possibly unaware he possessed, seeking to address people's perceptions of limitation, which Harrison would also acknowledge in 'Within You, Without You'. Like 'Strawberry Fields . . .' and Harrison's own *magnum opus*, 'A Day In The Life' is a timeless masterpiece that stands outside of the time (and the concept) of the album. It also articulated something of the awakening experience from the illusion of *maya* that Lennon had begun to recognise on 'Strawberry Fields'. Appropriately enough, both songs carry a similarly strong, dreamily atmospheric vocal. The first rendition, in Martin's esteem, was marvellous. Even in its nascent form, Martin felt that Lennon's wonderful voice could invoke a spine-tingling sensation in the listener.

Majestic and momentous, 'A Day In The Life' could only have worked with John and Paul collaborating together. Lennon later admitted they could often be slightly wary of interfering with each other's work, and Paul's initial reticence about contributing to the song was partly based on its potential for greatness. However, Lennon acknowledged that the pair worked particularly well together on 'A Day In The Life', and constituted what many regard as their finest moment of collaborative achievement: "That was something. I dug it. It was a good piece of work between Paul and me."

McCartney later stressed the extent of his admiration for his bandmate's work: the process of developing this song clearly excited its co-author. "It wouldn't just be: 'Oh yes, professional person, we'll write this,'" McCartney enthused. "I'd learn the chords off of him, and we'd develop it."

Lennon had brought the original working version of 'A Day In The Life' to McCartney's Cavendish Avenue home. The two men duly adjourned to Paul's upstairs music room, along with a copy of the *Daily Mail*, from which its author had derived the song's initial idea and inspiration. "It was mainly a John song," McCartney would later recall. "John and I sat down, and he had this opening verse." Lennon had begun writing the song while sat at the piano in Kenwood with the paper propped up in front of him.

"The way we wrote a lot of the time, you'd write the good bit, the part that was easy, like '*I read the news today, oh boy,*' or whatever it was. Then when you got stuck or whenever it got hard, instead of carrying on, you just drop it. Then we would meet each other, and I would sing half and he would be inspired to write the next bit, and vice versa."

John and Paul share the microphone during a 1963 session at the BBC. Between 1962 and 1965 The Beatles performed for 52 BBC radio shows. FRANK APTHORP/DAILY MAIL/REX/SHUTTERSTOCK

The leather-jacketed Beatles – with Pete Best on drums – on stage at Liverpool's Cavern Club during the early months of 1961.
MICHAEL OCHS ARCHIVES/GETTY IMAGES

Ringo behind his kit during the session for 'She Loves You' at Abbey Road, July 1, 1963. TERRY O'NEILL/GETTY IMAGES

JPG&R pose in their Peirre Cardin collarless jackets, their classic 1963 image. HARRY HAMMOND/V&A IMAGES/GETTY IMAGES

John and Paul sit around waiting for the opening show of The Beatles 1963 Autumn Tour, Odeon Cinema, Cheltenham, November 1, 1963. FOX PHOTOS/GETTY IMAGES

John, Paul and Ringo in rehearsals at Studio 50 in New York for their appearance on the *Ed Sullivan* show, February 9, 1964. George, suffering from a sore throat, was being nursed by his sister Louise back at the Plaza Hotel.
FRED MORGAN/NY DAILY NEWS ARCHIVE VIA GETTY IMAGES

The Beatles disembark from a Pan Am flight after their first US tour, February 1964.
MICHAEL OCHS ARCHIVES/GETTY IMAGES

John and Paul at the piano on the set of *A Hard Day's Night* at the Scala Theatre, March 1964.
K & K ULF KRUGER OHG/REDFERNS

The Beatles fool around in the pool at their rented home at 356 St. Pierre Road, Brown Canyon, Bel Air, California, during their Summer US tour, August 1964. EXPRESS/ARCHIVE PHOTOS/GETTY IMAGES

His three colleagues congratulate John on passing his driving test, February 15, 1965, in the car park at Abbey Road studios.
DAILY MAIL/REX/SHUTTERSTOCK

Arriving at Portland, Oregon, on August 22, 1965, one of the engines in The Beatles' plane caught fire, a dangerous situation that the group joked about during press conference after the show at the Memorial Coliseum. GETTY IMAGES

Police strain to hold back fans as The Beatles arrive at Buckingham Palace to collect their MBEs, October 26, 1965. "How long have you been together?" asked the Queen. "Forty years," replied Ringo. TED WEST & ROGER JACKSON/CENTRAL PRESS/GETTY IMAGES

John and Paul arrive back at Heathrow Airport after a holiday in Greece, ostensibly to buy a Greek island, July 31, 1967.
CUMMINGS ARCHIVES/REDFERNS

A shot of the four Beatles taken during the 'mad day out' when they posed for photographs in various locations across London, July 28, 1968. MICHAEL OCHS ARCHIVES/GETTY IMAGES

John and Paul announce the formation of Apple at a press conference at the Americana Hotel on Central Park West in New York, May 14, 1968. GETTY IMAGES

John, Paul, George and Ringo perform together as The Beatles for the very last time, on the roof of the Apple offices in London's Savile Row, January 30, 1969. Yoko, wrapped up against the cold, watches from the sidelines, along with Apple staff. EXPRESS/GETTY IMAGES

"'A Day In The Life' started life as most of John's songs: he'd taken things from everyday life and used them as a lyric," Martin opined. McCartney recalled that Lennon had sketched out most of the song's opening verse, including its enigmatic first line, before letting Paul hear what he'd contrived. McCartney noted that Lennon had also written part of the second verse, before the two men felt inspired to write a subsequent verse together. "John got '*He blew his mind out in a car*' from a newspaper story," McCartney recalled of the song's covert drug reference. Meanwhile, 'A Day In The Life' also appeared to carry the impression of the coloured sensations of an LSD experience when Lennon sang '*He didn't notice that the lights had changed.*'

A jaded Lennon had also penned the song's dispassionate reference to an onlooker witnessing the spectacle of a victorious army in its third verse. This regarded his role as the reluctant soldier, Private Gripweed, in Richard Lester's film satire, *How I Won The War*.

Once Lennon had reached a point where Paul's input became necessary, he asked if he had a suitable idea to fill the song's middle eight. "Paul's [other] contribution was the beautiful little lick in the song: '*I'd love to turn you on,*' that he'd had floating around in his head and couldn't use." "But the moment I remember," McCartney fondly remembered, "was when we got to a little bit that he didn't have, where we sort of said: '*I'd love to turn you on.*' We looked at each other, and said: 'We know what we're doing here, don't we? We're actually saying, for the first time ever, words like '*turn you on*', which was in the culture *anyway*, but no one had actually *said* it on record yet."

As risqué a lyric as they had dared to write at this point, a flash went between their eyes; a knowing look of mutual recognition. 'Do it! Do it!' was their instinctive, unspoken reaction. 'Get it down!' Reflecting the era of American LSD guru Timothy Leary's provocative '*tune in, turn on, drop out*' philosophy, '*I'd love to turn you on,*' McCartney admitted, was intended to signify a path to the truth instead of drug-inspired 'revelation'. John and Paul then realised they needed something incredible to illustrate the sentiment of '*I'd love to turn you on.*' "I just sat down and thought, 'This is the song, man!'" an enthusiastic McCartney recalled. "That ['A Day In The Life'] was one of John's very good ones. We could go *anywhere* with this song; it was definitely going to go big places." As a rare and genuine opportunity to take the song into adventurous, unexplored territory, it also exhibited a sublime musical ambition.

Lennon had already devised the storyline through the verses and recorded a near-transcendent, heavily-echoed vocal performance. Having developed a gospel-like piano accompaniment, McCartney then contributed his own diary-like *vignette* to follow John's evocative, verse-closing refrain of '*I'd love to turn you on.*' He offered a matter-of-fact sounding middle eight which opened with the line: '*Woke up, fell out of bed.*'

"When we took it to the studio," Paul remembered, "I suggested: 'Let's put aside 24 bars and just have Mal count them.' In order to keep the 24 bars so that everybody knew when we were due to come back in to the song proper again, and to keep everyone together, Mal Evans stood by the piano counting out loud through the 24 bars in the middle of the song that were still blank." Paul was carrying the backing to the song, and this discordant sound was recorded while setting down the song's impressive grand opening chords.

Meanwhile, the decision to utilise the ringing alarm clock as a cue to start the next segment provided a segue into Paul's section of the song. Moreover, the alarm clock awakens the listener in a moment of realisation. 'A Day In The Life' constituted The Beatles' very own wake-up call, but suggested there is still hope for the dreamer and the more attentive listener. With its series of snapshot images of a life in a day that has been compressed into five minutes, the essence of the song was then condensed into two thrilling sequences of 24 bars.

"He said: 'I've got this song . . . '*Woke up, fell out of bed, dragged a comb across my head,*'" Lennon remembered. "That was a little bit I had that wasn't doing anything. I had this sequence that fitted and we had to link them. 'You can use it if you like,' McCartney told him. 'Put it in your one. Will it fit?'"

Lennon readily agreed, and with this song bite at the heart of their new composition, they began to build the song in mini-operetta form. They then had to find a way of joining their respective pieces together. It proved an exciting process as the duo's songwriting art reached its highest state. *Anything* could happen. "We connected them with a series of empty bars on either side of Paul's section," Martin later recalled, "before we came back into John's section as a reprise."

McCartney's vibrant segment of apparently humdrum routine offered a fulfilling and grounding balance to Lennon's cosmic-sounding musings. Artfully combined, they articulated a sense of duality in this unique song: two separate entities and narrative voices relating distinctly different realities. It was also a keen expression of Lennon and McCartney's personalities.

A languorous sense of space surrounds Lennon's stellar vocal presence, as songwriter James Taylor would later observe. "So detached, the narrow eyes viewing the cosmos over your shoulder. How could he be so into it, and so out of it?" Tastefully heightened by the scaling strings and graceful orchestral colour, this, like the song as a whole, was one of the greatest moments in their body of work: an audible glimpse of spiritual reality before returning to the material world. The orchestral strains represented a musical and conceptual link between these two worlds.

Of the lyrical inspiration for the song's final verse, Lennon drew upon a *Daily Mail* story about 4,000 holes in the streets of Blackburn, Lancashire. The article and the following piece on a performance at the Albert Hall provided inspiration, McCartney remembered, for this poetic lyrical montage.

As the song's closing line, 'A Day In The Life''s second insistence that '*I'd love to turn you on*', prefiguring the mighty closing orchestral attachment, ultimately revealed its higher meaning: an entreaty to illumination on the path to the truth. Lennon and McCartney knew they had to devise something special to convey this sentiment. "The Beatles had come to me," Martin later recalled, "and said: 'Let's have a big orchestral sound on this. Let's have a symphony orchestra.' My imagination was fired. A symphony orchestra! I could see at once that we could make a lovely sound." Making a great leap forward into symphonic sound was clearly appealing to the producer, and he opted for a 41-piece orchestra.

Paul wanted to bring the musicians in and encourage them to play whatever came to mind in the pursuit of a thrilling and spontaneous symphonic freak-out. "I said: 'You can't get an orchestra to come in and play *anything*,'" Martin frowned. "The Beatles had never needed a note of written music in their lives," he pondered in his *Pepper* memoir. "Why should anyone else?"

Given their increasingly high-flown musical ploys, Martin later admitted his concern over the group's musical indulgence and creative pretension during 1967. "But it was Paul's idea to have something really tumultuous on the song. He didn't know quite what it was he wanted, but he did want to try for something extremely startling."

McCartney was keen to use the whole orchestra as a single-voiced instrument, in the same spirit as the unison performance he had heard during an airing of Beethoven's Fifth Symphony, where the orchestra played the same notes and eschewed conventional chords. He'd already persuaded Lennon about an ambitious instrumental passage as part of Paul's enthusiastic *avant-garde* musical education.

The ethos which defined their creative approach, and which character-ised the times was that *anything* was possible – and it could all be incor-porated into The Beatles' music. The song's orchestral crescendo became a musical icon in itself, a famous soundbite beloved of Lennon. Influenced by composer Karlheinz Stockhausen's equally ambitious, conceptually abstract consciousness-raising work, McCartney also attributed the idea of the song's 24-bar section to composer John Cage.

Martin's orchestral brief for the symphony musicians was simple yet powerful: "You start by playing the lowest note in the range of your instrument as quietly as possible, and eventually going through all the notes in the range of your instrument, rising up to play the highest note as loudly as possible." Lennon's wavering voice, and his evocative phrasing of the classic '*I'd love to turn you on*' lyric, also inspired their producer when it came to organising this orchestrated response. "I thought this would be a great phrase to echo," Martin admitted, "so I wrote a very slow semitone trill for the strings, making a good introduction or bridge to the now famous dissonant orchestral climb that is unique to the song."

Martin knew that encouraging them to improvise was futile. He duly instructed them how to play their notated parts. "I suddenly said to them: 'Don't listen to the fella next to you. Make your own way up this huge climax. Go your own way through this 24-bar passage and ignore the playing of your fellow musicians – just make your own sound. If you find you're playing anything like the same note as the fella next to you, you're playing a wrong note.' It worked."

The Beatles also sought to transform the recording session into a special occasion. For the purpose of filming the orchestral overdub session at Abbey Road on February 10, the group and many of their friends wore psychedelic regalia ("outrageously flamboyant floral costumes", in Martin's esteem) in what was later coined as the the first major "happening" of the 'Summer of Love'. The Beatles invited numerous friends to enjoy the moment, including The Rolling Stones' entourage of Mick Jagger, Marianne Faithfull, Brian Jones and Keith Richards, The Hollies' Graham Nash, Donovan and Monkee Mike Nesmith. Defying musical convention and carrying a strong vibration of change, the orchestra followed McCartney's brief and made this unique journey in their own time, performing five separate and very different renditions of the orchestral crescendo.

Having reached the highest note at the close of the instrumental sequence, the listener was left suspended at the coda of this extraordinary song. A finale, or a grand flourish, the producer reasoned, was now required. Returning to Lennon's original inspiration of the distant sound of chanting monks for his memorable vocal work on 'Tomorrow Never Knows', Martin's initial idea was to end with a hypnotic-sounding, mass hummed note. When this didn't work, the producer shifted emphasis to a giant piano chord. "We managed to scrape together three pianos. You can hear my voice on the master tape counting in to the chord," Martin claimed, "so that everyone hits it at exactly the same time. We got everybody that was available to play a chord on the piano. Paul, John, Ringo, Mal and I crunched down on the same chord as hard as we could. We wanted the first impact of the chord to be there, but the decay to be very loud. As the chord started to fade, Geoff Emerick raised the gain [the faders] gradually, to keep it singing on. At the end of the note, 45 seconds into it, the volume level on the studio amplifiers was enormous."

The striking sustain of this reverberating E major chord, reputedly a signifier in Western music of a state of grace, was attached to the orchestral crescendo. The sound of the chord, Martin later commented, was lengthened in order to replicate a time-stretching, galaxy-seeking note. Having striven to attain a sense of higher consciousness, the song literally culminates in a musical place where it has ascended to heaven.

Thus, 'A Day In The Life' became the most effective demonstration of the complementary creative genius of the Lennon-McCartney songwriting partnership; a brilliant production effort on an incredible composition boasting an utterly original song structure and, of course, an ideal coda to the album following the reprise of the 'Sgt. Pepper' intro. Along with Harrison's explorative and other-worldly 'Within You, Without You', it sat outside the fictitious concept of its parent album, seemingly originating from a different creative source. These two sublime, ambitious songs and their sense of musical exploration almost overwhelm the rest of the album.

Five months after recording the monumental 'A Day In The Life', 'All You Need Is Love' effectively signalled a change along The Beatles' journey inward, as Harrison called it: musicians based in a studio rather than performers on a stage. Just weeks after the release of their hippy symphony *Sergeant Pepper* came The Beatles' single most important statement. 'All You Need Is Love' was a resolutely positive work which epitomised the spirit (and subsequently set the tone and mood) for the halcyon Summer of Love.

Having written separate compositions, Lennon's 'All You Need Is Love' (with partial collaborative assistance from his partner) was completed in 10 days during June. Both Ringo and Martin claim the song was written especially for the occasion. "I don't know if the song was written before that," Harrison insisted, "because there were lots of songs in circulation at the time." "It fits very well, so it might have been written especially for the show and once we had it, it was certainly tailored to suit the programme," McCartney recalled. "I've got a feeling it was just one of John's songs that was coming anyway."

Having spent several days recording an instrumental track for the song at Barnes' Olympic Studios, The Beatles were in adventurous and experimental mood in the studio. Lennon played banjo and harpsichord, McCartney performed on upright bass while Harrison tentatively plucked away on violin during the recording of this amorous anthem. Lennon believed this Beatles quartet had created something resembling a Bach-like *avant-garde* orchestral noise.

"Then we thought, 'Ah, well, we'll have some more [live] orchestra around this little orchestra that we've got.' There was no perception of how it sounded until they did it on the day," said Martin. During the preparations for their live television show, The Beatles sought to inspire proceedings in the free-spirited mood of a psychedelic-era recording session, and would sing to the accompaniment of symphony orchestra musicians in the studio.

Not leaving everything open to chance, Martin ensured that they had prepared a basic track for the later television broadcast. "It was good. The orchestra was there and it was played live. We rehearsed for a while, and then it was: 'You're on at 12 o'clock lads,'" remembered Harrison.

"It was a good day," McCartney recalled. "We went in there early in the morning to rehearse with the cameras, and there was a big orchestra for all that stuff with 'Greensleeves' playing on the way out of the song." Producer George Martin's arrangement included classically trained chamber orchestra musicians playing a trumpet score, keyboard pieces, cellos and violins from 'Greensleeves' and sax parts courtesy of 'In The Mood'. With a trumpet fanfare acting as a loving herald, the blowsy brass proved an inspired moment. "The man upstairs pointed his finger, and that was it," Harrison recalled. "We did it – one take."

PART TWO

LONDON & LOS ANGELES

CHAPTER FOUR

Listen To What The Man Said

HAVING travelled the world for three years giving people love through their music, The Beatles' timeless message was now transmitted via the world's first global satellite link one summer's day. The *Our World* broadcast on June 25 proved an incredible spectacle, linking 24 countries across five continents and intended, as the TV presenter grandly announced, to bring man "face-to-face with mankind". "There's plenty of people in England that haven't seen us," Lennon admitted at the time, "unless we do a world telly show and everyone watches at once through a satellite. That's the only way everyone would see us."

The Beatles' rendition of 'All You Need Is Love' was an iconic moment as they performed for an estimated audience of 300 million people, a phenomenal figure for the times. "Because of the mood of the time, it seemed a great idea to perform that song," Harrison noted of The Beatles' contribution to this most celebrated of summers.

"Someone said: 'It's your duty to do something about it, to try and change the world,'" Lennon would later recall. "And I was saying: 'Well, I've sang 'All You Need Is Love' to 200,000,000 people on live TV.' And The Beatles were always for love."

"The song presents the possibility of a perfect world," Walter Everett surmised, "and insists on the ripeness for change of the very imperfect world he [Lennon] saw around him, on its willingness to change."

With the whole world watching, The Beatles had but one message as their audience looked on: we need more love in the world. "It was for love and peace," an excited Starr later recalled. "I even get excited now when I realise that's what it was for: peace and love." "If someone thinks that love and peace is a cliché," Lennon would later opine, "that must have been left behind in the sixties, that's his problem. Love and peace are eternal," he insisted. A proud Starr later recalled Lennon's generous and peaceable lyrical spirit. "The world was trying to change. It was the attitude, the concept. And it was all for this loving feeling."

He also believed the song's sentiment was one to aspire to and live by. Due to its apparent simplicity and memorable *'love, love, love'* mantra, this song proved an ideal counter-cultural anthem. The Beatles sounded like a psychedelic choir as they recited the song's dreamily-delivered message. At the close, Lennon recited the famous refrain from 'She Loves You', which now sounded like a love song from another era. Floating on a confident one-note chorus, this heartfelt, five-word mantra of *'all you need is love'* imbued this anthemic song with its communal spirit.

Lennon and McCartney clearly enjoyed this unique studio occasion. But then, these *were* exciting times. This celebratory occasion was a colourful high watermark in their career, proving difficult to emulate. In keeping with fashionable sixties parlance, it was a beautiful moment, and Ringo clearly revelled in it. "You can see the happy faces. I had Keith Moon next to me. Everyone was joining in – it was a fabulous time, both musically and spiritually." "I remember the recording, because we decided to get some people in who looked like the love generation," George added as a swathe of famous musicians sat at their feet. Above them, a pink-and-white *yin-yang* symbol and a blue-and-green model of the Earth hung from the studio ceiling above a sea of garlands, flowers and balloons.

Staged during more idealistic times, The Beatles, Lennon later reflected, had often discussed their ambitious dream of hosting something similar to this global broadcast to promote love and world peace. "Everyone in London was there, and there was that feeling in the air," John enthused. "There were lots of possibilities then." The performance of their new song was the best means of delivering their hopes to the world. But if the world, as McCartney later claimed, was a problem, The Beatles were not. Having partially tailored the song to suit this auspicious occasion, they could hardly have created a more appropriate or positive message.

"There's nothing you can think of that can't happen," Harrison insisted in his final interview in 2001, before repeating the song's famous opening maxim: *"There's nothing you can do that can't be done,"* when we trust and believe in love. There's nothing beyond our capabilities, seemed to be the song's message: anything is possible because love can overcome any obstacle.

'There's nothing you can sing that can't be sung,' Lennon also proclaimed,

insisting love helped one to voice or articulate what has previously escaped you. As a song of praise, The Beatles had clearly been helped to find the right words to sing. Lennon then paraphrased a key gospel line when he sang that there is '*nothing you can make that can't be made*', paraphrasing John 1:3: 'Through him all things were made: without him, nothing was made that has been made.'

Providing an assurance that no one was beyond redemption ('*There's no-one you can save that can't be saved*'), the song also reprised Matthew's gospel text, and exhibited a spirited sense of renewed optimism. As one of its prime objectives, loving salvation was another key aspect of The Beatles' spiritual message. The cool refrain of '*it's easy*', meanwhile, was a casual yet confident aspect of their powerful message. '*There's nothing you can know that isn't known . . .*' suggested there was no end to our knowledge and awareness. Lennon then insisted that '*There's nothing you can see that isn't shown*,' again (perhaps unconsciously) drawn from a Biblical source: 'There is nothing hidden that will not be disclosed, and nothing concealed that will not be known.' [Luke 8:17].

"All we need is love," Lennon re-affirmed in one of his final interviews of this neat sentiment. "I believe it," he maintained. "I absolutely believe it." Unsurprisingly, Harrison later claimed that 'All You Need Is Love' constituted a musical exercise and "subtle piece of PR" on God's behalf. It was also one of their most important and significant statements, McCartney later agreed, "and hopefully it always will be. It's a *timeless* statement." Lennon firmly believed that the song would prove The Beatles right for believing in their message.

Manager Brian Epstein eagerly enthused over this inspiring song's message for the world. "It could hardly have been a better message. It is a wonderful, beautiful record."

"Our messages were subliminal," Lennon would insist eight years later. "Just reporting on the state we were in, looking back on it. It was part of a change in attitude, the psychedelic stuff."

'All You Need Is Love' remains one of their finest and most positive compositions, and their last great visible musical spectacle. It also served to demonstrate that a belief remained within the group that they could achieve *anything*: refusing to acknowledge creative boundaries other than those of their own chemically enhanced or musically inspired imaginations.

At the beginning of 1967, the group had realised that, in the absence of any forthcoming tour commitments, they would need something to fill that musical vacuum. "We couldn't reproduce onstage the type of music that we'd started to record," John had admitted during the making of *Sergeant Pepper*. "So we wanted something to replace them. Television was the obvious answer." It was around this point that McCartney's growing managerial acumen and ambition came to the fore, promoting the conceptual idea for directing their subsequent colour film project, *Magical Mystery Tour*. Paul maintained that no script was required for the type of film they were intending to make: spontaneity and improvisation would be the order of the day. "It was just a mad idea. I told them all: 'We're going to make it up as we go along. But don't worry, it'll be alright.' But we knew we weren't doing a regular film. We were doing a crazy, roly-poly sixties film, with '*I am the eggman*' and so on."

The *Magical Mystery Tour*'s energetic title track boasted a memorably bright and magnificent trumpet fanfare. Yet a lack of real group enthusiasm for either the song or the project meant it was shelved until the end of the summer. McCartney's pro-active approach to *Magical Mystery Tour* and their Apple enterprise was a concerted effort on his behalf to keep The Beatles going.

Lennon and McCartney had sat down together in Paul's St. John's Wood home to plan the film with just a piece of paper, and proceeded to divide a circle like the spokes on a wheel into sections: "It was a case of: 'We can have a song here, and a dream sequence there,' and they sort of mapped it out," Neil Aspinall recalled.

With McCartney keen to keep working lest the group should yield their *Pepper*-era momentum, there *was* a patent need for the group to recover something of their creative dynamism if they were to match the consistent quality of work they'd produced during the previous 18 months. George Martin was also concerned about the growing musical indulgence and lack of discipline in their recording work following *Sergeant Pepper*.

In his conversation with Harrison, Perry then pointed to the *Magical Mystery Tour* soundtrack, which included Lennon's psychedelically orchestrated 'I Am The Walrus', a genuinely revolutionary approach to music-making in the studio boasting an ambitious, stirring melange of strings, radio samples and backing vocal group. Recorded over seven weeks in September and October 1967, '. . . Walrus' was the first new recording The Beatles undertook after the death of Brian Epstein in August, and it found Lennon re-interpreting Lewis Caroll's *Alice In Wonderland* as novelistic poetry. "'. . . Walrus' is just saying a dream – the words don't mean a lot.

People draw so many conclusions and it's ridiculous . . . what does it really mean, '*I am the eggman*'?"

Another lyric, which later revealed the '*elementary penguin*''s identity as American poet Allen Ginsberg, concerned the growing Stateside popularity for singing the Hare Krishna *mantra*. Lennon would later admit he avoided straight commentary in order to encourage the same close lyrical scrutiny frequently accorded the likes of Dylan. One of Lennon's favourite Beatles compositions, '. . . Walrus' proved a high tide of inspiration and musical invention in what Ian MacDonald described as an "idiosyncratic protest song". "John's poetry in those songs is so great," Starr later enthused. "In one line, he could say what it takes most people a whole song or a novel to say with the same sharp bite."

A result of both wise and worldly inspiration and intuitive musical rationale, the *Blue* album continued with McCartney's 'The Fool On The Hill', a timeless piano creation blessed with an airy harmonic melancholy that also boasts a beguiling major-minor melody and ascending chorus. It was followed by the catchy, word-association-inspired 'Hello, Goodbye', written in random spirit on McCartney's harmonium. Notable for its Hawaiian-derived singalong coda, this jaunty song of duality boasted a plaintive melody and childlike simplicity.

Perry and Harrison then considered the second *Blue* disc, incorporating material from The Beatles' *White Album* and final two studio album releases. Lennon, for one, had a clear preference for the eclectic quality of the material which graced this double set over that of its predecessor.

Harrison later insisted that little thought was given to emulating the incredibly popular legend of *Sergeant Pepper*. "Things *were* always different, anyway: in just a matter of months we'd changed in so many ways there was no chance of a new record ever being like the previous one." There was also the creative conundrum of attempting to fit three men's music onto one collective piece of work.

Not only did Lennon prefer his own compositions to those that graced *Pepper*, but in returning to some form of musical simplicity, Starr claimed The Beatles rediscovered a greater group ethic in the studio. "There were a lot of tracks where we just played live, and then there were a lot of tracks that we'd recorded that would need finishing together." Contrary as ever, Harrison argued that the album involved a greater individual emphasis in the production of their wealth of new songs.

Most notable amongst the group's expansive Apple adventures of 1968 was the McCartney classic 'Hey Jude'. A majestic anthem full of uplifting, emotional clarity, it became one of The Beatles' most enduring achievements, eloquent, compelling and one of their most effective healing songs.

'Hey Jude' touched Lennon as much as it impressed him. As an astute judge of his colleagues' work, Lennon loved and admired the song, and singing these words, couched in a glorious evocative melody, helped address his own pain. He clearly appreciated Paul's lyrical efforts, and no doubt identified with the song's soothing sentiment.

'Hey Jude' emerged from McCartney's sympathetic mood during the fall-out from Cynthia and John's separation in mid-1968. "It was written by Paul at the time John was splitting up with Cynthia," Harrison recalled. "Julian was just a little boy – probably five years old – and Paul had gone out to John's house and been affected by seeing Julian." "I had known them for so long. I thought, as a friend of the family, I would motor out to Weybridge and tell them that everything was all right," Paul insisted. "To try and cheer them up, basically, and see how they were."

Fresh from his own split with Asher, McCartney had an hour's drive ahead of him that particular June day. "I started coming up with these words. In my own mind, I was kind of talking to Julian: '*Hey Jules, don't make it bad, take a sad song and make it better.*'" Paul's idea was an optimistic, hopeful message for Julian: "'Come on, man, your parents got divorced. I know you're not happy but you'll be okay. It'll be alright.'"

Having settled on the initial title, 'Hey Jules', *en route* to Weybridge, McCartney decided to modify it to 'Hey Jude'. Lennon always felt the song was directed at his own situation, with McCartney offering a veiled or tacit approval of his new life with Ono. "The words: '*Go out and get her*' – subconsciously he was saying: 'Go ahead, leave me', but on a conscious level he didn't want me to go ahead," John later claimed. McCartney, meanwhile, felt there was much of himself in the lyric's sentiment given his burgeoning relationship with New Yorker Linda Eastman. What's undeniable about 'Hey Jude' is that the two men's view on its merits, and their instinct for what did and didn't work, was rarely sharper.

McCartney had demoed the song on piano before he began the process of refining the song during late June and early July. Paul road-tested his new work at Abbey Road for the likes of Badfinger and Neil Innes and had clearly grown attached to the new composition. When he played it for Lennon, John's genuine enthusiasm far outweighed Paul's own uncertainties. "I thought there might be a little more to go. There was one passage which went '*the movement you need is on your shoulder*'. And as I was playing it, I looked at John and said: 'I'll fix that bit. I've used the word "shoulder" once already, and anyway it's a stupid expression. You know, I'll change that.'"

Despite this apparent lyrical weakness, Lennon surprised him by insisting that the song was all but complete. "John said, 'You won't, you know! That's the best line in the song.' He said, '*I* know what it means – it's great.' That was the good thing about John – whereas I would *definitely* have knocked that line out, he would say it's great. Then I could see it through *his* eyes. So when I play that song, that's the line, now, when I think of John. And I sometimes get a little emotional during that moment."

A clear Beatles single from the moment it was conceived, 'Hey Jude' was recorded at the end of July when work on the White Album was well underway. Engineer Ken Scott worked on the song at Abbey Road before the group decamped to Trident Studios, and on hearing the finished product, Scott was mightily impressed. "On 'Hey Jude', when we first sat down and I sang '*Hey Jude . . .*', George was answering every line," McCartney recalled, "and I said: 'Whoa, wait a minute now. I don't think we want that. Maybe you'd come in with answering lines later.' He was going: 'Oh yeah, okay, fine, fine.' He wasn't into what I was saying."

As MacDonald noted, the song's huge chords suggested a personal revelation on Jude's behalf, while the arrival of the song's middle eight sounded like nothing less than the dawning of the sun as Paul sang of taking '*a sad song*' and making it better: transforming their outlook and replenishing hope through love as he sang with increasing fervour.

Let love in when you doubt yourself, McCartney's song of spiritual resolve insisted, and the healing begins as 'Hey Jude''s comforting, lullaby-like rhythm unfurls into a joyous, gospel epiphany. Regardless of its narrative intent, the song boasts wonderfully touching and evocative lyrics, particularly the urge for the listener to '*Let her into your heart, then you can start to make it better*'.

As a song which aimed to move its audience through an irresistible rhythm that would be played out across the world, a simple yet monumental accompaniment from a 36-piece orchestra helped to realise McCartney's vision. "Seldom has such a simple refrain," Sounes acknowledged of the song's '*Naa, na na, na-na na-na*' coda, "sounded so powerful."

As Apple Records' first A-side release, 'Hey Jude' became The Beatles' biggest selling single, shifting over seven million copies and spending nine weeks at number one in the US.

Its B-side was Lennon's 'Revolution', a track overloaded with distortion that pushed the VU meter to its limit. "People seem to think that everything we say and do and sing is a political statement, but it isn't," McCartney insisted. "One or two of the tracks will make people wonder what we are doing – but what we are doing is just singing songs." 'Revolution' constituted one of Lennon's most famous 'message' songs and his first 'manifesto' missive. It was also one of his best.

The song's initial pacifist ideology was devised in the peaceful haven of Rishikesh, but 'Revolution' duly became an enduring yardstick to measure his subsequent left-wing, radical output in the early seventies. Written whilst under the influence of Transcendental Meditation, Lennon maintained faith in love and God to change things while we took responsibility for changing our thinking. As the anti-war movement grew in strength during an increasingly radical period, Lennon felt motivated to write about the revolutionary air as 1968 unfolded, and was happy with the song's contemporary appeal. His only vacillation came over whether to entertain violence ('count me out/in') as a means of revolutionary activity.

The rest of the group, however, were not too enamoured with a song containing a heated political sentiment as the next Beatles single. "The first take, George and Paul were resentful and said it wasn't fast enough," Lennon later groused. "But The Beatles could have afforded to put out the slow, understandable version of 'Revolution' as a single . . . but because of the fact that I was again becoming as creative and dominating as I was in the early days, it upset the applecart."

Lennon insisted that the left-wing underground's focus was on the lyrical espousal of non-violence ('count me out') as a solution, whereas the original's 'out/in' dilemma showed that Lennon was undecided. He would later be criticised for not being left-wing enough. Lennon, however, was explicit in his description of the song and his intention for communicating his views through 'Revolution'. "I wanted to put out what I felt about revolution. I had been thinking about it up in the hills in India. I still had this 'God will save us' feeling about it. 'It's going to be all right.' That's why I did it. I wanted to talk. I wanted to say my piece about revolutions."

McCartney's 'Lady Madonna', released while the group prepared to embark on their voyage to India, proved a strong moment of solidarity for the ideal figure of motherhood. Biographer Howard Sounes, meanwhile, believed the song conflated Paul's memory of his mother with the Virgin Mary in a boogie-woogie hymn. Originally inspired by the magazine photo caption of Mountain Madonna, the song's rolling, Domino-esque piano line, rumbling bass and his Presley-esque vocal were, MacDonald insisted, meant to ground the group following their LSD-inspired phase.

On its release in March 1968, the song represented a step away from the group's psychedelic material of the previous year, and the sound of the song's spirit clearly stemmed from Fats Domino. Although any semblance of "acid-fuelled unreality" was more suggestive of playfulness, particularly in the self-referential chain of Beatles song titles, the song famously features impatient jazz magus Ronnie Scott's growling saxophone solo.

Recorded against the ominous backdrop of Soviet military intervention in Europe and inter-band tension, the album opened with McCartney's rock reconnaissance number, 'Back In The USSR'. Truly, the *White Album* could not have approached lift off on a more promising note: the sound of a thunderous jet, a thrilling rock riff and a powerful McCartney vocal delivery drove this confident, humorous song. Owing a titular debt to Chuck Berry's 'Back In The USA', its greatest influence was as a melodic and lyrical Beach Boys pastiche, parodying 'California Girls' by listing the charming attributes of the Soviet female population in the song's bridge.

The *Blue* album also featured Harrison's 'While My Guitar Gently Weeps', initially conceived in India as a delicate acoustic ballad while its composer became increasingly immersed in meditation. The song subsequently became a more fully realised and emotive piece of work that ventured into heavy rock with a striking production and a solo by Harrison's friend Eric Clapton.

After McCartney's lightweight 'Ob-La-Di, Ob-La-Da', the *Blue* album continued with another Paul song, 'Get Back', full of grace, punch and a little daftness. With infectious solos from Lennon and keyboard player Billy Preston, it showcased The Beatles in smooth, grooving mode. "Billy Preston was a great help and a very good keyboard guy, and his work on 'Get Back' alone justified him being there," Martin later claimed. "He was an amiable fellow too, very nice and emollient. He helped to lubricate the friction that was there."

"I think we were working on a good track and that always excited us,"

Starr argued. "'Get Back' was a good track. 'Don't Let Me Down' also. They were two fine tracks. Quite simple and raw – back to basics." After being recorded as part of their Apple rooftop concert, 'Don't Let Me Down' was one of Lennon's most impressive late period Beatles songs. Recorded live in the studio, with a minimum of overdubs or studio trickery, it set the tone for John's style of recording for the next two years or so. Not unlike Dylan's 'I Shall Be Released' in the drama of its delivery, 'Don't Let Me Down' opens with a sublime chorus and hovers precipitously on two chords during the verse before descending back into John's cry from the heart. The song's warm sound and relaxed maturity was redolent of The Band's quintessential early recordings, and featured one of Lennon's most passionate vocals.

'The Ballad Of John And Yoko', a meditation on the Lennons' marriage story and the excitement surrounding their visits to Paris and Amsterdam, featured only John and Paul. George Martin also enjoyed the experience of working on the song. "It was just the two of them. It was hardly a Beatle track – yet it *was* a Beatle track."

'The Ballad Of John & Yoko' was a song which, as MacDonald also noted, either attracted admiration for its *chutzpah* or drew criticism for its autobiographical vanity. "Considering the bitterness of the *Get Back* sessions, and their legal dispute, their friendship was still strong, if under strain," MacDonald noted of the Lennon-McCartney bond at this point. They may have moved in separate directions once their bond had broken, but as Beatles their strength had enabled them to carry on their work. With *Abbey Road*, there came an album offering hope for their respective musical futures.

Spanning the final months of their career, Perry and Harrison then cast a thoughtful gaze over the final side of the *Blue* album. Lennon's Chuck Berry-inspired 'Come Together' was a unique piece of work: an anti-elitist, counter-cultural anthem influenced by the in-vogue Americana strains of Dr. John and The Band. "Nothing else on the album," MacDonald insisted, "comes close to matching the Zeitgeist-catching impact of Lennon's declaration that: '*One thing I can tell you is you got to be free*' – a call to unchain the imagination and set language free, loosen the rigidities of entrenchment." "'Come Together' is me, writing obscurely round an old Chuck Berry thing. I left the line in: '*Here comes old flat top.*' It is *nothing* like the Chuck Berry song," added Lennon.

McCartney, however, claimed that this up-tempo song bore such a close resemblance to the Berry rocker that he added a swampy organ and uncharacteristic-sounding roaming bass. Lennon would always champion the song, one of the very few Beatles tracks that he would ever perform again in concert, in New York in 1972.

Considering the strains that had begun to show in their relationship, McCartney's selflessness was admirable and his contributions helped bring Lennon's song to life. Long-term drug use may have enabled Lennon to experience certain revelations which had freed his mind and unlocked new potential, yet the song's more bizarre lyrics showed how much it had begun to govern his creativity.

The song title's unifying mood, however, encouraged the group to focus on the task at hand. With 'Come Together', The Beatles gave their all to create an inspiring, album-opening salvo. Lennon remained proud of the song, given his intention of inspiring hope and a need for unity during this period.

Abbey Road's strength also came through Harrison's finest Beatles material, including 'Here Comes The Sun', a beacon of springtime renewal and hope on the horizon following what George described as the group's "winter of discontent". The song's warm radiance and the illumination of a new day emerging was therefore most welcome.

The album also featured the classic elegance of Harrison's 'Something', its ambiguous title reflecting something of the splendour of devotional love which Harrison had begun to experience through meditation. The most accomplished song on *Abbey Road*, its ambiguous title mirrors the song's almost intangible sense of a love divine, and which inspired its ardent lyrics. 'Something' found Harrison imploring us to listen and learn, and then love will grow.

A timeless composition initiated on piano at Abbey Road in September 1968 at the end of the *White Album* sessions, 'Something' was written across a range of five notes and suited most singers' vocal capabilities. Released as a single in the summer of 1969, Frank Sinatra famously garlanded the song with no little extravagance as "the greatest love song of the century".

It also contained, in its second verse, arguably its author's finest, most elegant lyrical sentiments, a match for anything Lennon and McCartney had ever written. "George's 'Something' was out of left field. It was about Pattie, and it appealed to me because it has a very beautiful melody and is a really structured song," McCartney generously insisted. "I thought it was George's greatest track." "It *was* a great song, and frankly I was surprised that George had it in him," Martin also conceded. Lennon also proved highly complimentary about 'Something', considering it to be *Abbey Road*'s finest moment.

Until this point, McCartney argued, Harrison's album contributions had reflected the fact that he was a junior songwriting associate within the group. "John and I obviously would dominate – again, not really meaning to, but we were 'Lennon and McCartney'. So when an album comes up, Lennon and McCartney go and write some stuff, and maybe it wasn't easy for him to get into that wedge. But he finally came up with 'Something' and a couple of other songs that were great, and I think everyone was very pleased for him."

"I think the trouble with George was that he was never treated on the same level, as having the same quality of songwriting, by anyone – by John, by Paul or by me," Martin agreed. "I was the guy who used to say: 'If he's got a song, we'll let him have it on the album' – very condescendingly. I know he must have felt really bad about that. Gradually he kept persevering, and his songs did get better – until eventually they got extremely good. 'Something' is a wonderful song – but we didn't give him credit for it, and we never really thought, 'He's going to be a great songwriter.' The other problem was that he didn't have a collaborator. John always had Paul to bounce ideas off. Even if he didn't actually write the song with Paul, he was a kind of competitive mate."

The final three songs on the *Blue* album were taken from The Beatles' final LP, *Let It Be*, even though this was actually recorded before *Abbey Road*. Conveying a loving light of wisdom, the title track remains a special moment, a great healing song in McCartney's Beatles canon. '*When all the broken hearted people living in the world agree, there will be an answer*': when discord is replaced with harmony, McCartney sings, a reconciliation through love can unite us and bring a peaceful solution. '*For though they may be parted*,' McCartney sings, of their separation from God, perhaps, as much as each other, '*there is still a chance that they will see.*'

"So those words are really very special to me, because not only did she [Paul's mother] come to me in a dream and reassure me with them at a very difficult time in my life, but sure enough, things did get better after that . . . in putting them in a song, and recording it with The Beatles, it became a comforting, healing statement for other people too." Meanwhile, Linda McCartney's first attempt at a vocal role came on the chorus of this song. "There was a very high note in there," remembered Paul.

"She and I were at Abbey Road late one night, and I was fussing around putting on a harmony, but I heard one higher and I couldn't get it. And I said to her, 'Could you get that note?' And she did it. So that was a pretty cool start."

As their era-defining, swansong single, 'Let It Be' was a touching song that found its author a nervous and insecure man. McCartney's public image did not match that of the private figure striving to keep the group together at all costs. 'Let It Be''s four-square gospel rhythm provided musical balm, and has inevitably remained a touching, powerful staple of subsequent stage shows. McCartney is still moved by the audience's reaction to this spiritual song, providing a source of emotional succour during concert performances. Beach Boy Brian Wilson, a great McCartney admirer, has insisted that 'Let It Be' healed him whenever he heard the song. In a spirit of musicianly reciprocity, Paul has stated that Wilson's 'God Only Knows' remains one of the most beautiful songs ever written.

Meanwhile, Lennon's 'Across The Universe' found its author attempting to convey how light and a love which *shines before me like a million suns* expand as a seemingly limitless force, clarifying the point using vivid imagery. Articulating an illuminating message of love being sent across the universe, it provided an appropriate title for the song. "The words are purely inspirational and were given to me," Lennon candidly admitted, "except for one or two maybe where I had to resolve a line or something like that. I kept hearing '*Words are flowing out like endless streams . . .*' I don't own it, it came through like that."

Accomplished and poetically evocative, Lennon later claimed that it subsequently became a 'cosmic song'. "'Across The Universe' is one of John's great songs and has special words," McCartney would later acknowledge. In India, Lennon had meditated for long periods and felt vindicated in focusing his energy on conveying new truths for the good of others.

However, 'Across The Universe' required a stronger group accompaniment, and its musical power may also have diminished because of Lennon's lethargy while the group began to dissolve. Brought in to rescue the project after it had lain dormant for over six months, producer Phil Spector gave it the Disney string treatment with lullaby voices, much to Lennon's evident approval.

McCartney felt very differently, however, when Spector adorned 'The Long And Winding Road' with an orchestral accompaniment sound never heard before on a Beatles record. This nostalgic and wistful song found McCartney singing about a road as a path leading back to the heart. He has seen the road before in his search for true love, and it will always be there. All he needs or requires is a little guidance.

Designed as a standard for mainstream balladeers, the song was attempted at the Apple sessions for *Get Back*, and was left undeveloped until Lennon invited Spector to salvage the song the following year. The touching emotion found in 'The Long And Winding Road''s soothing, nostalgic calm combined to create one of the most beautiful songs Paul ever wrote. It also features some of his most poignant and evocative lyrics, and with such melancholic loving wisdom, the song proved a fitting finale to the group's career and to the *Blue* album.

Originally little more than a rudimentary piano and bass demo with a satisfying McCartney vocal, Spector utilised Richard Hewson's orchestration which, as Ian MacDonald noted, "flew in the face of the etched, incisive and anti-romantic idiom painstakingly created since the mid-sixties".

When McCartney heard Spector's overdub work on his delicate song, he was sufficiently enraged for it to prove a decisive factor in his departure from the group. "I know that Paul was very cross about 'The Long And Winding Road' being interfered with," said Apple insider Derek Taylor. "I took the view that nobody should have ever interfered with their music. That was to me — I don't want to say *shocking* — but wrong, certainly. And if you were McCartney seeing your work being altered — I can imagine the outrage!"

"Paul has been quoted as saying that he didn't want Phil Spector involved, or didn't like him overdubbing orchestras on 'The Long And Winding Road' and other tracks," Harrison later confided. "But I personally thought it was a really good idea."

"So now we were getting a re-producer instead of just a producer, and he added all sorts of stuff — singing ladies on 'The Long And Winding Road' — backing that I perhaps wouldn't have put on," McCartney later affirmed. "I don't think it made it the worst record ever, but the fact that now people were putting stuff on our records that one of us didn't know was certainly wrong. I'm not sure whether the others knew about it."

With so much animosity leading to the point of the long-in-gestation *Let It Be*'s release in 1970, The Beatles faced increasingly turbulent conditions in which to continue with their work. With relations deteriorating for a year or so, the joy of making music slowly ceased to inspire them.

"John was always very outspoken, and Paul, of course, was always trying to be diplomatic," explained Ray Connolly. "I did feel sorry for Paul when they began to fall out, because John was the sort of person who would tell the world everything, but it wasn't necessarily all that accurate."

Having enjoyed an often unspoken closeness as harmonious counterparts in creating their musical legacy, Lennon and McCartney were no longer in sync with each other by the end of the decade.

CHAPTER FIVE

Spread Your Wings

B ACK in a Los Angeles studio in early 1973, Perry and Harrison were concluding their discussion of the *Red* and *Blue* albums when Harrison intrigued Perry by insisting that it hadn't seemed appropriate that The Beatles' work should stop at this juncture. "It seems like the career took a little turn here because it's like, all of a sudden, there's some great stuff but it seems incomplete," he told Perry. "It doesn't seem right it could or should end there!"

Perhaps there remained an underlying feeling among the group that a sense of unfinished business needed to be addressed. "I think it was John's band and he froze them at their peak," Ray Connolly insists. "And by freezing them then, he made them current forever. I think they probably realised this as the years went on."

In their producer's esteem, the group certainly hadn't finished their work by the time of their final album. Martin went on record during interviews marking the 25th anniversary of *Sergeant Pepper* by insisting that The Beatles would have continued to do even greater things. "By that point," argues Ray Connolly, "they'd had so many incredible years. Their output was astonishing. The amount of work they did. I think they needed a year off." At least as far as Harrison was concerned, their career had taken a different path, leaving an unresolved body of work.

Harrison's post-Beatles life was dominated by the pull between financial security and spirituality, and between meditation and drugs. "His attitude to The Beatles was equally conflicted," Peter Doggett argues, "and in 1970, he really missed being in the group. He became increasingly aware of everything that he had lost by being a Beatle, whereas the other three became increasingly nostalgic." Throughout the seventies, all four Beatles made various negative aspersions about the band, although they were often in the context of promoting their latest solo ventures.

"They all knew their artistic and commercial standing was higher together than apart," Du Noyer adds. "But each had a stubborn pride in his own independent ability and a need to have that affirmed by the world outside."

Discussing the group's experiences was not always an easy proposition for Jim Keltner, who played on a raft of Lennon and Harrison solo albums during the seventies. "I would ask John and George a lot of questions. I think they were relieved to not have to be Beatles for a while," he maintains. "They would let me talk about it to a point, but you'd have thought John would never want to revisit that again."

Various obstacles, most notably the competition with his dominant, illustrious peers had prevented Harrison's work getting through. This eventually worked in his favour on the release of his debut solo album, the triple *All Things Must Pass* collection. Released in 1970, it contained much of the material he'd slowly stockpiled throughout the late sixties.

As well as the stately title track, it featured the international best-selling single 'My Sweet Lord', and a cache of other songs influenced by his spiritual leanings. 'Isn't It A Pity' lamented the struggle to recognise divine love, while the battle against *maya* and illusion inspired 'Beware Of Darkness'. It also included the spiritual wake-up call of 'Awaiting On You All' and the sweet yearning of 'I'd Have You Anytime', co-written with Bob Dylan during Harrison's stay at his Woodstock home in November 1968.

Meanwhile, Keltner had first met Harrison during a Gary Wright session in 1971 before meeting again at Lennon's Tittenhurst Park mansion while making *Imagine*. Harrison duly requested Keltner's services for the much-trumpeted Concert For Bangla Desh at Madison Square Garden in August 1971. "He put that whole thing together on his own by the power of his name, and what he represented to people. Everyone would do whatever they could for George."

Keltner was excited about playing Harrison's music with Ringo, and the musicians spent two afternoons rehearsing in a New York hotel. "He got this great band together, and he got Dylan which would have been impossible for anybody except George. George loved the fact I was so close to Bob, which would've been a real fascination for John."

Lennon later recalled The Beatles' dream of staging something equally ambitious to promote peace and love. "There was a feeling of that, like when we did the live broadcast of 'All You Need Is Love'. Everyone in London was there, and there was that feeling in the air, there were lots of possibilities then."

Unsurprisingly, Lennon was impressed by the organisational scope of Harrison's Bangla Desh concert, although he declined the invitation to take part after George demurred at John's request for Ono to appear onstage. Leaving New York for Paris, Lennon hoped for a subsequent opportunity to perform with Harrison, who'd also invited a visa-restricted McCartney to perform. But with Apple matters in mind, he declined to appear as Beatles reformation rumours circulated. "I must say it was more than just visa problems. George came up and asked if I wanted to play Bangla Desh and I thought, 'Blimey, what's the point? We're just broken up and we're joining up again?' It just seemed a bit crazy."

However, McCartney would later applaud Harrison's generosity of spirit in setting such an impressive benchmark for future musical endeavours on this scale. "He must be given credit for that. It was the first big disaster that rock'n'roll had responded to. Typical of George, he did it right."

"George was a real pioneer," writer and actor Michael Palin insisted. "Not only did he have the strength of purpose to say: 'I'm going to do what I can for this country in trouble,' but look at the people he got together. Dylan, Clapton. These brilliant musicians."*

After Klein had paid for Connolly's flight and subsequently been given the Lennons' hotel suite, Connolly looked after Ono's sister, Setsuko, in Yoko's absence. At this huge Madison Square Garden concert, Connolly found himself seated in the front row, perfectly placed for Starkey to wave his drumsticks in his direction. "The concert was fantastic, and what was exciting was being around Manhattan. It was absolutely buzzing, and everybody was excited to be there. It was a great thing for George to do." The writer maintains that it was local hero Bob Dylan, who Harrison's devoted friend Shyamsundar Das had attempted to contact on George's behalf, who stole the show.

Apprehensive yet relishing the challenge at hand, Harrison gave a quietly commanding performance, including sumptuous renditions of 'Here Comes The Sun' and 'Something', which lingered long in the memory, and his huge international hit 'My Sweet Lord'. "This song was

---

* Palin later visited Bangla Desh during his *Himalaya* TV series expedition, and reflected on the country's plight as Harrison's charity single played over screen footage.

a simple idea of how to do a Western pop equivalent to a mantra," he recalled. "I don't just want to hear about some Holy Roller shouting about him. That's why I wrote '*My sweet Lord, I really want to see you*,' because if there is a God, I want to see Him."

George twice strolled onto the stage in front of 20,000 people at Madison Square Garden on August 1 and greeted his friend, Shyamsundar, seated in the front row, with 'Hare Krishna'. He then offered a similar salutation to the crowd and to the Lord as he strummed the opening chords of his classic 'My Sweet Lord' before encouraging his listeners to chant '*the names of the Lord*' during 'Awaiting On You All'.

Of all The Beatles, it was Harrison, Bill Harry insists, who appeared to have been enriched by his experiences during the sixties. "George had suddenly discovered his confidence, and I think it was because of the people he was associating with," Bill Harry explains. "It gave him a belief in himself. Not just as a musician, but with the people that he met. I think it was very important, because they stretched him and his talent as a musician. George was great with the guitar, and he became experimental with the sitar. George particularly enjoyed working with Eric Clapton, and he was getting involved with Ravi Shankar and Indian music and then onto the Monty Python team. With his interest in films, you also have Handmade Films, some quite exciting things. George did some *incredible* things."

Klaus Voormann's memory of the period which produced this concert spectacle was surprising, given Harrison's spiritual journey at the time. "I called and said I was coming up, and I heard him say: 'Klaus is coming. Hide the dope.' I appreciated George for his weaknesses as well as his strengths, and I could tell he was embarrassed."

As engineering assistant on the *Imagine* album, Jack Douglas then undertook the intensive experience of the *Concert For Bangla Desh* film mix. "We did the whole thing over a two-day period. And it was an amazing experience to work with George, who was [calm] through it. He was *very* cool. It was very nice."

Amidst attempts to control his indulgences while maintaining a more devoted spiritual life, Harrison was bursting with creativity after this landmark concert. He wrote 'The Day The World Gets Round' just hours after the occasion, an optimistic moment inspired by his friends' musical generosity for the greater good. This was clearly an emotional period, not least because of the assistance he had received in ensuring its success.

After marathon recording sessions, *Living In The Material World* appeared in the summer of 1973. *Rolling Stone* heralded the album as "the most concise, universally conceived work by a former Beatle since *John Lennon/Plastic Ono Band*". It yielded hit single 'Give Me Love (Give Me Peace On Earth)', conflating the spirit of two iconic Lennon compositions, 'All You Need Is Love' and 'Give Peace A Chance' in his own "prayer and personal statement between me, the Lord, and whoever likes it".

"Whenever I hear 'Give Me Love . . .' on the radio, I always well up immediately," Keltner admits of the thrill of hearing a new Harrison song. "It's one of my all-time favourites of George's. I played on the album, and that was a great period for him."

Starkey also featured on the album, and Keltner insists that George's Beatle brother would have figured on far more of their own records if they weren't specifically 'solo' efforts. The Indian connection culminated in the *Living In The Material World* album and stayed with him for the rest of his life. Elsewhere, 'Don't Let Me Wait Too Long' was a joyous song of amorous and spiritual love, 'Who Can See It' reminded Harrison of American icon Roy Orbison's unique voice, while 'The Light That Has Lighted The World' found Harrison offering hope through the need for change.

Increasingly fulfilled in the knowledge that his voice was being heard, Harrison steadily became more adept at expressing his spiritual realisations in song. '*Got a lot of work to do,*' he sang on 'Living In The Material World', '*trying to get a message through.*' "I'm just pretending to be a Beatle," he had told one interviewer. "Whereas there's a greater job to be done."

'The Lord Loves The One Who Loves The Lord' was dedicated to Krishna Consciousness founder Srila Prabhupada, who inspired the album's title track, which also featured George's comical account of the group's formation. "Some people wrote saying: 'Well, the problem with The Beatles is that when we were all growing up, they were just tooling round the world in limousines.' Actually it was the reverse. We were forced to grow up much faster." A "profoundly seductive record," *Rolling Stone* concluded of Harrison's album, "an article of faith, miraculous in its radiance."

"I would think about George, and his constant search for God. He was such a young man," Keltner emphasises, "and he wanted to know more, and share it with the people he loved. I truly treasured our conversations." Aside from drawing songwriting inspiration from Indian sage Paramahansa

Yogananda's *Autobiography Of A Yogi* teachings, George utilised the clever eulogies or cryptic aphorisms found carved around his Victorian property. Songs appeared like debut album offering 'Let It Roll' and *Extra Texture*'s 'The Answer's At The End', which included an invitation to let the foibles found amongst his friends to pass.

SPRING 1971. A typical life in the day of John Lennon. Two old friends are found sat together, not at Friar Park, but in the kitchen of Lennon's own Tittenhurst mansion in Ascot. Cameramen are busy documenting the making of *Imagine* as musicians and studio crew mill around the room. George and John are side by side at a large oak table with Phil Spector. Lennon raises the issue of McCartney's latest lyrical offerings on his recent *McCartney* album, a comment which provokes clear derision from Spector.

In late 1970, Lennon had already dismissed McCartney's eponymous first album, stating his preference for Harrison's critically and commercially acclaimed triple debut album. "I think it's better than Paul's. I think it's all right, you know. Personally, at home, I wouldn't play that kind of music, but I don't want to hurt George's feelings," he told *Rolling Stone* editor Jann Wenner. "I don't know what to say about it. But when I listen to the radio, and I hear George's stuff coming over, well then it's pretty good." Politics had prepared the ground for *Plastic Ono Band*, Lennon maintained, "the same as 'My Sweet Lord' prepared the ground for George's album."

It was McCartney, however, who was first off the starting blocks even though many thought his first solo work was hasty and unrealised. Released in early 1970, *McCartney* was a self-penned, self-performed and self-produced homemade album largely consisting of promising, fragmentary songs that failed to find favour with the critics. As David Quantick opined of the album's DIY charm, its composer now appeared like "a man alone in a recording studio fiddling around with a few half-written songs and a load of instrumentals", while critical carping suggested that Martin's work on Paul's Beatles songs had made them more substantial than they actually were. Excelling as a touching melodicist who largely played to his strengths ('The Lovely Linda', 'That Would Be Something' and 'Junk') despite the album's unusual erraticism ('Every Night', 'Man We Was Lonely' and 'Kreen Akrore'), its standout track was 'Maybe I'm Amazed', a classic piece of McCartney songwriting and, according to critic Howard Sounes, a "powerful expression of uxurious love" for Linda, the woman who had ultimately saved him from a turn-of-the-decade depressive torment. It certainly failed to impress the gathering at Tittenhurst Park.

"Phil was there at some of the key moments with those two guys, and that says something," insists Keltner of their producer. "I just loved watching the way they worked together. George would talk about John, but not very much. We mostly heard about their relationship from people who knew them well. Cynthia Lennon had some really wonderful and remarkable things to say about their relationship. I thought it was fantastic. They loved being together."

The drummer describes Harrison's down-to-earth qualities. Funny and bright, he loved people and equally enjoyed sharing his knowledge and musical tastes. Yet he also had what the drummer calls a "tremendous bullshit meter. He could see through people from a long distance. I saw him do that all the time. George was certainly his own man, but John was powerful. Can you imagine what it was like to have John Lennon as the leader of your band?" Keltner pondered.

"George's relationship with me was one of young follower and older guy," Lennon later confided. "I don't want to be that egomaniacal, but he was like a disciple of mine when we started." "George was certainly the youngster, and when you're young, that means a lot," Keltner adds of the Beatles' lead guitarist. "But he and John and Paul were peers, working together."

Back in his kitchen, Lennon turns to an amused Harrison, and with Spector's assistance, starts to scrawl a variety of translations based on the maxim of '*make love, not war*', a key lyric that formed the working title of subsequent Lennon single 'Mind Games'. An early version of the song opened with this most encouraging phrase, imploring his generation to surrender to peace by laying down their arms and becoming soldiers of love instead. "*Faire l'amour*," John continues, "*pas la guerre*," before joking about the producer's French vocabulary, much to Harrison's amusement. Yes, Lennon insisted, love was still the answer, nurturing hope and waiting to watch it grow.

Seeing the former Fabs engaging in jestful wordplay was apt, given the late-period Beatles idealism and the spiritual and philosophical motifs that later graced the song. With its '*love is the answer*' proclamation, 'Mind Games' looked back to the spirit of *Rubber Soul* stand-out 'The Word'.

"John prescribed a global projection of the power of love," Du Noyer enthused about 'Mind Games', a song that was reflective of a more meditative Lennon. "The song's guitars were overdubbed into a quasi-orchestral lushness that marked a partial return to *Imagine* territory."

Lennon later recalled that, with The Beatles sending out messages as the sixties progressed, conveying a sincere message of love seemed an appropriate thing to do for a group to whom people looked for answers. 'The Word' was an explicit, almost semi-evangelic attempt to broadcast such a sentiment on record. "The word is 'love'. '*In the good and the bad books that I have read*,' whatever, wherever, the word is love. It seems like the underlying theme to the universe." Despite the critical voice of his detractors, Lennon appeared to encourage Beatles listeners that the love we know led the way to a greater, more liberating love.

Delivering a sermon of new-born sincerity, 'The Word' was an early prototype of the love ethic that later materialised during the Summer of Love.

The song also contained the rejoinder to spread love amongst the less enlightened. Allow love the opportunity to speak its voice, sang Lennon, and follow its direction. Give love a chance, he offered, because it will provide the answer, even if he did not know the process (later explored through meditation) for achieving it. Sitting opposite Lennon in his mansion kitchen, Voormann was also on hand to assist with another translation of what became one of the key motifs of 'Mind Games'. "The words he chooses are for everybody," argued Voormann during the *LENNONYC* documentary. "That's why they're so strong, and it's what people can relate to."

After the critical lambasting of *Some Time In New York City*, Lennon hoped (and expected) *Mind Games*, recorded in the summer of 1973, would turn things around. "He couldn't record for a while, because he read all the reviews and, as a musician, he couldn't handle it," May Pang subsequently admitted. "And he didn't come back until *Mind Games*, which was a year later. He just went into hiding."

"*Mind Games* remains listenable," *Rolling Stone*'s Jon Landau would write early in 1974, just weeks after the album's release, "which is certainly more than can be said for *Some Time In New York City*. What was moving when applied to his own life was unbearably pretentious when used to offer aphorisms concerning larger issues."

With its roots as a song going as far back as The Beatles' *Get Back* sessions of 1969, a demo of 'Mind Games' was recorded the following year at Lennon's Ascot studio under the working title of 'Make Love, Not War'. Lennon finished writing the song after reading the book *Mind Games: The Guide To Inner Space* by Robert Masters and Jean Houston. "Verbose assertions use the language of radicalism," enthused critic Chris Ingham, to emphasise the "message of collective consciousness." Pang was later asked about the significance of the song's spiritual references amidst what Ingham insisted was a "hazy blanket of hopefully mystical production". "He taught me about the *I Ching*, and how accurate it was, and what you get out of it," she recalled. "He was always looking for answers."

This would also include his interest in Zen philosophy and mystical belief systems, towards which she claimed Lennon was moving during his spiritual search of the later seventies. "Love has to be nurtured . . . and you have to work at love, you don't just sit round with it, and it doesn't just do it for you," Lennon would later insist. "You've got to be very careful with it. It's the most delicate thing you can be given. It's a very delicate situation." May recalled that before they suddenly escaped New York for the West Coast, Lennon informed her he was ready to enter the studio. Despite not having an album's worth of new songs ready for the forth-coming record, within a little over two weeks, Lennon had produced *Mind Games*. It was a key demonstration for an admiring May of John's creative, productive brilliance.

"We took our time getting the sounds," Ray Cicala reflected on the *Mind Games* period. "Even though we did it fast. John was open to mis-takes. If there were wrong chords or there were too many notes per bar, we would fix that, or re-do it. If anything might have been out of tune, we would go for the actual feeling of the song. He definitely has the overall picture, but doesn't know how to get there."

Lennon's new album also suggested a tendency or a concerted effort to cut loose from old studio strictures, acting as his own arranger and producer. He also employed new session men of the calibre of virtuoso guitarist (and later Ono squeeze) David Spinoza. Yet Lennon drew on similar chord progressions and instrumentation on earlier solo album efforts like *Plastic Ono Band* and *Imagine*. As ever, Lennon was serious with the music, and knew what he wanted.

Cicala's expertise was crucial around a raft of New York session men (with the exception of Keltner) for the making of the album. "In some cases, I'd take the cymbals away from Jim and overdub, because you can get a better tom-tom sound." Cicala's solution sometimes ruffled the drummer's studio sensibilities. "He'd say: 'You can't do that!' I'd say: 'Yes we can. Here, have a drink,'" he told *Sound On Sound*. "It was very free-and-easy: 'You do your thing, I'll do my thing,' and it was great. The musicians did anything we wanted, and vice versa."

Cicala also found that Keltner's drum sound sometimes inspired Lennon to change his vocal approach to a new song. As Cicula said, Lennon definitely had the overall picture, but didn't know how to get there. For the majority of the time, John would arrive in the studio with a completed song, before running it down for the group to learn the chords. "And he had the musicians that were great," Cicala insisted, "because they would play *with* him. They wouldn't try to change the direction. If he didn't like it, he would just say, 'There's too much going on, let's try it a little slower, or a little different,' or we would say it to him."

Pang ensured each musician had their copy of John's lyrics once they'd assembled in the studio. The creative process and the musical rapport between Lennon and his players fascinated her. "I always loved the beginning, getting the musicians into the room and they're looking at it, and they would do what John would teach them, and then they'd come up with their own spin on it. I loved the actual sessions. The interaction between the musicians and John; it was nice to see the mutual admiration."

"'Mind Games' was just natural," claimed Cicala. "The slide guitar, and anything [lyrically] that was changed, was changed in the studio."

"The seeming orchestra on it is just me playing three notes on a slide guitar," Lennon later proudly admitted. "And the middle eight is reggae. Trying to explain to American musicians what reggae was in 1973 was pretty hard, but it's basically a reggae middle eight if you listen to it."

Cicala believed *Mind Games* was a more accomplished work than its predecessor, *Some Time In New York City*. Once again, Lennon was writing in the studio, inspired by the musicians and the studio environment. Keltner insists John's powerful personality and masterful songwriting abilities also played their part. Lennon would claim the album contained no deep philosophical message to be uncovered by fans and critics. "I very rarely consciously sit down and write a song with a deep message. Usually, whatever lyrics I write are about what I've been thinking over the past few months. I tend not to want to change an idea once it's in my mind, even if I feel differently about it later."

In biographer Ray Coleman's esteem *Mind Games* marked an attempt to return to former glories. Peter Doggett claims, however, that the album's overwhelming mood of *ennui* charted a journey from "the political equivalent of a bull in a china shop to self-parody in 18 months. The title of the album said it all: Lennon was playing at being an artist, where in the past his life and his art had been virtually interchangeable."

On this transitional and occasionally thrilling album, aside from the classic title track, 'Out Of The Blue' was a gorgeously restrained, richly augmented song about his pre-ordained love for Ono, while the lushly string-laden 'One Day At A Time', "the strongest indication in years of Lennon's old-style craft," Chris Ingham enthused, offered a vulnerable vocal in a delicate *paean* to romantic dependence. 'You Are Here' attempted to bridge the East-West cultural channel, "as warm and poetic a love song," Doggett conceded, "as Lennon had ever written."

'Aisumasen' was a lurching, gospel-type ballad, which contained a long, agonising confession to Ono over his personal foibles. Elsewhere, the jazzy strut of 'Intuition' proved an uncharacteristically forgiving song of Lennon's, promoting music's positive power in dealing with life. "It was immediately appealing," adds Doggett, "and might have worked as a single, but there was little but good intentions and the power of positive thinking."

But it is 'Mind Games' which remains a particularly special song for Keltner. "I liked the way the chords moved, and I could just sing this one note, and hang on to it. I just kept singing the high string part. I just kept hearing this all the time. John said he decided to use it as I'd sung it so often." Keltner subsequently heard *Mind Games* again some four years ago while interviewing for a magazine feature. "I loved it," he admitted. "It brought back immediately the feeling I had recording it."

Lennon sits alongside Dylan, Neil Young and Harrison in Keltner's bracket of great songwriters. "If I'm involved in it, and if I find that song to be playing itself, that's a great song by a great songwriter. That's my criteria." Keltner still believed in Lennon's creative credentials, regardless of the accompanying album's disappointing commercial success. According to Douglas, Lennon would hear the chord structure for a new song and its lyrics would then slowly coalesce before reaching the studio, ready to record. "By the time he gets to the studio," the producer told the *LENNONYC* documentary, "he has maybe two versions. And they go through changes until the word, and the sound of the word, matches the chord and the sound of the chord in the rhythm."

Cicala also provided a key insight into the recording process. "A lot of the writing [for *Mind Games*] happened in the studio while the musicians were playing. He would be changing lyrics, making lyrics." With the band set up in the Record Plant studio in the summer of 1973, an inspired Lennon would position himself in the midst of the players, and would sing as the group played around him. Cicala would also stress the relative sobriety of the *Mind Games* sessions, in contrast with the tequila-fuelled recording of its contentious predecessor.

Lennon and Keltner, who was driving a Daytone blue Corvette at the time, would sometimes ride to the sessions together with Pang at the wheel of a rent-a-car. On another occasion, the drummer recalls Lennon handing Keltner a huge jug-sized bottle of vodka through the car window as they waited at the lights *en route* to the A&M studios in Los Angeles. "The songs [on *Mind Games*] were like a tailored suit. Right away, you would just slip right into them," Keltner enthuses. "Playing John's songs, like with any truly great songwriter, the song will play itself. *Mind Games* was like that for me, and the playbacks were so much fun."

As a clear highpoint, he heard an acetate of the title track ("destined to become a first echelon Lennon classic," Philip Norman surmised) on his home turntable in Los Angeles. "John came over with May. It was a great hang that night." Keltner took pictures of the occasion, with a humorous Lennon genuflecting in front of a giant Joe Cocker poster of *Mad Dogs And Englishmen*.

Mind Games had been scheduled for release in November, and Capitol had organised marketing and promotion plans at its West Coast office. But Lennon was just as enthusiastic about one of his favourite promotional pastimes, undertaking radio DJ duties in Los Angeles in order to push *Mind Games*. "While he had been with Yoko, he had been involved with all these semi-subversive activities, which had not given him a great reputation in America," recalled Apple aide Tony King.

"He said to me at the time: 'Look, I've got this album, what do you think I should do?' I said, 'Honestly, you've got to go out and make a few friends, because you've lost a bit of support because you've been involved with things of a controversial nature.' So he said: 'Fine, you organise it, I'll do it.' And he did." PR duties aside, King clearly enjoyed Lennon's company. "I found him to be the most stimulating person I've ever worked for, because he was so fast and so bright and so on the ball. We had some great times together. John was crazy about America – that was liberation to him."

For Lennon biographer Philip Norman, *Mind Games* suggested "a retreat from all the causes and victims they [the Lennons] had championed together and a return to the therapist's couch, this time on the subject of marriage rather than parentage and childhood." "*Mind Games* reveals another major artist of the sixties lost in the changing social and musical environment of the seventies," *Rolling Stone* later carped. Having initially been conceived under the working title of *Make Love, Not War*, the album's sentiment, Lennon surmised, was open to ridicule by a more sceptical, less naïve audience. "That was such a cliché that you couldn't say it anymore, so I wrote it obscurely, but it's all the same story," as he explained to *Playboy*'s David Sheff. "How many times can you say the same thing over and over? When this came out in the early seventies, everybody was starting to say: 'The sixties was a joke, it didn't mean anything, those love-and-peaceniks were idiots . . .' 'We had fun in the sixties,' they said. And I was trying to say: 'No, just keep doin' it.'"

"In the hands of an experienced pop producer," claims Doggett, "say, to pick a name at random, Paul McCartney, [*Mind Games*] could have been moulded into something as appealing as Wings' *Band On The Run* album, albeit with weightier ingredients."

Mind Games would be released in November 1973, just weeks ahead of Paul's classic-in-waiting, an album that became the definitive McCartney collection of the seventies. *Band On The Run* was also a work which finally silenced his press detractors, quelling public derision and satisfying his own inner critic.

That summer, McCartney had clearly set his sights on a markedly different, even adventurous recording location for the follow-up album to Wings' early 1973 release, *Red Rose Speedway*. Paul claimed that he was also following an in-vogue inclination for making music on distant shores. Having requested a full list of record company EMI's global facilities, he scanned an exciting catalogue of studios spread across the world. China and the carnival city of Rio de Janeiro were two early considerations, but then McCartney noticed the Nigerian capital of Lagos as a possible venue.

That's so far off the beaten track, he pondered. Something memorable or unusual is bound to happen, he reasoned – something that will inspire us after undertaking this African odyssey. The great musical rhythms and cultural traditions of this dark continent were also appealing, as were the possible benefits of recording abroad. "For me the attractions were artistic, instinctive. It was like: 'The music of Africa will colour our feelings, we'll be steeped in the ancient African rhythms' – that sort of thing." 'Let's do it,' McCartney enthused.

Fortunately, or unfortunately, McCartney and co were oblivious to the fact that it was monsoon season in Nigeria and the studio was only half-built to Western standards. Just for good measure, drummer Denny Seiwell and guitarist Henry McCullough unexpectedly quit the band just hours before boarding the flight to Nigeria in September. Biographer Chris Sandford, an old friend of McCullough's, informed this author that the guitarist had been something of a 'critical fan' of the group's leader at the time. A sometimes overpowering McCartney had, as in the past, over-stepped the threshold of acceptable musicianly etiquette by suggesting guitar parts for his colleague to perform once too often, and McCullough walked out of rehearsals of new material at Paul's Scottish farm in August.

The two men had never worked well, but then despite their clashing styles, Seiwell insists that if his bandmate had shown a little more enthusiasm for the group's work, things may have been different. "If I hadn't have moved at that time, I think eventually I may have been sacked," McCullough later admitted. "It's all very well getting in a Lear jet and flying off to Lagos, but at the end of the day when you get home you still have to eat." Financial concerns were also of paramount importance as he and his employer exchanged fractious words concerning the guitarist's pay.

"I said: 'Listen, can't we just postpone this trip and break in a new guitar player?'" Seiwell reasoned with Paul. "'We can rehearse a new guitar player, teach him Henry's parts, teach him the songs, so we can go into this project and play it as a band kind of live and then embellish it?' He said: 'No, no, no, we're just going to continue. EMI have set up the studio for us. We'll do it like *Ram*. It'll all be over-dubbed, but we'll make it good.' I thought, 'I don't want to do that again.' We had just spent all this time and effort becoming a real rock'n'roll band, and it was becoming very good. So between Henry leaving, the bad news of Denny and Jo, no contract one more time, I just took it upon myself to say: 'That's it!'"

When Lennon learnt of their defections, he took little interest in the re-shuffle of Wings personnel, despite noting their slight resemblance to the Plastic Ono Band. "Wings keeps changing all the time. It's conceptual. I mean, they're back-up men for Paul. It doesn't matter who's playing."

"I never quite worked out why, whether it's 'cos Africa was a bit far,"

McCartney later reasoned. "I think everyone was blissfully happy until they were asked to go to darkest Africa. It was like, you know: 'We'll come to rehearsal next Monday – but Africa? Are you kidding?'" Both Seiwell and McCullough would later regret their decision. "I kind of like the way we did *Band On The Run*," McCartney enthused with the benefit of hindsight. "The way we did it was something we've never done before, and it's very interesting."

McCartney wasn't quite as philosophical at the time, however. "I said: 'We're booked. *We're* going.' I wasn't cool about it. I was livid. 'Right, screw you. I'm gonna make an album you'll wish you were on.'" Puzzled and angry, the phone call was, a furious McCartney admitted, nothing less than a bombshell. "You can imagine me getting off *that* phone call. It was like: 'Ah. Okay. Try and hold your nerve; try and keep it together. What do we do now? Sod it, we're going.' And at that moment it was one of those: 'I'll show you. I will make the best album I've ever made now. I will put so much effort into it, because I wanna just prove that we didn't need you guys.'"

Paul, Linda and Denny flew to Lagos as planned, and McCartney was initially thrilled to have the chance of watching from the cockpit as their plane came in to land. "Down below is jungle, and there was a mist. It's perfect; it's Africa. The two pilots said: 'Can you see it?' We said: 'Are we even going to land?' It was very under-developed. When you're placed in that situation, you have to make a decision – 'Am I going to run home, or make the best out of this?' So we decided to make the best of it."

Recovering quickly from this unexpected development, McCartney was forced to rethink his whole *modus operandi*. Multi-tasking in the studio and forced to take control, he handled drum and lead guitar duties (alongside Laine) as well as bass, writing and vocals. "I'm an okay drummer. I've got a style and a feel. I like playing drums. So I knew if I kept it simple, I'd be able to cover it. So you'll notice the drums on *Band On The Run* are pretty simple. But Denny can play guitar – that wasn't too bad – and then I just thought, 'Well, I've done *McCartney*. I can drum, I can do this and that, and we'll just completely rethink the whole thing.' But it was full of difficulties."

"Paul's personality is that he likes to be positive, he likes to be up – and there's a strength there somehow – he doesn't like to share his down time with other people," Laine would later reflect on the album's making. "He likes to cope with it himself in private." Laine, for one, didn't appear to be too ruffled by this unexpected turn of events. "It didn't bother me. When you've been through what we've been through with different bands and different members, you just get on with it. It's not like, 'Hey! It's the end of the world.'" Laine later claimed the album had been made in the vein of studio musicians-turned-producers, rather than a band.

While McCartney had written new songs, demo recordings with the band hadn't materialised prior to leaving for Lagos, so plans were made to arrange them in the African studio. Having claimed the song arrangements were clear in his own mind, it was the revised recording methods for a three-piece band that presented the biggest challenge. "We would just get the three of us – me, Linda and Denny – to do a track and get the basis of the song, and then I would go back in and add the missing parts. I think the songs themselves were the same - it was the instrumentation and the arrangements that changed. But in a way I found that to be quite a good thing, because stripping things back is never the worst idea."

The track 'Mrs. Vandebilt', making liberal use of McCartney's playful lyrical and musical tendencies, concerned these fantasy outcasts looking for respite in a carefree jungle existence. It was certainly the one track most redolent of the environment in which the album was recorded.

Linda's vocal harmonies, meanwhile, came to be central to the Wings sound. McCartney remembered that Elton John and Michael Jackson later praised her work on *Band On The Run*. "I think we just became a better band. I'd figured out what I'd been trying to work out, which was: 'What was the Wings sound?' And once you had it, then you could be with it."

McCartney and his group encountered a rudimentary, unfinished studio in the port of Apapa, certainly not the type of EMI facility they had envisaged before departing England. There was also a faulty control desk, an absence of separation baffles and unbuilt vocal and sound booths.

It was little more than an outbuilding adjoining a basic pressing plant. Fortunately, former Beatles engineer Geoff Emerick was on hand to persevere with the tropical insects, limited technical situation and humble recording environment. "When you opened [the back door] you saw a couple of dozen shirtless guys standing ankle deep in water," he recalled, "pressing records in this small, steaming-hot room." Local carpenters rectified the sound booth problems, creating a suitably 'homemade' vibe during the monsoon season sessions. "Paul discovered that Lagos was not a paradise resort where he and Linda could swing on hammocks under coconut trees," recalls biographer Howard Sounes, "but a dirty, dangerous, disease-ridden city, sticky hot in the monsoon season."

Meanwhile, former Cream drummer Ginger Baker had been keen for McCartney to record what became *Band On The Run* at his own ARC studio in Nigeria. McCartney has always maintained the EMI-listed studio was his first choice. Having apparently agreed to spend one day at the Ikeja-based facility to pacify an irate Baker, the drummer claims to have salvaged the sessions on the former Beatle's behalf after the intimidating local musical magus Fela Kuti and his entourage took over the EMI studio. "The actual truth of the matter is that *Band On The Run* would never have been recorded if it wasn't for me. I said, 'It *is* Paul McCartney, we really can't do this,' and the sessions continued. They wouldn't have done it without my intervention."

McCartney had been subject to local discontent and suspicion over their musical motives for visiting Lagos. A notable cultural and political icon, Kuti believed McCartney and his group intended to 'exploit and steal' indigenous black music during the making of their new album. McCartney insisted that his intentions were honourable, and was hoping to promote this unbelievable music back home. The subsequent *Band On The Run* material clearly lacked an exotic rhythmic or melodic influence. "He [Kuti] showed up at the studio one day, and said: 'Westerners, you've come here to steal our music.' I played him a few tracks and said: 'Look, is this stealing your music?' He said: 'No, that's okay. I see you're not doing that.' It was going to become a little bit sort of dangerous, because he was quite a voice in Lagos."

Their presence in Africa barely made news in the local media. Given such testy encounters, it was something for which McCartney was later thankful. "It was good, because we were getting on with the work, and so we didn't have to deal with what it's like now, where every little move is documented." A growing sense of menace eventually materialised one night when Paul and Linda were accosted by a group of knife-wielding locals keen on purloining their Western trinkets of cameras, recording equipment and studio tapes. Having been warned (but subsequently ignoring the advice) not to walk through town at night, the McCartneys had been partying with their colleagues when they were stopped on the road by a group of men who appeared interested in more than just the former Beatle's autograph.

"There were about five guys in a car, and I kept thinking they were offering me a lift. I naturally put the most optimistic spin on this. I just kept saying: 'No thanks, mate' and bundling the guy back into the car. I said: 'You know what, this is so nice of you – but it's a beautiful evening and we don't want a lift. Come on, now. Get in the car. Get back in that car.' So then the car stopped again. Anyway, the doors swung open and five of them jumped out – one had a knife and Linda started shouting: 'Don't touch him, leave him alone, he's a musician!'"

Following such a challenging experience, one can hardly wonder at McCartney's sense of wanderlust or yearning for freedom, feelings which were beautifully captured in the wide-eyed, airborne vistas of acoustic ballad 'Bluebird'. Meanwhile, 'Mamunia', named after a Moroccan holiday hotel, would consider Mother Nature's agelessness as they toiled in foreign climes.

With McCartney eager to share the writing workload, Denny Laine had been encouraged to bring more songs to the table. Their first collaboration resulted in 'No Words', a minor ballad. The track was an amalgam of two Laine ideas that the former Moody Blue played for Paul, before McCartney fused them together and announced they now had a song. "I'm not like Paul, in that sense. I don't just write about everything that goes on. If he sees something, he writes about it. He tends to write more. He's got more of a work ethic than me."

Laine would later reflect on the collaborative strength of his working relationship with McCartney whilst making the album, and the enduring appeal of *Band On The Run*. "The thing about working with Paul is, being such a famous person as he was, such a recognisable guy, that it was difficult to be his equal if you like, as far as the public was concerned, but in the studio we were pretty much on an equal par. It had the best feel of all the albums, it had a kind of unity. It was me and him, in one period of time. I like the album because us two did it under a challenge to make it happen. We were under pressure, and something came out of it."

One of the album's earliest compositions was 'Picasso's Last Words (Drink To Me)', written on holiday in Montego Bay, Jamaica after Paul dined one night with actor Dustin Hoffmann. "And he happened to say, when I was playing guitar round at his house after dinner: 'Could you write a song about anything?' I said: 'Maybe . . . try me!'" A clearly impressed Hoffmann told McCartney how strongly he believed in the incredible creative gift of songwriting. On their return a couple of days later, Hoffmann handed Paul a copy of *Time* magazine which featured a poetic article on artist Pablo Picasso's passing.

Hoffmann considered it an ideal subject for a song. "In the article he supposedly said: 'Drink to me, drink to my health, you know I can't drink anymore.' I strummed a couple of chords I knew I couldn't go wrong on, and started singing: '*Drink to me, drink to my health,*' and he leaps out of his chair and says, 'Annie! Annie!' That's his wife. 'The most incredible thing! He's doing it! He's writing it! It's coming out!' He's leaping up and down, just like in the films, you know. And I'm knocked out because he's so appreciative."

Despite his earlier disgruntlement, Ginger Baker even played a percussive part in the song. "We were working in Ginger's studio – nice studio down there. We thought we'd do this 'Picasso . . .' number, and we started off doing it straight," recalled Paul. "Then we thought, 'Picasso was kind of far out in his pictures, he'd done all these different kinds of things, fragmented. Cubism and the whole bit.' I thought it would be nice to get a track a bit like that, put it through different moods, cut it up, edit it, mess around with it – like he used to do with his pictures."

Meanwhile, producer and orchestrator Tony Visconti was a man who'd relocated to Britain to follow his dream of understanding how The Beatles made their music. He believed that McCartney knew exactly what he wanted in terms of a specific sound in the studio. 'Picasso's Last Words' was a case in point. "The middle section has a French radio station on in the background. He had two clarinet players I wrote the parts for. Paul came out and interacted with them, and wanted them to play more plummy. Then he did what you do in these situations: he just sang it for them, which is better than using words like 'plummy', which don't make any sense."

When the group returned to England, they listened back to the Emerick-engineered material they had taped in Lagos. McCartney was impressed by the different sound they'd created in a fresh environment, having soaked up new influences in a foreign land. With Visconti's assistance, McCartney set about adding overdubs and string arrangements to the suite of new songs. "It started to get raw but professional, which was a nice mix," Paul later enthused. "We knew we'd got the essence of the album and could add to it back in London."

Visconti received a call from McCartney, asking him to write the string parts on seven songs for a 50-piece orchestra inside two days. It was,

Visconti claimed, the end of a long quest to find himself in the studio with one of The Beatles. The orchestral work, conducted at Air studios that autumn, was duly completed at short notice. "After an hour we told most of them to go home. It was a good work day for those guys." The signature orchestral parts on the album's epic title track took some time to perfect, however.

Meanwhile, the closing saxophone lick on 'Jet' took what Visconti insisted were at least 25 attempts to make into a seamless 'super sax' part featuring Liverpudlian Howie Casey, a member of Beatles contemporaries Derry & The Seniors. "Paul said: 'I *have* to have that lick, I *have* to have that phrase.' Visconti encouraged Casey to play the bottom notes to complement the higher sax phrase, enjoying the challenge of making the song work under pressure in the studio with McCartney. Casey's skills were also well utilised on the flighty pastoral 'Bluebird'.

McCartney recalled his surprise at a phone call from Richard and Karen Carpenter offering their seal of approval for 'Jet' after the huge-selling single's release. "They were like: 'Oh, great record, man!' So, you know, it was actually resonating with people. They were liking the stuff." With its obscure lyric – originating from an ode to the McCartney's family pony – 'Jet' was a galvanising, anthemic track which became a loving paean to both an individual and a state of mind. McCartney realised that they suddenly had a set of songs in 'Jet', 'Helen Wheels', the ambitious title track and 'Let Me Roll It' that people could identify with.

Having written an ingenious sequence of classic guitar figures during his Beatle pomp, McCartney clearly enjoyed the dramatic and distinctive riff of 'Let Me Roll It', one he later relished playing in concert by winding up the stage amps. It duly became a staple song of his live set. Discussing the title track's appeal to his younger fan base, McCartney later admitted that a vigilante or desperado spirit had been at play. "It was a nice idea that we were breaking out, being stuck inside these four walls, and then the song could break out, and get more fantasy to it. It was symbolic: '*If we ever get out of here . . . All I need is a pint a day.*' It was feeling like that, the whole thing. Because we'd started off as just kids really, who loved our music and wanted to earn a bob or two so we could get a guitar and get a nice car. It was very simple ambitions at first. But then, you know, as it went on it became business meetings and all of that, and eventually it was really not fun. So there was a feeling of '*If we ever get out of here*', yeah. And I did."

As far as *Rolling Stone* were concerned, *Band On The Run* found McCartney traversing a middle ground between "autobiographical song-writing and subtle attempts to mythologise his own experience through the creation of a fantasy world of adventure. If the listener were to ignore the music and the skill with which McCartney has developed his theme," Jon Landau's review stated, "the entire enterprise might seem banal. But he holds the record together through the continual intimation that he enjoys the search for freedom more than he might enjoy freedom itself."

"*Band On The Run* is lyrically slightly weak, as usual, but musically it has an energy and cohesiveness lacking from [its predecessors]," biographer Howard Sounes concluded. McCartney would later admit that it felt as though the group had made something special. "It felt like we'd cracked it," he'd proudly assert, "and the strange circumstances of making it. It was quite a crazy project, really." Wings had suddenly come together and they had finally found a recognisable style for the group.

"What we had been trying to do worked. And also, what I'd seen in Linda – what I thought was there – finally came out. The albums that came after that were still different, but now that we were more popular, we discovered what our fans liked. So then that's your style. I think that's what happens with bands – it certainly happened with The Beatles and with Wings: you start off imitating people and just goofing around, trying to find out what works and what doesn't work."

Paul was finally enjoying solo success at the same level as John and George. Wings had won credibility with their new album after McCartney had written the theme song to the 1973 James Bond film, *Live And Let Die*, which was nominated for both an Oscar and a Grammy. Having followed this up with *Band On The Run*, Wings became a celebrated stadium band with A-list figures endorsing their work. The album became a worldwide number one hit, going triple platinum in the US and later transforming Wings into one of the biggest stadium acts of the seventies. And yet McCartney made some candid, almost disparaging comments at the time about his eventual double Grammy-award winning album. "I reckon I've made some bum records in the last couple of years. I like them, and they're all okay, but the things I've been through in the last few years aren't very conducive to inspiration."

However, Visconti recalled McCartney's joyous expression during the final stages of work on the album at Air. "Paul had a big smile on his face the whole day. It was probably something that he'd been dreaming about.

This album was the first that was approaching the magnitude of a Beatle album." It was certainly greeted as McCartney's most focused and coherent work, with one reviewer noting that its frothy self-confidence was reminiscent of The Beatles, but without the emotional grounding provided by Lennon and Harrison at their most productive. The album became the UK's biggest-seller in 1974, and Paul now seriously rivalled Lennon as an artist in his own right.

"*Band On The Run* is a great album," Lennon enthused in a rare moment of clear solidarity for his old partner's work. "It's Paul McCartney music. And it's good stuff. It's good Paul music." With his comments coming in the wake of the inaugural Beatles convention in September 1974, Lennon also believed McCartney's latest work was an enlightening affair. "There's definitely something musical happening there. It's very 'awake' music, and I've started listening to it again, and I'm digging it."

"It [*Band On The Run*]'s important for me, because it was really the first time we had a big hit," McCartney would later enthuse. "It was important for Wings, it introduced Wings to a lot of people, a new generation of people. They talk about it as an iconic album, whereas I often think of *Sergeant Pepper*. That was nice, especially as we'd been trying to be the band after The Beatles. So finally, we made it and went on tour in America and had a big success there." However, McCartney had launched Wings in order to play live but now faced an unexpected quandary: he had no live band with which to perform his finest and most successful post-Beatle material.

While McCartney finally prospered with Wings, Lennon was constantly searching and seeking to improve in his own work, admitting that *Mind Games* was a satisfactory work of "rock at different speeds". Free of the political dogmatism of its predecessor, it reprised the introspective nature of his earlier work. "Someone told me it was like *Imagine* with balls, which I liked a lot."

Despite insisting that his new, melodic and equally optimistic record was a superior work to that of *Imagine*, Lennon's opinion has clearly not withstood critical scrutiny or popular revision. "No, there's only one *Imagine*," producer Jack Douglas told Michael Epstein in 2010. "There isn't a weak point in the whole album. Talk about being in the right place at the right time." With hindsight, *Mind Games* had emerged from a period when Lennon began listening to critics' voices and the public's reaction. This was ultimately an exercise in making a pleasing album of sporadic brilliance that lacked genuine continuity.

May Pang has since recalled that Lennon had little confidence in his own voice, an incredible situation which certainly baffled John's young *beau* during the making of *Mind Games*. "It took a while for me to rebuild that with him. I would say: 'You have a great voice.' And he would say: 'It's not that strong, I don't sing that well.' I would say: '*What*?' That had been going on a long time before I was his girlfriend."

"If I put reverb or echo on his voice that was too much, he'd say: 'Don't take it off!' We recorded with all that repeat echo," engineer Roy Cicala told Michael Epstein. "We used to actually put the reverb or the delay on the track, and nobody could touch it after. I think it was his sense of insecurity that he had," Cicala insisted, "because everybody is insecure to a certain extent."

Keltner, meanwhile, recalls the distinctive quality of Lennon's voice, whether in conversation or at the microphone. When John spoke or sang, the drummer maintains, you listened. Greg Calbi, a former engineering *protégé* of Cicala's in New York and now senior mastering engineer at Sterling Sound, recalls a studio conversation between Lennon and Capitol Records' Al Coury, urging him to re-take a vocal. "I remember thinking: 'Here is one of the greatest rock'n'roll singers . . . I can't believe I'm hearing this!'"

Having temporarily left New York for Los Angeles in mid-September 1973, Pang recalled Lennon was the new kid on the block in untested musical territory. This was a very different environment in which Lennon would attempt to write and record. Yet Los Angeles initially provided Lennon with a sense of exhilaration. "John loved the sun, the water, so he began to relax and he felt rejuvenated," insisted Pang, who had begun to feel uncomfortable in the Big Apple after being encouraged by Yoko to initiate a relationship with Lennon.

John had finalised work on *Mind Games* in the autumn and began promoting his new album ahead of its November release. Journalist Chris Charlesworth first met Lennon in mid-October while enjoying music business mogul Lou Adler's company at a club on Hollywood's Sunset Boulevard. Adler was Carole King's mentor and the owner of the Bel Air mansion where Lennon and Pang were staying and where Charlesworth would conduct his first interview with the former Beatle a few days later. Lennon stressed that he had no plans for live appearances as he was obliged to wait until his visa and immigration issues were resolved. Entrancing Charlesworth with his light Scouse accent, Lennon began asking questions about politics, music, McCartney and life back in England.

The two men talked for an hour about Lennon's new album, his love of the States, his visa problems, the recent *Red* and *Blue* albums, the current music scene, and his relationship with Paul, George and Ringo. Lennon admitted an enduring fondness for McCartney's most cherished Beatles compositions, including the timeless *Revolver* classics 'Here, There And Everywhere' and 'Eleanor Rigby'. Like many of his contemporaries, Lennon privately (if not publicly) always regarded McCartney's musical gifts as incredible. Drawing on his accomplished, semi-professorial skills as a composer, the rest of the group could only admire McCartney's enviable ability to create such beautiful melodies in a memorable series of classic love songs. His capacity to share this gift left The Beatles with a rich and timeless musical legacy.

"One of the nicest moments I remember from those years was when John said he liked 'Here, There And Everywhere' better than any of his songs at the time – there were those little things." McCartney, after all, possessed the musical capacity to make people's hearts sing. Lennon would also have relished the chance to thank McCartney for the love within the music which he gave to the world. He may not have conceded as much at the time, but it was also a pleasure for Lennon to hear McCartney sing.

Ultimately, despite their competitive relationship, Lennon may have regretted this reticence about expressing his enjoyment of much of Paul's best work, and the beauty of many of his songs. As with 'Hey Jude', McCartney made a deep impression on Lennon with 'Here, There And Everywhere', a song which saw Paul express his true capacity as a romantic writer. "This was a great one of his," Lennon admitted. Articulating his blissful vision of a mutual belief in undying love, Paul envisages a future of unlimited potential for everyone that's waiting to materialise. As he looks forward, he is keen to convey the hope that we can experience this sensation. McCartney could often be a little guarded because of the characterisations in his songs, unaware that Lennon had wanted him to be more open and expressive. Here, however, his enigmatic narrative displayed his real lyrical gifts. On such warm and touching melodic form in this blissful paean to higher love, McCartney was without peer.

"We played it on a tape cassette," Paul remembered, "and he just sort of said: 'Oh, I *really* like that one.' That was very rare for John. He didn't throw compliments around, so I remember thinking: 'Oh great, it must be good!' I respected that he liked it." Paul later recalled Lennon's slight lyrical input in completing the song, one which clearly caught the renowned American balladeer Art Garfunkel's ear. "To me, the song is so stunningly sublime," he admitted, "that I am just intimidated to touch it."

Producer George Martin was also enamoured with this McCartney classic, later applauding its gentle, simplistic beauty. An elegant, well-crafted piece of writing, McCartney enjoyed the song's structure and melody. "I like it because it folds back in on itself through the middle eight. Each verse takes a word. Here discusses here. Next verse, there discusses there, then it pulls it all together in the last verse, with 'everywhere'." McCartney would rate it as arguably his finest Beatle composition, and as a covert Beach Boys pastiche, certainly one of the most enjoyable writing and recording experience of his Beatle career. Meanwhile, Lennon also admitted that he now spoke to one of the other former Beatles every two weeks. "I've talked to Ringo a lot recently because he's just moved into my house at Ascot, which is nice because I've always got a bedroom there. I haven't talked to Paul since before he did the last tour with Wings, but I heard *Red Rose Speedway* and it was all right." Feeling somewhat nostalgic, Lennon was spending time with Starkey and communicating with both McCartney and Harrison. John would also be eager to play the DJ and spin some of his favourite songs. "He'd tell me: 'I feel like a kid again!' so it was almost a natural progression," claimed Pang, "to go back to what inspired John to make music in the first place."

But for Elephant's Memory, Lennon's ongoing battle to remain in America proved an immensely frustrating period. As the group continued cashing their retainer cheques, they remained none the wiser over their collaborative future with the former Beatle. Van Scyoc remains convinced that if the group had figured in the making of John's *Rock 'N' Roll* album instead of an impressive cast list of A-grade sessioneers, the resulting record would have been a happier and more productive venture.

"We were on the East coast, and Phil didn't want to do it with us because he didn't think we were worthy. He wanted to get right back into the star-stream again, that whole LA scene. If John and Yoko had stayed together, then maybe he could have talked Phil into coming back to New York and doing it with us. We talked about doing that kind of album all the time. We were a strong live, rock'n'roll band, and we'd already been playing those types of songs in rehearit would have been the perfect match."

134

CHAPTER SIX

Midnight Special

ERRATIC productivity in a wilder musical environment would subse-quently characterise the drunken or chemically addled winter period of 1973 during Lennon's much-mythologised *Rock 'N' Roll* sessions with Phil Spector. "One of the greatest sessions of all time," Spector can be heard to joke on a session bootleg, "history is in the making." "The *Rock 'N' Roll* album was made in a studio in LA, with dozens of musicians who were drunk and stoned, with Phil in the middle of it," photographer Bob Gruen recalls. "People were yelling, and it was chaotic, just as rock'n'roll should be."

Lennon would later claim that this was a project which he and Spector had envisaged many years earlier, enabling him to reconnect with the songs which inspired him as a singer rather than a writer. Excited by the concept, he was considering the type of material he would like to tackle. "Whenever I'm in the studio, between takes, I mess around with oldies. I even used to do it in the Beatle days, so now I'm finally getting round to doing a 'John Lennon sings the oldies' album."

Lennon admired his production hero, but the experience of making *Mind Games*, he insisted, had been a valid education in producing his own work. "There was nobody to lean on, and this was a good exercise for me. I always control everything anyway, but this time I thought I'd do it all on my own. The only reason I make albums is because you're supposed to. I haven't really got into somebody's album since I was into Elvis Presley and Carl Perkins, and even then singles were always the best."

The resulting album attempted to be all things to Lennon and his critics too: a reconnection with his adolescent musical education, a safe retreat from the artistic frontline, and a re-filling of the cup from his favourite source. "Perhaps he imagined that the commercial success of *Rock 'N' Roll* might reawaken his creativity at a time when his songwriting well seemed to be dry," claims Alan Clayson, "and he was being made constantly aware that his best work was behind him." Or, as Peter Doggett argues, the album may have signified "an easy opportunity (or so it seemed) of avoiding a lawsuit with Morris Levy over the 'You Can't Catch Me'/'Come Together' plagiarism accusations". Lennon made his artistic motive for the album clear early on.

"I just finished *Mind Games* when I started the new album, and I just wanted to have some fun. It was so soon after *Mind Games* that I didn't have any new material. I wanted to just sing and not be the producer. I thought: 'Who's the one to do it with?' and I thought of Phil Spector. We went down to the Record Plant and started cutting and, well, it got pretty crazy . . . it really got wild at times. But we managed to cut seven or eight in the end before it collapsed . . . which is the only way to put it." Lennon was also keen to remove himself from the pressure of producing serious 'art' or facing tiresome enquiries about whether his songs were about him or Paul.

At the close of his interview with *Melody Maker*'s US correspondent Chris Charlesworth, Lennon dealt with the age old rumours of Beatles reunions with evasive aplomb. "There's always a chance," he said. "As far as I can gather from talking to them all, nobody would mind doing some work together again. There's no law that says we're not going to do something together, and no law that says we are. If we did something, we'd do it just for that moment. I think we're closer now than we have been for a long time. I call the split the divorce period and none of us ever thought there'd be a divorce like that. That's just the way things turned out. We know each other well enough to talk about it."

Lennon's only stipulation for what became *Rock 'N' Roll* was that Cicala would be present to engineer (and later mix) the sessions. "He became like a brother and a friend to me," said Cicala, who later served as an engineer on all of Lennon's seventies albums. "I really didn't want to go [to LA], because I knew it was going to be chaos, and I might end up never going back home to New York. So, I told John that and he said: 'Well, bring your family.' It was pretty crazy," Cicala confirmed during his *LENNONYC* interview. "John was drinking anything that was available. I went through a bottle a day. I don't know how we didn't die. But the record came out. That's another messy record, but it's great, the *Rock'n'-Roll* album. It's wonderful."

Keltner expresses similar amazement that not only Lennon but the musicians and production staff had survived this self-indulgent period. "Whatever you want to call it," Keltner emphasises, "to come through that, not many would be able to do that. But that's the fantastic thing: we got to see that with John. The world *did* see that."

Having considered only one man suitable to helm the project, Lennon insisted that Spector should assume control of the sessions. Had Lennon been sole or even co-producer (or if Spector had completed the work on the project), the *Rock 'N' Roll* album would have been a markedly less troublesome affair. "In this case, John was going to give him the job of producer on the album," Pang recalled. "Phil did ask him: 'Do you really mean that?' John should have taken the hint, as it were." Lennon had had an artistic vision of assuming the mantle of singer once again, much like his producer's wife Ronnie Spector fronting her group, happy to concentrate on his own performance. "John is not a frontman," insisted bassist Klaus Voormann. "He knew that's what people want. 'Okay, I'm gonna take this part.'"

Lennon simply wanted to be the singer in the band again, and sing all his favourite songs with years of experience and rock'n'roll gusto to inspire him. "After all those recent sermons to humankind, political tracts and painful explorations of his psyche," reasoned biographer Philip Norman, "it would be almost a rest cure to record some '*ooh – eee – baby*' songs that are meaningless for a change."

Despite his naïve intentions, this was not how the sessions materialised. "I should have seen what was happening when he [Phil] would come over to our house to go over songs and make arrangements," Pang ruefully recalls. "He'd come at night when everybody had already gone to bed and then he'd leave before dawn." Unsurprisingly, Lennon was kept in the dark about the material they would be performing. "I only went into the studio to do one thing, and you can tell this to John Lennon," Spector later reflected with no little grandeur. "They were making records, but I was making Art . . ."

Lennon's previous experience was completely at odds with the erratic sessions conducted under Spector's tutelage as 1973 drew to a close. "Phil had always been on target," Pang stresses, "but suddenly he wasn't, and it really threw us off. We were on his turf." One of the reasons behind Spector's changing attitude and tardiness was found in his growing eccentricity. "Phil would show up late for the sessions because he would do things like having a make-up artist paint a 'shiner' on his eye and tell everyone that John punched him. Or he would come in dressed as a doctor or in a karate outfit. He had a wand with a light at the end of it. It was something bizarre every night. It hindered the sessions."

One night, Lennon and his studio crew were sat around listening to a playback when they heard gunfire. Amidst screams and general pandemonium, Spector was found stood with a gun in his hand as goaded roadie Mal Evans attempted to wrest it from his grip. Lennon was, Pang claims, stood with his fingers to his ears as he pleaded: "Phil, if you're gonna shoot, don't mess with me ears. I need them for listening."

"Spector would steal the tapes after we recorded," Cicala remembers. "He would bring his old Rolls-Royce up to the door, and he would put all the tapes in the trunk of his car and take them home, in the fear that someone would take them. But he was a very eccentric person." Spector would later famously disappear with the master tapes from these legendary sessions, before Capitol Records eventually retrieved them at a cost close to $100,000.

Before returning home to an incredibly hectic Record Plant schedule, Cicala recalls Lennon's large coterie of musical sidemen booked into Studio B at A&M. With space for just 18 musicians on the sound board, a group of anything between 25 and 30 players (basically a rhythm section extravaganza) had to be accommodated. Pang remembers that 27 musicians arrived on the opening day of the sessions. "We were both taken by surprise. There was a bunch of musicians and nobody knew what they were doing." Spector failed to appear for three hours, setting a tone of incredible unpredictability that would subsequently mark this musical venture.

"It was very difficult," Pang admits. "In certain ways it was great but at times it was tough, because Phil wouldn't tell us who was coming to the sessions."

It was becoming clear that the disciplined approach to studio recording that had enabled The Beatles to flourish during the mid-sixties was changing. A significant portion of the subsequent Spector-produced material was not used, due to his 'Wall of Sound' recording ethos. If any one of the musicians was playing badly during a live take, it would present a problem. "He would put everything into a reverb chamber, with delay, and he would come up with a sound. Live recording was his thing, and he tried to do the same with John," Cicala recalls. "Phil kept going into the Wall of

Sound, but John liked the old rock'n'roll sound, the old Jerry Lee Lewis sound, and I think that's when a lot of the arguments came out. Phil wanted to do it his way, but John hated it. Not on *every* song; in some cases. I think John would win, and Phil would give in. John would be looking at him and they would get at it, and we would break it up."

Spector's Napoleonic complex proved a huge challenge for Cicala in the confines of the control room. The ensuing legend that has grown around this diminutive man has not been exaggerated. "He'd just carry on talking while we were cutting tape, from one take to another, so I'd ask him to leave and he'd do so. We had a mutual respect . . . Thank God!" Cicala's resolutely positive engineering approach ('*Let's do it – nothing's impossible*') found him plugging keyboard players into mike leads that ran from tape machines. But it was worth it. "I mean, when those musicians cooked, man, it didn't make any difference if the sound was Class A. It was all about the feel."

"Phil Spector was funny. He was like Lenny Bruce, he was so funny. It's a shame people only think of him as being crazy. John would get drunk, Phil would get drunk, and we would get drunk and pretty soon it was like a party. All kinds of people would come to the sessions," recalls Keltner who was delighted to encounter Hal Blaine, one of his drumming heroes.

Production politics aside, the sessions were populated by a thrilling retinue of musical talent, including Steve Cropper, Dr. John and Leon Russell. "Joni Mitchell was recording in the other studio. When she found out that John was recording in the studio we were in, she was coming in all the time," Pang adds. "She would bring in other people. One night it was Warren Beatty and David Geffen. Musicians were always coming through the door: Elton John, Cher."

"The sessions would soon become hedonistic marathons," claims writer James Bay, "peopled by a vast, ever more inebriated cast of musicians, liggers and inquisitive superstar visitors."

The first song attempted for the album was Lennon's version of 'Bony Moronie', a song he dedicated to Pang. "He called me out of the control room to sit at his feet as he sang it to me. It was wonderful." In much the same way that he would later do with the album's successor, *Walls And Bridges*, Lennon had already 'heard' the album's sequencing in his head. Gene Vincent's 'Be Bop A Lula' had already been designated as the album's opening track. "John loved the skiffle sound, the echo," Pang maintains. It was one of the songs that John played onstage at the Woolton

Parish Church Garden Fete on July 6, 1957, the very day on which he first met Paul McCartney.

"At one point he said that he'd like to do an album of oldies, music that was the basis for *his* music. All the good stuff, Chuck Berry, Little Richard . . . you name it. He wanted to pay homage to the people that he admired, that he grew up with," says Pang. One of the *Rock 'N' Roll* sessions was postponed when Lennon's hero Chuck Berry paid the thrilled Beatle a visit. "That was a wild night. We kept waiting and finally John said, 'So, Phil, is it Chuck Berry? I bet you it's Chuck.' The next thing we know, Phil's butler comes to the door and announces 'Mr. Charles Berry.' Chuck starts coming down the steps with a blonde on each arm and Phil turns out the lights. John runs up to him and says: 'Chuck, it's great to see you! Phil, turn on the lights!'"

Berry was one of Lennon and McCartney's idols, and when it came to making the difficult selection of the most appropriate material to cover, Pang and Lennon knew that Chuck would be listening, having hung out together as the sessions commenced. Jim Keltner believes that if either Lennon or Spector had exhibited a little more self-control, *Rock 'N' Roll* could have been a brilliant album. "Fats Domino, Little Richard, Chuck Berry – you gotta love those songs. Those are the songs they grew up with."

Having been reprimanded for breaching copyright when appropriating the '*Here come old flat top*' lyric from Berry's 'You Can't Catch Me' on the *Abbey Road* opener 'Come Together', Lennon subsequently recorded Berry's original as part of a legal settlement with catalogue owner Morris Levy. "Even back then, we thought we would win," Pang insists, "but John didn't want to go back to New York for a court case because we had gotten Phil back into the studio [in LA], and that was the reason for the settlement." In rather deft style, Lennon covered 'You Can't Catch Me' in a manner reminiscent of his own song. "The original recording was too short, lasting only two minutes, so Spector did a 'Strawberry Fields'-type edit – the song actually starts all over again to give it more length."

In the case of *Rock 'N' Roll* Pang recalls: "John just wanted to sing the songs that had influenced him in his life. If you listen to the album you hear two distinct sounds: one very lush, where he was drunk. We tried to change the vocals as much as possible. It was very difficult with the Wall of Sound because everything is in the same room and it leaks." While Lennon sought a rock'n'roll sound redolent of Jerry Lee Lewis and the

American heroes he wished to honour, Spector had naturally brought his own inimitable Wall of Sound production ethos to the mix. Creative conflict, at least in terms of age-old 'musical differences', was inevitable. "We tried to split the difference, which is a difficult thing to do, and that's where a lot of the arguments started," Cicala claimed. "John and Phil often screamed at each other. John would win and Phil would give in. Phil wanted to do it his way, and John hated it."

Pang would often have to confront an aggravated Spector, struggling to handle a headstrong twenty-something woman intent on defending her lover. "I don't think he was looking for anything except a good record. Something that would do the songs justice from his perspective: John's way of singing and his arrangement." But as Pang also recalled, the chaotic atmosphere of the sessions would often run into the non-recording days. "Everybody wanted to be partying constantly. Even if we tried to slow it down, somebody would pick up the speed on it."

"The drinking started right away," Cicala confirmed, "or, at least, an hour into it. I myself took it a little bit easy sometimes, because I was the designated driver. But then again, if you didn't indulge you couldn't get with it in that company. So, I would partake, too." Lennon, Cicala claimed, was often drinking a bottle of Dewers a day, or anything that was available.

"John is rather uncontrollable and he did what he wanted to do. He was very difficult to influence, and no one was going to put a leash on him," recalls Gruen. Spector's behaviour had set the tone, drinking a bottle of liquor a night before the rest of the assembled cast followed suit. "From that point on," Pang insisted, "we couldn't get Phil back on track."

The sessions took place at A&M Studios until a drunken musician emptied his bottle into the recording console, an incident that precipitated Lennon and co's swift exit. Nine songs were recorded in sporadic sessions between October and December before proceedings ground to a halt. A disappointed Lennon was unaware of the incident at A&M before the sessions subsequently switched to the Record Plant West studio. This wasn't the way he worked. "Every day it was a bottle of Scotch each, or good whisky," Cicala recalls. "The sessions would start late afternoon, and go on until three or four in the morning. And they were great sessions."

"Everybody was drinking, getting out of their minds before the sessions," Pang remembers. "And that was something that John and I were not used to. John's way of working was that he would come into the studio and do the work. If you wanted to go drinking or take drugs, you did it *after*, not during his sessions. But we both thought that it wouldn't last; that it wouldn't be every day of the sessions. People didn't want to go home, because there were drinks there. Everybody wanted the freebie, and it was on John."

Pang, meanwhile, struggled to keep Lennon away from the drug temptations on offer amongst a group of often wildly self-indulgent musicians. "John was fine. He was not a drunk. He wasn't drinking every day. It wasn't remotely like that. He was having fun with the guys, but the only person who got in the paper was John."

"John and alcohol together was not a good idea, *ever*," recalled Jack Douglas. "He'd get drunk and I'd want to escape. He'd make me the designated driver. If he went out, people would want to touch him, and that fed on itself."

After rehearsals were undertaken in September at Morris Levy's upstate New York farm to re-work the largely unusable Spector material, the *Rock 'N' Roll* album was eventually finished during a week to 10-day session at New York's Record Plant East studio in late October 1974. A year on from the sessions and in much more focused, business-like fashion, Lennon was clearly keen to complete the project. "John wanted *Rock 'N' Roll* to be a fun album; a fun experience," Pang recalls. "It became a 'chore' album because of everything that went down in getting the record completed and to the public."

Lennon was, like McCartney, a huge Little Richard fan. The "powerhouse medley", as Pang later described it, consisted of 'Rip It Up' and 'Ready Teddy', strong performances with superlative drum work that found the former Beatle in fine voice on treasured material. Much like 'Slippin' & Slidin'', another classic Little Richard track that made the album, these songs had been performed by the novice Beatles and revived memories of their Teddy Boy period. "In paying tribute to his musical-childhood background, Lennon sounds like he's forgotten he used to perform material like this seven nights a week," Jon Landau emphasised, "and that he used to record it several times a year. He's forgotten that most of today's rock audience came to Little Richard and Chuck Berry through The Beatles' versions of the music."

Promo copies of the song had been pressed as a possible single but were later shelved. Plans involved including 'Ain't That A Shame' as the flipside. Taught to John by his mother as she played the banjo, this was Lennon's first piece of musical tutelage. The song clearly retained its sentimental value more than 15 years later. Having encouraged the nascent Quarry Men during their stage performances and taught John new tunes, she became something of a muse, an almost dreamlike subject of his unconditional love and adoration. Her death duly shattered him, and inevitably drew him closer to his junior friend and creative partner McCartney, who lost his own mother at the more tender age of 14.

Lennon would also attempt to teach Pang to play this Fats Domino number. "Obviously the song had a lot of fond personal memories for John, and it was important for him to record. It has fond memories for me as well." 'Do You Wanna Dance?' was one of the album's minor moments, a slow-tempo rendition of the Bobby Freeman original. "The song stands for all the gems left behind by rock's minor heroes," enthused *Rolling Stone* critic Landau. Pang, who featured in the studio 'choir' that sang on the chorus, noted the song's distinct Jamaican reggae feel, one of Lennon's enduring musical passions.

Buddy Holly was one of Lennon's teenage idols and 'Peggy Sue' was loved for the inimitable stuttered vocal styling and its attendant echo. Here, Lennon stayed close in spirit to the original. McCartney would have been pleased, if only from a purely financial perspective, since he'd recently purchased Holly's song catalogue. "What a clever move that was," Lennon insisted just after the album's release. "I hope he gives me a good deal. I don't care who gets the money. With Paul it's cool, 'cos we're pals, and even Klein's all right really. I'm not gonna get much money from this album anyway."

Later to rue the haste with which he had recorded his part, bassist Klaus Voormann made a rare vocal cameo on Lennon's fine rendition of the Sam Cooke standard 'Bring It On Home To Me'. The track was paired with 'Send Me Some Lovin''. "John liked the transition from the first song to the second," Pang remembers. "During rehearsal, everybody was throwing in their two cents about the song, and John loved the idea of making it a medley with 'Send Me Some Lovin''." Pang was fascinated that she shared similar, vintage rock'n'roll tastes with those of Lennon. This mutual musical love was apparent with the inclusion of Rosie & The Originals' 'Angel Baby'. Lennon later informed presenter Bob Harris that this phenomenal track remained one of his all-time favourites. (Lennon and Pang's favourite song was the Little River Band's 'Reminiscing'. "Every time I hear this song I think of us," she would later admit.)

Lennon would later insist that Spector's choice of 'Just Because' proved an ideal album coda. But the impromptu dialogue at the end of the song wasn't, as Pang confirmed, a case of Lennon saying goodbye to his audience or his recording career from the confines of the Record Plant. Paradoxically, an unreleased segment, recorded in October, included warm greetings to all three of his former Fab colleagues. "He was just playing around as John always liked to do. It actually lasted a lot longer, too, and included hellos to Paul, George and Ringo which showed his true state of mind back then. But he saw himself as a DJ on the radio back in the fifties, and he was signing off for the night. It just fit the moment."

As Charlesworth recalls, Lennon would often announce his presence on the telephone during this period by using the pseudonym, Johnny Beatle. "I did 10 tracks in three days [October 21–24], all the numbers that I hadn't got around to with Phil," recalled John. "I had a lot of fun, and mixed it all down in about four or five days. My one problem was whether it sounds weird going from the Spector sound to *my* sound; from 28 guys down to eight. But they match pretty well I think. So there it was, I suddenly had an album."

Having eventually produced nine of the tracks himself, the album was rush-released the following February to combat Morris Levy's un-authorised *Roots* record of the sessions. "John never promised Morris any-thing. And John did not say that it could be put on his record label," Pang insisted. While Lennon had given Levy an unmixed album tape, it was not one of sufficient quality for mass distribution. "John did say to him that he thought the idea of selling LPs the way Morris did, through TV ads, was interesting. But John told him, no matter what it came down to, he was signed to Capitol and they were the only ones who would release it."

Rock 'N' Roll eventually reached number six on both the British and Stateside charts. "That's another messy record," claims Cicala, "but it's great. It's a wonderful record." It also provided Lennon with an impressive Top 20 success with a cover of Ben E. King's 'Stand By Me'. Released in March 1975, the self-produced, straight-ahead contemporary rock'n'roll track, captured on film a week or so later during a classic TV performance on *The Old Grey Whistle Test*, is one of Lennon's finest moments on record. King would subsequently applaud the stylish arrangement of this most accomplished version of his song.

Pang, meanwhile, had given her all during some difficult times whilst making an album that was important to Lennon. "When it [*Rock 'N' Roll*] first came out, people didn't know what to make of it, because they had heard about what had gone on in the sessions. John was going to rise above it, and he did what he had to do to put the album out." The album liner notes showed that Pang, traditionally credited as production co-ordinator, had earned the more meaningful accolade of 'Mother Superior'. "I was there to help him through it, and John wanted me to get special credit for that. We'd gone through the whole year-long saga together, so I'm glad it came out."

Following the completion of the *Rock 'N' Roll* album, Lennon would be, at least contractually, a free agent from Capitol, and McCartney's own obligations were also ending. While Lennon and McCartney had experienced a more difficult time during the early seventies due to their (apparently) fractious estrangement, when talk had turned to a prospective Beatles reunion, Lennon reflected something of the quandary that faced him and the rest of the group. "Imagine if we did get together," he mused. "Think of the scrutiny we would face. Could we fit the dream people had of us?" Yet memories were fond and the wounds were healed, Lennon later told journalist Elliot Mintz. So much so that the prospect of reforming the group could not be dismissed outright. "It's quite possible. I don't know why we'd do it, but it's possible," he enthused rather cryptically. "If it happens, I'll enjoy it."

"The fall-out from The Beatles was very painful for each of them," Paul Du Noyer explains, "both in the sense of old friendships turning sour, and in the sense that none of them could really transcend that revered legacy. While they could never forget the bitterness that it caused, they could overcome it." Yet Lennon was unsure he'd want to be responsible for initiating any reunion. That, he admitted, would be a matter of instinct. "If the idea hit me tomorrow, I might call them and say: 'Come on, let's do something.' If it happens, it'll happen. If we do it, we do it. If we record, we record. I don't know. As long as we keep making music . . ."

Following the release of *Mind Games* and with Beatle relations improving, McCartney had attempted to reconvene the group for a meeting in New York that December. "I rang John up, and John was keen to do it. He was going to fly in today from LA to New York. Great. I was going to be here; John was going to be here. Then I rang Ringo, and Ringo couldn't figure out what we were actually going to say, outside of 'Hi there'. He didn't want to come all the way to New York from England. So he was a bit down on it. Then I called John and he said he was talking to George, and George was having some kind of visa problems. So it's a bit difficult to get the four of us together. But it will happen soon."

Perhaps a financial settlement may have encouraged a much closer friendship before a musical reunion took place. But would a Beatles reunion during the mid-seventies have been driven more by financial necessity than creative inspiration? As the seventies progressed, all four Beatles were mindful enough of the importance of reforming the group to not let money influence their decision. "In a way," Doggett insists, "I don't think that creativity would have made up their minds one way or the other. It would have been a decision based solely on emotion, and friendship." Despite having been a supporter of 'Something', his finest songwriting effort to date on *Abbey Road*, Harrison claimed that Klein was perhaps *the* major stumbling block to a Beatles reconciliation.

George was reported to have told Apple's Allan Steckler (the man who had introduced Lennon to Record Plant producer Roy Cicala in the late sixties) that the only way The Beatles could have reunited at this point was if Klein was no longer involved in the group's affairs. George also insisted that both he and Starkey were ready to play together, and was quietly confident that Lennon could be persuaded too.

McCartney told *Rolling Stone* in early 1974 that, business issues notwithstanding, he was ready to play too. But what was the significance of Klein's removal as a perceived obstacle to a Beatles reunion? While its symbolism may have been vital, there were no practical reasons why their soon-to-be former manager needed to be out of the way, claims Peter Doggett. "With Klein still in place," he maintains, "there was no way for McCartney to return to the fold without admitting that he had been wrong to take legal action against the other Beatles."

"The thing about Paul was, he was never wrong," Connolly explains. "In a sense, he always thought he was right, and we all think that. But with all the major decisions about The Beatles, he *was* right about Allen Klein, and right about what songs should be the A-sides."

Where a potential route to Beatle reconciliation was concerned, McCartney's lawyer Lee Eastman agreed with the general view amongst the group: a financial settlement might beget a revived friendship before any musical reunion took place. "First, they have to sever their economic interests. Then they could be friends. Then, finally, they might play together."

"There was an awful lot of money made," McCartney told *Rolling Stone* in early 1974, "and none of it came to us, really, in the end. Virtually, that's the story. So I'd kind of like to salvage some of that and see that not everything's ripped off." McCartney certainly felt that Klein's departure had opened a vital channel of communication. "The only thing," he would claim, "that has prevented us from getting together again has been Allen Klein's contractual hold over The Beatles' name."

Getting rid of Klein, he insisted, was a painless piece of conciliation on the part of the other Beatles. It was also a prudent move should any future reunion take place. "I think that, like everyone else around The Beatles, and maybe The Beatles themselves, Lee Eastman underestimated the psychological barriers that prevented the four men from getting back together," claims Beatle historian Peter Doggett. "To a Beatle outsider, it probably seemed simple: sort this problem out, and this desired result will happen. But that didn't take account of the years of emotional baggage that couldn't be removed that easily." And McCartney was clearly optimistic about the opportunity Klein's departure might present. "There were no practical reasons why Klein needed to be out of the way," wrote Doggett, but its symbolism was vital.

A year after a Beatle trio reconvened for the 'I'm The Greatest' session, much had happened in the careers of the former Fabs. Following his growing commercial success with *Band On The Run*, McCartney had been asked by an ABC TV interviewer early in March whether The Beatles' myth could be recreated anew. "We might do bits together," he emphasised. "We don't know yet. I think once we get our business problems sorted, there's every chance we might just feel like getting together to do something. I wouldn't like to say what."

Both Lennon and McCartney had been seen backstage renewing their friendship at the Academy Awards in March, a day after Paul cautiously approved the viability of undertaking future Beatles work. A loose creative collaboration certainly seemed plausible given the experience of Starkey's 'I'm The Greatest' session in early 1973. Shortly after the December release of *Band On The Run*, *Rolling Stone* interviewed McCartney in early 1974. "There's certain things we could do quite quietly and still produce some kind of ongoing thing," he insisted. "I don't think you'll ever get anyone to give up all their individual stuff now; everyone's got it going too well now. I wouldn't rule everything out, it's one of those questions I really have to hedge on."

When McCartney had released the stand-out *Red Rose Speedway* single 'My Love', Lennon called the song "simple and unaffected" in his humorous, mock 'press release' back in early 1973. The song was also notable for the gleaming improvised solo by frustrated guitarist Henry McCullough, who found himself standing in the studio with just a guitar and 50-piece orchestra for company and a decidedly uncertain McCartney looking on. Paul had always preferred Henry to learn his pre-written parts for the songs, but fortunately for all concerned, McCullough proceeded to play the solo of his life on what became a major US number one single.

Work on the parent album had also been conducted at George Martin's AIR studios on Oxford Street under the auspice of a less-than-enthusiastic producer, Glyn Johns. McCartney had sought to be considered as one of the guys during the making of the album, Johns recalled, which didn't last long amongst a group of frequently stoned musicians who, he considered, were too awed by his presence to question his musical judgement. The producer also felt that McCartney needed Lennon at this point, if only as a musical equal to critique his ideas and quash his grandiose tendencies.

When talk of renewed partnerships came into the fray, he also drew the comparison between himself and his erstwhile partner and that of Jerry Lewis and Dean Martin. "Should Dean Martin and Jerry Lewis have stayed together because I used to like them together? What is this game of doing things because other people want it? The whole Beatle idea was to do what you want, right? To take your own responsibility." McCartney made a similar comparison a year later in March 1974. He reminded inter-viewer Scott Osborne that Jerry Lewis now had his own career since their split. "It's a bit like that with me and The Beatles," he insisted. Lennon's viewpoint would, however, gradually change as 1974 developed. "Not long afterwards, John kept a civil tongue in his head when he and Paul met for a drink in Los Angeles," Clayson recalls. "Afterwards, it was reported that Paul mentioned he wouldn't mind working with John again on a casual basis, and John saying how wrong it had been for The Beatles to have split so decisively."

Keen on seeing The Beatles' legacy restored to something approaching its former greatness after their temporary rifts, McCartney told *Rolling Stone* he was hoping for a greater measure of co-operation between the former members as 1974 unfolded. If it proved permissible, Paul even mooted his hopes for a new creative collaboration. "I've got a lot of ideas in my head what I'd like, but I wouldn't like to tell you before I tell them. But there might be things, little good ventures we could get together on, mutually helpful to all of us and things people would like to see, anyway."

With former members focused on their individual careers and agendas,

Paul responded to the question about recurring Beatles reunion rumours. As for McCartney's perspective on his partnership with Lennon in the wake of creating his finest hour with Wings, memories were fond. "I like to write with John. I like to write with anyone who's good."

Crucially, fresh hope was apparent too. Paul clearly believed the granting of his US visa early in 1974 was a promising development for any hopes of a Lennon-McCartney reunion. The physical distance that had separated John and Paul, and prevented them from re-establishing their friendship, was no longer such an overwhelming barrier.

For critics and fans alike, it seemed a promising state of affairs. In practical terms, the granting of McCartney's US visa after his wrist-slapping drug conviction seemed to be vital in terms of renewing his friendship (and any new speculative musical partnership) with Lennon. Back then, it had appeared that physical distance was one of the main obstacles to the renewal of their musical partnership. With Lennon reluctant to leave the States for fear of being unable to return, McCartney could now begin travelling to the States, enabling the two men to be in the same country at the same time.

But this promising development, Keith Badman insists, didn't appear to carry the same significance for John. "It was only when they were both in the same country that Lennon (especially) and McCartney came up with other reasons for stalling a reunion," Doggett reflects, "suggesting that the problem over visas had just been a convenient excuse."

McCartney now began to make a series of increasingly frequent visits to Lennon as 1974 unfolded. Suddenly, any new creative musical enterprise didn't seem so unlikely. "I couldn't physically write a song with John; he was in America. He couldn't get out. I couldn't get in. But now that's changed, so whole new possibilities are opening up." Anything could happen. Little could Lennon and McCartney have known that, just three weeks later, they would be sharing a studio once again for the first time in more than four years.

With Lennon's chaotic *Rock 'N' Roll* project having ground to a halt after Spector's disappearance with the session tapes, in early 1974 Lennon was seeking a new musical project in which to involve himself.

Harry Nilsson was admired by all four Beatles and had been since the very early days of Apple in the late sixties, and Ringo had reintroduced Lennon to Nilsson after the two Beatles spent time together in LA. For a period, Starkey lived *chez* Pang and Lennon, who later penned a song for his forthcoming *Goodnight Vienna* album. Shortly after the mayhem that defined the *Rock 'N' Roll* sessions was abandoned at the turn of the year, the drunken craziness characterising Lennon and Nilsson's lives needed a suitable creative focus in order to provide a musical purpose.

"I went on to do the Harry Nilsson thing and I tried everything to get the [*Rock 'N' Roll* album] tapes back, even just hanging around LA to see if Phil would get better. I couldn't think what to do, so I did the album with Harry while I was waiting." Still in the throes of his fabled 'Lost Weekend', Lennon suggested continuing the concept of adolescent musical nostalgia by producing an eclectic album of their favourite songs that included Bill Haley's 'Rock Around The Clock' and Bob Dylan's 'Subterranean Homesick Blues'.

Unsurprisingly, their self-indulgences continued to spill over into work on the subsequent album, *Pussycats*. "He was there to make music," insisted engineer Dennis Ferrante, "but the craziness is what it was all about."

"The main thing was we had a lot of fun," said Lennon. "There was Keith Moon, Harry, Ringo and me all living together in the house and we had some moments. But it got a little near the knuckle. That's when I realised: 'There's something wrong here. I mean, this is crazy, man!'"

Exacerbating the disorganised atmosphere which surrounded the album's making, Nilsson was plagued with vocal problems, a throat complaint no doubt triggered by his alcohol-fuelled lifestyle. "He loved a party, he could really sing, and he was such a musical artist," says Keltner. "He was great to play with, and John loved him very much," with a notable paternal or managerial quality to their bond. "All the artists who were songwriters loved Harry. But Harry partied too long."

Having suddenly woken up and realised his precarious position amidst a drunken crew of good-time musicians and friends, Lennon straightened out and proceeded to complete the album. He also contributed a new song, 'Mucho Mungo', to the project. Paul Simon and Art Garfunkel, who hadn't sung together for four years, were also rumoured to be present during the sessions. As unearthed tapes tend to suggest, they may even have provided *ad hoc* vocal support. Before the duo left the studio, there seemed to have been low-key tension on Lennon's part over Simon's vocal harmonies during a version of 'Rock Island Line'.

Lennon was understandably pleased that, on *Rock 'N' Roll*'s release, American radio was at least giving Nilsson's album an airing. "I guess that it was his first production, and he was very proud of the fact that he had produced the *Pussycats* album," New York DJ Dennis Elsas informed me. "It wasn't the height of either John's or Harry Nilsson's career, but he's very happy to play a track from it, and happy to talk about it and dismisses the little bit of trouble he got into in LA, and says thanks to Harry for putting the record in the window."

Pang and Lennon had already entertained the likes of Nilsson, Moon and Starkey. But they were now surprised to welcome a new addition to this gathering of British rock pageantry. With Lennon largely bereft of musical direction and creatively unfocused during the wildest moments of his 'Lost Weekend', it seemed an auspicious time for Paul McCartney to re-enter his life. McCartney's re-appearance duly offered John a sense of stability, while providing a reconnection with his musical past during a period of turmoil.

"There's no doubt that he enjoyed being back in contact with his old friend," Doggett argues, "without the emotional traumas that adding Yoko to the equation might have produced. And the same applies, perhaps even more so, to Paul. But as with any old friends who have moved on, that pleasure had to be balanced against the fact that both men's lives had changed: there was no way that they could be as important to each other as they had been in the late fifties and for much of the sixties."

Badman, meanwhile, simply believes that McCartney was more interested in rekindling their relationship than Lennon was. "I knew it [music] was important to him [John] and I wanted him to go back to his roots and have a good time," Pang would later admit. "I knew those things would be good for him and give him pleasure. Seeing John on such a high made it all worthwhile. I remember us visiting Keith Moon one day and him telling me: 'This is the John I remember and the John I knew. I'm so glad he's back and you're with him.'"

Being present at these West Coast sessions, McCartney's memories are of a wild and eccentric indulgence. "I went out there and he [John] was doing *Pussycats* with Nilsson and Keith Moon and Jesse Ed Davis . . . Harry Nilsson was a lovely boy, but he went to excess. Keith Moon, another lovely boy who went to excess. They were fairly wacky guys making that record! This was LA crazy . . . three beautiful total alcohol nutters plus John, forget it! Even the location is perfect . . ."

Lennon claimed it had taken time for the wounds to heal following his distant relationship with McCartney during the early seventies, mainly conducted through posturing press statements and subtle musical responses in their songs. During the early seventies, the two men had experienced a more difficult time due to their supposedly fractious estrangement. Yet Lennon now conversed regularly with McCartney during this period according to Pang, with whom John had become romantically involved after his estrangement from Ono. "Perhaps people felt Yoko was the problem," Cicala would later admit. "I don't think anybody liked Yoko at the time. They felt she'd broken up The Beatles."

A pivotal moment in the history of post-Beatles reunions, and an unexpected yet much-anticipated studio reconciliation, occurred between Lennon and McCartney at LA's Burbank Studios on March 28. Directing the first night of recording sessions for Nilsson's new album, *Pussycats*, Lennon had just laid down the first day's basic tracks and was sat behind the board in the control room as he listened to the playback. Most of the Burbank personnel had left for the night. Jim Keltner, Ringo and Keith Moon had gone home, while bassist Klaus Voormann had also departed.

Pang claims that she and John were about to leave when out of nowhere, she looked up and happened to see Paul and Linda McCartney walking through the studio door, having decided to drop in unannounced. "I said, '*Paul and Linda*? What are *they* doing here?!' John turned round and said, 'What?!' I couldn't believe it. It was just: 'Hey, what's going on here?' We had no clue he was coming."

The two men hadn't seen each other for three years, and those who remained in the studio waited anxiously to witness Lennon's response. He greeted his old sparring partner warmly, and the meeting bore none of the previous antipathy between the two since The Beatles' split. "Valiant Paul McCartney, I presume?" the host jested with his familiar visitor. "Sir Jasper Lennon, I presume," came the reply. "It's very difficult to remember those days, because it was all a bit crazy and everyone was getting out of it," McCartney later recalled. "But yes, John was doing some recordings in Los Angeles and I showed up."

With McCartney joining forces with Lennon again, Pang witnessed their re-acquaintance at first-hand. Paul's Burbank cameo, which occurred at their only post-Beatles studio jam, would prove an unforgettable moment. Considering all John had said about Paul over the past few years, this private meeting was surprisingly friendly. The warmth that existed between the two men was clearly deeper than any petty residual vendettas.

Having arrived late, Paul and Linda were surprised to discover the day's recording session had already finished. The other musicians that remained were winding down as they hung around in the studio. While eager to talk, Paul was even keener to play, evidently enthusiastic to make music with Lennon again.

Taking the initiative, Paul and Linda were keen to begin a jam session. "John told him that they were done for the night," Pang has since recalled. "But even so I could see him and the band adjusting to the idea." Paul slowly edged his way towards Starkey's kit, where Ringo had been playing just hours earlier. Picking up the drumsticks, adjusting the set-up and sitting on the vacant stool, McCartney yelled: "Let's play!" "All of a sudden," Pang enthuses, "we have a drummer." Comfortable enough in each other's presence, yet no doubt weary from the evening session, Lennon eventually agreed to a jam excursion with his former Beatle brother: Lennon was well aware of the numerous sets of eyes in the room, focused in on the two former Beatles sharing the same studio space for the first time since 1969.

In no time at all, Lennon picked up his guitar while his studio colleagues began to plug back in. Following McCartney's lead, they began to jam alongside session pianist and hoarse, drink-ravaged singer Nilsson and guitarists Danny Kotchmar and Jesse Ed Davis. They launched into a ramshackle rendition of 'Midnight Special'. "It sounded great," Pang recalls, "they were all tooting away, and even John was grinning. You could see these jaded musicians standing there in shock, staring at the two Beatles. They didn't skip a beat, just went right into it."

The jam session also featured Bobby Keys on saxophone, May Pang and Mal Evans on tambourines while Linda McCartney sat in on Hammond organ. "I jammed with Paul. I did actually play with Paul," Lennon told British TV interviewer Bob Harris almost a year after the event. "We did a lot of stuff in LA. There were 50 other people playing too, and they were all just watching me and Paul." Their reunion, according to Pang, saw the two old comrades re-engage as if they had rehearsed the previous day.

Meanwhile, the impromptu session crew were bereft of a bass player after Voormann's earlier departure. Pang later recalled: "Somebody from another session had heard we were looking for a bass player just for a jam. He threw his session over for a once-in-a-lifetime jam with John and Paul." One rumour suggested the unknown bassist was Ed Freeman, a roadie for the opening act on The Beatles' controversial American tour of

1966. "Clearly the greatest pop music phenomenon that ever was," Freeman proudly attests. "I tuned their guitars for them onstage before they came on. I didn't really know any of them very well personally, except for George Harrison. The more that is written about them, the better."

Apparently working on another session elsewhere in the studio complex, he was believed to have arrived in time to play in this exalted company. "I've heard that before, that I played bass on that session, or that I even produced it. I did neither. I wish that rumour, and all the others I've heard were true, but they aren't." Freeman did, however, hang out on a Spector-produced Lennon session in Hollywood for the *Rock 'N' Roll* album, and was present at the subsequent party that lasted long into the night at the late engineer Gary Kellgren's house. McCartney's surprising appearance was not the only major musical shock that night. As the jam unfolded, word spread throughout the Burbank facility about what was happening. Pang recalls a door opening, and being stunned to see Motown legend Stevie Wonder walking in to check out the action. Having begun work on the follow-up to his recent Grammy award-winning *Innervisions* album, Wonder stopped by to join in on electric piano.

As the musicians limbered up, Lennon rambled through an improvised, stream-of-consciousness lyric entitled 'Never Trust A Bugger With Your Mother', referencing his prolonged wait for Green Card status before reciting various Stateside locations. Compelled to take control of the session and grousing over the unfocused jam ("Somebody's got to be boss here, right?") Lennon quietly complained about the sax players' sound. He then recalled recent jam session fodder by the likes of Fats Domino, whom Lennon had seen in concert at Las Vegas' Flamingo Hotel the previous summer in the company of Apple PR Tony King. "Fats came over to John and said: 'Oh, I'm really honoured to meet you.' John said: 'No, *you're* the man I've come to see. You shouldn't be honoured to meet me. I should be honoured to meet *you*.'"

McCartney then suggested that the assembled crew attempt Bobby Day's 1957 hit 'Little Bitty Pretty One', but Lennon didn't seem too interested. A brief excursion was made into The Shadows' instrumental 'Midnight' before Lennon disengaged from attempts at a further run-through. A sense of exasperation on Lennon's part was undeniable, despite the unique occasion unfolding in the Burbank studio that night. "If somebody knows a song we all know, please take over," he insisted. "I've been screaming for hours . . . who's got a mike beside me? C'mon, somebody join in!"

This brief, impromptu session has been criticised as an undercooked echo of Lennon and McCartney's musical chemistry and former glories, with no sense of it being a precedent-setting occasion for future collaboration. "It is a little better if we think of a song we all know. Give Stevie a vocal," Lennon urges, before requesting some alcoholic or chemical assistance. "Come on, let's do something!" he calls impatiently as McCartney and Wonder's voices waft across the tape. After suggesting they attempt an ambitious 12-part harmony to 'Stand By Me', Lennon asks for a show of hands from those who know the song. "Let's not get too serious," he suggests to his studio colleagues. "We ain't doing nothing but sitting here together," he scolds, "and anyone who gets bored with me, take over."

"Turn the vocal mike up again!" Lennon then hollers, berating the sound engineers and encouraging Wonder to make his presence felt. "McCartney's doing the harmony on the drums. Stevie might get on it there, if he's got a mike," as the studio players await a Beatle-Motown alliance. Notable in the music business for his aversion to drug indulgence, Wonder sounded in fine voice on the night. His appearance certainly brought a sense of order to the chemical studio fug. Having manned a Fender Rhodes organ for the remainder of the session, he was, unlike his colleagues, firmly on his musical mettle. Taking the lead on a brief rendition of Sam Cooke's 'Cupid', Wonder switches to a rich, earthy take on '. . . Chain Gang' against Nilsson's ragged, distracted backing. After a couple of false starts and some brusque complaints about the poor sound quality, Lennon eventually begins a biting version of 'Stand By Me'. Paul's distant harmonies and Nilsson's hoarse rasp pierce the mix as the song finally finds some momentum.

After berating the studio engineers, the session includes Lennon's scathing rendition of McCartney's Little Richard forte, 'Lucille'. They then performed the traditional Leadbelly song, 'Take This Hammer'.

As a unique studio occasion, Lennon and McCartney's first recorded session for more than four-and-a-half years featured some awkward moments of mutual musical indecision. Whether their jam session represented a tentative step along the path toward a prospective reunion or not, it affirmed something of their old rock'n'roll rapport. Unfortunately, the session was not photographed. In one respect, it was the sound of two former partners reconnecting again in the studio amidst less than ideal circumstances. Given the session's impromptu spontaneity, and in the face of critical reaction, Pang has since complained that the late-night session, subsequently issued as the *Toot And A Snore* bootleg, was never intended for public consumption. "No one was doing this for recording purposes. It was meant just for the group to get together and have fun after a recording session. We didn't even realise the tape was running."

Regardless of the tape's quality, it has since become a valuable document of a long-awaited (and much-anticipated) musical moment. "Neither Lennon or McCartney were thinking they were making history or taking part in a historic reunion," Peter Doggett believes.

Occurring at the height of his fabled 'Lost Weekend', Lennon was unrecognisable to McCartney as the man he'd last worked with on *Abbey Road* five years earlier. "It was a little bit strange, John and I, seeing each other at that time," Paul would later state. "It was a strange session. The main thing I recall is that someone said, 'What song shall we do?' and John said, 'Anything before '63. I don't know anything after '63.'"

Discussing which songs they should attempt, Lennon can be heard insisting on material drawn from his adolescent musical education. "It's got to be late fifties," he argues, "no later than '63, or we ain't gonna know it." Striving to find a song which everyone knew how to play, the idea of jamming on old rock'n'roll songs, Pang later recalled, was second nature due to their familiarity with this material.

For chronicler Keith Badman, Burbank constituted "an extremely loose, crazy, drug-fuelled, impromptu jam session; a musical get-together between friends and people who just happened to be hanging out there." As the *Let It Be* sessions attest, Lennon had previously enjoyed ramshackle studio affairs such as these. The two men duly attempt to revive some of the classic American fifties standards which had initially provided such rich inspiration.

In the wake of McCartney's *Band On The Run*, and as something of a reconciliation with the past, did this session represent an opportune moment for the two men to think about reviving their musical bond? "It was a hail-fellow-well-met evening of coded hilarity and mutual nostalgia about the old days rather than the presentation of any serious avenue for a professional reunion," Alan Clayson insists. "Regardless of quality, it wasn't the harbinger of any permanent liaison. Nonetheless, there lingered enough fond memories of The Quarry Men, Hamburg *et al* for further get-togethers, musical and otherwise, with John outside the context of the prevailing business over division of the Apple empire."

Not unlike many other drug-fuelled jam sessions, it may have passed into vaguely recollected folklore if not for its illustrious cast and the subsequent taped document. "It's so funny that people have only just found out about Paul and John's jam session," Pang told journalist Vicky Ward in New York in 1997, the year when the session tapes first came to light. "I wrote about it years ago," she sighed, "but no one ever took much notice of what I said."

This may not have proved a wholly satisfying occasion, but neither John nor Paul would have left Burbank that morning thinking it had been a missed opportunity. Paul Du Noyer maintains the experience did not deter the two men from trying again at a later date. "I'd guess they knew the real test would be writing together again, or at least vetting one another's new songs, as per The Beatles' later routine, rather than casual jamming on old standards."

Having reunited with McCartney, it wasn't until later that year that Lennon admitted he'd lost his negativity about the past. "John never really talked about Paul," Keltner insists, "and he never really talked about George, who *would* talk about Paul. I never spent that much time with Paul, so I didn't get to know him very well. People used to ask me, usually producer types: 'Why do you suppose you never worked with Paul? Why do you think Paul never wanted to play with you?' And my standard answer was: 'Why would he?' I mean, just because I was there with John and George, it didn't mean he would have to have me there with him as well. And I'm not sure I would either, based upon the fact that it's okay, so let me find another way."

Keltner never played with both Lennon *and* McCartney, but hung out with Paul during visits to the Record Plant in Los Angeles. On one occasion when the two men played drums together at the facility, Paul broke a drumstick and then the snare drum head on Starkey's kit with a mallet he'd lifted from Keltner's kit-bag. The drummer recalls exclaiming in horror: "Man, you broke the *Ed Sullivan head*!" A nonplussed McCartney simply shrugged, insisting he'd buy the drummer a replacement. Starkey had used it during The Beatles' legendary, generation-defining appearance in February 1964 on the *Ed Sullivan Show,* a seismic moment in American culture.

On March 22, Lennon and Pang moved into a rented beach house at

625 Palisades Beach Road in Santa Monica, a Spanish-style mansion where John and Robert Kennedy had once entertained Marilyn Monroe. The house evidently restored John's appetite for music and his old work ethic, and quickly became a popular *rendezvous* for the cream of LA session musicians and British rock celebrities. Having borrowed equipment from Burbank Studios to use at the beach house, Sunday night jam sessions featured Nilsson, Ringo, Keith Moon and Klaus Voormann amongst others. Lennon subsequently invited McCartney to attend a Sunday night jam session on March 31.

"I was a bit surprised, having heard all the stories of their rocky relationship, how quickly they resumed their warm friendship," Pang later recalled. "Whatever the business problems they had, they did not bring it into the house, or have conversations about it. That was left up to their respective lawyers to work out." Importantly, there was no hint of animosity. "Everyone was sweet," she insisted, "and everything was cool again." Pang also recalled the musicians attempting a handful of numbers during this loose and relaxed private session.

The following day, shortly after Paul and Linda had left for their nearby hotel, Ringo and Keith arrived for work on Nilsson's album after carousing into the early hours of the morning. Starr immediately noticed his set-up had been adjusted and wanted to know who was responsible. "Paul's been here. He was here last night," John told him. "He played 'em."

Famously fussy about his drums (they loomed large in his legend, after all), Ringo sulked: "He's always messin' around with me things!" May witnessed Starr's comments, wryly noting that their exchange suggested they'd never left Liverpool. The Beatles, she marvelled, never lost their working-class sensibilities. "That was the amazing thing about them," she wrote. "That's how they saw themselves and acted with each other." While Lennon claimed they had remained 'working class' and chosen not to abandon their Liverpudlian accents to enhance their prospects, McCartney admitted he was proud of his humble background and still considered himself a part of the working class. "Maybe I should have adapted," he mused in 2012.

Around midday on April 1, Paul and Linda returned to the beach house that had hosted the previous night's revelries with their children, Heather, Mary and Stella. John was still in bed when McCartney arrived, and his new lifestyle seemed to cause a bemused Paul some slight alarm. "He was a teenager again," McCartney reflected. "He was just being his old Liverpool self, just a wild, wild boy. Linda and I had kids so we'd be up early. We wouldn't be just lying in bed until three in the afternoon, which is what John was doing. It was everything he'd always wanted to do in Liverpool . . ."

Once Lennon had eventually risen, McCartney recalled taking John into one of the rooms at the back of the beach house. The two men exchanged pleasantries, and were happy to see each other. Paul found John in a mellow mood due to his docile routine.

Having surfaced from his noonday slumber, Lennon eventually joined them at the poolside, where McCartney was enjoying the company of familiar faces. Keith Moon complimented him on his drumming work on *Band On The Run* following the last-minute departure of Denny Seiwell in September. Nilsson attempted to entice McCartney into sampling some angel dust, who politely (and wisely) declining his offer. "He seemed to understand," Paul recalled. "But that's how it was there."

Meanwhile, Moon assistant Peter 'Dougal' Butler and Pang took photos of Ringo and Paul relaxing together. McCartney positioned himself at the piano for most of the afternoon, playing a medley of Beatles songs and some standards. Ringo seated himself besides McCartney, enjoying the moment and offering vocal support. Pang also took a photo of Lennon and Starr together, but no photo has surfaced of all three former Beatles together. Knowing the beneficial and pleasurable effect it would have on John, Pang had regularly encouraged him to hook up with Paul and Ringo. "The four guys were brothers. Whenever they would meet, it was like no time had gone by."

It was here on a sunny afternoon that John and Paul were photographed together for the very last time. Dougal Butler's Polaroid picture of Lennon and McCartney showed the two Beatles reclining by the poolside, looking relaxed as they engage in casual conversation, Paul shading his eyes from the sun as they talk. The mood, May has recalled, was relaxed, light and friendly. This, she claims, is how it worked and was where they were really at. Here were two guys enjoying each other's company, picking up from where they had left off some four to five years ago. They acted, Pang insisted, "like brothers that hadn't seen each other in a while."

"Certainly, it re-affirmed their friendship after a fashion," Clayson argues, "not least because their personal dynamic was such that utterances un-amusing to anyone else would have them howling with laughter on the carpet at Lennon's villa in Santa Monica."

"Let's see each other again," McCartney ventured to his old partner before leaving the gathering. Following the McCartneys' departure, Lennon turned to Pang and said: "You know, I sometimes worry about George and Ringo. Never about Paul. The guy's just so *together*."

Lennon claimed he had also invited Harrison to join them at this Sunday evening gathering, but the guitarist was apparently involved in recording sessions with Ravi Shankar at A&M Studios. While all four Beatles were apparently together in LA simultaneously, George was unable to attend. "He still had some trouble getting in and out of the States," Lennon would later comment. "There were three of us and everybody says: 'Beatles getting back together.' Hey! Hey! We can't even *meet*, man! We can't even get the four of us together for a meeting, let alone play! The other month, Paul and Ringo and me met in LA and we wanted George to be there, but they wouldn't let him in at the time."

After the day's impromptu musical gathering, Pang overheard Lennon tell Nilsson: "Wouldn't it be fun to get the guys back together again?" In the minds of Nilsson and Pang, there was no doubt which 'guys' Lennon was referring to. Reconciliation was clearly at the back of Lennon's mind, even at this stage of proceedings. Four weeks after jamming with McCartney, Lennon was seen onstage at the March Of The Dimes concert in the company of Harry Nilsson, announcing the latest whereabouts of his former Beatle colleagues from the stage.

It seems interesting that, as his notorious 'Lost Weekend' proceeded, Lennon moved away from an outright dismissal of a Beatles reconciliation. He began to demonstrate a nostalgic fascination and enthusiasm for playing this classic material with his former colleagues. While all four Beatles went through similar changes of heart during the decade, Lennon was more public about his thoughts in frequent interview sessions during 1973–74. Having agreed to a further *rendezvous* with McCartney, Lennon was, according to Pang, giving serious consideration to his private plan of re-convening the band live onstage. "We talked about reuniting The Beatles. At one point he wanted to do it. For the heck of it. Because there wasn't any pressure, any contracts. He'd say: 'That'd be fun.'"

Following an initial discussion between Lennon and Starr about a one-off live reunion, Lennon disclosed to select insiders during late spring about behind-the-scenes plans for a small, unpublicised Beatles concert. Also featuring Harry Nilsson, it would ideally be staged in Syracuse, upstate New York that autumn. "We wanted it to be close to New York City, but not in the heart of it, where it would be a bit too crazy," Pang

160

later wrote. "John did enjoy his time there in 1971, so he just thought that if this were to happen, Syracuse might just be the spot. He would talk about it with Harry Nilsson."

Each Beatle's contribution was enthusiastically debated. Despite the timeframe involved for all four men, Lennon knew that a focused approach would prove successful. Nilsson, naturally, was more than keen to participate. Other musicians' involvement was also discussed. Lennon's sincerity about bringing The Beatles back together, Pang recalls, was not in question. Unsurprisingly, it received a warm response. "I think there was a possibility. We all talked about that too, of the boys getting together for a couple of gigs here and there. Not a tour, but for a sporadic one or two gigs. But everybody's schedule didn't work. But believe me, there *were* talks."

Each Beatle's contribution to their live return was, however, initially discussed in casual debate involving Pang, Lennon, Starr and Nilsson. However, as Pang stressed, each Beatle had individual career plans or schedules. "This would have taken four different heads, four different parties, to make it work. Everybody had their own manager, lawyer, or whatever else you want to call it . . . it was definitely more about the timing."

Yet, with Harrison's *Dark Horse* tour across North America scheduled for November and December, Starr promoting his new album and with McCartney looking to rehearse material for a new album, none of the group seemed able to commit to bringing these live plans to fruition. Mal Evans, Ringo and John were together in Los Angeles at this point. Lennon knew that if he focused on making a musical reunion happen, it was always possible. And so by mid-1974, it seemed that The Beatles' famous songwriting core had largely resumed their friendship.

What truly mattered now was how the two men felt about their burgeoning relationship, and not their respective guises of commentator or songwriter. But did a repaired Lennon-McCartney friendship during the early summer of 1974 mean the two men were readying themselves to revive their creative partnership the following year? If nothing else, they were certainly ready to start *thinking* about it. Lennon duly returned to New York with Pang in late April, seeking to reconnect with something more worthwhile than the value of his own sense of celebrity.

PART THREE

NEW YORK

CHAPTER SEVEN

A Good Friend Of Mine

FROM the point of the handshake which sealed their collaborative song-writing partnership in a Liverpool mews in the early sixties, Lennon and McCartney had ambition. As he told *Rolling Stone* in 1984, Paul was seduced by the romantic image of collaboration as seen on the silver screen. "All those films about New York songwriters plugging away at the piano – 'We'll call it "Alligator Symphony"': what a great idea!' And they all go to California and get drunk. That always appealed to me, that image."

When their songwriting collaboration began, Paul had clearly envisaged the two men becoming an equable partnership. "I know they loved the idea of Rogers and Hammerstein, and even Goffin and King," critic Steve Turner told me, "and they saw themselves as a team. Most of the early songs were either written together, or started by one of them, and then finished together."

"John and Paul were beginning to write their own songs and Brian played [publisher] Dick James some tapes of theirs. Dick got the rights to the single 'Please Please Me', and all the subsequent songs too," Neil Aspinall recalled during The Beatles' *Anthology* documentary series. "We were all pretty naïve back then, and I think that The Beatles have all since regretted the deals they got into regarding song ownership." All of the songs that Lennon and McCartney would write (originally credited as McCartney/Lennon and published by Dick James) during the next three years would go into Northern Songs, set up to honour their ambition of owning their own publishing company, with an option to extend the agreement for another three years.

"We were desperate to get a deal. It's like any young novelist who wants to get published. We just signed this thing, not really knowing what it was all about," claimed Paul, "and that is virtually the contract I'm still under."

"Northern Songs is a long term thing, and it rests on Paul and I writing songs until we're 60," Lennon added at the time. "Unless something happens, there's nothing to stop Paul and I writing hits when we're old. It's so profitable and, anyway, we're good friends – there's no reason on earth why we should give it up."

According to Ian MacDonald, it was in September 1962 that their partnership came into full swing as a recognisable voice of real originality. This was a business-like partnership that clearly took their writing craft seriously. Their intention, which rapidly became clearer with impending success, was not merely to be competent but to keep improving. "John and I were a songwriting team and what songwriting teams did in those days was write for everyone – unless you couldn't come up with something, or wanted to keep a song for yourself and it was a bit too good to give away."

Jointly crediting their songs to Lennon and McCartney was an early decision they had made in part due to their aspiration towards achieving a Rodgers and Hammerstein-like status. "We'd heard these names and associated songwriting with them, so the two name combination sounded interesting," McCartney later recalled. "I wanted it to be McCartney/Lennon but John had the stronger personality, and I think he fixed things with Brian before I got there. That was John's way. I'm not saying there is anything wrong with that; I wasn't quite as skilful. He was one-and-a-half years older than me, and at that age it meant a little more worldliness."

McCartney recalled attending one meeting and being told that they should henceforth credit their songs under the Lennon-McCartney bracket. "I said: 'No, it can't be Lennon first, how about McCartney/Lennon?' They all said: 'Lennon/McCartney sounds better, it has a better ring.' I said: 'No, McCartney/Lennon sounds good too.' But I had to say: 'Oh alright . . . sod it!' – although we agreed that if we ever wanted, it could be changed around to make me equal. But by now, we'd achieved our aim, we'd become like Rodgers and Hammerstein. We were now a songwriting duo."

McCartney would arrive at Lennon's house in search of inspiration, often with little more than a song title. Once they had an interesting title with which to intrigue people and as a creative starting point for any new song, they were halfway there. Exchanging chords and ideas on their guitars or on piano, a song would come within two to three hours. Without the luxury of cassette demos of new songs, memorising new compositions proved an invaluable discipline. Unsurprisingly or not, there were no rules or compositional criteria which they used to create new material.

"We write them anywhere, but we usually just sit down, Paul and I, with a guitar and a piano or two guitars, or a piano and a guitar and George. It's all the combinations you can think of, every combination of two people writing a song. And we obviously influence each other, like groups and people do." As part of a largely imaginative and inventive process, the two men frequently bounced ideas off of each other, emulating and mirroring each other as equal partners, able to sense when the other needed direction on a new composition. "Usually, one of us writes most of the song and the other helps finish it off, adding a bit of a tune or a bit of a lyric," Lennon recalled. "If I've written a song with a verse and I've had it for a couple of weeks and I don't seem to be getting any more verses, then we either both write or he'll say: 'We'll have this, or that.'"

As long-time musical soul-mates, they'd been through so many experiences together and had always triumphed. It was a friendship and alliance which defined them both. A very real love, writer Chris Salewicz claimed, existed between them. "It was a very close bond between us, quite a big one," claimed McCartney. "We came together professionally afterwards. And as we became a songwriting team, I think it helped our intimacy and our trust in each other. Eventually, we were pretty good mates."

McCartney also insisted that distinguishing between a hard-edged John number and soft-centred Paul song ('Paul does ballads – John does rockers') was a fallacy. "There were certain songs that were very much mine and others that were definite collaborations with John," McCartney would later explain, "where we'd actually sit down and spend three hours. Then there were ones that were very much John's. I think it roughly splits somewhere down the middle."

A very real fraternal love existed between them. It was something, however, that Lennon had never verbalised. Even complimenting Paul on his new material was an unusual act that Lennon's partner unsurprisingly cherished. "John was always having to put up a front," claimed McCartney during a 1997 interview. "It was only later, when we stopped working together, that I realised that. When we were private and together there was no need for that, and he could be a real soft sweetie, which took people by surprise."

Nevertheless, this superficial toughness inevitably created a false impression of Lennon for the outside world. "One of my great memories of John was when we were having some argument. I was disagreeing and we were calling each other names. We let it settle for a second, and he lowered his glasses and he said, 'It's only me' and then he put his glasses back on again. To me, that was John. Those were the moments when I actually saw him without the façade, the armour, which I loved as well, like anyone else. It was a beautiful suit of armour. But it was wonderful when he let the visor down, and you'd just see the John Lennon that he was frightened to reveal to the world."

Lennon certainly didn't relish being labelled as a cynic, or known as a cynical character, while McCartney was more than capable of exhibiting such tendencies himself at times. "Paul can be very cynical, and much more biting than me, when he's driven to it. Of course, he's got more patience, but he can carve people up in no time at all, when he's pushed. He hits the nail right on the head, and doesn't beat about the bush, doesn't Paul."

McCartney agreed: "I could often be a foil to John's hardness. But it could be the other way round too. People tend to have got it one way, but John could be very soft, and I could do the hard stuff. It was funny. The myth developed that I was the melodic, soft one and John was the hard, acerbic one."

McCartney clearly relished and cherished the wonderful experience of writing with the talented and quick-witted Lennon. "Deep down, he was a great person to know. He was a very charismatic guy. I was a bit of a John fan; I think we all were. And I think we had a mutual admiration going on there."

On arriving in America for the first time in 1964, they were asked about the songwriting process for their hit-making material: 'Who was responsible for the words, and who handled the music?' "We said: 'I do them some days, he does them another. It depends,'" recalled McCartney. "We would swap. They asked us: 'What's your formula for hits?' We said: 'We hope we never find one. It would get very boring.'"

They clearly enjoyed their working relationship which, McCartney insisted, was the great secret of their success. "We read each other, and we knew each other's history. We had a bond that we never talked about. These kinds of things gave us a strength."

"When The Beatles were against the world, I did have the co-operation of a good mind like Paul's," Lennon later admitted. "It was us against them."

Lennon and McCartney had shared what critic Mark Hertsgaard described as a "miraculous state of grace" for a number of years, one which had elevated them "to another dimension, superior to any individual creation as they set about crafting arguably the finest body of popular musical work, an almost perfect encapsulation and representation of the period."

For McCartney, it was incredibly difficult to imagine any other potential collaborator matching, let alone emulating, the creative rapport he had shared with Lennon. "He was no slouch, that boy. He was pretty hot stuff. And so was I. So the two of us together, we gelled. We started off writing very simple songs together. Gradually, the songs got a little more complex, a little better as we learnt our trade."

On balance, and in terms of their musical and personal chemistry, the two men were clearly good for each other. A sense of equality and enjoyment in an intelligent working relationship was also crucial. If this hadn't been the case, it's unlikely they would have endured as a songwriting partnership. Although they worked as part of the same team, theirs was a challenging creative rivalry: their self-confidence as writers enabled them to develop while they thrived on this sense of competition. "This rivalry," MacDonald opined, "was the secret of the continuing upward trend in the quality of the work."

While McCartney had a great need to perform, Lennon had a strong urge for self-expression. "I'd have a separate songwriting John Lennon who wrote songs for the meat market, and I didn't consider them – the lyrics or anything – to have any depth at all. They were just a joke. Then I started being me about the songs, not writing them objectively, but subjectively." "The song is what remains. I honestly believe in the song more than the music," insisted Starr, privileged to have watched the songs develop, "and John and Paul wrote some amazing songs."

The competitive rivalry between the two men essentially reflected their contrasting adolescent relationship, in order to create a song. "There was a little competition between Paul and me as to who got the A-side, and who got the singles," Lennon later noted. "If you notice, in the early days, the majority of singles – in the movies and everything – were mine. And then, only when I became self-conscious and inhibited, did Paul start dominating the group a little."

McCartney agreed with his former partner. With extreme ego and ambition yet to surface and proliferate, the group's artistic growth would soon escalate through the combined factors of musical ability, personal unity and emotional toughness. "You could, though, almost touch the rivalry between them," George Martin claimed. "No sooner would John come up with an outstanding song than Paul answered him back with a winner in the same vein. It was typical of the way they worked as a songwriting duo. Creative rivalry kept them climbing their individual ladders. And kept The Beatles on top."

McCartney later stated that a random compositional technique offered more scope for perfection than a safe approach or established songwriting formula. 'Crafted' songs were clearly not without merit in comparison to those which had 'arrived' by more unconscious means, or via what Lennon termed as 'the spirit'. If they ever began to establish creative writing rules, they were often prone to break them.

"I think if Paul had learned music 'properly' – not just the piano, but correct notation for writing and reading music – it might well have inhibited him," Martin insisted. "He thought so, too. Once you start being taught things, your mind is channelled in a particular way. Paul could think of things I would have considered outrageous. I could admire them, but my musical training would have prevented me from thinking of them myself."

"Occasionally, we would write things totally separately, and finish them up together," recalled Paul. "John and I wrote together just short of 300 songs. We would meet up, sit down to write and three hours later, we'd have a song . . . and *never* did we have a dry session. We never came away without a song. We *always* wrote a song. Looking back, I feel blessed to be the guy that wrote with John." McCartney's wife, Linda, has noted the great sense of creative electricity between the two men. They had also shared the enviable ability of being able to finish off each other's songs.

"Lennon and McCartney wrote fluently together when the mood or the situation took them," Ian MacDonald noted, "but they wrote as least as much, and sometime more, apart from each other." I asked Ray Connolly about some of the strengths of the Lennon-McCartney partnership in the early sixties, first as songwriting collaborators before developing into musical competitors. "I think the most fantastic quality that they had was they were brilliant editors of each other's work. I think everyone needs that, and it's a shame that it was something they lacked later on. There were some tracks on Paul's first album, all they needed was for John to say, 'Are you sure about this?' And he never had that after."

McCartney would later describe the thrill of his collaborative union with Lennon in unequivocal terms. "I'm sitting in the room with John, him with me. Believe me, we're both pretty good editors. We were young turks. We were smartasses, and we did some amazing things. I would love him to be here now, saying: 'Don't do that!' – or, more wonderfully, 'That's great!' So yeah, I really had the greatest writing partner. What John and I normally do is start off songs on our own . . . I go away and write something or he does. If I get stuck on the middle eight, I know when I see John he will finish it for me.

"He'll bring a new approach to it, and that particular song will finish up half and half, Lennon and McCartney. It really will be a 50-50 job. We would sit down opposite each other with our two guitars. And because I was left handed, when I looked at John I would see almost a mirror image of myself, so we could clearly see what each other was doing, almost what you were doing yourself."

Theirs was clearly a symbiotic yet complicated relationship. Essentially, the differences in their compositions illustrated the contrast of their relationship and personality traits. "I think the great thing about their partnership was Paul's melodic instincts and John's cleverness with words," Connolly continues. "They were able to give each other ideas and spark each other off, being close together and listening to each other. I think the editing thing is what they missed later on. That's where they were at their best, offering each other ideas. When one would say: 'Where do we go from here?' The other would say: 'Why don't we do this?'"

"No one knows what really went on," Linda later insisted. "I guess when you work together for that long, it's going to get crazy. And it got crazy." As many fans and critics would concur, Paul's musical gifts were (and remain) incredible. His attributes of smooth, melodic sophistication were complemented by John's rhythmic and lyrical edge. "He had much more musicianship in him than any of the others did. Paul had the makings of a great composer," claimed Martin.

The two men were, in Martin's esteem, both complete yet complementary writers whose songwriting acumen blossomed in breathtaking fashion. Their eventual familiarity with (and growing command of) studio technique after mastering their craft, where the harmony and the overall sound was initially so important, was a crucial factor. They composed their new work in astonishingly short time, utilising their growing knowledge in developing these exceptional songs. Nothing was wasted: the economy of language, meter and phrasing was seldom bettered or equalled.

For music critic Joshua Rifkin, there was much to be commended in the attractive compositional architecture of their songs. "At some time, harmony and voice leading are the main focus," adds Walter Everett. "At others the interplay of rhythm and meter is centre stage – at others, the recording process itself is primary." Over time, the songwriting act would be treated with the same intensity as the recording process, with the two becoming increasingly entwined. The studio subsequently became an instrument in itself for The Beatles. Observers have noted that their level of perfectionism in the studio was at times confounding, due to the complete feel of much of their work. They were not the only ones to use the studio in this fashion, but the effects were germane, more relevant, and always had a purpose.

Unlike his partner, McCartney's newly written songs displayed a free-ranging melodicism which required little harmonic support from Lennon. Paul's natural acumen for composition often prevailed over songs more closely directed by their lyrical sentiment. As he would increasingly demonstrate in his work, McCartney was becoming a master melodicist with a growing preponderance towards sophisticated songcraft. (As an introduction to this facet of McCartney's writing, the melodic and harmonic structures of the verses to early composition 'You'll Be Mine' are worthy of further consideration.) As a prelude to many future Beatles compositions, the song's melody contained both an upper and lower voice, and demonstrates something of Paul's melodic gift, and the interaction between melody and harmony.

Everett claimed McCartney's entertainment-driven approach to writing enabled him to develop a "focused musical talent" as part of a new popular songwriting lexicon he did much to enrich. What's more, McCartney also developed a more refined approach to (and understanding of) harmony and theory. Nurturing a gift for melodic expression which at times bordered on genius, Paul admitted in late 1966, as he moved towards the sophisticated height of his songwriting development, that with a finely tuned ear he could often detect a whole song in a single chord. "I think you can hear a whole song in one *note* if you listened hard enough. But nobody ever listens hard enough."

"There's something about chords in a song that can take you to a place," he explained in more detail in 2007. "They may not be complex, but there can be something in the tonality of them that take you to what the vocal becomes." The sound of the chord, therefore, would often affect the singer's unconscious or intuitive approach to the sound of the words in a song, effectively being able to 'hear' the requisite vocal once they have heard the chords.

McCartney, of course, remained a less confessional storyteller than Lennon, and has a structure in his work few pop songwriters can boast, let alone equal. "The difference between John and Paul at the time, early on, was clear. John was a pure rocker. And with Paul, he loved Fred Astaire and he loved the type of music that his father played," claims Bill Harry. "He loved musicals, and he loved performing ''Til There Was You'. His taste in music tended towards traditional musicals. In that way, there was a complete difference in their musical likes." A clear characteristic of the Lennon-McCartney symbiosis was the fact that the contradictory aspects of their songs seemed to answer each other.

McCartney and Lennon saw eye to eye musically, John would later recall, particularly in their formative songwriting days. They worked well together, he insisted, because they both enjoyed the same forms of music. Part of the genius of the Lennon and McCartney songwriting partnership was also their intrinsic ability to make something new and different out of their eclectic cadre of source material.

Additionally, Paul's superior education in music (thanks to his father's piano playing and amateur jazz band musicianship) would give The Beatles an edge to their musical development they might otherwise have lacked. "He was always playing pop and jazz standards and Paul picked things up from him," Lennon later recalled. "In the early days, we'd write things separately because Paul was more advanced than I was. He was always a couple of chords ahead, and his songs usually had more chords in them. Some of Paul's he wrote separately. We wrote together because we enjoyed it a lot sometimes. It was the joy of being able to write, to know you could do it. There was also the bit about what they would like. The audience was always in my head."

"From our earliest day in Liverpool, George and I on the one hand and Paul on the other had different musical tastes," Lennon reflected in 1971. "Paul preferred 'pop type' music, and we preferred what is now called 'underground'. The contrast in our tastes, I am sure, did more good than harm, musically speaking, and contributed to our success." As a competitive partnership, it was also a diligent and industrious combination whose hard work enabled their scope for artistic expression to grow and improve over time. As Pang reassured Lennon, when they were together they were unbeatable. "No other songwriting set-up outstripped Lennon and McCartney in terms of consistency of quality or sheer aural fantasy," Ian MacDonald observed of this duo's revolutionary work. "Their partnership acquired greater expressive force and articulacy as it developed. They were, and remain, the measure of popular music in their time."

"Some people analyse songwriting. I've never known about it. It's fingers crossed, every time I sit down to do it," McCartney admitted. "I just dive right in and hope for the best, and it seems to work." Sometimes the harmony that McCartney was writing would be in sympathy with Lennon's melody, and would subsequently become a stronger melody to carry the song. "When people wrote out the musical score, they would ask: 'Which one is the melody?' because it was so co-written that you could actually take either."

A unique and special writer blessed with his own share of greatness, Lennon prized truth over beauty and proved an ideal collaborator for McCartney, adept at producing material with an unusual depth. Aside from his creative presence in their long-standing musical partnership, McCartney would understandably miss Lennon's matter-of-fact feedback too, perhaps his only true equal. In the same manner that Lennon had once looked to his kindred spirited art-school confidante Stuart Sutcliffe for the truth, so McCartney relied on Lennon's formidable presence, not only as a critical foil to his exuberance but as a perfect creative counterweight.

Paul had also helped to balance John's personality too, loosening his toughness and yet energising his indolence. On a more introspective level, the softness that Paul saw inside John was the same characteristic which Lennon saw in McCartney's exterior. Likewise, the toughness Paul observed in Lennon's countenance was the same characteristic Paul admitted to drawing on within himself at times. Here was a mutual recognition of the interchangeable characteristics that no doubt drew them together. Paul later agreed that he and John were like two sides of the same person.

"On the surface, I was very easy-going, always accommodating. That came easy to me. That's how I'd been brought up. But, at certain times, I would very much be the hard man of the duo. At certain moments, I could bite. But that would be when no one outside the group was watching. John would allow me to take that role, because it enabled him to drop his guard and be vulnerable. On the surface, he was this hard, witty guy, always on hand with a cutting witticism. But really, he was very soft. John was very insecure. Ultimately, we were equals."

"John and Paul were extremely good friends; they loved one another really," George Martin explained. "They shared a spirit of adventure, and a modest childhood ambition: they were going to go out and conquer the world."

Having led the way in communicating The Beatles' musical message, Lennon and McCartney's decade-long prolificacy was simply astonishing, increasingly so given the perspective of four decades' worth of hindsight. "In all the years I wrote with John, I can't remember a single occasion when we didn't come up with a song," Paul later revealed. "At worst, we'd write at least one every day. It all happened at an amazing pace. Because it had to."

Given such fascinating insight into their working relationship, it's small wonder that Paul believed he and Lennon, two men who would expand the horizons and vocabulary of popular music, were so fortunate in finding each other. McCartney was later asked about their bond. "I like collaboration, but the collaboration I had with John . . . it's difficult to imagine anyone else coming up to that standard," he admitted in 1984. "I can't imagine anybody being there when I go: '(sings) '*It's getting better all the time*' . . . I just can't imagine anybody who could chime in: (sings) '*It couldn't get much worse.*'"

They were a right- and left-handed alliance, seeing eye-to-eye during their formative musical development, and harmonising together also proved a musical manifestation of an unspoken closeness. The seemingly contradictory aspects of the creative approach to their co-written songs provided complementary answers to the musical questions they asked of each other during their collaboration. Lennon and McCartney were a classically productive combination who were blessed with an energising competitiveness that defined their relationship.

"I don't think John ever felt he was better than me, and I don't think I ever felt I was better than John," Paul would later claim. "Certainly when we worked it would have been fatal in a collaboration for either of us to ever think that. It was just that I brought a certain 50 per cent, and John brought a certain 50 per cent." The two men were, in Martin's esteem, both complete writers whose songwriting acumen and eventual familiarity with and growing command of studio technique, where the overall sound was initially so important, was a crucial factor. "Seeing music as a vehicle of thought and feeling," MacDonald opined, "Lennon stressed expression at the expense of formal elegance, which held no interest or value for him *per se*."

Lennon insisted that he maintained "a professional songwriters' attitude to writing pop songs", turning out a certain style of song for a single or for another artist, a separate creative enterprise whose lyrics were not considered to have any great substance or depth. "And also they'd say: 'Well, are you going to make an album?' and we'd knock off a few songs, like a job. Though I always felt the best songs were the ones that *came* to you. If you ask me to write a song for a movie or something, I can sit down and sort of make a song. I wouldn't be thrilled with it, I find it difficult to do, but I can do it. I call it craftsmanship. I've had enough years at it to put something together, but I never enjoyed that. Even with songs that they considered to be 90 per cent complete, there was always a missing ingredient added in the studio."

As a rhythm guitarist, the accents and the articulation in Lennon's playing consequently influenced his writing. His natural songwriting tendencies were towards rhythmical strength: seeking to create a sound whereby the harmonies shifted over the top of the melody. As a diary-like writer who composed over a small range of melodic intervals, Lennon's songs were closer to the intonation of speech than song, and would become an expressive force in a harmonic context.

With the group enjoying the discovery of new chord sequences during the development of their songwriting art, it subsequently fuelled their musical spontaneity. As a result, both Lennon and McCartney's music would commonly set in motion deep and sympathetic vibrations amongst listeners. The mood and the sound of Lennon's lyrics often closely corresponded with the song's melody, yet he would consistently claim that his words were, at least during their earlier compositions, virtually irrelevant. Having heard a chord structure in his head, Lennon would often be sparked into writing by a set of words or 'sound words', and would later present musicians with a chord sheet and attendant lyrics to match.

With such impressive creative credentials in mind, McCartney later realised the daunting task that subsequent collaborators would face in following Lennon's lyrical and creative genius. The influence of their combined musical legacy would undoubtedly have discouraged some artists from even attempting to write with McCartney. Having often stressed that he wasn't seeking a songwriting successor to his former partner during the ensuing decades, it wasn't something he would rule out. "If I happened to fall into a situation where I felt comfortable writing with someone, I definitely wouldn't say no to it." McCartney still found it hard to explain what he (and no doubt others) considered the 'great mystery' in his coming together with Lennon. Something, it seemed, had ensured a sufficiently meaningful first meeting.

Paul has subsequently spoken of the warm, close and loving relationship he enjoyed, not only with Lennon but with his fellow Beatle colleagues too. "We used to say: 'I love him,' on interviews. I think we really did, genuinely," Paul told Michael Parkinson, who appeared alongside Clement Freud and boxer John Conteh on the *Band On The Run* album cover, "and I still do." It was one of the key reasons for his gratitude about the re-making of their relationship as the seventies progressed.

During the summer of 1974, Lennon had enjoyed reconnecting with McCartney, and their strengthening friendship could naturally be seen as a vital precursor to any hopes of a prospective musical reunion. Pang would later admit that she retained the ambition of reuniting the two estranged writing partners, with a long-term view of engineering a Beatles reunion. Pang also knew that Lennon was keen on welcoming Paul back into his life. Lennon and Pang's relationship was a helpful factor in John's *rapprochement* with Paul who, unlike Ono, had no history of tension with Pang.

For Paul, John and May represented an old friend and his attractive young partner. May also helped John to realise the importance of his old bonds of friendship. Bill Harry agrees that a lot of the credit goes to Pang for encouraging Lennon to renew the bond with his son. "John was changing as a person," he insists, "and May had encouraged him to reconnect with old friends again. I think if he'd stayed with May and not gone back to Yoko, he would have got back together with Paul. I think it was inevitable. I think John was excited by it, and he was struggling to get out of that situation."

Throughout the early summer of 1974, May and John frequently saw Paul and Linda in New York. "I got along great with Paul and Linda," Pang later enthused. "They were terrific." The McCartneys were regularly having dinner with the couple, and John and Paul enjoyed a series of Beaujolais-fuelled reminiscences about the group's early glory days in Hamburg and Liverpool. During these nostalgic, friendship-enhancing occasions, they drank wine and remembered their tough, myth-making initiations. "'Didn't we have fun in Hamburg? Remember that day on tour?' And we did all that trip," Lennon would later reflect. "I look back now with fond memories." "John and Paul were always one-upping each other, like brothers," remembers May, a vivacious and easy-going woman.

Another of these wine-fuelled evenings spent reminiscing about The Beatles' formative experiences took place in June at the plush Pierre Hotel on Fifth Avenue, close to Central Park. Lennon had already spent time here in April, working at speed to write new material for his forthcoming *Walls And Bridges* album in a frenetic burst of creativity. His work here, critic Philip Norman concluded, "suggested relief to be back in the river-girt citadel of Manhattan".

Melody Maker journalist Chris Charlesworth was also in attendance one night, along with Keith Moon and his assistant, Peter 'Dougal' Butler. "Keith, Dougal and myself rode in a limousine [from Madison Square Garden] to the Pierre, instructed the driver to wait and headed up in the elevator," Charlesworth recalls. "John seemed pleased to see Keith. They'd been pals back in London in the sixties. In truth, Keith was a bit of a Beatles groupie, and John was one of the few people on this earth who could tame his wild behaviour, simply because he respected John so much."

Meanwhile, the McCartneys had first met May in California, but the two couples became more relaxed with each other later that year in New York. Pang, meanwhile, actively encouraged these Lennon-McCartney *tete-a-tetes*, and John relished recalling shared memories of their testing apprenticeship. One summer evening John played Paul a copy of 'How Do You Do It?' on their apartment stereo. Taken from his growing Beatles bootleg collection, this was a song bypassed in favour of their debut album title track, 'Please Please Me', as the group's second single in 1963.

Lennon had sung lead on their recording of the Mitch Murray song against general group indifference during the studio session in September 1962. The group also strenuously resisted their producers' wishes to release what he considered a sure-fire chart-topper. Following his unsuccessful pleas, Martin agreed not to release it. "A classic!" McCartney later joked in 2012. "We were wrong!" Thankfully, The Beatles stood firm and decided to write their own material.

It also seemed that Lennon's time with Pang helped him to rediscover a sense of The Beatles' importance in his life. Having witnessed John and Paul's reconciliation at first-hand, Pang knew that Lennon was impatient for certain things. He was also open to spending time and relaxing together with Paul in their East 52nd Street penthouse apartment in New York, his most homely abode during his separation from Ono. Lennon and Pang also visited the McCartneys at the city's Stanhope Hotel. "The first time they ever visited us in New York, the doorman called up and spoke to John. John said to me: 'Oh my God! Paul and Linda are downstairs. Can you handle that?' And I said: 'Yeah so? What's the problem? There's nothing to handle. They're your friends. Send them up.' The two of them [Paul and Linda] would pop up and visit all the time," Pang recalls. "The fans out there thought that John and Paul didn't talk for years, but he was always over."

Lennon may have feigned a characteristic nonchalance about McCartney's numerous visits to their apartment, but this shared feeling of nostalgia seemed to offer Lennon a sense of belonging. "So we got back together again," McCartney would happily reflect. "It was lovely." Lennon and McCartney would enjoy a penthouse view of the East River from John's balcony. For John, it was reminiscent of Liverpool's River Mersey and growing up in the city. "New York City's affinity with Liverpool made him nostalgic," biographer Ray Coleman claimed. And it was on the very same balcony that Lennon was startled to experience his first UFO sighting in August.

Lennon and Pang had returned home from the studio on a sweltering Friday evening, August 23, at around 9 p.m. Feeling hungry, they decided to order pizza. While they waited for their food, Lennon walked out onto the apartment's balcony terrace, "dreaming around in my usual poetic frame of mind", he conceded, in the dark heat of the night. Smoking and relaxing as he looked out to the East River, he suddenly turned his head, looked left and happened to see something moving in the sky about 100 yards away. At first, he saw a bright light which he thought may have been a billboard light. Even a perilously short-sighted Lennon could have seen this mysterious object without his lenses. 'What *is* that?' he thought. Was it a helicopter? Is it a balloon? Maybe it was the Blimp, he pondered, as he attempted to rationalise what he was seeing.

Lennon's initial instinct, beyond one of shocked surprise, was to enjoy this incredible experience and tell Pang about it later. Feeling sure she would struggle to believe him, he called her name with increasing urgency so she could witness it for herself . . . and to ensure he wasn't seeing things. "It was *there*," he insisted later when he recounted the event to the press.

179

"I didn't believe it either. It was *there!*" Pang was stood in the bedroom when she heard John's call to come out to the balcony. "I was in the other room and I hear him yelling for me. He yells again, and I run out to him and when I get out there, I see this thing hovering over our heads. It was so fascinating. I thought, 'What is that?!' John said: 'You're seeing what I'm seeing!' I'm like, 'Oh my God', I start freaking out because I know exactly what this thing is. John was like, 'Isn't this great?'"

"One part of me thought: 'That's a UFO, you know,'" Lennon later admitted. "You don't expect a Martian in the sky." "I said: 'Oh my God, It's a UFO!' I was so freaked out," Pang remembers. "I kept screaming: 'It's a UFO! It's a UFO!'" John and May stared at the craft as it moved slowly, taking its time flying in the dusky sky. Cars on the street below were clearly audible, as were the helicopters across the water, but this mysterious object floating directly above their heads made no discernable sound. Total silence also heightened this sense of intrigue.

Flying low, barely above the height of the apartment rooftops, the UFO hovered, coasting quietly like a tourist, Lennon later recalled. When it moved over the rooftop of the adjacent building, a shimmering heat haze was visible beneath the craft. "It was the size of a two-man Lear jet," Pang later revealed. "It was so close we could see the rim of it. It was circular, and had white lights going on and off around the edge, and one solid red light on top. The bottom was this dark grey metal. We watched it for a good 10 or 15 minutes. I think it was surveying, checking out what was going on. I'm staring at it, looking through binoculars."

Pang then attempted to take some photographs of the craft with surveillance film fitted in her camera. However, the dark night made the resulting images appear over-exposed. During one subsequent TV interview, Pang presented a drawing of the craft to the camera that Lennon had made shortly after the incident. It seemed that no one else in their neighbourhood witnessed the experience. "Amazingly, not one of my neighbours looked out of the window, or turned their lights on to check. Later, I realised that most people would probably have gone away for the weekend since the city was so scorching that summer."

Pang watched the craft float down the East River, before it sped up and then slowed down as it travelled towards Brooklyn Bridge. When it reached a midway point out on the water, it halted. Quite unexpectedly, it then disappeared straight up into the night sky. The awestruck couple phoned their friends to inform them what had happened. Photographer

Bob Gruen remembers things a little differently. He claims Lennon recalled seeing blinking lights through his living room doorway. The photographer also recalls Lennon telling him the flying saucer was reminiscent of the UFOs made popular in fifties sci-fi films. "As the saucer started floating downtown he shouted to it: 'Wait! Come back, come back! Take me with you!' But it floated away."

Pang later saw a second UFO in the company of one of their friends. "I always believed in the existence of other beings but that just brought it home for me. I've always believed there was life elsewhere, and I can't believe we're the only beings in the universe. I learnt to always look up in the sky and you just don't know what you'll see." Lennon may not have been taken on a strange vacation, but he did board a plane the following day to Los Angeles to visit Ringo and record a new song for his forthcoming album.

Where the work of his former partner was concerned, Lennon had apparently been impressed by Al Coury's efforts in making a success of McCartney's latest album. "I must not take the credit on *Band On The Run*," Paul later admitted. "Al Coury, Capitol's ace plugger, rang up and told us: 'We want "Band On The Run"! We want "Jet"! We want 'em off!' And he's such a good spieler, this fella, that I'll say: 'Well, it sounds like sense. No skin off my nose, try it,' and it just kept coming back up, much to my delight. The majority of people don't know *Band On The Run* is out unless there's a single.

"If someone says: 'This is the single from *Band On The Run*,' then everyone knows it's out. That's the power of the single. You go into a shop and they say: 'Well, it's on an album, do you want that?' and they say: 'Oh, is it?' The communicative value of a single is the big thing."

The best moments from *Walls And Bridges* and *Band On The Run* would certainly have made a very strong Lennon and McCartney pairing on record at this point, with the two men producing some of their best independent work to date. After being invited to stay with Lennon at the Dakota during earlier album sessions, Keltner would often stare out the window of apartment No. 72, located on the building's seventh floor which overlooked New York's Central Park, and think, " 'Hey, I'm up here with John!' "

On more recent visits to New York, Keltner has stood on the corner across the street, at 72nd and Central Park, and looked up to Lennon's four-bedroom apartment and remembered those days. Keltner has always cherished the time he spent in John's company, and fondly recalls the period which would produce *Mind Games* and *Walls And Bridges*. "We used to have some great times coming back from the studio. We'd have some real great conversations, and it's something I treasure. He was so interesting and smart, and always talking about amazing future plans. And we had so many things in common, musically and stuff."

One morning, Keltner stood in the kitchen of the Dakota apartment making breakfast. Lennon ambled in to join him, and the two men began discussing glasses. "He asked me if mine were prescription. I told him they weren't. So he said: 'Why do you wear those things then?' I got used to hiding my eyes. I was so self-conscious I wore glasses. And he said: 'Well, that's crazy.' And I said: 'Okay, let me try your glasses on.' And I put his glasses on, and it was just like looking through coke bottles! I remember I tried on Bob Dylan's glasses once, and they were exactly the same!" Keltner was shocked to realise how short-sighted Lennon was. "And when the record [*Walls And Bridges*] came out, when I got my copy of it, I couldn't believe it. It had that picture of him wearing those five or six pairs of glasses!"

New York photographer Bob Gruen had taken photos of a multi-spectacled Lennon at short notice, before they appeared on the new album's artwork. "I shot 12 rolls of pictures, with all those different expressions. It was easy to take John's photos," he told *LENNONYC* director Michael Epstein. "He wasn't awkward or shy. He'd done thousands of photo sessions before."

Having invited Gruen to his East 52nd Street apartment, a location the photographer visited a number of times during Lennon's separation from Ono, Lennon had wanted to forego the time and expensive process of a photographic studio session for the new album cover. He opted instead to use the roof of his apartment as the setting for a simple, yet striking, art director's brief: a series of profile shots that could be made into a playful, interchangeable collection of facial expressions. These included shots of Lennon wearing glasses and sunglasses, although Lennon's eyes, Gruen marvelled, were still visible through them all. After finishing the session for the new album artwork, Lennon then suggested they take a further series of photos on his apartment roof in preparation for album publicity.

During the *Mind Games* session the previous year, Gruen had stopped *en route* to the Record Plant near Times Square. He duly purchased a clutch of NYC T-shirts from a sidewalk vendor, one of which he handed to

Lennon. "I remembered that I had given him a shirt. They weren't sold in a store. When I would see them, I would buy a few, because I used to wear them all the time. We had the whole New York skyline all around us, and I asked him if he still had the T-shirt that I gave him. He said that he did, and he went off and put it on, and he looked pretty good."

Following their rooftop shoot in the late summer of '74, the T-shirt image soon became an iconic part of Lennon's American legend. "We took a series of pictures which have become some of the best known photos of John ever taken," Gruen acknowledges.

Back in 1971, Gruen had heard through the grapevine that Lennon and Ono had left the St. Regis Hotel, their first makeshift 'home', and moved in to Greenwich Village's Bank Street. Composer John Cage, who had inspired McCartney's experimental ambitions on 'A Day In The Life', was their neighbour. "It [the apartment] had a door which opened onto the street," remembers Gruen. "It was almost like going into a farmhouse. A bit of an office area, couches, kitchen area, a two-storey white bedroom, spiral staircase, white room, and it had one of the biggest TVs I've seen."

According to Van Scyoc, there was nowhere else Lennon would have wanted to be. "He was living there on Bank Street at the beginning, and round the block was Magne Graphics. They loved it here, the recording studios; there were so many things to be interested in." But this wasn't a case of Beatlemania – no one would envisage knocking on the front door of this modest apartment and screaming when he appeared. Life there became a series of exciting moments. Soon after Harrison's Concert For Bangla Desh in 1971, Bob Dylan had been an early visitor to their apartment. He duly took the Lennons on a tour of their new surroundings, pointing out the plethora of artistic activities that were on offer.

Lennon also enjoyed conversing with the local all-day delicatessen owners and fruit stand workers in Greenwich Village, who were happy to treat him as a regular guy. "I regret profoundly not being American, and not being born in Greenwich Village. That's where I should have been born," he confided to Jann Wenner in his infamous *Rolling Stone* interview in 1970. "But it never works that way. Everybody heads towards the centre; that's why I'm here now . . . this is where it's happening."

"You'd have David Peel and the musicians, journalists and media crews and a lot of people who'd just walked in off the street to say 'Hello,'" Dan Richter recalled. "John and Yoko were brilliant," Peel later told Ray Coleman. "They knew how to ad lib quicker than anybody I've ever met.

What they liked doing best was getting things done quickly. They hated wasting time. John was open-minded, learned a lot, he had access to a lot of people, and he always listened. He wasn't as committed to the radical thing as a lot of us, because he was a Beatle. He could make a call and get things done. When you are close to John Lennon, the guy's so powerful and aware of the world events that you start losing your own identity. Being so close to him for a year or so was good and bad, you know."

"I'd just arrived in New York and all these people, Jerry Rubin, Abbie Hoffman, David Peel, they were right on the corner when I was going out for a walk in the Village," Lennon later explained. "It was that kind of community. I loved it. At the time, though, it was a good scene and they meant no harm."

"He wanted to communicate with people on an ordinary level," wrote biographer Ray Coleman. "New York, and the crowd he was introduced to by Jerry Rubin seemed to offer that, coupled with the radical politics preached by Rubin and his friends. It was John's automatic haven for the early months in the Village."

Van Scyoc would often arrive early at rehearsals during the 1971–72 album sessions for *Some Time In New York City*, and enjoyed hanging out with Lennon in the Village's bohemian streets. "We'd be going down to the deli or the fruit stand. I would tag along, and he would know the guy at the deli. If someone recognised him, they would just say: 'Hi John, how are you doing?' They wouldn't stop and hassle him. They would just acknowledge him. I used to record a lot at Jimi Hendrix's studio on 8th Street, and it was considered as a place where we might record at one point. The Village sucked you in. There was a lot of politics happening, and you'd walk around Washington Square Park, and people stood on the corner. A big discussion on Nixon would break out, 'cos something had happened that day, or in the papers." Life among the Greenwich Village hippies, wrote biographer Ray Coleman, "was a natural diversion of fun and freedom for John. He wanted the freedom to stay in New York. The pulse of the city was right for him."

A little *risqué* at the time before the city was eventually revitalised during the ensuing decade, the Village was an exciting place to be, its cobble-stone streets reminding Lennon of Liverpool. "There were a lot of stars running around," Gruen recalled, "and they were respectful of people like that. And I think he felt that freedom." Gruen also argues that the press refrained from attacking the Lennons as heartlessly as their British counterparts. "They were off the main glare of the spotlight when they came to New York, and there were a lot of other weird artists. Yoko's friends with a lot of them, people doing interesting artistic things."

New York also represented the centre of the creative world at the time. Lennon wanted to be part of the city, rather than feeling removed by living in the suburbs. Gruen also believes that Lennon enjoyed being immersed in the *avant-garde* art scene by becoming comfortable as an independent artist. "You can re-establish and reinvent yourself. Yoko took John to see people like Andy Warhol, Ornette Coleman, Charlotte Moorman and a lot of her friends." Lennon and Ono met artists, poets, politicians and activists. "When John got to New York, it started to turn into an artist's haven," Adam Ippolito said, "and gave the opportunity for young people to move in."

"While in New York, there's these fantastic 20 or 30 artists who all understand what I'm doing and have the same kind of mind as me," Lennon enthused. "It's just like heaven after being here [in Britain]. She [Yoko] felt the country would be more receptive to what we're up to . . . in the States, we're treated like artists. Which we are! Or anywhere else for that matter. But here [in Britain] I'm like the lad who knew Paul, got a lucky break, won the pools, and married the actress." Excited and elated, Ono felt they should stay, and she effectively sold Lennon on being in New York after they walked the city and explored all its hidden qualities.

Aside from the occasional visit to the trendy Studio 54 ("It wasn't the kind of place John would hang out," Gruen says. "He wasn't going out every night") and a music industry hangout called Ashley's, Lennon would often drink in a nondescript bar on the Upper East Side after recording sessions. Van Scyoc recalls frequenting Chinatown eateries when Ono was hungering for Oriental food, and his favourite local restaurant, Home, on Manhattan's Upper East Side. "It was a macrobiotic restaurant, and we knew the owner there. We'd played there a couple of times with Elephant's Memory, and John enjoyed the place very much. It was good food, and it was just perfect to hang out there after a session."

"We used to go to a place called Smith's Bar," recalls Cicala of their less austere diet, "and we used to walk up 44th Street, half a block from Record Plant. It was on the corner of Eighth Avenue and 44th Street. It was amazing, the food that was in there. *Nobody* knew who he was. There were many things like that. We'd go up to Eighth Avenue and get a hamburger, or order sushi on a Friday."

"I think what he *really* liked about being here," observes Gruen, "was having a certain freedom to walk around. John liked the fact he was anonymous. He could walk around New York, and ride a bicycle around the Village. He could walk down the street in New York. If you're famous, people see you, but they don't bother you. If you see someone walking around New York who looks like Robert Redford, well, it probably *is* Robert Redford. He felt comfortable here, he could walk across the street without people freaking out. He took taxis, he walked in Central Park, and people asked him for autographs, but people didn't really bother him. We did that a number of times, and he liked that. He ran into musicians." On one occasion, an awestruck fan yelled: 'When are you getting The Beatles back together?' at which Lennon jokingly glanced at his watch, signed the autograph and carried on.

Lennon's love of the city's bohemian allure, Van Scyoc recalls, was just as strong. "One morning at seven o'clock, we had just finished up [at the studio], and I assumed John and Yoko were getting in their car. [John] had a kind of bodyguard who would drive him back up town to the Dakota at that point. I was driving up the road and I see them in the middle of Eighth Avenue, trying to hail a cab. I picked them up and said, 'What the heck are you doing? Get in the car, I'll take you home. Didn't your driver come? What are ya thinking?' It's cool during the day, but not early in the morning on Seventh Avenue. 'You're a Beatle for God's sake, c'mon!' I had to rag him out a little bit on that one."

This feeling of freedom was much greater than it had been for Lennon in England. "I think the press left him alone in a sense, and I think he found it a breath of fresh air that he could come here and live a normal life," Gruen adds, "and not have the newspapers making fun of him. You can always get something done, and things move kind of fast." John loved the speed and the largesse of New York City. It was the only place, Lennon told pianist Nicky Hopkins soon after relocating to the city, that could keep pace with him and his life.

"It's going at a tremendous speed. I don't know why, but it's that kind of tenseness," Lennon admitted to British interviewer Bob Harris when discussing life in the city in 1975. "There's the same quality of energy, of vitality, in both cities. New York is at my speed. I like it 'cos it's 24 hours." Gruen reminded me during our interview that, true to legend, it's still the city that never sleeps. He had been understandably thrilled both to see (and spend time with) Lennon and Ono at an Apollo Theater benefit concert. The young photographer was scarcely able to believe his luck. "I liked their movies a lot. I thought The Beatles were cool. There was nothing not to like."

He also admitted his pride in the image he captured of John in front of the Statue Of Liberty in 1974: a poignant, powerful symbol of America welcoming foreign artists to its shores. '*The Statue of Liberty says "Come!"*' Lennon sang on 'New York City', the title track of his topical political long-player and his apparent ode to life in the Big Apple.

"A solid, rousing rocker," Paul Du Noyer opined of the album's title track, "the best defence witness in the case of *Some Time In New York City*." *The US v John Lennon* documentary film features footage of John and Yoko aboard a boat, offering a peaceful salute to the beckoning iconic statue shortly after their arrival in September 1971.

Lennon began writing the song at Bank Street in Greenwich Village, a Chuck Berry inspired rock'n'roll diary, in critic Peter Doggett's esteem, "of what happened when the Lennons hit New York. At the heart of the song was John's liberation at having escaped England . . . and its refusal to see beyond the myth of The Beatles in approaching John's more recent work. New York City, a melting pot of races and ideas, had taken the Lennons to its heart; the song was Lennon's vote of thanks."

Co-director John Scheinfeld, for one, was not in the least surprised about Lennon's love affair with the vibrant city. "First of all, there's much to love about New York and America. The lifestyle he and Yoko experienced in New York was perfectly suited [to] their personalities and desires," he claims. "In so many ways New York and John Lennon was a perfect match."

For Lennon, feeling at home in New York, he was steadily at one with this great city, redolent of Rome at its height. "America is the Roman Empire and New York is Rome itself," he told one writer. "It's the Rome of today, a bit like a together Liverpool. I imagine New York is like London must have been in the Victorian days when Britain was at the height of its power. The American Empire is now what the British Empire used to be. America now has the empire of the world . . . it has that quality about it. Fortunately or unfortunately, they speak English, so I just fitted in. I'd always like to be where the action is. The seventies are gonna be America's."

Despite the city's incredible capacity for visual thrill, Lennon acknowledged to TV presenter Bob Harris something of the brooding tension he discerned at street level. "It's almost the difference between Liverpool and London, and London and New York. To me it's no tenser than London or Liverpool was. I like New Yorkers because they have no time for the niceties of life. They're like me in this." Lennon also loved the city's wit too, reminding him of home.

Lennon loved New York. For him, it was the hottest, and the fastest, city on earth. But what was it about New York City that inspired or excited him enough to want to stay? "He obviously enjoyed living here, but it wasn't something that we chatted about as friends," Gruen acknowledges. "He didn't say, 'I'm so excited to be here.' He seemed pretty comfortable with himself here, whenever I saw him. I don't know how he felt, because I never asked him."

The Lennons also savoured its cobbled streets and the busy pace of downtown life. New York was tough, and there were easier places to live. But it was a solid place and New Yorkers, Gruen argues, like to survive. More satisfyingly, they also like to succeed. "If living here for four or five years makes me a New Yorker, I am a New Yorker," Lennon reported after settling into the city. "I don't wanna get too nationalistic about New York – it's the best place I can think of to live, but everywhere is somewhere."

Lennon later told New York radio DJ Dennis Elsas about the enthusiasm he received for his residency case in the city, and his determination to remain in the metropolis he loved. "I think people are a bit cooler in New York. People will wave or the taxi drivers will say: 'Are you still here?' or 'Good luck' or all that jazz about immigration . . . I love it here, and that's why I'm fighting so hard to stay here in New York. I'm still here, and I don't have any intentions of going. I don't harm anybody. I've got a big mouth, but that's about all. I think there's certainly room for the odd Lennon or two out here."

As reflected in the *US v John Lennon* documentary, Lennon's sense of belonging in the States (and his determination to stay there) made this American chapter of his life so compelling and dangerous. Lennon would famously state that after meeting numerous (possibly native) New Yorkers who complained about the city's environment, few would actually take the step of leaving the Big Apple. Lennon was always happy to defend New York, not least because of its sincerity as a city. For him, it was a place that had everything.

Klaus Voormann believes that Lennon was in thrall to the excitement of the city as a multi-racial, cultural melting pot. "It's pretty hard to pinpoint what an American is," Lennon later ventured. "They're all Italian-Americans or Irish-Americans or African-Americans or Afro-Americans. It's *nice* here."

Lennon felt at home amidst the vital blend of artistic bohemia and fast-paced urbanity that it offered, once he'd relaxed and adjusted to the fact that he'd left England. For him, this was the whole point of the city, something he believed many had overlooked or misunderstood. "I've been living here for three years in New York, and hopefully I'll be living here for a long time to come. I'm living here for my psychic well-being," Lennon later insisted shortly after the birth of his son, Sean. "I write in a cocoon – when you come out of your cocoon it's wonderful, with all this madness to look at and play with."

This was the place where the music he loved came from. He clearly felt comfortable making music in New York too. "I seem to be the guy in New York that all the Englishmen say 'Hi' to. Which is good, when Mick [Jagger]'s in town, or Paul's in town, when anybody comes, I love it. All the rockers come and say: 'Hey, what's happening?' I'm supposed to show them what's happening. They already know – most of them, anyway. There's still plenty of studios and musicians. There's a lot of action here, a lot of good musicians," Lennon informed Bob Harris in 1975. "What was great for me was to see John be pleased," Keltner told the *LENNONYC* documentary team, when asked how it felt to play on the sequence of John's New York-based albums. "If you're a musician, and you're playing on someone's record, that's what you're there for. You can only hope to be that in spades. That's why I ended up working with him for so long."

Keltner remains an avid fan of the album material that constituted the start of Lennon's creative and commercial upswing. He duly produced *Walls And Bridges* during the summer of 1974, a creative period which Keltner still recalls with affection. "Everything I've done since I left England has been at the Record Plant. They're a good bunch there," Lennon told Elsas. "He loved recording here in New York," Gruen explains, "because he kept doing it over and over. He worked with Roy Cicala and Jack Douglas. They were very much regular, solid guys and he worked with them from then on."

Douglas, an assistant and engineer on much of Lennon's seventies output, felt that his wealth of Beatles experience ensured his sessions were amongst the easiest he'd ever produced. Lennon's observations on what was happening during the creative process were always solid and constructive. "All those guys were fantastic," Keltner enthuses, unstinting in his praise of Lennon's control-room colleagues. "Everybody was so talented. All the engineering was great: Roy Cicala was great, and Shelly Yakus."

Cicala insists that nobody knew about Lennon's Record Plant sessions, one of the many major artists to record at this most prestigious of studios. It was certainly never advertised, and Lennon would often arrive through the facility's freight entrance. Lennon loved the studio's down-to-earth authentic rock'n'roll environment, with its mirrored consoles characterising a facility blessed with the world's best equipment and engineers. Often liable to take five at the back of the studio during all-night sessions, Yakus still regards his work with Lennon as a defining moment in his studio education.

After all, Lennon had spent much of the last few years as an almost exclusive studio musician, following his fantastic schooling at Abbey Road. ("George Martin is listed as one of the great producers of his time, and rightly so, because he produced The Beatles," Keltner reminded me during our conversation.) With this in mind, Yakus could only hope to give Lennon what he needed. "I wanted it to go smoothly. It was a very professional session, so you do your best to make everybody happy and come up with a sound that works. [They] turned out to be really terrific sessions."

Yakus' later production partner and studio assistant, 'Little' Jimmy Iovine, agreed with this assessment, insisting the *Walls And Bridges* sessions were amongst the most professional he'd ever known. "John knew what he wanted. He knew how to get what he was going for. He was going after a noise, and he knew how to get it. His solo thing had an incredible sound to it. He really had his own sound."

Iovine also believed that one of the reasons for popular culture's ongoing fascination with Lennon was his willingness to look in places other artists didn't dare to explore. As Gruen points out, Iovine turned out to be one of the American recording business' biggest names and most powerful men as the wealthy owner of Endoscope Records. "This is the guy that would come to me in the morning and say: 'Hey Jimmy, you wanna coffee?' And he'd fetch me one, bless his heart," adds Keltner. "He's got a good sense of humour, and when I remind him of those things now, he has a good laugh."

With around a $60,000 budget, Pang recalls Lennon booking time at the Record Plant in June. Al Coury, the Vice President of Promotion and A&R then appeared at the studio with news for Lennon. He was now in possession of the long-lost *Rock 'N' Roll* session tapes. "Phil had apparently had an auto accident. Only he knows whether he did or didn't, but that's what the story said," claimed Pang. "That was the end of it then, because he'd got the tapes and I didn't get them back until two days before I went into the studio to cut *Walls And Bridges*."

According to Pang, Lennon had no interest in these chaotic recordings with work on a new album project about to commence. "When I did get into them, I found that out of the eight [tracks] there were only four or five that were worth using. The sessions had 28 guys playing live and a lot of them out of tune, which is too much, even for rock'n'roll. So I didn't know whether to forget it or carry on, but I hate leaving stuff in the can. In the end I decided to finish it off and produce the rest myself."

They would prove to be painful listening come the end of the *Walls And Bridges* sessions, and would necessitate a trip to Morris Levy's upstate New York farm to rehearse further material for the abandoned, Spector-produced album. Despite this early distraction, a well-prepared Lennon completed the whole, self-produced *Walls And Bridges* project with ease inside two months. Unhappy about wasting money, he was focused and driven in the studio.

"When you walked in, you knew who was boss," Pang declares. True to form, Lennon's strict work ethic, no–nonsense approach and insistence on punctuality was also required of his colleagues. "He'd expect you to be there on time. [If] he said a session was at seven, he meant seven. He wants you to be ready, so get there before seven, so when it was time to play, it was time to play." Engineer and producer Dennis Ferrante also argues that Lennon was not a man keen to waste studio time. "He was there to make music. That state led to musical creativity, which in turn made great music."

Regularly making changes to a song while recording in the studio, Lennon would rehearse his new material and then run through a new song to demonstrate what he'd composed. Guided by feeling and instinct, if he noticed a mistake but was happy with the song, he'd leave it in. Just as importantly, Lennon respected his studio colleagues. "He'd play what he had, and then he'd let the musicians do their parts," recalls Pang, a fascinated studio spectator. An experienced Lennon was happy to let the musicians play through and do their own thing on his new songs. As Voormann attested, Lennon believed in his colleague's abilities, and never told the bassist what to play on a studio session. "I always play what I thought fit the song. With John, you had the feeling that he had trust in you."

According to Keltner, Lennon loved to explore, to see what happened in the studio during the recording process. Discussing their sound with studio guitar players, he clearly knew what he was looking for. The fact that Lennon was so familiar with his own material was a key factor in *Walls And Bridges'* musical effectiveness. "As a session musician, you're used to going in and hearing a song and hitting it. But if the artist is really well-rehearsed, and knows how he wants his songs to go, and he can play them well, that goes a long way."

When Lennon was in work mode, Pang insists, you knew it. On this album at least, musicians hoping to indulge in a little dope, coke or alcohol would have to wait until the job was finished. Gruen confirms that Lennon was actively discouraging any drinking until after the session. Another notable track was the Sinatra-esque, Los-Angeles-penned arrangement for the Vegas-like 'Nobody Loves You (When You're Down And Out)', Lennon's blowsy ode to the vagaries of life during his so-called 'Lost Weekend'. "I had been sitting on the song because I knew I would ruin it if I tried to record it at the time I wrote it – my head wasn't together enough to deal with it, so I just kept it in my pocket."

As one of the album's musical highlights with its lachrymose guitar solo, Lennon's seen-too-much vocal weariness is well-executed, retaining a twist of resignation over what he's witnessed and experienced. 'Scared', on the other hand, is a tense, haunting track exploring Lennon's fear of ageing, loneliness and empty success. "Brilliant and chilling it may be," Du Noyer surmised, "but only the sincerity of John's delivery prevents it tipping over into melodrama." "That's how I felt when I wrote the song," Lennon admitted in late September, "but I'm perfectly happy now, thank you."

Meanwhile, the melancholic yet uplifting 'Bless You' seemed to address love's interchangeable quality and its unpredictable capacity for joy. "A lot of couples' experience of love, and the way love changes," Lennon explained while promoting the album, "doesn't remain the same all the time. Love comes in mysterious forms, its wonders to perform. This expresses one side of that." "It's a beautiful song," Pang told Lennon after hearing a playback of the sumptuous, floating track he'd written for Ono. "Every chord sequence seemed to awaken echoes of their previous work together," critic Philip Norman claimed.

Lennon considered 'Bless You', along with '#9 Dream', to be the finest efforts on the album. Allied with the likes of 'Surprise Surprise . . .', these songs demonstrated a return to a more inspired song craftsmanship. "He knew what worked when he heard it," says Cicala. "You know, John wasn't a Bach musician, and when he played the piano his chords might be simple, but the feel? Forget about it! He was incredible. What's more, when he'd go in front of the microphone and start singing, all of a sudden the melody might change. It was amazing."

Held during mid-June and July at the Record Plant, the *Walls And Bridges* sessions were characterised by a marked sense of sobriety on Lennon's part. Having returned to New York in the spring, the wildness and drunken chaos of Los Angeles was eschewed in favour of discipline and soda drinks. "In LA we had to get drunk to keep up with everybody else who's drunk," recalls Cicala.

"We weren't drinking in New York. Maybe we'd go out for a beer. Simple. We realised the LA scene was dangerous for us." Gruen, for one, was intrigued by the metamorphosis he saw in Lennon after he'd dropped the drink. "I woke up one day, and thought, 'What is this? I wanna go home,'" Lennon would later admit in reflection on this turbulent period. "So finally, I sort of stopped drinking. I come back to New York because I wanted to get myself out of LA, and out of the bottle, and then I found myself producing *Walls And Bridges*."

Wisely opting not to repeat the experience of utilising a swathe of A-list studio musicians, Lennon chose to work with a tight, experienced crew of session players for the new album. "We had the greatest musicians in the world, right?" Cicala laughed during his *LENNONYC* interview. Voormann denied that his presence on the sequence of Lennon's seventies albums was based on their old Hamburg friendship. Lennon still enjoyed Klaus' bass playing, just as he still admired the respective abilities of guitarist Jesse Ed Davis, drummer Jim Keltner and pianist Nicky Hopkins, players who had sat in on most (if not all) of Lennon's solo output.

The drummer, who had played on everything since *Imagine* including *Mind Games* and the *Rock 'N' Roll* album, claimed he was simply doing the job that Lennon liked. Keltner recalls Lennon's classic approach to making records was a joy to experience at such close quarters. "He came into the studio with his guitar, or he would sit at the piano. He would sit and sing, and play it, and yell out bits people should pay attention to. He'd very rarely say anything to me or to Klaus, the rhythm section. He'd give a lot of direction to guitar players and to the keyboardists, and he knew his arrangements. He was very specific with his arrangements."

Pianist, organist and string/brass arranger Ken Ascher was also an integral piece of the studio ensemble, conducting what Lennon wittily coined as the 'Philharmonic Orchestrange'. Lennon had initially intended to record the songs in stripped-back fashion, without ornamentation, before deciding to add strings and horn arrangements. Shining as pianist, vocalist and guitarist, Lennon's crew of seasoned session men had developed a relaxed personal chemistry and exciting musical rapport, and would, critic Ashley Kahn correctly noted, "help translate the songs inspired by an eight-month hangover into a coherent musical statement".

Photographer Bob Gruen was fascinated by Lennon's change in temperament. He believes the recording process saw a different approach in attitude and lifestyle. "John was much more focused, and he seemed to have grown up. He was taking life much more seriously." Determined to work hard and be serious about making (or salvaging, according to Gruen) a more accomplished successor to *Mind Games*, Cicala insists the higher calibre of work owed much to the lack of alcoholic indulgence. "It was recorded well. I was straight, John was straight, the musicians were straight. The quality was there because we were all sober, and we had to focus. And we were *really* focused."

"It's a beautiful production," Lennon later told British journalist Ray Coleman of a work which, he enthused, had been completed in typically rapid fashion. One of the keys to this endeavour was the fact that Lennon had led his musicians through two days of rehearsals of new material prior to recording. "It made a colossal difference," Lennon insisted to the same writer. On the third day, Lennon continued to develop and fine-tune the material at hand.

"Everything started going like clockwork," Cicala insists. "We'd do one track a day, one song a day. He was writing in the studio, and the next day we would come in and listen to the previous song that we recorded the day before. We'd love it, and went on to the next song. We'd only do one song a day. So I'd say, in five or six days, we did the basic tracks. And then from there, we did vocals and then we did solo guitars, the way everybody else in the world records," he laughs. In 30 days, Capitol Records had the album. "They wanted the record of *Walls And Bridges* very fast," Cicala recalls.

What worked for Lennon on this album, critic Peter Doggett maintains, was finding a creative space far enough removed from a fraternal, post-Beatle competitiveness with McCartney and the intense relationship he had shared for the past five years with Ono. "I think it's a shame that he didn't take the opportunity to explore his own brand of creative freedom beyond that album."

Most music critics interviewed for this book claim *Walls And Bridges* was a strong, worthy effort, given the context of mid-seventies pop-rock. This was not an album that was ever going to shake the world on a musical or emotional level. While it carried the feel of contemporary popular soul ventures in places, critic Peter Doggett sees it as "a joyous reminder of why we loved John's music, rather than a reason for any new listeners to become converted".

"These are great tracks," Badman also enthuses, "especially '#9 Dream'. It's easily one of his best." Despite his reservations about the album's musical merit and emotional weight, *Walls And Bridges* proved arguably Lennon's most artistically satisfying album since *Imagine*, a work which left *Mind Games* and *Some Time In New York City* rightly in the shade. Sounding ready in places to be more loving on record, Lennon had clearly left the earlier, political rebel-rousing behind him too.

Keltner retains a strong affection for 'What You Got', one of his most treasured songs in the decade's rock canon. "Jesse Ed's guitar sounded great, and John loved it," the drummer recalls of his willingness to find a new percussive sound, with the help of engineer Shelly Yakus. "When I look back, I had no other reason but to do it for John." "Short on poetry," Du Noyer observed of the song in his study of Lennon's work, "but is satisfyingly stuffed with drama."

Having enthused about the pace at which he completed this impressive successor to *Mind Games*, Lennon also revealed something of his keenness to reconsider his past. "I can see The Beatles from a new point of view," he told Ray Coleman. "I was thinking only recently, 'Why haven't I ever considered the good times instead of moaning about what we had to go through?' So, y'see, all that happened when I blew my mouth off was that it was an abscess bursting, except that mine as usual burst in public. When we did a tour as The Beatles, we hated it and loved it. There were great nights and lousy nights. It wasn't all pie and cookies being in The Beatles: there were highs and lows, but the trouble is, people just want big mouth Lennon to shout about the lows . . . I've got perspective now, that's a fact."

One thing which helped him to find this perspective was a long drive across America, with an armload of Beatles cassettes for company in the car, re-acquainting himself with their remarkable body of work. That summer, journalist Chris Charlesworth saw Lennon's affectionate humour for the group for himself at a private party held on New York's Upper East Side. "I remember watching John autograph an Italian Beatles album at this party, and instead of just signing his name, he added dialogue in bubbles coming from each of The Beatles' mouths on the live shot on the front. George's bubble read: 'Anyone fancy a curry after the show?' Paul's read: 'Come on lads, we need to rehearse more.' Ringo's read: 'What song are we playing?' In his bubble John wrote: 'I'm leaving to form my own group.'"

Lennon now appeared to have developed an unlikely fascination for what had happened to him as a Beatle during the sixties. "I've started taking an interest in what went on while I was in that fish tank. It must have been incredible." Having revised his opinion of the group, the weight of their history and reputation seemed to have lifted sufficiently for him to appreciate their artistic value. Lennon had also resolved to enjoy the Beatles legacy.

"A couple of years ago, I might have given the impression I hated it all, but that was then. When I slagged off the Beatle thing in the papers, it was like divorce pangs, and me being me . . . Now we've all got it out, and it's cool, I just wanted to shoot my mouth off to clear it all away." Lennon even admitted that he had begun to accumulate Beatles memorabilia, after Elton John presented him with a set of animation dolls from the *Yellow Submarine* film. He was clearly beginning to adopt a new mindset regarding his past.

CHAPTER EIGHT

Sweet Bird Of Paradox

JOHN had spoken of his experiences as a Beatle during the early seventies soon after participating in Primal Scream therapy, and now disowned many of his bitter outbursts. While he had often denied the plausibility of any opportunity for The Beatles to reunite, Lennon's thoughts now turned, Peter Doggett maintains, to the rapport he'd shared with "the only men who understood what he'd been through".

"Together we would sound exactly the same," Lennon insisted when asked about the musical expectations he might have, "only better, because we're all better now, you know. I'm sure if we ever did anything, it would be in 1976, when the EMI contract runs out. In what form we play together again, I don't know. It's been a physical impossibility [for us all] to be in one place at one time. I couldn't leave here, 'cos I wouldn't get back in. George and Paul have problems coming in – they have to ask permission a few months in advance. The most that's probably been here is three now. It's my immigration and Paul and George's immigration problem that's kept us from even sitting in a room together, although we've done it in different combinations of the four."

But what was the overriding factor during the second half of 1974 which suggested to Lennon that a musical reconciliation with McCartney was a viable idea? Perhaps it was a change in perspective on his Beatle past, his separation from Ono or his new relationship with Pang. Lennon's old partner had decamped to Shop Sound studios in Nashville, Tennessee that summer, attempting to rehearse his newly re-configured band. During what amounted to a working holiday, the group rented a ranch, rode horses and entertained Roy Orbison during McCartney's birthday barbeque that June.

Wings now included former Thunderclap Newman guitarist Jimmy

McCulloch, a talented yet challenging and highly-strung young man with attitude. Taken to growing feisty while inebriated, he reduced Linda to tears after one critical attack on her musicianship. He and McCartney also experienced friction, as Denny Laine reminded Howard Sounes. "I liked Jimmy, but he was a lot of trouble. He and Paul clashed a lot." English drummer Geoff Britton had also been recruited, groomed into a state of readiness ahead of recording a new album later that year.

"When I'm in a place, it's not uncommon for me to want to write about where I am. Being in Nashville, I wanted to use a couple of local guys," McCartney later explained to Paul Gambaccini. "I never worked with a Nashville steel guitar player, and I had to have a bit of material I could bring in and ask them to do. This bloke named Buddy took us out to Printer's Alley, which is a little club district." The group would also be filmed whilst rehearsing in the city's studio, the subsequent live footage being readied for inclusion in Wings' *One Hand Clapping* documentary.

Meanwhile, Lennon put serious consideration, as The Beatles always had done, into the sequencing of *Walls And Bridges*. He was emphatic that the track-listing for the album simply *had* to be right. On a visit to the Record Plant studio while spending time with his father in New York, Lennon's 11-year-old son, Julian, became an impromptu drummer during the contractually obliged recording of the Lee Dorsey classic, 'Ya Ya'. The original, produced by Allen Toussaint, had been recorded in the same New Orleans studio space which McCartney would soon occupy.

This spontaneous-sounding snippet of the *Rock 'N' Roll* track was included as *Walls And Bridges'* closing cut. "If I'd known, I would have played better," Julian informed his father, either unaware the tape was running, or that his spontaneous contribution was intended for inclusion on the final album. "By slowing the track down and over enunciating," critic Jon Gerson insisted, "Lennon makes 'Ya Ya' into a children's song."

Significantly, Pang would be instrumental in encouraging John and Julian to re-establish a stronger father-son relationship. Meanwhile, Lennon played a decidedly off-kilter piano rhythm and offered a perfunctory vocal. "You can hear John say at the beginning of that one: 'Okay, let's do "*Sitting in the la la*" and get rid of that,' which was a joke," Pang recalls. However, the joke's target, Morris Levy, was not amused. The song was one of three 'settlement' tracks recorded from Levy's catalogue as part of a legal agreement.

Walls And Bridges subsequently enjoyed strong commercial recognition during the autumn of 1974. The album boasted a panoply of styles in the mode of *Imagine*, but lacked the lighter sense of cohesion that its classic predecessor could boast. It was, in Pang's estimation, akin to The Beatles' own *White Album*, its mixed emotional palette colouring a strong series of contemplative songs. Most importantly, the album appeared to mark a return to his personal songwriting ethos. This parallel to the Beatles' double LP also included Lennon's re-engagement with his favourite, most mystic numeral.

Yet '#9 Dream''s fluid, string-laden beauty was about as far removed from the dense, tape-loop soundscape of 'Revolution #9' as it was possible to travel. Lennon was later asked about this past and present connection by New York's WNEW DJ, Dennis Elsas. The album's title was a reference to communication, wide enough in scope to broach the varied themes of the assembled songs.

Having joked about the concept, Lennon claimed the phrase was over-heard on a public service announcement during a late-night movie. Having initially assigned the title *Walls And Bridges* to his work-in-progress classic '#9 Dream', he later admitted: "I tried to fit it in anywhere like a jigsaw, but it didn't seem to fit any of the songs, and I hadn't written anything."

Much of his new material clearly went through a rapid series of title changes until just prior to the album's release. He'd later proudly inform *Melody Maker* editor Ray Coleman during a studio playback that *Walls And Bridges* would rectify the critical backlash which greeted *Mind Games*. It did, however, suggest that media opinion was still influencing his musical choices. "As long as I'm going through something, I've got some-thing to say," Lennon would still insist after the album's release. "As long as I'm writing songs, I know where I am."

Despite the album's often unhappy genesis following the directionless 'Lost Weekend', Lennon was relieved to be writing prolifically once again. "Let's say this last year has been an extraordinary year for me per-sonally. And I'm almost amazed that I could get anything out. I had the most peculiar year. I'm just glad that something came out. It's describing the year, in a way, but it's not as sort of schizophrenic as the year really was. I think I got such a shock during that year that the impact hasn't come through. It isn't all on *Walls And Bridges* though. There's a hint of it there. It has to do with age and God knows what else. But only the surface has been touched on *Walls And Bridges*, you know?"

Given the intensive work ethic Lennon had displayed in making the album, there had to be time for humorous distractions. As Side A of *Walls And Bridges* was sent up to the mastering suite, Lennon and engineer Greg Calbi, taught to master by Cicala, decided to play a practical joke on the engineer.

Having convinced him that the album's tape reels had unwound, Cicala found them piled high on the floor as he walked into the studio. Once the furious engineer had driven halfway back home to New Jersey, he received a call from John on his huge car cell phone after coming through the Lincoln Tunnel. "They were laughing like you wouldn't believe, like it was the funniest movie in the world," Cicala recalls. "But they were joking because they weren't drinking." Always able to recognise Lennon's passion for music, Pang recalls John's pleasure and pride in the finished product. *Walls And Bridges* was an album which Lennon would energetically promote.

During the autumn of 1974, this amenable former Beatle could be found in a nostalgic frame of mind. In September, he took the encouraging step of publicly declaring he would like to record again with The Beatles. He would reiterate this a few weeks later, as though time had helped him to realise just how much his Beatle past had meant to him. Band relations, Lennon claimed, were warm in the autumn, with all four members happy with each other. It was a positive portent. In the weeks just after the release of *Walls And Bridges*, congeniality and not tension characterised relations between the former Fab *freres*. At this point, Lennon was unsure how any musical *rapprochement* would transpire. But there was one thing he was sure of: their coming together would have to be a stimulating experience in order to create something new.

There was no intention of resurrecting any past musical image, or revelling in some collective, rose-tinted glow for the sake of the past. That would never have been a Beatles thing. "It would have to be interesting to us musically, otherwise there'd be no point. We don't want to do it just for old times' sake."

Pang, meanwhile, was grateful to have spent so much time with Lennon as she witnessed his interactions with the other Beatles. "They were great guys and he loved them all. They had a love like you wouldn't believe. He cared for his brothers. He was okay with all of them, including Paul. It was great." Following his recent studio session with Starkey, he had found his old drummer friend to be in fine fettle as he completed work on a successor to *Ringo*.

"He's doing his next album, which sounds like it is going to be another winner, and he's in good form," Lennon told radio DJ Mark Parenteau. A few months previously, Lennon and Starkey had taped radio commercials for each other's albums [*Goodnight Vienna* and *Walls And Bridges*], the kind of co-operative gesture that Lennon would never have considered with McCartney or Harrison.

In the same month as *Walls And Bridges'* eventual release, Harrison had launched his new Dark Horse record label. Lennon would joke on air that George's venture may prove the only plausible avenue for releasing new Beatles material. After *Walls And Bridges'* late September US release, Lennon gave an entertaining series of promotional radio and TV interviews. They provided an enlightening and revealing account of Lennon's thoughts on the exciting prospect of a Beatles reconciliation. Lennon did, however, outline the current obstacles preventing any creative reunion.

Walls And Bridges went platinum within around a month of its release, and Lennon soon found himself at the top of the album charts. "Confident about the merits of his work, he threw himself into an exhaustive campaign of self-promotion," Albert Goldman confirmed in his controversial account of Lennon's life. "On radio and in print, he sounded thrilled to be alive and to have experienced and survived his spectacular past."

While Lennon was putting the finishing touches to *Walls And Bridges* at the Record Plant, a Capitol Records employee, a friend of New York DJ Dennis Elsas, made an exciting offer to the young Beatles fan. "'Why don't you try to come to the Record Plant studio on Tuesday night,'" he was urged, "'and I can probably get you into the control room to see John – there's a recording session unfolding, but there's no promise of meeting him.'" Elsas didn't need to be asked twice. "So I get to the studio," he recalled in the *LENNONYC* documentary, "and my first view of John is through the glass. I'm just sort of watching, and they were really in the final stages of putting the odds and ends together for the album . . . I am *this* close to a live Beatle. Oh my God, I can't believe it! I am like every teenager . . . whatever. Inside my head, I'm screaming: 'It's John Lennon – it's The Beatles!'"

Having been introduced to Lennon and shaken the former Beatle's hand, there was little time to talk. In the moments before Elsas left the studio, he mentioned to Pang that he would be happy to have Lennon on his radio show to help promote the new album. Elsas was naturally dubious that anything would materialise, seeing as no Beatle had ever visited the station's Manhattan studio before.

A few days later, Pang called the WNEW building to inform Elsas that John would be happy to come to the station. He took the call while stood in the music library. "And she says: 'When would you like him?' and I'm no fool. I remember I'm on the air Saturdays and Sundays, two 'til six. 'How about Saturday at four?' figuring that that's a good time to have him on. And she says: 'Yeah, I think that will work.'" Elsas was reticent about promoting this event on air, while FM policy was decidedly cool on heavy plugging.

Mid-town Manhattan's WNEW FM, one of the leading rock radio stations, had never been graced by a visit from a Beatle. "They wouldn't have heard him on the radio, because the radio he did in the seventies was with Yoko, and it was more politically based, and with KHJ [with whom Lennon had appeared the previous day] it was more Top 40." Elsas informed his listeners when the show opened at two that he had a special guest that Saturday in late September. Listeners were encouraged, in time-honoured fashion, to stay tuned. John introduced himself on air at 4 p.m. in humorous style: "Surprise, surprise! I am Dennis' surprise."

No photographers or media reporters had awaited Lennon's arrival outside the WNEW building in mid-town Manhattan, located on the corner of 45th Street and Fifth Avenue. "No-one knew he was coming," Elsas laughed. "*We* didn't expect that he would be coming!" Having refrained from announcing Lennon's forthcoming appearance due to his wariness about it ever happening, Elsas was unsure whether Lennon would arrive in a limousine or something more befitting a Liverpudlian working class hero.

"I wouldn't be surprised if he's come in a taxi, because he refers in our interview later to being in a taxi when he talked about his immigration. He turned to the taxi driver and said: 'Take me to the airport,' or whatever the joke is." "The last time I was on the way to Record Plant in a taxi, I heard it on the radio that I had 30 days to get out," Lennon told Elsas. "So being jocular, I said: 'Drive me to the airport, Sam,' and we were laughing about it." "I can't leave here," he later commented more seriously on his situation. "I don't want an award at 60* telling me how wonderful I used

---

* John was being unusually prescient. The music industry's zeal for presenting awards, so widespread in the 21st century, had barely got off the ground in 1974.

to be, but not quite wonderful enough to be allowed to live here right now."

In an echo of his recording ritual when visiting the Record Plant, Lennon entered the building through its freight entrance at around 3.45 p.m. "And when the moment arrives, the freight elevator operator, Jose, had the secure phone line into the studio and says: 'Your guests are here.' I really remember grabbing the album *Chicago II* and playing the 16-minute track and making sure (and hoping) that it doesn't skip. I went down, and there was May, John and his friend Richard [Ross, restauranteur]."

A keen Lennon brought along four of his favourite, semi-obscure 45 records to share with the WNEW audience. Elsas hadn't known what to expect. "May said to me: 'John would like to bring some of his own records,' and I thought: 'What does he mean by bringing some of his own records? Does he mean his own John Lennon albums?' But what he brings is 'Watch Your Step' by Bobby Parker. And John is not only comfortable, but he's actively enjoying participating in the DJ side of it."

With Lennon sat across from him behind the turntable, Elsas admits to being overwhelmed by the experience of being in Lennon's presence. "People ask me: 'What was he *really* like?' And for the two-plus hours I was with him, he was witty, charming, and he was straight. He didn't appear to be on any drugs, or drunk or anything like that, and he was relaxed." Lennon made Elsas comfortable, and the conversation became more serious as talk turned to life in New York and his immigration battle.

As Elsas insists, Lennon's time with May was a very specific moment, encouraging him to undertake a great deal of media work during the period following *Walls And Bridges*' release. "He and May are interested in coming and promoting their forthcoming album. In the first half hour, he's very focused on the album, and we talk about who's on it, who recorded it, the names of the musicians and the Record Plant. And at some point, I guess he made me feel comfortable enough so that I can open the door to all these wonderful little stories."

In increasingly relaxed mood off-mike, the two men casually began to discuss The Beatles. "And it's the great moment for me – even as a young man, I'm a pretty professional guy. At the front of my head, I know that John Lennon is there. I'm such a huge Beatle fan, and want to ask all these questions." Lennon began to discuss 'Revolution #9' after Elsas had given 'Day Tripper' an airing. 'I Am The Walrus' also came under consideration.

Elsas was a childhood fan of The Beatles, a part of the societal change that swept through America in the sixties. The group's break-up, for him, was recent history. As it would transpire, it remained unfinished business for his famous guest too. Elsas was thrilled to see that Lennon was a genuine fan of his old group, having shed the personal and political rebellion of his early seventies, post-Janov output. "During those first years, he was being that angry guy: '*I don't believe in Beatles, I just believe in me.*' I realised that he was still a Beatle fan, and we didn't know how he, or they, felt about each other. But what does everybody *really* want to talk about? Are they getting back together?! People still love talking about it. Up until his death, anyone who had grown up with The Beatles wanted to know whether they would get back together. And up until that point, you at least sense that they are not opposed to it."

After insisting that group relations were presently warm and amicable, Lennon intuited Elsas' follow-up question. "And he knows that I'm about to ask the question, and sort of pre-empts it." "'Are they getting together?' Well, we'd have to be on the Dark Horse label the way things are going!" he laughed in response. "If you say no, it's a negative, they all hate each other. If you say yes, it's *Rolling Crawdaddy Cream* says: 'They're getting together,' or Harry [Nilsson]'s bringing them together, or something. There's always a chance we'd work together, because if we see each other, we tend to fall into that kind of mood. But I can't see us touring or anything like that. We've never discussed it. I could see us making records. Why not?"

There were no definitive plans in place, Lennon admitted, primarily because the four men had not been in a room together for five years due to immigration problems and visa restrictions. "Ringo I've seen a lot of, because he's been over here recording. In the middle of my album, I just took a break and went down and did a track I'd written for Ringo on his new album, and then I went to Caribou and sang 'Lucy In The Sky . . .' with Elton John, and then came back and finished my album off. George I haven't seen, but he is coming over in October to rehearse, so I'll go and see him then."

Any ongoing speculation about a Beatles reunion to date had been just that: speculation. "We're not going to do it until the royalty rates improve, or we're not going to do anything until the contracts are up in '75 , '76 . . ." With his commercially minded Beatle persona to the fore, he admitted they would be naïve to record any new work before 1976. "John says in my interview that he felt comfortable walking around the streets of

New York," Elsas revealed to me from his Westchester, upstate New York holiday home, not far from the Woodstock peace festival site.

The DJ believes the city afforded Lennon the chance to reinvent and rediscover something about himself in the process. Elsas recalls spending two hours in the company of an amenable and open Lennon that day. This was a witty, relaxed and charming man who was proud of his new work. "I think what you hear in retrospect that day was *the guy*. He's there, you can hear it in his voice, and in his jokes. Albert Goldman wrote a pretty cutting biography of Lennon. He never spoke to me – but on the page where he describes my interview with John, I don't know that he uses the word 'sullen', but had he listened to the same interview that everyone tells me that they love so much? In retrospect it flows almost seamlessly, it just comes together." It was a wonderful, unscripted experience for Elsas, who retained the music sheets and interview tapes for posterity.

What Goldman actually wrote in his controversial *Lives Of John Lennon* was not as demeaning as Elsas recalls. He would even congratulate Lennon on "the last great public demonstration of his wit" during this Saturday afternoon performance in Elsas' company. "Unlike his appearances on film or on TV, where the lights, cameras and the voyeuristic focus of the media made him uncomfortable, John's situation in a broadcasting studio – alone, invisible, surrounded by soundproofed walls, and in command of a microphone – was ideal for unpacking his mind and playing his favourite word games. Not only could he spin his treasured records from the good old days, but he could discourse upon them in a manner that often blew everybody's mind."

Goldman would also stress that during this period, Lennon had come to realise how in-demand he was. "That was why all the new superstars were trying to inveigle him into appearing on their shows or cutting tracks on their latest albums." More astutely, he also reasoned that Lennon was experiencing a second, miniature wave of Beatle-esque adulation, focused through the more decadent lens of seventies rock culture.

"When all the evidence of John Lennon's state of being during the latter half of 1974 has been assembled, it becomes clear that he was enjoying a unique period of felicity. For though he had known many spasms of joy and triumph in the course of his astonishing career as a pop star and in the early days of his relationship with Ono, the basic tenor of Lennon's life had been punitive and unhappy."

Meanwhile, one of *Walls And Bridges'* more contentious and meaner-spirited moments, 'Steel And Glass', represented one of the album's stronger, more insidious cuts. A slower-tempo rehearsal with sketched-out lyrics had featured Lennon on acoustic guitar. However, a piano demo of the song, included markedly different lyrics. In September 1974, Lennon admitted the similarity between the song's sinister sax riff and the guitar lick from 'How Do You Sleep?'

"I fall back on myself. I like repeating a word or lick I like from another song." This time Lennon's lyrical snipes were directed at Allen Klein. "Paul and I are just good friends, as they say. We've seen more of each other this year than we have for the last three years. We've spent some time together. Like a novel writer, I use other people as examples. People thought it had something to do with Paul, but it certainly doesn't."

Meanwhile, Pang insists that McCartney's anthemic *Band On The Run* number 'Let Me Roll It' had inspired the *Walls And Bridges* R&B instrumental filler, 'Beef Jerky'. With suitable irony, McCartney's track used a vocal echo more readily associated with his former bandmate. He later denied that the song was a coded message to Lennon.

"It was one of those: 'You're not going to use echo just 'cos John used it?' To tell you the truth, that was more [about] rolling a joint. That was more at the back of my mind than anything else." *Rolling Stone* critic Jon Landau acknowledged the song as a clear tribute to Lennon's hard-hitting and expressive *Plastic Ono Band* era guitar work. "He re-creates it with such precision, inspiration, enthusiasm and good humour," Landau opined, that it seemed McCartney was capable of performing Lennon's music just as well as John.

"But I *know* he can do better than *Walls And Bridges*," McCartney insisted of his former partner's latest work following the album's release. The vitality of The Beatles' legacy, which he rightly regarded with pride, was never far from his mind. "I heard The Beatles' 'I Am The Walrus' today, for instance, and that is what I mean. I reckon '. . . Walrus' is better. It's more adventurous, it's more exciting."

A highlight of their colourfully eclectic Summer of Love *Magical Mystery Tour* soundtrack, '. . . Walrus' remained one of Lennon's favourite tracks due to the thrilling variety of its constituent parts. "I remember John saying to me: 'You know what's at the end of the song, don't you?'" Elsas recalls. "And of course, I didn't know that it was *King Lear*." The quotation from a BBC radio play had, Lennon recounted, been a happy accident. "That was live radio that was tuned to some BBC channel all the time, and it was interesting to mix the whole thing with live radio coming through."

While promoting his new album, Lennon told Detroit DJ Mark Parenteau: "I produced 'I Am The Walrus' at the same speed I produced 'Whatever Gets You Through The Night'. If there's a quality that occasionally gets in the way of my talent, it's that I get bored quick unless it's done quick." Meanwhile, Pang later claimed that the '*Somebody please help me*' lyric found on 'Going Down On Love' was a direct reference to the title track of The Beatles' second film, *Help!*. While a number of subtle Beatles references populated *Walls And Bridges*, Pang's relationship with Lennon now precipitated a gradual change of outlook on his Beatle past.

Producer Jack Douglas, with whom Pang retains a solid friendship more than 30 years later, insists that Lennon clearly had strong feelings for his younger lover. "In that year-and-a-half [of their relationship], you see that the bright side was quite bright, and John had a lot of fun." An ideal candidate for an Ono-approved relationship, Lennon and Pang's partnership was clearly beneficial, something that went further than anyone close to the couple could foresee.

"Yoko thought that it would only last two weeks and that things would go back to normal," Pang would later insist. "But what Yoko didn't count on is that John and I would fall in love with each other."

"I went to May and said: 'Look, I think you have to accompany John to LA. I have things to do here, and I'm not a very good wife, you know.' I didn't say: 'Do it' or anything," Yoko insisted. "It was just to be an assistant, to go there. But I knew what might happen. Because he was never without anybody."

"It was practical to send his secretary May Pang with [John] to look after him [in California]. I suppose Yoko knew it was likely there would be intimacy between the two of them," claimed Elliot Mintz. "And Yoko believed May could handle it. May did not smoke, drink, take drugs, she was not part of any weird Los Angeles orgy scene."

Cicala reluctantly admits that he saw the Lennon-Pang liaison as little more than a fling at the time. "It was my recollection that Yoko asked John to go with May, alone, knowing that that would happen. It was only a short time. May came out to LA, and whatever happened, happened. May came to me, and she was excited that John had got her a new car. I expected to see a 350 Ferrari. It was like an old Firebird." Lennon may have described Pang as his sweet bird of paradox in song, yet she was, given the translation of her Chinese middle name of Fung Yee, a phoenix.

It seemed appropriate, having come into his life with the avowed intent of lifting him out of the darker moments of his 'Lost Weekend'.

She also encouraged thoughts of resurrecting The Beatles and representing hope for the dreamer inside John. Lennon felt free with her, and Pang claimed she took great pleasure in helping him rediscover something of his gregarious and humorous artistic persona. As author Albert Goldman argued, Lennon had found a sense of love and devotion in Pang, an "indefatigable aide" in his work, and someone who was keen to make him happy.

Pang has often spoken with clarity about her views on the enduring Lennon-McCartney friendship. But how influential was her contribution, as Lennon's lover, in helping to create the right circumstances for the two men to reunite? To her credit, Pang was instinctively aware of the benefit Lennon would derive from reconnecting with old musical *compadres* McCartney, Harrison and Starkey. She was also impressed by the knowing sense of humour and sharp wit which had entertained so many people during the last decade. "What he [Lennon] exuded was this personality. He was funny . . . he was *so* funny. Sometimes he didn't mean to be funny, but he *was* funny. He had wit. He was clever. It was the way he did things. He'd make fun of himself. He had charisma."

"John was a nice guy, and he *was* really funny. He was so grounded and perceptive, and I always felt I would learn something," Gruen happily recalls. "In person, John was so much like himself in the movies, and he comes across as he was in life. He was quick with the one-line jokes, he could say things that were confrontational. He would say something of the moment, but then turn it into a pun so that it wasn't offensive."

Voormann, of course, had seen a different side to Lennon since the very earliest days of Beatles popularity. "John was funny, sarcastic, and very uptight at times," Klaus admitted. "But we had a great time."

However, Lennon's complexity and May's relatively callow years meant that the former Beatle's more difficult moments and moods may well have passed undetected by his younger *beau*. Gruen, meanwhile, was certainly surprised to hear news of Lennon's involvement with the attractive young Pang. But Lennon was keen to stress he still maintained a close relationship with his wife, despite living with May. "May did a good job of being John's secretary, which wasn't easy. He never said to me that Yoko kicked him out, more that they discussed it and Yoko asked him to move out." Gruen adds that, on one occasion, Lennon had paid for Pang to take a shopping trip so he could talk to Ono alone. Journalist Ray Connolly was equally surprised at this development. "Yoko rang me one afternoon, and told me that he had gone off with May Pang, which was a bit of a shock. And that was a very strange conversation." Ono and Pang, Keltner observes, were very close at one point in the early seventies. The drummer also argues that May had involved herself in John's life in such a way that not everyone approved of or agreed with. To her credit, Pang always seemed prepared to occupy a junior role in her relationship with John. "May wasn't Yoko, which was important because she didn't carry any late sixties baggage," asserts Doggett. "And she was genuinely positive and supportive towards everything John did. There was no sense, as there might have been with Yoko, that May was suddenly going to say: 'That's all very well, but what about *my* work?' That's not a criticism of Yoko, who had her own artistic agenda."

"Without exception, everybody who knew them as a couple," Philip Norman commented in his Lennon tome, "remembers May as a wholly positive influence at a time when John most needed it: kind, sweet and almost supernaturally unselfish."

"May contrived a quasi-fictional scenario in an attempt to give form to a relationship that was not there," Mintz coolly claimed to the contrary. "From the moment John met Yoko, to the last hour of his life, she was the only woman who shared his love."

One of the first tracks Lennon penned upon returning to New York, 'Surprise, Surprise (Sweet Bird of Paradox)', was written for Pang after they enjoyed their first night of passion in the autumn of 1973, shortly after the completion of *Mind Games*. Devoid of the more overwrought emotional candour found elsewhere on the *Walls And Bridges* album, the song offers affirmation of a new lease of life for its writer and his young muse. "Far from the hell-on-earth 'Lost Weekend' he was supposed to be having, Lennon sounds inspired, happy and relaxed," Chris Ingham surmised.

But as an earthy testament to their physical, loving intimacy, one of the key lines: '*She gets me through this God-awful loneliness*' suggested something more profound, even redemptive about their relationship. Part of the concise electric guitar demo for the song was retained in the final middle eight. A later acoustic demo more closely resembled the re-worked material. When Lennon went in to the Record Plant to tape the new track, sections of the demos were dropped in the studio. The song also features harmony vocals from Elton John, who spent an arduous three-hour session perfecting his part, struggling to emulate Lennon's unique phrasing. 'Sweet Bird Of Paradox' is also the song that Pang keeps closest to her, and one of her fondest memories is of hearing the song for the first time. After John informed her he'd penned a song in her honour, he waited for a suitably private moment before picking up his guitar and singing the song in front of her. Pang was stunned. "I was so floored I never responded. I just sat there smiling and shaking my head while he started singing, *'Just like a willow tree . . .'*" It would be one of the first of Pang's many treasured memories of listening to Lennon play for her, at home and in the studio.

As an artist, Lennon was most comfortable in his own surroundings, and Pang insists that he would have loved to have made music in a studio at his New York home. Pang hasn't needed to continue playing John's music to remind her of the love that they shared. "I know he wrote 'Surprise Surprise . . .' for me," she admitted in a 1997 interview. "That's enough." Lennon had apparently written the song with The Diamonds' 1957 hit 'Little Darlin'' in mind.

Walls And Bridges remains a meaningful record, one which Pang was pleased to have contributed to and partly inspired. Lennon later confided to US journalist Larry Kane that his time with Pang was perhaps the happiest period of his life. As a professional, May was hard working, loyal and a lover of John's music. On a personal level, she was clearly a big stabilising influence on John during arguably his most prolific period as a solo artist. With an increased curiosity about his Beatle past and the intriguing prospect of a group reunion, the beneficial effects their relationship had on him, as a man and musician, were becoming clear.

Pang would argue that Lennon was battling a sense of guilt because he was enjoying so much freedom, creating a sense of longing for what he'd shared with his former Fab colleagues. "I think my biggest influence was that he didn't take that many drugs when he was with me. Instead, we'd go swimming in summer time with his son, Julian. We'd drive out to Long Island, go to the grocery store and do simple things.

"I spent a lot of time with May Pang during the 'Lost Weekend'," Voormann recalled. "She was always very sweet." "The high points were when he was working, or we'd just be at home relaxing," Pang also remembers, "reconnecting with Paul and Linda, Ringo, George and lot of musicians that knew him early on."

Their partnership appeared to both liberate and relax Lennon, facilitating a gradual yet striking rethink. He also appeared to be ambitious and driven. Apparently happy and settled, and having embraced the love of his younger companion, new opportunities seemed to be presenting themselves to Lennon in a hugely beneficial manner. It was down to him to accept these chances. Good things were starting to happen, and Lennon would soon collaborate with contemporary artists who were more than happy to share in his revived artistic glow. It seemed to indicate the wisdom of his decision to stay with Pang, as it became clear that Lennon was more accessible during their year-and-a-half together than in the rest of his solo career.

Fascinated by exploring the feelings that frequently inspired his music, and with sloganeer sermons and political polemics apparently behind him, Lennon had rediscovered a stronger sense of emotional expression. Like McCartney's *Band On The Run*, *Walls And Bridges* represented a reconciliation with the past, building on and re-shaping their Beatle experiences.

"Today, Lennon knows that neither dreams nor their puncturing is the answer," *Rolling Stone*'s Ben Gerson opined. "There is no neat answer." "*Walls And Bridges* happened pretty fast, but then all of John's stuff happened pretty fast. I loved every song on the album," Keltner admits. Not least the timeless '#9 Dream'. "Musically, it was special for a lot of reasons. It was one of those mesmerising songs. It's a reason to be immersed in the music: John's music somehow *sounded* just like John."

One spring morning in New York, John Lennon awoke from a vivid, other-worldly experience. His mind was filled with refracted images, and the language of dreams. Reaching instinctively for his yellow bedside pad and Flair marker pen, he scrawled down a string of esoteric words. Fresh from this beguiling daze, he also noted the subconscious fragments of an intriguing melody. From this account would come one of his most timeless compositions. '#9 Dream' found Lennon surrendering to his higher artistic instincts in one of the most inspired and divine-sounding piece of music he ever created.

John told May that he'd heard two women, presumed to be his lover and his estranged wife, echoing his name. On hearing a song being sung in spirit, Lennon witnessed two female spirits engage in a surreal dance. "One of the women in the dream was actually his Aunt Mimi," Pang claimed during conversation with Radio WBAI in New York in April 2013. "In the dream he had, he heard her voice." Mimi's voice was represented by May in the song, although it would, in turn, later be mistaken for Ono. "He woke up and wrote the whole song, which he literally dreamed up," Pang would later relate. "And it always comes just as he was going to sleep. All these lines came swirling into his head, and he had to force himself back up to write them, or else it's gone by the morning."

Pang clearly admired Lennon's thrilling aptitude for wordplay, taking simple phrases and creating what became great songs. Having been fortunate to observe Lennon writing lyrics on numerous occasions, his inspiring writing technique obviously fascinated her. "He had what you call God-given talent. He was so gifted that he could turn whatever he wrote into a song." Every so often, John stopped to play May what he had written to gauge her reaction. "I would watch him and think: 'These are very simple words, but the way he phrases it is *amazing*.' He was such a quick thinker, and words came so easily to him. He used to doodle and to write down anything – and *everyone* and *everything* inspired him – and these jottings would eventually turn up in his songs."

'#9 Dream''s creative life had begun as 'So Long Ago', its title taken from the song's opening line, before Lennon briefly toyed with the more obscure working title of 'Walls And Bridges'. It didn't fit the song, and would eventually be used to title the accompanying album. Lennon, Pang recalls, was focused, if not 'trance-like' during the song's creative process. Lennon's production, and the song's ethereal sound and mood lulled the listener into his dream. Bathed in its tactile, golden glow, the song recounts a sense of aural and visual bliss. Having ventured down the sidewalk, time and place blurred as Lennon entered a surrealist landscape of shimmering foliage and streams of sound. As a complement to the dreamy vision which partially inspired him, the song's tranquility was pitched somewhere between golden slumber and thrilling higher awareness.

In his dream, Lennon had also heard the strangest of mystical refrains: '*Ah, bowakawa, pousee, pousee . . .*' Defying meaning or translation, the exotic phrase clearly excited him. Uplifting the listener through its airy allure, a chorus of ethereal voices chant this other-worldly refrain during his enraptured trance. This phrase eventually became the song's *falsetto* chorus, and was also sung at the song's coda. Lori Burton, one of Pang's fellow Record Plant studio backing singers (coined the '44th Street Fairies' by Lennon) encouraged John to place a French accent on the final four syllables of this *risqué* phrase. This had followed concern from Capitol promotion man Al Coury's comments about a likely lack of airplay. And it worked, Burton's then-husband, Roy Cicala, recalled. "John listened to us. In fact, he listened to just about everything."

As an eager musical medium, Lennon openly admitted to his receptivity as a channel for the 'music of the spheres', the same music which, he once claimed, surpassed all understanding. The song carries an appropriately cosmic quality. "John was so in tune. You know, a lot of this is youth," Keltner confides. "Everything is a young man's game. When you've reached a prime age, there's a sense of invincibility. It's an unforgettable experience, being in the presence of genius," he enthuses.

As Lennon's poetic *piece de resistance*, critic David Cavanagh claimed the song represented a linguistic rebirth following Lennon's celebrated realism period of the early seventies. To his biographer Philip Norman, '#9 Dream' proved a veritable "hymn to the mystic numeral". "Everything around him seemed to come in nines," Pang reminisced. "It was his lucky number. John was always into the spiritual side of things, including his music."

Lennon would later classify '#9 Dream' as an account of a psychedelic experience, a startling, inspiring verification of his own experiences. "We try and describe the dream to each other," he asserted, "to verify what we know, what we believe to be inside each other." While his lyrics displayed disbelief at the blissful experience, they were tempered by true faith. Lennon also tried to convey a sense of unreality for the listener. Lennon's sentiments ('*What more can I say?*') strove to describe this sense of rapture, and to articulate this speech of the heart. '#9 Dream' was memorably described by David Cavanagh as a "dream song which became a dream in itself, by recounting the dream which inspired it".

Early song lyrics featured an account of his dream imagery, although the chorus had yet to arrive. As memories of an enthralling experience floated through the song, Lennon was revisiting and reconnecting with his past. The song's opening line, '*So long ago . . . was it in a dream?*' from which it took its initial working title, hints at his fonder recollections of the Fab Four. '#9 Dream' also carried what writer Paul Du Noyer claimed sounded like a hushed *maha mantra* blessing for John's old compatriot, George Harrison. If so, the gesture represented an affirmation of their distant bond. In the same way that Lennon would honour Paul by singing 'I Saw Her Standing There' in November onstage in New York, spiritually if not lyrically, '#9 Dream' symbolised the extension of a musical olive branch to Harrison.

Simply put, Lennon loved being in the recording studio. The experience, Pang readily admitted, often took her to another level too. "He was ambitious, and he wanted to make music. If he had the musicians there," she insisted, "he meant business. He's *got* to get the track done." As one of the last tracks to be recorded for his finest solo album since *Imagine*, Lennon re-wrote his own musical rulebook in creating this inspired paean. Having recorded acoustic guitar demos of the song, Lennon then combined a literal and poetic approach in developing the song. Lennon would often give his musicians lyric sheets with corresponding chords for them to play.

"He would be singing the song and then change the lyric, and it just came out naturally," Cicala admits. The song took just 15 minutes' writing time in the studio, with Cicala shouting '*take nine*' each time the tape rolled for a new run-through of this classic-in-waiting. On other occasions, recalled Dennis Ferrante, "he would run the tune down for the band and after about 45 minutes, the band would be ready to put it down. Then we would record any guitar overdubs or other instruments and be ready to put down John's vocal." '#9 Dream''s ethereal air also came from the sumptuous echo and delay on Lennon's vocal. "John's voice was so bright," Jimmy Iovine enthused of Lennon's famous sound, "that it sounded incredible on it."

"He didn't like to hear his voice plain, so I had to put effects in his headphones," claimed Ferrante, "and the more he heard them, the better he sang. And he couldn't sing without it. I mean, if he heard himself in the headphones plain, he would just stop singing. And I'd say: 'Aren't you going to sing?' And he'd say: 'Nope, not until you put that effect on.' I said: 'Oh-*kaay*' and then he'd start singing like a little bird. He'd just sing his heart out. After that, we put on the background vocals and whatever little nuances were needed, like May saying 'John' in the chorus."

"John brought me in to the studio and said: 'I want you to do this part,'" Pang recalls, "and to make it sound really ethereal, he took the lights down so I could get into the mood." As Lennon recalls the audible warmth of soul-wakening music, Pang's hushed voice echoes in and out of earshot, a veritable angel whispering John's name at his side. Drawn into the fray upon hearing '*Somebody call out my name*', this lyric was reversed and reused in the second verse, following the words '*music touching my soul*.' Pang then whispers '*John*' against gentle acoustic and soft-keyed piano accompaniment from Nicky Hopkins.

Paul, Ringo and George with a cut out of the animated John at a press screening for the *Yellow Submarine* movie at the Bowater House Cinema in Knightsbridge, London July 8, 1968. MARK AND COLLEEN HAYWARD/REDFERNS

Yoko, John and Paul at the premier of *Yellow Submarine* at The London Pavilion in Piccadilly Circus on July 17, 1968. Afterwards they attended a celebration party at the Royal Lancaster Hotel where the disco was renamed the Yellow Submarine for the occasion, a name it would retain until someone decided copyright was being infringed. CUMMINGS ARCHIVES/REDFERNS

John and Yoko outside Marylebone Magistrates' Court on October 19, 1968. John was charged with possessing cannabis and obstructing the police. "We'd been in bed," he said. "Yoko ran into the bathroom to get dressed... so they got us for obstruction which was ridiculous because we only wanted to get our clothes on." EVENING STANDARD/GETTY IMAGES

Paul and Linda after their marriage at Marylebone Registry Office, March 12, 1969. A luncheon reception afterwards at the Ritz Hotel was attended by Princess Margaret and Lord Snowdon among others. Paula Boyd, Patti Harrison's sister, handed Margaret a joint in full view of everyone. C. MAHER/DAILY EXPRESS/HULTON ARCHIVE/GETTY IMAGES

John and Yoko, with Apple executive Peter Brown as witness, during their wedding ceremony at Gibraltar on March 20, 1969. They remained on Gibraltar for just 70 minutes before flying back to Paris where they were staying at the Plaza Athenée Hotel.
EVERETT/REX/SHUTTERSTOCK

John and Yoko promote 'Bagism' on Thames Television's *Today* show with host Eamonn Andrews, April 1, 1969. Note the date… BOB AYLOTT/GETTY IMAGES

… of more import was John and Yoko's 'War Is Over' Peace Campaign during December 1969. Here they are with a poster on the steps of the Apple offices in Savile Row. GETTY IMAGES

Paul and Linda with their daughter Mary and Linda's daughter Heather from her earlier marriage to John Melvyn See.
JAMES GARRETT/NY DAILY NEWS ARCHIVE VIA GETTY IMAGES

Paul, sporting a full beard, and Linda arrive at the High Court of Justice on February 19, 1971, to break up the Beatles partnership. GETTY IMAGES

American drummer Jim Keltner, who played on albums by John, George and Ringo during the seventies. GETTY IMAGES

John, with Yoko and Elephants Memory, appearing on the *Mike Douglas Show*, on February 14, 1972. Having taped several songs earlier in the month, John and the group appeared on five consecutive shows between February 14 & 18.
MICHAEL OCHS ARCHIVES/GETTY IMAGES

John, with Yoko and Elephants Memory, on stage at New York's Madison Square Garden during the One To One Concerts, August 30, 1972. JORGEN ANGEL/REDFERNS

John with May Pang, Yoko's assistant, who became his companion during 'The Lost Weekend' period between 1973 and 1974. ART ZELIN/GETTY IMAGES

Paul with Linda, London, 1974. Eyebrows were raised when Mrs McCartney became a member of Wings but Linda faced down the cynics with aplomb thanks to her easy-going nature. MICHAEL PUTLAND/GETTY

Paul fronting his group Wings at the Capitol Theatre in Aberdeen, Scotland, on September 22, 1975, during the UK leg of their Wings Over The World tour. Left to right: Jimmy McCulloch, Denny Laine, Linda and Paul. MICHAEL PUTLAND/GETTY IMAGES

John and Yoko on the streets of New York in 1978. Fatally, John felt safe strolling in the neighbourhood where he and Yoko lived on the West Side. THE LIFE PICTURE COLLECTION/GETTY IMAGES

Keltner, meanwhile, was impressed by the track's memorable drum sound. "I've heard a couple of different versions, but I believe that someone in the control room accidentally unplugged one of the compressors on the drums, and it made a distant sound. I loved it." Lennon, Cicala insists, would often take the feelings from the drummer and the bass player, and use them to help him with his music. Anxious to offer help in order to make the track work, Voormann recalled Lennon's concern about an elusive quality to the song.

"He said: 'Something is missing. I don't like it.' It's always like that. He has the idea, he has the song, and sometimes he says he doesn't know. I said: 'Why don't we do a part in the middle where it gets very dreamy, with no drums going through, just a real break, and you do it real simple and easy?' And he tried it, and he said: 'That's great, that works.' And that's how we got '#9 Dream' done."

After the basic track had been recorded, Pang recalled Lennon encouraging her input into the song's string sound. "Orchestrally, what was I feeling? Did I like it? Were there enough instruments going on?" She then suggested the subtle cello strains be given greater prominence in the mix. Lennon immediately turned to Cicala and urged him to bring them up. Yet Cicala claimed it was the introduction of violins which helped to transform '#9 Dream' into a whole different picture. "If we had to put violins on, that would be an arrangement, the pureness of an arrangement, but not in the rhythm section," he added.

Clavinetist/electric pianist Ken Ascher's sublime string arrangement and orchestration duly enhanced the song's compositional beauty. Its gorgeous, Eden-like melody, meanwhile, resulted from Lennon's reprise of the beautiful string arrangement for Harry Nilsson's *Pussycats* cover of Jimmy Cliff's 'Many Rivers To Cross'. "I thought: 'This is a tune, you know,'" Lennon later insisted, "and it was such a nice melody on the strings." In partial homage to Harrison's idiosyncratic guitar style, the song began with celestial wah-wah slide guitar courtesy of Jesse Ed Davis as timeless strings swept across a serene acoustic backdrop. After the tracks and overdubs were put in place, "we would mix, and the rest," Ferrante recalled, "is what you hear".

'#9 Dream' remains a billowing gem of orchestrated ecstasy. Echoing Lennon's voyage into the dream realm, the song's luminous setting was a place of rich, interior experience. Located in the singer's own heart, critic David Cavanagh insisted it was a place where *every* fan of music had been.

Lennon producer Jack Douglas later echoed the general critical and commercial consensus that it remains one of Lennon's greatest songs. An ambitious, inventive choice of single, it would, appropriately enough, reach number nine in the US charts early in 1975.

Having relocated back to New York with Pang, a gradual transformation occurred in Lennon's perspective on The Beatles' legacy. Lennon subsequently moved away from outright dismissal of a reconciliation, and began to demonstrate a nostalgic fascination and enthusiasm for playing their classic material with his former colleagues. With all four Beatles going through similar changes of heart during the decade, Lennon was more public about his thoughts during frequent interviews of the period.

He insisted that persistent enquiries about a Beatles reunion from taxi-drivers *en route* to the West 44th Street Record Plant studio usually consisted of: "'Are you guys gonna play together again?' In what form we play together again, I don't know . . . it's been *my* immigration and George and Paul's immigration problem that's kept us from even sitting in a room together, although we've done it in different combinations of the four."

During the transitional year of 1974, Paul enjoyed enormous success with *Band On The Run* while John would reach the top of the singles chart with 'Whatever Gets You Through The Night'. Having praised his former partner's work, there was now a feeling that the two men were artistic and commercial equals for the first time in five years. "At other times in the decade," Doggett added, "one or the other of them would have felt they were in an inferior position in commercial terms."

"John never really talked much about Paul," Keltner claims. "I never spent that much time with Paul, so I didn't get to know him well. He was basically in another world."

Ever since the Concert For Bangla Desh triumph in the summer of 1971, George had felt a certain inevitability about venturing back out on the road. It was a feeling which grew, and subsequently led to his challenging autumn 1974 tour to promote the *Dark Horse* album, helping to spotlight Ravi Shankar's music to largely appreciative American audiences in the process. Asked about Harrison's ever-deepening involvement with the wonders of Indian music and his apparent remoteness from contemporary rock'n'roll circles, Lennon agreed that his former bandmate seemed increasingly ostracised. "If you're surrounded by people who aren't rocking, then you just forget what it is. And he *is* so involved in the Eastern trip . . . you know, if you don't listen to the radio, know who the current artists are, the latest records . . . if you switch off from that you don't know what people listen to, which happened to me in England!"

After 'Whatever Gets You Through The Night' had fared moderately in the UK charts, Lennon had felt compelled to request regular record company dispatches of the current Top Ten from home. With the likes of Showaddywaddy, Status Quo, Queen and Alvin Stardust populating the charts at this point, it was a very different proposition from the American scene, and Lennon was shocked at the current penchant for 'glam' rock'n'roll pastiches. "I was just: 'My God, three years!' I had no idea what was going on there. Now I get them to send it over every few months . . ."

When his extensive *Dark Horse* tour commenced, Harrison quietly thought to himself: "What am I doing? It was such a big tour. I felt for three years the presence of this tour in my subconscious, and it's been deep down and slowly bubbling up to the surface and it's like a lot of forces and energies. In a way, I decided to go on tour, I suppose you could say that. But in reality, it was just outside energies and maybe subconscious desires."

Having finally been persuaded by George to join him on tour, the US jaunt featured Keltner in a supportive role. The financial travails surrounding his eventual agreement to play, and his purchase of a new Mercedes ("George said: 'Why don't you take a car instead of the money?'") partly inspired Harrison's subsequent *33 & 1/3* composition 'It's What You Value'. Keltner had decided not to tour anymore, and explained to Harrison that he wouldn't be accepting his invitation.

"George had kept calling me. I kept saying: 'No, I can't make it,'" the drummer recalls, Harrison persisting in his request for Keltner to join the touring team. "If George had toured all the time, he'd have had it down, man," the drummer later told *Uncut*. "He would have known how to pace himself, and he could've gone out in stronger shape. He had a great band, he assembled some great musicians, he broke all the rules in a beautiful way – like having Ravi – and he did really well, except that these were crazy days. Let's be honest, drugs were a problem."

Given the length of time since Harrison had last toured America, he had understandably lost touch with his audience base in the prevailing eight years. Becoming distanced from the early seventies musical scene in the States, he had had little time to familiarise himself with the latest chart competition. He was also unsure about the most favourable locations to include on his touring schedule. George had initially wanted to see North America by train, or even more obscurely, by camper van; a leisurely tour which would allow him time to experience the places in which he would be performing, rather than relive the pressurised and restrictive Beatle touring experience.

"Instead," he would later admit, "it got to the point where I thought: 'I might as well do it in one shot,' and get into the motion and do as many as possible. I didn't have any of that old fear that I thought I might have. If I'd sat back and thought about it, I would have been petrified and would never have done it." Harrison later admitted that on his return to Friar Park, such was his relief at being back on familiar territory that he simply retreated into the gardens of his huge estate.

As far as his interest in reuniting with his former bandmates was concerned, during the *Living In The Material World* and more testing *Dark Horse* period of 1974 his urge to re-group was always minimal, having always been keen on following his own path. "As he said himself, The Beatles started to split in 1964," insists Keith Badman, "and he wanted out at an early stage, so why would he want to return, unless for monetary reasons, which he did later in his career?"

Despite the fact he hadn't seen him since March the previous year, Harrison maintained in October that his relationship with John was currently good. "He's in great shape," he told one reporter. While Lennon had seen almost nothing of (and rarely spoken to) Harrison in the past three years, Starr insisted that the one creative bond that needed remedying was that between Paul and George.

Time had yet to fully reconcile their musical differences. While an undercurrent of musical tension persisted with McCartney, Harrison claimed that things were friendly between him and Paul after meeting in October. "It doesn't mean everybody is going to form a band," he added with caution. "Paul is a fine bass player, but he's a bit overpowering at times. I'd join a band with John Lennon any day, but I couldn't join a band with Paul. That's not personal, but from a musical point of view."

In late November, George discussed Paul in a radio interview, later condoning him for 'ruining' him as a guitarist. "I'd rather have Willie Weeks on bass than Paul McCartney . . . having played with other musicians, I don't think The Beatles were that good . . ."

Having survived press criticism from Lennon, McCartney took

Harrison's comments with good grace. "I think the others are great. I'd always stick up for them. I don't agree with George. I don't think The Beatles weren't any good. I think they were *great*." Yet a contrary Harrison was ready, so he claimed in early December, for The Beatles to boldly knock down the barriers obstructing a reunion. The following week in Washington, a characteristic note of caution re-appeared when Harrison insisted that he was having more fun with his current band of musicians. "George is entitled to say that," Lennon observed early the following year, "and he'll probably change his mind. We can all change our minds. I don't take any of my statements or any of their statements as the last word on whether we will. And if we do, the newspapers will learn about it after the fact. If we're gonna play, we're just gonna play."

Lennon, Pang remembers, had begun feeling good during late 1974, a point adequately proved by his numerous interviews and TV appearances during the period. An appropriate *impasse* in his ongoing relationship with McCartney had also been reached. It seemed the timing was certainly right for a reunion. The Beatles' former press agent, Tony Barrow, later sensed that the tantalising prospect of reuniting with McCartney had remained in Lennon's mind, a man with whom he shared so much history.

"I don't think either party was against it happening," Barrow later stated. "They'd had their petty quarrels. But the relationship between Lennon and McCartney was like brothers." As a fraternal bond and defining friendship, time had clearly begun to heal the wounds during a period of reconciliation. In early October, Lennon enjoyed a friendly yet frank interview with WABC host Howard Cosell. Reflecting upon the Beatlemania phenomenon, he also discussed the old 'divorce pang' feelings over the group and his relations with George, Paul and Ringo.

"It was mainly fear – we were uptight with each other. We liked working together. We are good friends, we're quite happy. We spent time over a bottle of wine reminiscing. We're all doing well with our records. We were leaning on each other for a long time." Invitingly, he also stressed that a reunion was now quite possible. "Whether we do live performances is another matter. It's quite feasible we might make records together."

While admitting he had spent little time with Harrison in the preceding, post-*Imagine* years, he was looking forward to reconvening ahead of Harrison's *Dark Horse* tour. Intriguingly, he also highlighted the fact it had been five years since he'd worked with McCartney. For the first time,

Lennon was now seriously contemplating a reunion. "We get on fine," Lennon told the press in October after turning 34 and celebrating his birthday in an exclusive New York club.

"When we meet, there's no tension between us. You can tell by the charts how well we're doing professionally. Like anyone, they have their ups and downs. We all had our little pains when we split up, and that was probably basically down to fear. However much we wanted to be independent, it's quite hard to be independent after ten years of being locked in each other's arms as it were. It was quite an experience for all of us, but I think we've all got over that. We're gonna be friends for the rest of our lives."

Lennon had spent more time with Starkey, he told Jim Ladd, than any other Beatle in the last two years due to his regular visits to the States. And while he considered the prospect of playing live again, the notion of performing for free may have been an idealistic sentiment. "As long as I'm having fun, I don't care what it is or what it's for. It's amazing, but my biggest kick is still making music. For the last six months, say, my biggest buzz is still writing those songs, and to say what I want to say, express whatever it is, and recording them. I was 34 yesterday. I'm too old to be doing this, and then I think, 'That's dumb.'"

Artists, Lennon explained to Ladd, are a mirror of society, sitting back, observing events and commenting on them. It was, he stressed, an important role, and was something that artists should not be afraid to admit. While Lennon was wary of accusations of naïveté whenever his peace 'crusade' was highlighted during this more ostentatious decade, he reiterated his ongoing belief in his hopes for peace.

"I believe that we get whatever we project, and somehow I believe that. Projecting love and peace: that's what I want, so when I project it, we'll get it. If there's any change to be made, it has as much to do with attitude and projection of thought as it does to change. What is it we're talking about? Social order where everyone is happy? What are we looking for? Perhaps the best thing is looking for less pain. I don't know, it's so hard. People say: 'You sang about peace, John, but we never got it.' But what would have happened if we *hadn't* said that all together?"

Lennon still saw himself singing songs that reflected the feelings of the ordinary man, keeping a beacon lit for the next generation. During the rest of these post-birthday party musings, he defended much of his earlier fascination and involvement with Maharishi Mahesh Yogi and Primal

Therapy. He was also aware of the public's reaction to his changeable attitude towards such movements.

"It was all helpful, surprisingly enough, although I understand it when people say: 'One minute, he was with Maharishi, then he's doing that, then that.' Meditation and Primal Therapy helped me in the period they were there, and they're still there, but I don't sit around meditating each morning. I use the techniques I learnt in Primal Therapy to get in touch with my feelings if I'm getting choked up. It's every man to his own trip."

CHAPTER NINE

Statute Of Liberty

TWO weeks later, around October 23, McCartney could be found in New York ahead of his latest press conference. Harrison, meanwhile, was preparing for his own media call on the West Coast at the Beverly Hilton in California to promote his lengthy American concert programme. "I understand The Beatles, in many ways, did nice things and it's appreciated that people still like them," George insisted, aware of their role in filling a space for people in the sixties. It was one which the public had increasingly begun to miss. Lennon certainly didn't envy the fact that Harrison was about to undertake such an extensive nationwide tour during the remainder of the year.

John, meanwhile, had returned to the studio, entering the Record Plant for a week to complete the *Rock 'N' Roll* project. Its eventual cover had an intriguing origin. May Pang had attended the inaugural Beatlefest convention in mid-September. Event organiser Mark Lapidos had consulted Lennon in person about organising such an event after the two men met in Central Park that summer. "I decided to do something about it. He [John] really liked the idea, and put me in touch with people who might be able to help. John nearly even came to the first one to pick the winner of the charity raffle and see who won his old guitar."

Lennon and McCartney both supplied guitars for the event, while Ringo sent signed drumsticks. The celebration was staged at New York's Commodore Hotel, and false rumours suggested that Lennon had made an appearance. Pang had been sent on John's behalf to buy up any intriguing memorabilia on sale. "*I* can't go, so go and check it out," he encouraged her. "I think it's great . . . they must be the people who buy the re-packages, because some of them are only 14 or 16. I mean, it's good for business, isn't it? And if we ever did anything together, there they are, waiting. It's nice to know."

Melody Maker journalist Chris Charlesworth was also at the convention, and when he met Pang, she asked his advice on what she should purchase. "I knew that John was keen to collect Beatles bootlegs but since I didn't know what he already had, I wasn't sure what to recommend," he says. "But I reasoned that John wouldn't mind having more than one copy of a bootleg, so she invested in several that I thought John might like."

A year earlier, Lennon had waxed lyrical over a bootleg of the group's Decca audition in Charlesworth's company. He was, it seems, an avid collector. "It's beautiful. There's us singing 'To Know Her Is To Love Her' and a whole pile of tracks, mostly other people's but some of our own. I got copies made from this Decca audition and sent it to them all [the bootleggers]! I wouldn't mind actually releasing it."

More importantly, Pang had also purchased some original pictures of The Beatles in Hamburg which had been taken in 1960 by photographer Jurgen Vollmer, who was also present at the convention. Pang called Lennon from the Commodore with news of meeting his old friend, and was promptly invited over to their apartment. "John was so happy to see him, and vice versa. We got a print of that classic photo of John to use on the [*Rock 'N' Roll* album] cover and Jurgen was thrilled."

The iconic black-and-white cover photo in question featured Lennon stood leaning in a Hamburg doorway underneath a superimposed luminous sign. Three young Beatles, in the shape of Paul, George and art school bassist Stuart Sutcliffe, were seen blurrily trooping past their group's leader. "The art director at Capitol came up with that after they got Jurgen's photo, and John told them what he wanted," Pang remembers. "That photo really represented the time, the songs, and what the album was about."

Late October is a time for ambitious new ventures. Just weeks before Lennon makes his fabled appearance at Madison Square Garden with Elton John, heavy morning traffic jams a bustling 60th Street, located between Fifth and Madison Avenues in New York. John and May are taxi-bound, *en route* to fulfilling a business appointment before getting stuck in the horn-honking congestion of the Big Apple. Lennon had earlier attempted to reach McCartney in order to arrange dinner for the evening. However, Paul had already left his hotel.

"It was really quite funny," remembers fellow passenger Pang, who was about to celebrate her 31st birthday. "John goes: 'Oh my God.' And he looks in the cab next to him, and who's in the cab? Paul and Linda! And he rolls down the window and he's yelling: 'Hey, Paul! We tried to get you this morning.' Paul says: 'We're on our way to see Lee,' his father-in-law. And John goes: 'Yeah, we're on our way to Capitol.' Paul goes: 'Maybe we'll have dinner later.'"

As the two taxis start to move once the traffic begins to flow, Paul and John attempt to keep their conversation going, sticking their heads out the window as they try to make arrangements for later that evening. It is a comical incident and a poignant one. This happened to be one of the last times they'd see each other before Lennon became a father for the second time the following autumn.

Friend Bob Gruen was on hand at the end of the month to take what became one of the most iconic photos of Lennon in New York: flicking a two-fingered peace sign in front of the great Statue Of Liberty monument on Ellis Island. "He enjoyed having his picture taken everywhere. I was kind of proud that I did suggest going to the Statue Of Liberty," recalls Gruen, "which was dramatised during his deportation case when they were trying to throw him out. The Statue Of Liberty was a great symbol of the fact that we should be welcoming artists like John, and I was very happy that he wanted to do that. He'd never really suggested places to photograph him. I'd mainly photograph him at the recording studio or at home."

The following day, Lennon told UK journalist John Blake that he was keen for his former bandmates to record together again. Inevitably, with growing hopes and new creative ambitions for some form of Beatles reunion, their past legacy was never far from view. "The Beatles nostalgia and 'getting-back-together' bit goes on as much here as it does there [England], maybe more . . . are you kidding? I do a lot of radio when I have an album out – and all the people who call up want to know when . . . from Minnesota to Los Angeles to New York . . . to the hippest and coolest, they want to know when and if and what it's gonna be like."

Days after recording a radio commercial for Ringo's new album, Lennon and Pang attended the premiere of the *Sergeant Pepper* stage show at New York's Beacon Theatre in mid-November. "At the *Sergeant Pepper* opening it was announced: 'He's going to be there,' so it was Beatlemania going on," Lennon recalled with both shock and surprise. "I got a fright because I really didn't know what I was letting myself in for. I got the *deja vu*, as they say, because it was *Hard Day's Night*. But that's because it had been manufactured, and it was *Sergeant Pepper* and they probably expected all four."

This hysteria over a Beatle appearing in town seemed to both amuse and concern him. Outside the same theatre the following day, Lennon was filmed for what became the 'Whatever Gets You Through The Night' video, pointing towards a musical poster bearing the legend of Lennon & McCartney. Another shot found him posing with a fan, clutching a street sign for 'Sergeant Pepper Way'.

There could be no doubt: Lennon had swung into a new groove and was gaining fresh impetus from the sudden sense of career revival. By mid-November, and for the first time since he had left The Beatles, John stood at the top of the charts. *Walls And Bridges* and its first single, 'Whatever Gets You Through The Night' had both reached number one.

Again, Lennon was photographed during this dynamic period of commercial activity, alongside a copy of the *Billboard* Hot 100. "We made it!" he wrote in a note to Pang at the time. 'Whatever Gets You Through The Night' had been the last composition written for the *Walls And Bridges* album. In his musical mindset, Lennon heard a derivation on the contemporary chart hit, 'Rock Your Baby'.

Lennon had derived the title phrase from late-night TV evangelist Reverend Ike's show whilst channel-surfing. His muse was suitably awakened as he looked for new material to complete the record. Prone to jotting down conversations or intriguing phrases, Lennon placed no limits on what would inspire his songwriting. "John loved it and said: 'I've got to write it down, or I'll forget it,'" Pang recalls. "He always kept a pad and pen by the bed. That was the beginning of 'Whatever Gets You Through The Night'."

Gruen would often encounter Lennon, a rabid TV enthusiast, sat in the bedroom while reading, being interviewed or entertaining friends, a television on constantly as a background accompaniment to his daily life. "The TV was just on. He loved his Monty Python, he had it flickering all the time. I didn't like it. *He* liked it."

"I love the millions of radio stations and television channels and the piped TV movies I can get and things like that which you can't get in England," he'd told *Melody Maker* the previous year. "And they talk an American version of English on TV, and it goes on all night. But beyond that, there's not much difference."

Yet 'Whatever Gets You Through The Night' was not a song that

Lennon would be keen to play live, he told Detroit radio in late September. Having admitted that he was now enjoying the music-making process again, he seemed more anxious to return to the studio than hit the stage. 'Whatever Gets You Through The Night' would feature harmony vocal and piano accompaniment from Elton John, who'd visited the studio with his Apple label manager, Tony King.

The two men had first met in October during the *Rock 'N' Roll* sessions in LA, and Lennon admired his versatility as a musician and writer. Lennon had been cogitating on how to embellish the near-completed track when his friend promptly arrived. "I was fiddling about one night and Elton John walked in – you know, we're all good friends – and the next minute Elton said: 'Say, can I put a bit of piano on that?' I said: 'Sure, love it!' He zapped in. I was amazed at his ability: I knew him, but I'd never seen him play. I was pleasantly surprised how he could get in on such a loose track. A fine musician, great piano player. I was surprised at the way he could add to it and keep up with the rhythm changes – obviously, 'cos it doesn't keep the same rhythm . . . And then he sang with me. We had a great time."

While Elton's presence in the studio was a great morale-booster for Lennon, he also played his part in helping John secure his only chart-topping single of his seventies career. Elton's manager, John Reed, subsequently complained to Roy Cicala about his client's diminished presence after their harmony had been recorded around the same mike. "I said: 'Well, who's the main artist here?'" Cicala remembers. "He said: 'John,' and I said: 'Right. I know Elton is the artist, too, but if we bring that piano up, that's all you're going to hear on the radio.' He wasn't happy, but the rest is history. The record was a hit and you could hear Elton very well on the radio."

Urged to release the song after taking a consensus of opinion on the album's most suitable single fodder, 'Whatever Gets You Through The Night' was, despite Lennon's assessment of its 'wild and rough' appeal, destined to be a hit single. Via a mutual friend, Elton also managed to glean a tentative promise from Lennon that if the song reached the top of the US charts, he would join him onstage at Madison Square Garden as part of his next US tour. With the strong instinct that the song would never reach number one, Lennon agreed. When it did, he nobly stayed true to his pledge and nervously agreed to play.

"I don't know if there were rumours," Gruen confided to me about

Lennon's appearance at the Garden, "but it was kind of a surprise," he admitted. "It was *certainly* a surprise to me when I found out in the afternoon."

"I didn't want to come on like Dean Martin, doing my classic hits. I wanted to have some fun and play some rock'n'roll," Lennon admitted. He performed his new hit song, along with a rendition of Elton's version of 'Lucy In The Sky With Diamonds' (to which Lennon had contributed studio vocals and guitar) and 'I Saw Her Standing There' on Thanksgiving Night, November 28. "He [Elton] suggested 'I Saw Her Standing There' and I thought 'Great', because I never sang the original of that. Paul sang it and I did the harmony."

Lennon's famous quip from the stage paid tribute to his "old, estranged fiancé" during an electrifying occasion. "I'm not against live performances, but I haven't got a group and I haven't put a stage show together. I'm just not keen on it right now, but I may change my mind."

Gruen will never forget the joyous roar of approval and lightning-like blast of energy which greeted Lennon's arrival onstage that night. "But for the audience, when John came out onstage, they just went wild. Elton John is a very exciting performer and the show was fantastic. When John came out, it just went over the top. The crowd were cheering and John sang onstage with Elton, and he was really smiling."

Despite his nerves, Lennon had fun with his friend onstage, later describing the night as a heady experience. "It was just a weird feeling being up there alone. But I knew Elton, and I knew the band, and it was just a one-off thing." "John would never make another stage appearance," biographer Philip Norman noted, "but in this final one he never felt more loved."

Lennon would later joke with Bob Harris that being onstage wasn't something he'd like to do for a living. Performing, he candidly admitted, was not his greatest thrill as he approached his mid-thirties. "I might do odd TV, or TV specials where I can control the thing . . . like in the studio. See, I like to see it. I like to have something afterwards. After the concert you don't get anything – you either get cash or a headache." Having sustained arguably the most prolific period of his solo career to date, Lennon had renewed old acquaintances, was relevant again in an artistic and commercial sense, and had rediscovered a sense of musical expression that went beyond sloganeering or emotional cleansing.

Having spent the weekend with Starkey a week or so after the Garden show, Lennon promised to plug his new album. He even started to resemble a '68 vintage Beatle once again. When he was asked about hopes of a live reformation in early December on American TV, he surveyed the imperial spectacle of a crowded LA Coliseum, a sight which he declared "made rock concerts look like tea parties", while pondering its merits. "You never know, you never know . . . if it looked like this," Lennon pointed to the vast crowd, "it might be worth doing, right?!" He also joked about being subjected to a rendition of 'Yesterday' on arriving at the LA venue. He clearly hoped that he wouldn't be faced with continual reminders that McCartney had written such an instantly familiar song.

Any Beatles reunion, it seemed, would be predicated on the need for all four men to want to play together at the same time. Having initially rejected any thoughts of a Beatles reconciliation before softening his stance during 1974, Lennon was now enthusiastic about the more enduring prospect of a new Beatles recording session. As Harrison insisted in 1976, they wouldn't be reuniting in order to make money, and would need to want to be together as people, as friends, and have a need to want to make music. Then, he asserted, the rest would fall into place. Lennon had met comedian Jonathan Winters that same night, and future president Ronald Reagan was also seen in his company, explaining the finer subtleties of American football.

George experienced his own summit meeting after being invited to the White House on December 13 to meet President Gerald Ford, who had been handed a job which, Harrison sensed, he didn't particularly cherish. "I could look him in the eye, and I felt that he was a decent human being, a really good guy, and it gave me hope for America and for the world, because the world is influenced a lot by America. America has such influence on the rest of the world."

Before offering his trademark peace salute in front of the Statue Of Liberty, Lennon had voiced similar sentiments about the positive potential of his adopted homeland just weeks earlier. "I think if there's any hope in the world, America is it. It has the energy and everything else, and that's why I want to be here. I feel comfortable, and I feel at home here. America is what I was brought up on, and it feels natural for me to be here. The music is international, and it sounds like a cliché, but it's true."

Lennon also claimed the New York public offered spiritual support too. With an abiding sense of keen observance, Harrison was also inspired by the raising of people's consciousness in the States since the sixties. He was amazed at the incredible changes he saw across Texas, for instance, after playing venues in Fort Worth and Houston. "It's like it was four or five years ago in San Francisco or Los Angeles. The feel of the people, and the way they look, and the way they act. It's great." Harrison was also reintroduced to Ford's son Jack, who he'd met backstage during the intermission of his Salt Lake City show on November 16, the very day on which Lennon topped the *Billboard* charts. "Somebody said: 'President Ford's son is here. Do you want to meet him?' I said: 'Sure, sure. I'll meet anybody!' He doesn't have to be the President's son."

Having been pictured in front of the White House alongside his father, Harry, sitar guru Ravi Shankar and acclaimed organ/pianist Billy Preston, Harrison told the assembled press about his forthcoming tour-closing plans once he'd flown to New York the following day. "The next move will be Madison Square Garden, then I'll go back to the [Plaza] hotel. Then it'll be Madison Square Garden *again*. After that? I don't know . . ."

Harrison and Lennon's rapport, meanwhile, was being rebuilt after a period of estrangement. With Lennon ensconced in America, Harrison's visa problems had restricted his Stateside visits prior to his solo US tour in the autumn. Looking forward to seeing Harrison during the course of his *Dark Horse* tour, Lennon had considered meeting him during rehearsals on the West Coast. "I don't think he'd be too much fun before he goes on tour. And he's going to be wound up. He's the first one of us out on the road."

Dealing with the media circus, autograph-hungry fans and pulling a band together in time to go out on the road would not, his former bandmate noted, be easy. "It's not like having a band and saying: 'Okay, let's go', and calling Bill Graham and being ready to go." Lennon also sounded far from enthusiastic about participating in George's lengthy nationwide sojourn during a guarded interview in October. "I'll just read about it in the papers, and hope it goes well. I'm sure it will, you know."

I asked Beatles chronicler Keith Badman whether Harrison's experience of the critical reaction to his solo American tour may have encouraged a more benevolent frame of mind regarding a Beatles reconciliation. "Quite the opposite," he said. "I think it reminded him how much he hated being asked about the past, and his audience's need for him to relive it. If it had been a storming success, I think he would have felt much easier about working with the other Beatles."

Despite Lennon's comments, their sense of distance and the lack of communication, a special, unspoken bond had persisted between the two men. Lennon later claimed that Harrison had less respect for himself than John did. Perhaps Lennon's affection for Harrison was, like that for Paul, something he could never voice. Yet Harrison could just as easily cherish Lennon as chastise him. In late October, Harrison insisted he'd have no hesitation in joining a group which included Lennon in its ranks, a clear validation of their enduring musical and fraternal bond. "George and John were close," Pang insisted of a friendship which had survived public and private tensions. "They were brothers. There was no animosity." She also recognised the extraordinary bond which George later acknowledged in 'All Those Years Ago'. "I finally saw how much George really looked up to John . . . that's what I was trying to explain to people."

Years after the event, Harrison would later claim The Beatles' dissolution had been one of physical separation rather than spiritual severance. George had insisted that he'd enjoyed an instinctive understanding of what John had wanted (or was doing) when his thoughts had turned to peace. Since their perception-enhancing LSD experiences of the mid-sixties, the two men had enjoyed an increased sense of fraternity. An unspoken kinship and sense of spiritual solidarity duly developed between these two friends and musicians.

Their relationship would, for a time, be strengthened through their meditative practices. "Just by the look in his eyes I felt we were connected," Harrison opined. Their intriguing bond was strengthened during a shared journey of inner realisation towards higher consciousness. "John and I spent a lot of time together from then on," Harrison would later recall, "and I felt closer to him than all the others. I understood him, and I believe our thoughts were much more in line with each other."

After spending years in their company in the studio, I asked Keltner about the differences between a post-Fab Harrison and Lennon session. For the drummer, it was the parallels between both men's music-making approach that seemed more important. "They were both able to sit there with a group of musicians and play and sing them their songs beautifully. They played their instruments superbly, and they could both convince you. You would go in, and you would hear the song right away.

"To hear a song, and have it hit you with the impact that's needed for your total involvement, that makes all the difference. All the great ones that I've ever worked with have been like that. And if you can do that, you stand a chance of making a great record. Every sense is working at a peak, and that's the way it was with John and George. I was with them at that moment in their lives, when they were unstoppable." "He [John] got such a high from playing," Pang recalls of the period, "that I loved watching him work."

Lennon recalled that he and Harrison had attempted to communicate at the New York Plaza Hotel between December 14 and 20 before George's tour-closing dates at Nassau Coliseum and Madison Square Garden. "I hung around the Plaza for a few days," he admitted, "but it was hard." Harrison and new girlfriend Olivia Arias met Lennon and Pang directly after disembarking their plane from Washington DC on December 14. A decade on from The Beatles' first arrival in the States, Harrison was reconciled with Lennon at the same hotel which hosted them on their historic visit in 1964.

Like Keith Moon, Harrison was pleased that Lennon was with Pang, and told them so that night. "He definitely spoke what was on his mind," May would later remember. "I hold a special place in my heart for George."

Harrison then invited Lennon and Pang to the evening show of his Coliseum concert in Long Island the following day, December 15. "The show I saw was a good tight show. The band was great," Lennon later recalled. "George's voice was shot, but the atmosphere was good, and the crowd was great. That night the band really cooked. I saw the one without Ravi [Shankar] because he had had a heart attack. My personal opinion was that even though I know what George was trying to do, I don't think it worked with Ravi . . . I mean, I'm no one to say what works and what doesn't work really, but my personal opinion was that he would have been better without." Harrison later visited Lennon at the Dakota in the mid-to-late-seventies, no doubt encouraged to see hundreds of Indian albums stored in his record collection.

In the face of mounting media criticism directed towards Harrison's touring enterprise, Lennon insisted: "I want to see George do George. I'm with the kids . . . whether it's George Beatle, or George Ex-Beatle." Despite playing 'While My Guitar Gently Weeps', 'Something' and 'In My Life', Harrison clearly didn't want his tour to turn into a Beatles nostalgia experience. "I respect George, but I think he made a mistake on the tour," Lennon observed. "From what I read and heard, one of the basic mistakes seemed to be that people wanted to hear old stuff. George wasn't prepared to do that and I understand him." John had planned to see George in

October when he arrived in the States for tour rehearsals, but he had to wait until December, when the *Dark Horse* tour neared its *dénouement*, before they were reconciled.

Having socialised with Harrison at the Plaza and watched him perform the following evening, Lennon was buoyed by the Beatle-flavoured spirit of the moment. As adept as ever at publicity, Lennon briefly promoted his *Walls And Bridges* album and plugged the release of new single '#9 Dream' in front of the NBC TV cameras on December 16. More importantly, John publicly stated his intention of working with Harrison later that week. When asked by the host what this possible collaboration may consist of, Lennon explained that George was playing two tour-closing performances at the prestigious Madison Square Garden. "We might have a laugh," he grinned into the camera. "It's the last night of his tour." Significantly, he also stressed that the two men were still good friends. A sense of *esprit de corps* was pervasive as 1974 drew to a close.

With no little sense of fraternal pride, Lennon drew genuine satisfaction from the former Fabs' individual achievements. Harrison, McCartney and Starkey could all boast current chart entries with their respective *Dark Horse, Band On The Run* and *Goodnight Vienna* albums for the first time since The Beatles' split. "I'm pleased everybody is doing well, and I'm glad Ringo has got a good niche," John enthused. "I'm always going to look after Ringo and make sure he wants for nothing as long as he lives."

"I was a big fan of John's. I always felt he had the biggest heart," Starr would later insist. "He wasn't the cynic people thought. He had the biggest heart and he was the fastest." But what about Lennon's former partner? "I often worry about George and Ringo, but never Paul," John continued. "Why do I need to worry about him for? I know Paul's going to be okay. He's so *together*."

When asked if the celebrated 'feud' with McCartney had been blown out of proportion since the early seventies, Lennon confirmed that any antagonism was a thing of the past. "The Beatles had a divorce, and Paul and I were always out front, and so our celebrated feud was 'Lennon-McCartney'. We wrote the songs, it was bigger." Whether or not fans read in print how much they appeared to hate each other, it was, Pang assured the press, only business tensions. This was not a personal vendetta.

In the spirit of the moment, Lennon appeared keen to adopt a more conciliatory tone. "We were actually probably very nervous about suddenly being on our own. Although we all wanted to get away from each other after being in a room together for 10 years, you know?" Any feelings of antagonism had now dissipated, and the four men were closer than they'd been since 1968. At this point, aside from Harrison and McCartney's ongoing musical differences, it seemed that their intentions and personal relations began to galvanise the four men towards something new.

"As a sixties myth, The Beatles would long outlive its too human *dramatis personae* but, in the mid-seventies," claims Allan Clayson, "whether these four mortals as individuals sold records or not did not yet depend upon commercial viability." Any mid-seventies Beatle reunion was predicated on the need for all four men to want to make music and to play together at the same time. "For us to do that, we'd have to do more than just resurrect what went on in the sixties," Lennon emphasised. "Whatever format would have to be interesting to us musically, otherwise there'd be no point. We wouldn't want to do it just for old times' sake."

The Beatles' career retrospective film, *The Long And Winding Road* and its years of accumulated footage also came up for discussion. Lennon mused that The Beatles still existed, but didn't work together. The following week, he joked while in Harrison's company that it was still near impossible for the four members to convene in the same room. Telephone discussions or newspaper commentary seemed the only feasible forum for discussion.

Yet a real love still existed between them. "It was the last time," Pang later recalled of this Beatle-friendly period, "he [John] spent any quality time with his musical brothers."

Meanwhile, Harrison later claimed he could still detect an unspoken link with Lennon during their final meetings in New York, one of which occurred just four days after Lennon's televised declaration of support for his old bandmate.

In Lennon's eyes, a clearly tour-weary Harrison seemed a little erratic following the demands of his *Dark Horse* sojourn. The fact that they hadn't met for some time due to Lennon's ongoing residence in New York hadn't helped matters. John had seen little of George since they had worked so well on *Imagine* ahead of Harrison's triumph in New York in the summer of 1971. While attempting to communicate properly with each other for the first time in three years at the Plaza, Lennon insisted that business matters had always interfered with personal pleasure, partly due to their reliance on lawyers to mediate their messages. Their sense of distance was compounded further by the familiarity John enjoyed with Paul in New York and with Ringo in LA as 1974 had unfolded.

While Starr had refused to travel to New York for fear of receiving a deposition from Klein, Madison Square Garden was rumoured to be staked out with men waiting to deliver subpoenas to Harrison. According to Lennon, their former manager was chasing George across New York, claiming that Harrison was busy running down back elevators to evade Klein's representatives. Even Martin Scorsese's acclaimed film biopic included footage of Harrison scampering down flights of the Plaza's stairs. It would certainly prove a hectic, emotional day on December 19.

Not only was there the signing of the defining Apple agreement to contend with, but George attended the NBC TV studios to record a version of 'Dark Horse' before his opening performance at the Garden. Lennon's attempts at reconciliation seemed to involve making amends for his absence as a friend since moving to America. After the Nassau concert, Lennon reassured Harrison that if he needed his help, he'd come and work with him. "At one point," Pang remembers, "he was going to get onstage and play with George, to help his mate since the tour was not going so well."

In Pang's account of Lennon and Harrison's mid-December meeting in *Loving John*, she claimed her partner had tried to be accommodating and generous towards his old friend. In her portrayal, George was attempting to keep his long-supressed resentment and hostility at bay. "A long hour went by, filled with off-and-on talk about the tour," she wrote. "Then John finally hinted that he would be willing to play with George when he appeared at Madison Square Garden. 'Well, maybe I can come and help ya,' he said. 'That'd be nice.'"

Harrison and Lennon tenuously agreed that John would join George onstage later in the evening during his performance at the Garden, despite John's nerves at the prospect and his lack of preparation. When the critically-controversial tour reached the venue during the weekend of December 19 and 20, Lennon agreed to make a cameo appearance alongside his former bandmate. Failing to support Harrison would be unfair, he reasoned, after playing the same stage with Elton John just weeks earlier. There would, however, be little time for rehearsal. "I didn't want it to be a case of the great John Lennon jumping up and just banging out a few chords," he reasoned.

Yet playing with Harrison at least afforded Lennon the opportunity for a very public show of reconciliation and hope. It ought to have been a moment for renewal in the live arena. A critically maligned Harrison needed a lift at this point: Lennon was the man who could have provided some timely support to George amidst a critical maelstrom. "The guy went through some kind of mill," Lennon admitted. "It was probably his turn to get smacked. The public, including the media, are sometimes a bit sheep-like and if the ball starts rolling, well, it's just that somebody's in, somebody's out. George is out for the moment. And I think it didn't matter what he did on tour."

Meanwhile, the long-anticipated meeting for the signing of what Lennon called the 202-page 'Famous Beatle Agreement' was scheduled for December 19 in the salubrious *environs* of New York's Plaza Hotel. With the McCartneys flying in especially for the occasion, arrangements had been made for the Apple agreement to be signed in Lennon's home town just days before Christmas.

While the McCartneys had brought portable recording equipment to film this historic occasion, one man would not be making an appearance on the night. But it wasn't a case of stage fright. Starkey had already signed his quarter of the papers at home in England, and opted not to travel to the Big Apple. His lawyer and business manager were present instead. Ringo was, however, reachable by phone as he awaited further news.

With rich irony, an entire floor of the Plaza had been the group's place of residence on their historic arrival in America in February 1964. "As Rome cherishes the Coliseum," wrote *Love Me Do* author Michael Braun with no little sense of grandeur, "and Paris the Arc de Triomphe as symbols of a more glorious day, so New York feels about the Hotel Plaza."

A large suite full of Apple businessmen and legal representatives had been booked as the signing ceremony beckoned. Harrison and his own lawyer and manager sat at a huge table, joined by McCartney's own legal family team, the Eastmans. Apple's Neil Aspinall was also present, along with company lawyers representing the English and American teams. Lennon had sent his lawyer, Harold Seider, to be present. As time began to pass late into the night, and the gathered representatives grew anxious about Lennon's whereabouts, Harrison then voiced what appeared to be a unanimous opinion amongst the congregated Beatle family. "*Where's John?*" Harold Seider left the suite and contacted Pang with an urgent last minute phone-call.

Lennon refused to take the call after locking himself in his apartment suite. Pang asked what was wrong. "I'm not going to sign the agreement," he replied, much to May's astonishment. She was left with the unenviable task of informing Seider that Lennon would not be attending the meeting. Her news was greeted with silence. Lennon was unhappy with a number of points in the agreement, and was adamant that he was not going to sign the agreement on that chosen day.

"John wouldn't show up," McCartney remembered as his old song-writing partner stewed in his apartment. "He wouldn't come from across the park!" Harrison clearly took umbrage at Lennon's non-appearance, ordering him to join the Beatles gathering. "George got on the phone, yelling: 'Take those shades off and come over here, you!'" McCartney would later recall. "John still wouldn't come over." While Lennon's absence from the meeting left his old colleagues in limbo, it was an incensed Harrison who appeared to feel the snub most acutely. Already feeling the effects of a harsh critical reaction to his exhausting *Dark Horse* tour and suffering with vocal problems thwarted by throat strain, Harrison finally snapped. "George picked up the phone and called John," Pang remembers. "I answered and asked if he wanted John, but he barked: '*No!* Just tell him whatever his problem is, I started this tour on my own, and I'll end it on my own!' before slamming down the receiver. John was listening over my shoulder."

Having shouted at Seider along with many of the other lawyers present in the room, Harrison's anger at John for not signing at the appointed time and place could do nothing to change Lennon's mind. "He had a balloon delivered with a sign saying, 'LISTEN TO THIS BALLOON'," marvelled McCartney. "It was all quite far out." Pang knew this wasn't the sole reason for Lennon's decision to abstain from the signing ceremony. He announced with no little *chutzpah* that an astrologer, likely to have been contacted at Ono's insistence, declared that the stars on the day weren't right for him to sign. "The numbers weren't right, the planets weren't right, and John wasn't coming," Linda McCartney later claimed. "Had we known there was some guy flipping cards on his bed to help him make his decision, we would have all gone over there. It's beyond words. It's mind-boggling."

The incident also illustrates Lennon's ambivalence about ending The Beatles' collective legal partnership. Just as The Beatles were preparing to sign the settlement papers, Lennon had begun to express his desire to get them back together. The deep irony of the situation demanded that Lennon needed to sign it so they may be in a better position to come together. In simple terms, Lennon was loath to sign his group's own disbandment notice, despite the business-related pressures faced by his former colleagues.

With no sign of Lennon and a plethora of unsigned documents spread out in front of them on green baize tables, McCartney looked decidedly dejected with the affair as he put pen to paper. Harrison muttered each member's name as if in a primary school roll-call, sounding irritated and impatient at the flustered politeness of the suited executives. "Only a brief document or two left," he is reassured as they sift through the agreement in front of them. Harrison leant back from the table, pen in hand. "For the record, I'd just like to say," he glared at the camera: "These are more papers that *I don't know what they say* that I'm signing."

"George and I are still very good pals," Lennon later admitted, "and always will be, but I was supposed to sign this thing the day of the concert. George got a little angry with me for not signing it, and he decided to finish the tour as he started it."

According to Pang, George was just George. Lennon had been on good terms with Paul and Ringo but sadly, his relationship with Harrison clearly needed repairing. "He always viewed him as his kid brother. Since he and John were equally stubborn, George was the Beatle that John really needed to come face to face with." After a while John apologised, and when asked why he wasn't there for George, John replied: "I'm here now."

Keltner believes that Lennon's strong, fraternal influence on Harrison's thinking and his attitude was crucial. "The way John did things in the world, and the way he handled his Beatledom – I think that George was very affected by that."

Lennon was subsequently not invited to watch or participate in George's show. Ominously, Lennon had told Chris Charlesworth back in October 1973: "When I did the Madison Square Garden show, I had a sort of *deja-vu* feeling that I'd done it all before, and this was no better or no worse than it had ever been before. It felt strange and I felt like a robot doing the same thing over and over again."

"Somehow or other, I was informed that I needn't bother to go to George's show. That was cool by me," an off-hand Lennon insisted to *Hit Parader* with a year's worth of hindsight, "because I'd just done Elton, but I didn't want to do George because it was expected. I had already seen the concert in Nassau, so I wasn't really planning to go to Madison Square Garden anyway. He probably made the right decision."

Live concerts, though, had never really been his forte, even if his former bandmate was onstage. "I'd only go because they're friends, you know. I don't really enjoy sitting in shows, whosoever they are, because you either have to go backstage with all that hassle, or sit in front where you get all that looking at you. I prefer records, I always did. I always liked the studio, always the best. I like the record. Records is what I was hooked on."

The McCartneys, meanwhile, were believed to have appeared at Harrison's show heavily disguised in Afro wigs and moustaches. Following the somewhat fractious reactions during the previous night at the Plaza, the McCartneys arrived at John and May's Sutton Place apartment on the morning of December 20 in consummate PR mode. Paul was clearly keen to smooth out the business differences that had sufficiently unnerved Lennon into not signing the group's business agreement.

"Paul, I have to say, was great, very supportive and concerned about John," Pang would later recall. "The upshot was that everyone went over to Lee Eastman's office, of all places. Paul was sort of the head boy, Lee the headmaster. John laid out the problem, and from that point on, things were worked out. And he [John] said: 'There's a few things in here I just don't want to do.' And Paul said: 'Okay, let's try and work it out.' And they did."

Peace was thus restored. One of the factors influencing Lennon's resistance to signing the document was the finality of actually ending The Beatles partnership. Yet this needed to happen, not only to create a sense of resolution, but in order to help foster the right circumstances in which they might reunite.

A few weeks later, in February 1975, Lennon argued that he now had a new perspective on the prospect of playing Beatles material again. "And I think George will see that. If he doesn't, that's cool. That's the way he wants to be." During one December meeting in New York as Harrison's tour closed, tensions between the two men reached a head. Having complied with his business decisions over Allen Klein and acquiesced to his musical vision during the prevailing years, George's frustration towards Lennon for not being there when he really needed him was palpable.

Pang believes George's resentment, which clearly created a genuine tension of its own, had been accumulating for a long time. Where was Lennon, Harrison wondered, when he had been preparing for the

Concert For Bangla Desh in New York, something which John's boldness as a Beatle had inspired him to organise and realise? Each outburst was met with an almost identical reply from Lennon: 'You knew how to reach me.' In this moment, George wanted (and needed) to look John in the eye.

Asking Lennon to remove his sunglasses, John promptly did so, replacing them with his spectacles in an effort to pacify him. This served only to rile Harrison into throwing John's trademark spectacles to the floor. According to her account, Harrison was as furious and angry as any man Pang had seen, even frightening the no-nonsense Lennon off his guard. "It was exactly the kind of situation that John usually ran from. But I could see in that moment that he loved George enough to remain calm and still as George drilled away at him. John had virtually ignored him, a fact that pained George deeply." (On another occasion at his Dakota apartment in the late seventies, Harrison witnessed something troubling in Lennon's eyes. He saw an urge within John to articulate something which George felt he was simply unable to do.)

Backstage at Madison Square Garden, however, Julian Lennon and Pang had apparently spoken amicably with Harrison and Aspinall, who had also flown over for the signing. Harrison's dark mood eventually gave way to relief at finishing this lengthy and incredibly demanding tour. After attending Harrison's final Madison Square Garden show on December 20, Julian informed his father that George had forgiven him, inviting him to his end of tour party at New York's trendy disco, the Hippopotamus club/restaurant, located on East 62nd Street near First Avenue.

Weeks earlier, the club had hosted a party in mid-November which had been attended by John and May to celebrate the off-Broadway opening of the *Sergeant Pepper's Lonely Hearts Club Band* musical. Harrison, Lennon and McCartney were all in attendance that night at the Hippopotamus, and shared a warm embrace, according to Pang. In all probability, this was the last time that all three men gathered together in the same room.

Most importantly, Harrison and Lennon had made their peace, and all was forgiven. "I saw George after the Garden show [December 20] and we were friends again. But he was surrounded by the madness that's called 'touring'." Harrison's stress had been particularly clear, characterising his most recent dealings with John, but everything appeared to have returned to relative harmony, with their tensions ironed out following the previous night's friction.

"As soon as George saw John, he hugged and kissed him. 'Please forgive me,' he said. 'I wasn't feeling well last night. I didn't mean to get upset.' It was as if the previous night had not occurred. Yet again I realised how unpredictable they all were!" Spending time with Harrison, Pang noted an undeniable sense of fraternal concern on Lennon's part. "I like him. I love him, we're alright," John confided during an interview the following year. "I don't really want to make a big deal out if it."

By the end of 1974, Pang claims that Lennon was far from an embittered cynic about his former band mates. More to the point, John was clearly sentimental about them. "I saw all of them," May says. "We had three in one room in each instance." Together in New York, Pang claimed the friendship between Lennon, McCartney and Harrison had been re-instigated, with John close to all former Beatles. "And you would never in a million years think that they had problems. The friendship was still there. John was really close with all of them. Despite what was said in the press, and even by John himself at times, he loved them like brothers."

Keltner recalls regularly asking John and George about their time together as Beatles. The two men truly were brothers, the drummer insists, interacting with a real fraternal intensity. "They had great moments, and then they had moments of real division, the way a family is. They would be disappointed with each other for various things, and frustrated with each other. In any group of people, it is inevitable. There's no perfect situation. Especially when you have brilliance like they had."

Having made their peace, Harrison and Lennon were then reconciled on air during an entertaining shared radio interview in New York. Their old, familiar rapport was palpable during an early morning conversation on December 21 with LA's KHJ radio station. "The time was 5 a.m., and the time was right," the station announcer declared, as the 'musical master' Harrison awaited Lennon's arrival in his New York hotel suite following the Hippopotamus club party.

As far as his lengthy North American tour was concerned, this was a journey that he felt, deep inside, he'd simply had to make. "It's like a lot of forces, outside energies and subconscious thoughts. I have a lot of concepts which I wanna get rid of. I've been so busy working this year." During their interview, Lennon had insisted Harrison's restricted entry into the States (based on visa access) had rendered any full Beatle conciliation a limited prospect. A husky-voiced Harrison emphasised the importance of upholding positivity despite the onset of negativity. Aside from his post-tour fatigue, he'd rarely sounded so upbeat. "There are so many records I never hear, not because I don't like them, but because I'm so busy making records I don't get to hear them."

George also re-affirmed his faith by paraphrasing a contemporary Maria Muldoor song: '*I've tried praying to God and the saints on high, and I know they hear me . . .*' Appropriately enough, he discussed the joyous inspiration behind the creation of 'My Sweet Lord', before providing an insight into Lennon's role in his songwriting development. "I was alongside John or Paul as they were writing things. I can think of a million times when I wrote a few lines or verses to 'Eleanor Rigby', or something else too. John helped me, in as much as he gave me a tip. He was just being observant, and that is: once you get in the motion of starting a song, try and finish it and complete it."

According to old Liverpool friend Bill Harry, Harrison hadn't sought to collaborate with either Lennon or McCartney on his own material, but was simply seeking assistance in writing his own songs. "George was still developing. He was the most talented guitarist, and that talent got John to accept him into the group. I think that, eventually, gave him the backbone to write songs. But the songwriting, initially, took second place. John adamantly refused to give him any help, but Paul could be more helpful if it was needed."

Biographer Ray Connolly concurs. "It's much easier, if you're a song-writer, to have your mate with you. You can play off each other. They were probably neglectful, and they could have been a bit more thoughtful. I could understand how George felt left out."

Harrison later complained in interview about not receiving sufficient credit for his lyrical contributions to Lennon and McCartney's work. Bill Harry empathised with George's predicament, even suggesting to Harrison during The Beatles' early days in Liverpool that the reticent writer team up with Starr in order to further his abilities.

He also believes that Harrison had felt dominated (if not overwhelmed) by the famous songwriting team. "It was always difficult to get his songs accepted, because of this big battle between John and Paul. I think it was hard for him, because they wrote so much, and were always playing ideas off each other. They also wrote a lot of their numbers separately. If John wrote a number, it would be under Lennon and McCartney. If Paul wrote a number, it would also be under Lennon and McCartney. But they always rushed to get their numbers [recorded] first, when they had a new project."

While McCartney and Lennon had led the way in communicating The Beatles' message, it had always proved difficult for Harrison to contribute. "When I first started writing songs, it was presented to me like this: 'Do you want your song published?' And as John and Paul's songs were being published by Dick James, I said: 'Yeah, OK, I'll have my songs published.' So I signed this contract, thinking, 'Great, somebody's going to publish my song,' and then years later, I'm saying, 'What do you mean, I don't own it?'"

In time, Harrison was destined to provide a subtler influence upon the group, and his work became greater as the years passed. Harrison also began to feel a greater sense of fulfilment in the knowledge that his voice could now be heard. Gradually becoming more prolific as the sixties progressed, Harrison had steadily written a retinue of new compositions in between Beatle projects, songs which did not appear on subsequent albums.

"That's why he had enough to do his double album," Harry argues, "because there were so many songs he'd written that he'd not been able to get on Beatle albums. You had great things from George, and he'd had to put up with things like 'The Ballad Of John And Yoko'." "The songs of George's that *were* recorded, like 'Not Guilty'," Connolly adds, "could have been put on an album." An intricately harmonic song about conscience and anger, in MacDonald's esteem, it showed Harrison's frustration at the pervading unhelpful mood in the studio between his colleagues.

After entering Harrison's Plaza Hotel suite in voluble fashion, 'the one and only' John Lennon was introduced to New York's KHJ radio listeners by Harrison during their shared interview. With Beatles banter on their mind, the duo were swiftly reminiscing about their old group's incredible legacy, and discussed the group's old musical magic. "There's lots [of Beatles songs] that I thought were pretty good," George admitted, "and there's lots that I thought were sensational. I enjoyed the ones which were *inventive*. Which were *new*."

Harrison also displayed his generosity by discussing some of John's finest work. He began by praising the overlooked commercial potential of their debut album highlight, 'There's A Place'. "We made a record, and John wrote a song. And we evaded, or avoided, making it into the next single," he reflected. "Someone else did it as a single and we just did it as an album track . . ." Sounding rueful that the song had languished as the penultimate track on the *Please Please Me* album, Harrison clearly considered the song (the first to be recorded at Abbey Road during their historic 12-hour session) had sufficient commercial appeal as a follow-up to 'Please Please Me'. "It was like the one before," he explained to his old bandmate, "with the mouth organ and all that bit."

This passionately-delivered song's immediacy, poignancy and authentic contemporary live sound, MacDonald noted, provided the listener with an "inescapable strength of feeling". 'There's A Place' also proved an early signpost of the direction Lennon would take in expressing his fascinating interior life in song through psychedelic revelation and, later still, meditation.

Given the song's espousal of the virtues of seclusion and peace of mind, 'There's A Place' was a song which appeared to arrive ahead of its author's own wisdom. "This was the difference with what we were writing," McCartney later recalled of this co-composition. "We were starting to get a bit more cerebral." The song also described an interior place that Harrison would, through meditation, realise was timeless and spaceless. This wasn't the first time that Lennon had been reminded of the song. At the end of September, he'd been drawn into comparing its melodic appeal to that of Todd Rundgren's 'I Saw The Light'. "Nothing," musicologist Ian MacDonald claimed, "better demonstrated the speed at which The Beatles found themselves as writers than through this stirring period piece." Moreover, this Forthlin Road composition's "raw intensity made it sound especially original, almost as if it already existed in a version by some other artist."

Harrison also applauded Lennon's blooming artistry on 'Norwegian Wood'. "I *felt* where it was coming from," he admitted of a track which first featured his idiosyncratic sitar style. He'd also enjoyed the aural and sonic revelations of Lennon classic 'Strawberry Fields Forever', which, to its creator, still sounded like a big production. Harrison also defended Lennon's memorable, yet momentary, denouncement of The Beatles on his *Plastic Ono Band* album track 'God' in 1970. George remained a little aggrieved that Lennon had been denied the right to change his mind on the matter. Characteristically, John had retracted this statement some two years later. Assuming the role of DJ for Los Angeles' KHJ station back in September 1974, a snatch of Lennon's *'I don't believe in Beatles'* lyric circulated over the airwaves, prompting him to insist that, yes, he *does* believe in them.

★　　★　　★

After the business tensions of New York, Lennon and Pang were keen to enjoy a more convivial, joyous environment in which to unwind as Christmas approached. John, May and Julian headed for Florida on December 22 to celebrate the festive season, staying at the Polynesian Hotel in the Disney World resort. Minder Mal Evans was also present to enjoy the thrills and colourful spectacle of the famous theme park. Lennon was duly photographed, with Pang at his side, in the appropriate attire of a Mickey Mouse T-shirt.

Lennon and Pang also took a ride on the park's monorail system. Their jaunt, John remembered, occurred on perhaps the most crowded day of the year. "I was sitting along with everyone else, not being recognised, and I heard someone with his back to me say that George Harrison was there today. The guy was leaning on me, and he'd heard that a Beatle was there somewhere. He couldn't see the wood for the trees."

Harrison had actually visited the resort some three years earlier in the company of Ravi Shankar and actor Peter Sellers. While Lennon and Pang settled into their holiday surroundings, a new Harrison single, taken from his critically maligned *Dark Horse*, hit the shelves. 'Ding Dong' rang out the old and welcomed the new as 1975 beckoned. The accompanying video showed Harrison in all manner of Beatle-era regalia, fast-forwarding through a procession of the group's rapidly changing identities.

What's more, new signs of Beatlemania were appearing as Christmas beckoned. Excerpts from a stage show, written by Liverpudlian Willy Russell and entitled *John, Paul, George, Ringo and Bert* were broadcast on BBC TV, duly infuriating McCartney once he had returned home from New York. The footage he saw on screen depicted him and not Lennon as the protagonist in the break-up of the group.

"The success of the musical, though, and the interest in making it into a movie, showed how potent The Beatles story remained," Sounes argued. "Paul's strong reaction to the play demonstrated how deeply he felt about the way his part in history was represented, something that would become a veritable obsession." Rather less enticingly, the weighty volume of legal documents awaiting Lennon's signature arrived at the hotel, Pang remembered, courtesy of an Apple lawyer. John had until the end of the year, or the duration of their vacation, in which to put pen to paper. "John was the last one to sign it. He held out because he didn't like certain clauses in the contract. When they finally changed it, the lawyers brought it down to us in Disney and if you look closely, you can see the other three signatures."

Many may not agree, but Lennon felt the setting suited the occasion, amused by the fact that the Beatle dissolution saga should reach its *denouement* in the colourful splendour of a Disney theme park. It was a place, to borrow a phrase he'd once used to describe his old writing partner, of pizzas and fairy tales: a mass, low-brow culture of candyfloss and cartoon characters. The signing, Pang maintains, was a sad occasion but one which also represented a sense of progress for the four Beatles, with an eye to future collaboration. "I think it freed them up from certain contractual obligations and made it so they could eventually come back and maybe work together under better circumstances if they wanted to, without feeling that they *had* to."

Additionally, the four men had the choice to do what they wanted, as individuals in terms of their own careers, instead of remaining contractually obligated to working together. This sense of closure may have led to a rejuvenation of the group in a new musical setting. It would, Pang later insisted, give Lennon a new relationship with his Beatle brothers. When Lennon eventually sat down to ink his signature on the large sheaf of legal papers on December 27, he knew that this was it. Having started the group, he ensured that he would be the one (at least on paper) to bring it to a close. Pang took photos of the moment when Lennon signed.

"'Take out your camera,' he joked to me. Then he called Harold to go over some final points." Lennon hung up, and gazed out of the window of their hotel room. Pang could sense him playing over the whole, decade-long Beatle experience in his mind. This was the band that had helped invent pop culture, changed people's lives and subsequently changed the world. "He finally picked up his pen and ended the greatest rock'n'roll band in history by simply scrawling 'John Lennon' at the bottom of the page."

PART FOUR

NEW ORLEANS

CHAPTER TEN

Down South In New Orleans

WHEN the final legal links that had bound The Beatles were officially relinquished in a London hearing, McCartney emerged as a victor, thoroughly validated in his view on the business conduct of former manager Allen Klein. The following day, January 10, the McCartneys left Heathrow Airport on a flight bound for New York. Wings' latest single, 'Junior's Farm' was riding high in the *Billboard* charts as Paul prepared for his forthcoming studio project. Just a few days before flying on to Louisiana, the McCartneys arranged to have dinner in a New York restaurant with Lennon and Pang the following evening.

After enjoying their evening together, they returned to Lennon's swish apartment. McCartney waited for his moment before disclosing an interesting proposal for his old partner to consider. "Oh, Linda and I are going down to New Orleans . . . Thinking about going there to record an album. We'd like you to meet us there." Lennon was clearly receptive to Paul's new album project. After McCartney reminded John of his plans before leaving their apartment, Pang recalled Lennon's enthusiasm for travelling to the Deep South to watch Paul record.

Despite Paul's invitation, Lennon seemed unaware of the possibility of the two men recording together. However, May insisted that, deep down, Lennon had realised that the two former partners were now ready to work together once again. For years, this had often seemed an unlikely prospect, but May now sensed that it could happen, with Lennon increasingly open to discussing working with Paul. "He talked about it a lot. He was really thinking about it," Pang enthused. "It was so fantastic."

For Pang at least, a musical reconciliation between the two men now appeared close to fruition. It may have been a long distance to travel, but there now came the real opportunity of undertaking a trip to New

249

Orleans. After inviting John to the studio before travelling to Louisiana, Paul would quietly (and privately) hope for Lennon's arrival in the Deep South as January wore on. Pang remained wary of raising the issue and thereby turning Lennon off the idea. "But he kept bringing up the trip," May recalled in her memoir, "and each time he mentioned it, he grew more enthusiastic."

While Paul settled in and relaxed in New York's vibrant metropolis before readying himself for the journey to the Louisianan delta, Lennon was busy penning an in-joke-laden missive to his old Beatle friend Derek Taylor the following day, Sunday January 12. This pun-strewn *communique* relayed his thoughts on making the long sojourn '*to New Orleons to see the McCartknees*'. The following day, Lennon entered the Record Plant studio to work with Cicala on a session for '#9 Dream' backing singer Joey Dambra's band, Dog Soldier. Having repeatedly been asked what form any speculative Beatles reunion might take, Lennon believed that getting relaxed in the studio would be the best option for any future music-making policy. What's more, Lennon's musical confidence now matched his sense of artistic and commercial ascendancy.

Back in December, a nervous David Bowie had called on producer Tony Visconti in New York for moral support ahead of his meeting with Lennon, his slightly puzzled hero, at the Sherry Netherlands Hotel. Bowie had arrived in town to complete his new album, *Young Americans*, at the city's Hit Factory studio. Later describing Visconti as the "complete producer", Pang and Visconti's meeting led to their eventual marriage and the birth of their two children, Sebastian and Lara.

This pleasant, if slightly awkward, scenario continued in early January. With the McCartneys having arrived in New York, they decided to visit Lennon at his apartment one evening. The quartet duly took a cab to the Pierre Hotel, where Bowie enthusiastically played Paul and Linda and May and John a test pressing of his *Young Americans* album.

Bowie certainly seemed keen to rouse Lennon's interest in his new record. Yet he may also have sensed Lennon and McCartney's growing friendship and increasing closeness at the time. Like McCartney, Bowie was keen to work with John at this point. He also informed Paul that he'd like his considerable expertise on new material that he would be recording later that week, product that would ultimately involve McCartney's former writing partner. It's possible that during this particular get-together in New York, McCartney first ventured news of his journey to New Orleans.

"That night," Pang recalls, "he [David] played the album for Paul and Linda, even though John and I had heard it already, in lots of different states." Bowie spun a mix of his new album while enlightening his guests about the process of achieving his 'plastic soul' sound in Philadelphia, with the assistance of singer Luther Vandross. He then played the album again. "I could see Paul getting restless," Pang would later admit. If the two men had listened carefully, they would have recognised a familiar line emerging from the speakers: '*I heard the news today, oh boy,*' an almost direct lift from their co-written Beatles masterpiece, 'A Day In The Life'. According to Bowie's girlfriend Ava Cherry, Alan Clayson claims, "the dialogue was rather confrontational, deteriorating to the point when Paul snapped: 'Can we hear another album?'"

Bowie ignored McCartney's request and proceeded to play the album again. Pang recalled that John politely told him: "'David, it's a great, great album . . . is there anything else we can listen to as well?' David looked devastated. John hadn't noticed Paul had made almost exactly the same remark a few minutes earlier. David said, 'Excuse me for a second.' He marched out of the room."

When Pang and Lennon returned to their 52nd Street apartment later that night, Bowie was quick to telephone and voice his dismay at Lennon and McCartney's brusqueness. A diplomatic Lennon apologised for any offence that had been caused, smoothing over any ruffled artistic feathers while congratulating his friend on his new work.

Lennon's letter to Derek Taylor also included news of Bowie's request during this telephone conversation to work on a cover of Lennon's late psychedelic Beatles classic. "Next minute he says: 'I'm doing "Across The Universe" . . . you wanna come on down?' So I said: 'Alright, I live here', so I popped down and played rhythm. It was just: 'I'm doing your song, wha' d'ya say? Do you want to come?' 'Alright, I'll come.'" Bowie frequently discussed Lennon amongst his friends, and while John was friendly and enjoyed his company, he remained slightly puzzled by his admiration.

Perplexed by Bowie's choice of cover material, Lennon nevertheless eagerly agreed to his young hero worshipper's offer of a studio session at Electric Lady around January 15. Lennon was certainly grateful, if a little intrigued. '. . . Universe' remained one of his favourite compositions, but he had never been satisfied with the version of the track he'd cut with The Beatles in early 1968, or with Spector's later, orchestrated efforts to remedy the song for subsequent album release in 1970. Lennon used universal themes of light, love, space and wisdom as a means of conveying his feelings.

The original version of the song had possibly required a stronger musical accompaniment, its diminished power due in part to Lennon's lethargy and the group's growing, collective apathy. "He loved being in on the recording," session engineer Eddie Kramer later recalled, "and just playing guitar – he was a ridiculously good rhythm player."

"I was so excited about John," Bowie would later remember, "and he loved working with my band, because they were playing old soul tracks and Stax things. John was so up, had so much energy. It must have been so exciting to always be around him."

While Bowie's version of the song omitted the original's meditational entreaty, Lennon, Doggett wrote, "generously heard him out, adding distinctive guitar touches to the spaces where his *jai guru dev* mantra had once been".

'Across The Universe' encapsulated something of Lennon's feelings when he first became aware of the true power of meditation. In India, he had meditated for long periods and enjoyed its benefits. He later claimed he'd always be grateful to Maharishi for explaining the process of Transcendental Meditation.

Married to the ethereal ambition of its melody, the vast scope of its lyrics, which Lennon later claimed had arrived through an inspiring state of meditative awareness, is certainly special. They were arguably the most accomplished he ever wrote. "I'd kept hearing these words over and over, flowing like an endless stream," he later recalled of the song's poetic ambition and sense of self-realisation. "Such an extraordinary meter and I can never repeat it! It's not a matter of craftsmanship; it wrote itself."

"'Across The Universe' is one of John's great songs. It has special words," McCartney would later insist of this illuminating, quasi-cosmic creation.

The Maharishi had encouraged Lennon to use the more embracing, life-affirming lyric *'meditation will change your world'* instead of Lennon's more downbeat assumption. Like 'Revolution', it was a song which showed an urge to make a difference, although the change Lennon sang of came from within before exacting change in the external world.

As a fan of disco at the time of the Bowie session, Lennon's current musical passion informed his work and inspired his playing on a subsequent new composition. "The guitarist had a lick, so we sort of wrote this song. It was no big deal, it wasn't like sitting down to write a song," Lennon recalled. "People always say: 'What's he doing with David Bowie or Elton John?' I'm doing it because it's fun!" According to Tony Visconti, Bowie had played the subsequent recording of 'Across The Universe' to Lennon, who was sufficiently impressed to agree to his request to collaborate on new material. It would prove a fast-paced session, in which Lennon and guitarist Carlos Alomar sketched out guitar parts, quickly inspiring Bowie to pen new lyrics after overhearing a half-spoken vocal phrase from Lennon as he strummed away in the studio lounge.

"After isolating the track, we found that when John recorded his acoustic guitar part, it seemed that he liked to rest his chin on the guitar and breathe loudly," recalled Alomar. "David mentioned how it sounded like he was saying 'fame'. I countered that it was just heavy breathing. But his insistence that John was saying 'fame', led him to go home and write the famous lyric which later became 'Fame'."

"Whatever stimulants he [David] was taking didn't affect his ability to be creative," said engineer Eddie Kramer, who was present when Alomar started playing the riff, adapted from a Rascals song, 'Jungle Walk'. Lennon was playing around on the acoustic in the lounge, singing a couple of lines from a disco hit over the top of the same one chord vamp. "So he was working it, and David walks in and hears that," says Pang, who remembers Bowie leaving the room and returning with a complete set of lyrics within 20 minutes.

"He heard what I was doing, and commented on how much he liked it and how funky it was," Alomar remembered. "David encouraged John to lay an acoustic guitar track down and he did. I had much work ahead of me and my possible overdubs were still fresh in my head. To my delight, when David returned, he loved all the guitar overdubs. He recorded a guitar line and the song was completed."

Pang recalls Lennon and Alomar had begun by jamming on a funky riff derived from a track entitled 'Foot Stompin'. The song proved, according to writer Paul Du Noyer, "a bleak meditation on the barren nature of celebrity, made as John was walking away from stardom and Bowie was rushing to embrace it. The one disillusioned, the other ambitious, they were scarcely singing from the same hymn sheet, but the match of old master and young pretender was effective." The song became Bowie's first number one the following September, and he regarded Lennon as nothing less than "the last great original".

According to Pang, Lennon was as delighted as David at his subsequent chart-topping success. "He had that competitiveness with the other guys [i.e. McCartney] and he thought it was great." Alomar would later work with McCartney on his *Press To Play* album in the mid-eighties, and recalled the comparative experience of working with the two former Beatles. "I had a great time meeting and working with Paul. He was wonderful and allowed me great freedom to come up with anything, and play on any song I wanted."

McCartney appeared keen to speak about his Beatle days during their working partnership. "Linda was very sweet as well, and a good time was had by all. When it came to working together with Lennon and McCartney, it is like John was a city kid, and Paul was a country boy. But they were both not only fun, they were funny. I enjoyed working with them both equally as well."

No doubt excited by this spontaneous collaborative experience just hours before McCartney left New York, Lennon now actively welcomed the opportunity to write new material with his old partner. Following the session, Lennon spent the next two weeks considering undertaking a studio reunion in the Crescent City. With thoughts of working with McCartney firmly to the fore, Lennon apparently returned to the Record Plant on January 22, producing a re-arrangement of 'You Can't Do That' for Dog Soldier.

According to his partner, Lennon was in good spirits as the new year dawned. Seemingly happy and settled, the couple were planning to buy a cottage together in Montauk, Long Island, and had taken Julian along to view the property. "Alive in '75 is my new motto. I've just made it up," he told journalist Peter Hamill in early February. "I've decided I want to live. I'd decided I wanted to live before, but I didn't know what it meant, really. It's taken however many years and I want to have a go at it."

Just a few days after this Record Plant session, Lennon earnestly began seeking guidance on renewing his prodigious songwriting partnership with McCartney. At his 434 East 52nd Street apartment one morning in late January, John asked May for her much-valued opinion on resuming their collaboration. Lennon had already consulted Pang on his plan to return to the studio and commence work on a new album, which had tentatively been pencilled in for an autumn release.

Lennon's creative juices were clearly fermenting during the early weeks of 1975 as he looked ahead with confidence to producing a successor to *Walls And Bridges*. "I'm writing well. So I'm happy. I'm always at it," he enthused. "The best stuff usually comes out on impulse. Or inspiration. And I hardly have to think about it. But I am always writing. In the back of my head, or if somebody says something, I'm storing it away – a line, or an idea. There is never a moment when I'm not writing, almost."

Growing increasingly intrigued about working with McCartney again in the studio, it was one morning in late January, towards the end of the second week of Paul's work at Sea Saint, when Lennon stood in the kitchen as something played on his mind. "I've got to ask you something," he ventured. "I want to ask you a question."

Having intrigued May, he then stunned her in an understated yet unforgettable moment. "What would you say . . . what would you think if I was to start to write with Paul again?" It was a casual yet earnest enquiry about the virtue of renewing their prodigious, world-changing collaboration. Having stood with her back to John, Pang turned round and looked Lennon straight in the eye.

"Do you think it would be a good idea?" John reiterated.

"Write with Paul? Are you *really* thinking about that?" Pang beamed.

"I'm just asking you. What do you think?"

"Are you *kidding*?! I think it would be a *great* idea, John!"

Pang wanted nothing more than to see the two men reunite. Imploring John to summon the courage to travel to New Orleans, she urged him to renew their creative alliance. With a prevailing sense of his old insecurity, Lennon needed to know why Paul's invitation seemed such a good idea. "Well," Pang began, "solo-wise, you guys are good, wonderful," something to which their respective efforts in the early seventies attested. "But when the two of you get together . . . just look at all the Beatle stuff you two created," she enthused.

As an artist, Lennon's fascination with the exploration of his feelings had increasingly driven his music, while his instincts would frequently influence his creative decisions. As a collaborative partnership, Lennon and McCartney had proved a wonderful combination, one that had created a special working rapport. Pang reassured John that, as arguably the finest songwriting team of them all, they had been unbeatable.

"I think Linda put her finger on it when she said me and John were like mirror images of each other," Paul later confided. "Even down to how we started writing together, facing each other, eyeball to eyeball, exactly like looking in the mirror. That's how songs like 'I Want To Hold Your Hand' were written."

With The Beatles striving to clarify themselves on record in the mid-sixties, the likes of 'We Can Work It Out' had called for people to take on board their message. While they weren't providing 'answers' as such, one sensed their urgency to remind people about their original purpose: love. Having needed time in order to heal a friendship which had defined both men's lives, an appropriate point in their reconciliation had been reached. The timing seemed right for a musical reunion. Pang suggested the simplest, yet most suitable, premise for them to reconvene and create musical magic once again: both men wanted to do it, and without the pressure of a Beatle contract, no one was forcing their hand.

"For them to return to each other, and do what they wanted when they felt like it," May insists, "was a lot easier to deal with. It was just the nervousness of it all," Pang felt, a point which Lennon had made weeks earlier on the *Today Show*. Lennon simply offered a thoughtful 'Okay' before considering his options, pondering the prospect of an event which had inspired three years' worth of speculation. Having gathered his thoughts, Lennon had made his choice. "You know what?" he announced to a delighted Pang. "Let's go down to New Orleans and visit Paul and Linda. I've never been, and I'd like to go!"

Offering a fresh creative start, a positive Lennon was genuinely keen to put plans in place to convene with McCartney. Pang was equally enthusiastic about this prospect, and had worked hard for this moment. Once she had ensured that Lennon reached the studio, she hoped the inevitable would transpire. "John was thinking about going back with Paul, and wanting to write with him. I was encouraging him about it, and John thought it would be good. We were talking about going to see Paul, and that's how it would have been."

While her husband had grown increasingly keen to write with John again as the seventies progressed, Linda later intimated that there had always been hope of a Lennon and McCartney reunion. "They loved each other. They were friends and carried on being friends, and it's deeper than any of us will ever know," she insisted. "They weren't opposites; they were *so* alike. You read about history and you know that's not what really went on. The press made out they didn't like each other, but to work together for that long, it's pretty clear they had to be such close friends.

But it's always much easier for the press just to dismiss it."

By 1975, The Beatles' friendships had been firmly restored, and any animosity had long since receded. The previous half decade's-worth of petty personal and business-driven antagonism appeared to have been consigned to history. What's more, some of the old proximity of Lennon's friendship with McCartney had been slowly restored. Having observed the process of their reconciliation at first hand during the previous summer, Pang believed that Lennon and McCartney were ready to work together again. Despite the sense of expectation, McCartney's hope of renewing their creative collaboration became a viable proposition.

They still shared a genuine mutual affection, and could enjoy each other's company once more . . . as long as recently resolved business issues or management disputes were kept out of the frame. Both men were presently enjoying recent commercial success with their respective releases. Yet despite the restored credibility and commercial resurgence produced by *Band On The Run*, McCartney had begun to recognise his new career remained shaded by the creative force he had once been as part of a classic songwriting partnership.

Perhaps he also realised that what his music lacked at times was the original, often unconventional, input of his former partner. Linda had already observed the same competitive sense of fraternal one-upmanship later witnessed by Pang. "All I could do was sit there, watching them play these games. John and Paul both had problems, and they loved each other, and boy could they have helped each other. If they had only communicated! It frustrates me no end, because I was just some chick from New York when I walked into all of that. God, if I'd known what I know now. . . ." Not only did Linda encourage Paul to reach out to John, she also attempted to convince Lennon to work with her husband again.

McCartney's premise for his old partner's visit to Sea Saint was: come down and visit us, and watch us record. Having already spent two weeks in the Crescent City, Paul would happily welcome John back into the creative fold. Pang was convinced that if Lennon reached Louisiana, something new could be initiated. She also felt sure that McCartney would do the rest and bring Lennon back into the studio. It's possible that Paul, and John, too, privately anticipated an opportunity to play, write, or even record together again.

With May urging John to follow his instincts, both men needed to seize the moment if a Lennon-McCartney reunion was to be realised. Events had certainly synchronised to create an opportunity for *something* to happen. At one time a wonderfully unlikely proposition, the chances of the two men writing and recording together again, for the first time in over five years, now looked possible. Things appeared to be moving towards a moment of transition. Becoming more content with his past, Lennon was reconnecting with the influences that had driven the best of his work, not to mention the musicians and friends who'd made it or inspired it. A sense of momentum was unmistakeable.

Having played with Paul in March, recorded with Ringo in LA in August, and reconciled with George in New York in December, the next step seemed to be to write new material. For Lennon, The Beatles clearly had unfinished business. Given his readiness for revisiting their classic musical legacy and keen on following his instinct, Pang believes that a Lennon-McCartney session might have developed into a Beatles reunion.

Revelling in New Orleans' rich, attractive musical heritage and no doubt influenced by producer Allen Toussaint's deft touch, McCartney duly became part of the studio's illustrious clientele. "Paul treated everybody with a wonderful respect," the American musical maestro Allen Toussaint enthused from his Deep South office during our mid-summer interview. "And it had a lasting effect on everyone here. You couldn't have picked a better subject to write about."

McCartney had last visited the city in whirlwind fashion 10 years earlier, passing through in a day after The Beatles had played a typically brief half-hour set at the City Park Stadium in September 1964. "I'd never been to New Orleans, except on tour when we never saw anything except the inside of a trailer," McCartney told biographer Chris Welch. "The only thing I remembered about New Orleans was the vibrator bed in the motel. And it was sweating hot." They'd had no time for sightseeing, travelling via a motorcade escort from the city's International Airport to the Congress Inn Hotel along the Chef Menteur Highway.

The group later met Fats Domino after their show. As Paul recalled, the great man wore an impressively-sized star-shaped diamond watch. With Beatlemania at its height, the group later recorded three songs by local rhythm-and-bluesman Larry Williams, a lucrative royalty opportunity for the Crescent City writer. Having initially wanted to travel to the city for recording sessions around the time of Thanksgiving the previous year, McCartney's current preoccupation with distant recording locations (Nigeria) and musical capitals (Nashville) had led him to the Louisianan delta of New Orleans. As Wings started recording sessions for their new album, they attempted the unenviable task of following the commercial bonanza of *Band On The Run*.

The album may not have been great, *Rolling Stone* argued on its release, but it was certainly a good piece of work that was clearly worthy of merit. McCartney claimed that he and the group had wanted to record in America once they had found a suitable studio. The options included Tennessee's hallowed musical capital, the Big Apple and LA. The Crescent City's rich heritage, ornate locale and lively vibe therefore seemed an astute choice. New Orleans seemed to offer the perfect setting for what McCartney wanted to achieve with his new work. The city's Dixieland and trad jazz roots had produced world-class icons like Louis Armstrong and had proved an unparalleled melting pot of black-and-white rhythm and blues. Aside from the balmy weather of this legendary city, Paul's intentions were to seek a greater flexibility and more fluid, bluesy sound for his flourishing pop-rock group. While McCartney wanted to be in New Orleans to draw from the city's deep well of musical inspiration, Lennon had been keen to revisit his musical past on *Rock 'N' Roll*. There was also a mutual sense of musical aspiration, another promising factor in the reunion equation.

A New Orleans native, Sea Saint studio's co-owner, producer and arranger Allen Toussaint first met Marshall Sehorn some years earlier, having arranged a successful recording session in the city for Bobby Marcias. Sehorn had already proved himself a good producer and astute businessman. The 40-year-old, who hailed from North Carolina, was a likeable, go-getting guy with a true zeal for his work. One notable discovery in his guise as talented R&B scout was Wilbert Harrison, whose version of 'Kansas City' impressed McCartney.

When the two men were re-acquainted, Sehorn approached Toussaint, keen to work together in some capacity. "What about a 50/50 partnership?" he enthused.

Known as something of a smart, no-nonsense businessman, they formed production company Sansu. Sehorn appeared to provide a perfect counterpart to Toussaint's quieter, artistic nature. What's more, people easily took to his demeanour. It was, as other observers have noted, a winning combination of business expertise and creative vision which helped to re-affirm New Orleans' place on the American musical map. As consummate professionals and endearing individuals, their partnership proved, in similar vein to a certain Lennon and McCartney, one of huge mutual influence in their professional lives.

As a man who helped to bring the New Orleans sound to the national stage, Toussaint also left his mark on the city's contemporary R&B scene. Skilled in keeping pace with the funk and soul revolution of the sixties and seventies, he simultaneously helped consolidate on the city's R&B traditions. An all-round musical eminence, Toussaint had already written and produced a string of mid-sixties soul classics (including 'Ride Your Pony' and 'Working In A Coalmine') for the legendary Lee Dorsey, while penning new material for Jessie Hill, The Neville Brothers, Ernie K-Doe and chart hit-makers LaBelle, who provided the studio with their biggest international success.

Just weeks after the *Venus And Mars* sessions had been completed, Toussaint told writer David Nathan that each project he tackled was the most important thing at that time. "And it's what happens when I'm in the studio, when I'm creating and working. What happens afterwards, that's beyond my control. Naturally, you want what you do to do well, but all you can do is strive to do your best when you're actually in there creating. Whoever is there at that time, whatever is special about them [becomes] most important."

Various Toussaint-penned songs were covered by The Yardbirds, Bonnie Raitt, Herb Alpert and Glen Campbell. Allen also groomed the influential instrumental funk house band The Meters, who duly recorded some of their most successful work with the producer.

Situated on the city's Rampart and Dumaine Streets, New Orleans' prime recording facility had been Cosimo Matassa's J&M studios. Having hosted the likes of Fats Domino's Imperial recordings and boasted fabled drummer Earl Palmer in its house band, the studio subsequently ceased trading as a new decade dawned. "If Cosimo hadn't closed," Toussaint maintains, "we would never have built Sea Saint in 1971." Located on Clematis Avenue in the city's Gentilly district, Sehorn and Toussaint's co-owned, state-of-the-art studio rolled tape for the first time two years later. "By the time Paul came," Allen explains, "we had a good reputation as *the* place to be in New Orleans."

Two days after Toussaint celebrated his 37th birthday, and with Carnival season beginning in earnest, some suitably sultry weather greeted McCartney and co upon their arrival at Sea Saint on January 16. Nestled in a residential neighbourhood at 3809 Clematis Avenue, away from the vibrant hoopla of the city, McCartney entered the small, modest-looking white building as he prepared for the first day of a six-week session that would run until February 24. Local fan Gina Fontana, for whom McCartney was a swoonsome teenage idol, was thrilled to discover the studio was less than a mile from her home. A feature in the local press had provided details of the studio's location.

"The reason I knew Paul was coming to town was because of a small article in the afternoon paper. It said Paul was coming to record an album at the Sea Saint studio. They were to stay in New Orleans for a little more than a month." Media attention drawn to McCartney's arrival also extended to a TV announcement that the former Beatle would be spending time in the city to record his new album. An excited Fontana had learned that McCartney was due to fly in on Monday January 13, before the local press announced a delay in his arrival.

Fontana visited the studio on Wednesday, only to realise that Paul had arrived in town the night before. His presence at the studio was also eagerly awaited by locals. An hour later, a large white limousine drove down the street. Fontana was convinced she was about to witness the arrival of her hero. When the car pulled up, McCartney was nowhere in sight. Fontana returned to the studio on Thursday, but Paul had still not arrived. Arriving at the studio the following afternoon, other fans began arriving an hour later, and at 3 p.m., Laine, McCulloch and manager Allan Crowder arrived, signed autographs and posed for photos.

McCartney was on his way, his colleagues assured them. Fans were poised with their cameras and the excitement was tangible. An hour after his band's arrival, McCartney drove down Clematis Avenue at high speed. "He drove up, and everyone ran to his car. It was like 1964 all over again. Everyone was wild – they were pushing and shoving, and Paul kept trying to get out but the crowd wouldn't let him." With a perfect view of her hero, Fontana recalled McCartney's terrified expression. "He finally got out the car with one big push. His first reaction was to scream: 'Get out of here. What is this?!' The crowd started to move back, and Paul started to make his way through."

Wearing a blue pin-striped suit over a purple *Band On The Run* T-shirt, Fontana clung on to McCartney before he made his way into the studio. She was speechless at her brief encounter. "I had actually seen him, touched him, and talked to him. It was really a dream come true. Everything had happened so fast." Fontana returned to the studio later that night and the

McCartneys emerged from the facility just before midnight. "Paul was so at ease with everyone. He didn't rush things at all. He signed autographs and posed for pictures. He kept making all these cute faces. He had the McCartney charm on full blast."

Swiftly addressing the issue of McCartney's freedom around the city, Sehorn had purchased a car for Paul to use during his stay. Marshall's presence around the studio was, it transpired, more noticeable than that of Toussaint during the sessions. "There was nothing stupid about him," engineer Alan O'Duffy insists. "Marshall organised the thing, and he was a good guy when it came to getting things done, which is another good aspect of it. I'm sure it was very wise of him to buy it, because how else is Paul going to get around? Looking back," the engineer recalled, "it was absurd because the style was a Lincoln Continental, with a long bonnet and boot. It was a six-seater." New Orlean fan Fontana claimed they'd hired a White Delta 98 convertible, and photographs taken during the sessions showed Paul at the wheel, with his young daughters sprawled across its spacious seats.

One subsequent studio photo shows Paul working intently over the desk at Sea Saint. Sat beside him was O'Duffy, undertaking engineering duties on the album. Successor to legendary engineer Eddie Kramer, the former Olympic studio stalwart wasn't a confidante, or part of the former Beatle's 'inner circle' whilst residing in the city. "But I *was* there in New Orleans," he recalls, "and had a part in making this beautiful album." O'Duffy recalls arriving in the Crescent City ahead of the group in order to prepare their studio. "Patti LaBelle's 'Lady Marmalade' had just been a big hit, which had been done in that studio. We had some ex-Vietnam vets helping us set up the studio the way I wanted it. The outstanding thing about working with Paul is: 'Let's set up the drums, and bass and guitar and have a good time,' and I'd done a lot of that."

Like Fontana, local musician John Taylor had been informed that Paul was coming to the Crescent City in order to record his new album. Sea Saint studios was just three blocks from Taylor's girlfriend's house. Keen to ascertain if the rumours were true, Taylor took a chance and drove into the studio's small parking lot. Already feeling nervous, Taylor was then astonished to be greeted by a familiar, famous face. "A car pulled alongside of mine. I glanced over and it was Paul and Linda. I was in shock, but they looked at me, smiled and waved. I got out and walked toward them. Paul shook my hand and said: 'How are you, this fine morning?' I said: 'Great, you are really all right.' And he said, 'I hope so by now.'"

Taylor claims he met the couple each day for the next few weeks during the recording sessions; taking photos outside the studio, collecting autographs and enjoying the rare opportunity of fraternising with a Beatle. "Paul and Linda look so happy and excited with making the album," Taylor said. Toussaint, meanwhile, insists there wasn't an overwhelming media frenzy of journalistic attention surrounding the studio, despite numerous media outlets contacting Sea Saint to gain access to McCartney for interviews. "Marshall and the people in the front office saw to it that that didn't happen," Allen recalls. "It wasn't that sort of scene, [with] that sort of paparazzi around the studio. We didn't have that problem."

However, members of the local media soon discovered McCartney's new accommodation, spending hours hanging around his hotel, attempting to glean any information from McCartney about his work at the studio. Paul would offer a quick wave, a comical face or a curt nod for the waiting media.

Paul had opted for the plush Le Richelieu Hotel, situated at 1234 Chartres Avenue, deep in the old world environs of the city's colourful and romantic French Quarter. While the traditional carnival processions had skirted the area for the last two years, at the opposite end of the street was the renowned, much-eulogised Bourbon Street, whose sights, sounds and restaurants had made New Orleans famous. "He wanted to have the whole New Orleans experience," Toussaint insisted. With a procession of celebrities staying at Le Richelieu through the years, the live-in owner's office was rumoured to be papered with autographed photos.

While cutting the album, the McCartney family lived like residents, occupying one of the Richelieu Hotel suites for five to six weeks. A corridor upstairs led down to two rooms, and Paul had taken both suites. And because this was a former Beatle, the door into the corridor had a guard. "Paul didn't like the idea of a guard being there. He's a very low-key guy, who doesn't do any nonsense," O'Duffy insists. The engineer took the apartment adjacent to McCartney. "I always remember having breakfast on the veranda. And I used to have raisin bran, something 'pretend healthy', and then head off to the studio."

Friendly and often accommodating, McCartney also schmoozed with local press in a neighbourhood bar packed with curious onlookers. "He was exceedingly witty, bright, and talkative," a young news writer for the city's

NBC station insisted. Seeking local inspiration, Paul began appearing around town with the Wings entourage, and was seen frequenting French Quarter restaurants, jazz hangouts and popular clubs. Tipitina's was New Orleans' most-noted live music venue, considered to be one of the finest of its kind in America. McCartney was also believed to have befriended many of the city's local artists.

"In New Orleans, we have a different taste to the rest of the country," Toussaint explained to me one August afternoon from his Crescent City office, "and maybe even to the rest of the world. Paul knew so much, and he was truly a lover of the music that was made here. He had love for the musicians, and a lot of respect and a great love for the history of New Orlean music."

"The New Orleans scene, the R&B thing, was great," Paul enthused in 2001 when reflecting upon his Big Easy recording experience. "Even though you didn't use the style of the town you were in too much, it still influenced the way you felt about the music, and added to the spirit. I think it always rubs off a bit, just in the kind of arrangements and who's there. There's a couple of tunes we've got brass on, and it's New Orleans brass," relishing the joyous sounds of the Crescent City's finest. "It's great, it's like they're revving up all the time. They're brilliant."

Even guitarist Jimmy McCulloch was effusive in his praise of their recording experience. "The brass players from New Orleans had fit in. They gave it a good kick." Paradoxically, McCartney would claim the sound of their subsequent album didn't reflect its environment. "I couldn't tell you. It's just your opinion. Everybody says something different about every track anyway," he told his biographer Chris Welch.

McCartney clearly felt musically comfortable with the re-configured Wings line-up that arrived in Louisiana, charged with the task of producing a follow-up to *Band On The Run*. "I had written *Venus And Mars* songs in Jamaica – we were getting around a bit in those days! – and had the album pretty much mapped out," McCartney recalled. "Jimmy had written one of the tracks ['Medicine Jar'] with a mate of his. We'd been in Jamaica before we went to New Orleans, and for the first time ever, I'd got all the songs together like a scroll that went from here to the end of the room. So I had all that together, and we just went and turned up and started recording."

This may well have included the brief title track, and the segue into the glam-pop stomp of 'Rock Show'. The four sheet, poster-sized scroll, featuring a number of compositions that included lyrics, music and arrangements, was presented to Alan O'Duffy at the start of the mid-January sessions. McCartney later claimed that four of the album's songs were programmed in the same mode as the 'mini opera' on *Abbey Road*. "I start off with an idea," McCartney explained to Gambaccini. "'Rock Show,' boom. '*Long hair*' . . . well, where else? Madison Square. 'Rock and roll', well, that rhymes with Hollywood Bowl. Often these things that turn out to be great afterwards are just searches for a rhyme."

The song had clearly been conceived with one eye on the American stadium market too, a clever concept that would introduce the band into the world of the rock arena during the following year. Whilst in Jamaica, McCartney's exposure to the Marvel comics series on a weekend market stall also inspired the humorous sci-fi escapade, 'Magneto And Titanium Man'.

"The drawings are great. I think you'll find that in 20 years' time some of the guys drawing them were little Picassos. I think it's very clever how they do it. I love the names, I love the whole comic book thing."

"Unfortunately, some of the non-love songs ('Magneto And Titanium Man' especially) on *Venus And Mars* are more galling and impudently silly than that pun," carped *Rolling Stone*. In discussing the album's merits upon its release that May, the magazine sounded a further note of concern. "What is really worrisome here is the almost gleeful enthusiasm with which he makes trivial anything meaningful."

Yet as Sounes rightly observed, "this sort of soft rock was what the market wanted". McCartney would later claim the group had written or developed most of the material before they reached Louisiana, including the impressively busy soul-funk of 'Letting Go' which featured fired-up local brassmen. As Peter Ames Carlin concluded, the song "traced the thin line between love and obsession; passion in all its dangerous, unhinged glory".

Along with McCulloch's 'Medicine Jar', the sublime ballad portrait of 'Love In Song' had been recorded at Abbey Road back in November, prior to the group's departure for the Big Easy. Paul was later asked if his fabled Hofner violin bass had been utilised on their new studio material. While not an ideal studio instrument, Paul had played stand-up bass on 'Love In Song'. Subsequent overdubbing work was carried out once they reached their Louisianan destination.

Meanwhile, photographer Sidney Smith, who was privileged enough to witness McCartney's gifted musicianship around the studio from behind his camera lens during the sessions, was clearly star-struck and deeply impressed. "I had previously met many musicians through my work with rock groups, but this was over the top." Smith attended just a few of the Sea Saint sessions, due in part to his wariness about over-stepping his boundaries with McCartney. "I was a 20-year-old kid who lucked into this incredible opportunity. I didn't just show up at the studio. I waited to be invited for photo opportunities. I was just trying to conceal my giddiness because I was trying to remain professional."

McCartney, according to Smith, was easy-going and kind in his company, and enjoyed being one of the guys in the studio. Yet his musical versatility truly captivated this besotted fan. Smith's critical faculties were certainly suspended once in the presence of his childhood idol. "Watching him record in the studio was amazing. He was involved in everything. The man is just a musical *savant*. An absolute genius. I really think he can play anything. [He was] a master of every musical instrument that he picked up," Smith enthuses, a dedicated young Beatle fan at the time. "And he wanted every take to be perfect. In my opinion, the man could do no wrong. I was truly impressed with everything he was doing during that time."

On the album itself, McCartney played piano, acoustic and electric guitar, with main lead duties taken by McCulloch and Laine. Weeks earlier, Smith had also enjoyed the privilege of watching another of his musical heroes, George Harrison, in concert at Baton Rouge, Louisiana. "*That* was special. While I did shoot some pictures at the concert, I went there as a paying customer, not as a photographer. Seeing Harrison onstage was like seeing my entire youth, my childhood and teenage years, playing itself out in front of me. That was a hugely emotional experience. And then three months later, I end up getting to meet and work with none other than Paul McCartney. That's why I was probably overly-cautious about being professional in front of McCartney. I couldn't have been more overjoyed."

There also seemed to be a suitably amorous air to studio proceedings where Paul and Linda were concerned. "Whenever I was present," Smith insists, "all that I witnessed was happiness and good vibes all around. The vibe was always fun and upbeat. Everyone was smiling and happy." O'Duffy also admits that the McCartneys were a warm and pleasant couple to work with in the studio. "At that time, when Paul and Linda were together, it felt like love was all around," Toussaint adds. "We were in love, and we wanted to be together. That was the central idea," McCartney later reasoned, "and then, 'If you're going to be in a band, you'll need to learn an instrument.' She'd played a bit of piano, but not since she was like a kid. I would show her basic stuff, and it was not exactly Tchaikovsky. It was pretty much three or four chords. So she would pick it up and she had a good sense of rhythm."

Rolling Stone, however, found the pairing of Paul and Linda on this record to be a difficult musical pill to swallow. "For all I know, the McCartneys may love each other passionately, but it is self-aggrandizement, not private ardour, that shines through the computerised smoothness of their insubstantial songs."

While the mysterious and elusive 'Spirits Of Ancient Egypt' was inspired after McCartney read a tome on the ancient history of the country, the light, fruity 'You Gave Me The Answer' suggests the group had absorbed the genuine New Orleans jazz atmosphere. "I know it's sort of a rock-and-roll album, but there's other things I like that aren't necessarily rock and roll," McCartney explained to journalist Paul Gambaccini. "On this LP, I thought I'd like to get some of that in, so 'You Gave Me The Answer' is real fruity, imagining tie and tails, my impression of the Fred Astaire era."

However, it was a little harder to discern a Crescent City flavour in the likes of future FM staple 'Listen To What The Man Said', "an example of slick, professional entertainment and carefully crafted 'product'," *Rolling Stone* later enthused, "deliciously catchy and creamily produced." It was also the type of song which McCartney's critics would carp over, partly because of the song's apparent breezy effortlessness. "I remember hearing 'Listen To What The Man Said' over and over," Smith recalls, "until Paul felt it was in the can. It was an absolutely great song."

McCartney was, as ever, seeking perfection. 'Listen To What The Man Said' also featured a brief and barely audible rap, allegedly from Toussaint, and a wonderfully improvised cameo from well-respected sax player Tom Scott after album operations had moved to Los Angeles. Its high, reedy sound would subsequently become a much-favoured studio hallmark of seventies sax recordings. His involvement appeared to have been an inspired, spur-of-the-moment occasion. "There's a funny story about that one,'" said McCartney. "It was one of the songs we'd gone in with high hopes for. Whenever I would play it on the piano, people would say: 'Oh,

I like that one.' But when we did the backing track, we thought we didn't really get it together at all. We let it stay and added some things on it, Dave Mason came in and we did a little bit of overdubbing guitars, and then we wondered what we could do for a solo. We thought it would be great to have a very technical musician come in and do a great lyrical solo. Someone said: 'Tom Scott lives near here.'

"We said: 'Yeah, give him a ring, see if he turns up,' and he turned up within half an hour! There he was, with his sax, and he sat down in the studio playing through. The engineer was recording it. He came in and I said: 'I think that's it.' He [Tom] said: 'Did you record that?' I said: 'Yes,' and we listened to it back. No one could believe it, so he went out and tried a few more, but they weren't as good. I think what he plays on that song is lovely and that, overall, it worked."

The urban, R&B-influenced sound of the impassioned 'Call Me Back Again' had a rough McCartney vocal reminiscent of 'Oh Darling!'. *Venus And Mars* also utilised a few of the conceptual techniques McCartney had used to produce a more continuous feel to *Abbey Road*, particularly the segue between 'Listen To What The Man Said' and the 'Treat Her Gently'/'Lonely Old People' medley.

Having contributed high harmonies to another unnamed song during the sessions, O'Duffy recalls the 'blessing' of singing harmony with Paul on 'Lonely Old People' during a studio rehearsal. He subsequently taught his part to Laine for the recording. He recalls his astonishment at hearing McCartney sing at close quarters: his high tenor impression of Pavarotti remains a lingering memory.

"'Lonely Old People' was very touching. Paul sang sitting at the piano with his wife, Linda, who was a wonderful lady, God bless her. He has a great voice, and knows how to work with his voice. He has a great way of singing, a great intuitive voice, which is very melodic. So he stood beside me at the back of the desk as we listened to the playback, and Paul was singing along to his own voice, practising and thinking of a harmony. And I can sing the cello part for an orchestra. I can spot these things, so I sang harmony with Paul."

The album would close with a cover of the twee television theme tune to *Crossroads*. Paul was asked about this unusual, typically McCartney-esque gesture during a press conference in the Crescent City. "It's after 'Lonely Old People', you see. They are sitting there in the park, saying: 'Nobody asked us to play.' It's a poignant moment. Then there's a little break and then 'Crossroads' starts up. It's just the kind of thing that lonely old people watch. It could just as easily have been *Coronation Street*, but we knew the chords to *Crossroads*. I just thought that it would be nice to do it."

McCartney played a demo of the song to 'Stash' de Rola, one of the Rolling Stones' former courtiers. He was startled to hear Paul's latest work, having enjoyed the thrill of being privy to *Sergeant Pepper* demos during the sixties. O'Duffy insists that McCartney's wealth of experience and incredible artistic and commercial success could easily have made him condescending towards others in his music-making demands. But Alan's studio experience proved quite to the contrary. "He's a lovely, lovely man and you could imagine he could be anything he wanted to be – he's been there, done that – and he could say: 'Who are you? You're just some engineer from a studio who made a hit record.' But he was completely the opposite, completely fun – 'Let's go, let's get on with it.' He might say: 'Well why don't we triple-track the backing vocals?' And I couldn't say: 'We don't have enough tracks, that's not technically possible.' He's Paul McCartney, he's been there."

With his engineer looking on, McCartney clearly appeared in control in his search for a specific and enthralling end product. But that didn't mean Laine, McCulloch and co weren't allowed full instrumental expression in the studio. It was, O'Duffy reveals, more a case of creative 'manipulation' in a musical sense, with Paul cleverly editing and refining the contributions of his band mates to get exactly what he wanted. "Oh, I agree with Alan," Smith concurs. "But it also seemed to me that Paul knew what he wanted to create."

CHAPTER ELEVEN

My Carnival

FEELING privileged to be a member of Wings while aware of his place in the musical ranks, newly recruited drummer Geoff Britton had been apprehensive about travelling to New Orleans. "It's a funny band, Wings. From a musician's point of view, it's a privilege to do it. From a career point of view, it's madness! No matter how good you are, you're always in the shadow of Paul."

"I think *any* musician working with Paul might consider himself to be in Paul's shadow," argues Sidney Smith, "and Geoff knew Paul infinitely better than I did."

Meanwhile, the personality clash that had been evident between McCulloch and Britton during Wings' 1974 sessions in Nashville became more pronounced. Britton would perform on half of the album tracks before ending his six-month tenure. His replacement was American drummer Joe English, who had been quickly auditioned and hired to complete the rest of the album's drum work. "It's funny. We lose a drummer named Geoff Britton, who's English," McCartney later mused, "and get in a drummer called Joe English, who's American." With the New Orleans influence in mind, "Joe drummed a bit funkier," Paul admitted, "than if we were back in . . . *Lancashire*."

With McCartney's album sessions entering their final fortnight, his friendship with Sehorn was strengthened when the Sea Saint co-owner organised a private party and press conference for the group on a riverboat cruise. Having arrived in style in a brace of white limousines, McCartney and his fellow band members wore top hats and paraded under pink parasols. They danced in the quayside sunshine to the accompaniment of the local Young Tuxedo Jazz Band, a rather dapper ensemble of trombone, tuba and saxophone players who'd been hired by McCartney to perform on the day.

As the crowds enjoyed the musical spectacle, McCartney handled the microphones and flashbulbs with customary aplomb. Meanwhile, the paparazzi gathered on the dockside prior to Wings boarding the boat. '*Viva New Orleans*' read the welcome banner as the McCartneys were ushered aboard past a Stars and Stripes. A press party was held at the beginning of the day before the boat set sail. The local media were also allowed onto the boat to undertake interviews, take photos and film the band.

Fledgling photographer Sylvia de Swaan, an artist enthralled by the city's exciting charm, had heard about their boat excursion in the local media. With her brand new camera, she arrived amidst a horde of seasoned staff snappers to capture the event. "New Orleans is a city where you get out and photograph masses of people for Mardi Gras. There were plenty of opportunities to do those kind of things, so it was delightful. I dressed up kind of smart and went along. And they [Paul and Linda] just let me in. It was fun, it was very crazy. I took photos on the pier, just before I got on the boat. And they said: 'Sure, come on in.' It was a big call for me."

Having been welcomed aboard, footage from the boat trip showed the relaxed former Beatle enjoying a dance and drink with the rest of his bandmates after sampling local cuisine.

Whilst sailing through Bayou country on the *Voyager* vessel, their journey took them along the course of the mighty Mississippi River. With a host of local musicians on board to provide entertainment, McCartney naturally found it impossible to pass up the opportunity of participating. One onlooker aboard the boat was Sidney Smith. "The Beatles were everything to me," he admits of a group who, like a million others, had strongly shaped his upbringing. "From the time I was nine years old, The Beatles ruled my life. I was just completely in awe of the fact that I was about to meet someone who was just in a different universe."

Smith had already been in contact with the respected New York-based music journal *Pop Wire* service. "They had used my photos to illustrate stories in several of their rock magazines such as *Hit Parader*," he recalls. Smith was eventually introduced to McCartney by Joe English, who had just been hired to replace Geoff Britton. Smith admits to having had no idea what to expect upon meeting this iconic musical figure. "I met Paul outside by the swimming pool of the [Le Richelieu] hotel he was staying at in New Orleans. He was gracious, kind, and extremely easy to speak with. He spent a while looking through my portfolio of photos I had taken of many of his contemporaries."

Smith clearly enjoyed the exciting, day-long boat voyage which produced a treasure trove of memorable images. He also faced no restrictions or limitations on what he could photograph. "I was the only photographer who was allowed on the boat once it set sail. I was capturing images that no-one would be able to capture. I was in seventh heaven."

With a swarm of press photographers and reporters stepping on each other's toes to get a picture or a quote, de Swaan clearly recalls this organised media melee. "Linda would say: 'Okay, let's relax and move over. Let's have a drink,' but I didn't get to talk to them. I shot rolls of film, and got some nice shots. A friend convinced me to take my pictures down to Sea Saint studios. I thought it was kind of preposterous, because there would be photographers from all over the world to cover it, so why would they want to use mine? They told me something went awry with the official photographer's film, and encouraged me to bring by the prints I had made."

In fact, Smith had suffered an unfortunate setback after a spectacular day of shooting exciting images of the group. "At the end of the day, when the boat arrived back at the dock, I put my camera bag down next to me and became a fan, just watching Paul play with the band on board. As I went to grab my bag to depart the boat, to my horror, it was gone. Someone had stolen my cameras as well as all the film I had shot that day. I was devastated." Subsequently, de Swaan's phone rang one day. "Someone was calling from London, the designer of the album, who wanted to use my photos for the album." Linda liked her photos and pushed for them to be used on the poster artwork.

While de Swaan and Smith had snapped away, an on-board news channel interviewer asked McCartney if he had a message for the city's populace during their annual celebrations. "Yes indeed!" he chirruped in local dialect. "*Maawwdi Graah!*" Asked for the latest news on the album reaching the shops, McCartney revealed that an April release date was likely. Had he thought of a title for their new work? "Not yet," he admitted, "but stick around, and we'll let you know . . ." "Keep smiling, we love you," Linda beamed. "Venus and Mars are alright tonight," she hinted with a grin. But the biggest question of all, which no interviewer would ever have considered asking at the time, was: would Lennon show up at Sea Saint?

Perhaps in honour of rekindling the flame with his old partner, the subsequent album's title track made reference to '*a good friend of mine*' who *'follows the stars'*. "The song 'Venus And Mars' is about an imaginary friend who's got a girl friend who's into astrology, the kind of person who asks you what your sign is before they say hello," McCartney would later explain of this Ono-like persona. Outside of McCartney's usual penchant for characterisation, this *could* be a coded reference to Lennon heeding to astrological advice before deciding against signing the recent Beatles' dissolution agreement a few weeks earlier. *'A good friend of mine studies . . . follows the stars,'* Paul corrects, perhaps recalling John's absence from the Plaza signing session the previous month.

Paul could hardly be blamed for being somewhat sceptical. If Lennon hadn't travelled from the other side of Central Park to meet his old bandmates a few weeks ago, would he really take the time to travel to the Deep South? Yet even after regaining the supposed security of his marriage, Lennon remained enthusiastic about the idea of reuniting with McCartney. John made one call from the Dakota to New Orleans in the opening days of February to discuss visiting Paul, but McCartney was asleep. Instead, John talked to Starr and Harrison about business in the wake of the Plaza signing session.

Meanwhile, McCartney had also been reading science fiction, and Asimov's *Foundation* was a distinct influence on the composition of the album title track. "I love the scope of it, the vision of it, because you can write anything," he told Paul Gambaccini. "The second time 'Venus And Mars' comes around, it says: *'Sitting in the hall of the great cathedral/Waiting for the transport to come.'* That's like in science fiction books, waiting for the space shuttle. 'Starship 21ZNA9', that's the kind of thing you'll find in Asimov. I like that, sitting in the cathedral, really waiting for the saucer to come down, to take him off to Venus and Mars or whatever."

Having resolved to name the track after the first two planets that came to mind, the first celestial pairing McCartney considered was of Saturn and Jupiter. But these two zodiac giants outsized his concept for the song. Saturn and Jupiter didn't have the same 'ring' as the classical pairing of Earth's closest neighbours. McCartney claimed he had remained unaware of Venus and Mars' proximity to Earth. You live and learn, he told one well-informed friend. 'That's great,' he thought, 'I'll put those in.' He couldn't go wrong. Broadcaster George Melly had assumed McCartney's inspiration had come from the artist Botticelli, something which Paul denied, claiming he wasn't even aware of Venus and Mars' symbolism as the goddess of love and god of war. In a further synchronistic occurrence,

McCartney later discovered that Venus, the morning star, and Mars had completed a rare conjunction in October in Lennon's sign of Libra. '*Your star is in the ascendancy*,' ran an early, astrologically inspired lyric. With the planets apparently in place that autumn, one can almost imagine McCartney sat in Sea Saint, pondering Lennon's possible arrival: awaiting a great moment when his musical dream of rekindling their partnership can transpire.

Toussaint, meanwhile, believes the arrival of a well-rehearsed Wings was in itself an exciting prospect. "Paul was so comfortable around the rest of the musicians that you didn't feel that awe of spending every moment in his presence. Everyone around them was comfortable. Paul was just one of the guys. So the thought of one of The Beatles being there wasn't prevalent at all times. And he was there for quite a spell. I must say, many people got to see him, and got to know him, and everyone felt the same. I think he [Paul] loved New Orleans music, and he knew about the local musicians who might not have been popular around the world, but still respected them highly. And from time to time, he would call on them for various things, and treated them royally."

"Just the fact that he had a constant flow of local R&B musicians visiting the studio while he was recording gave evidence to that," Smith confirms. "I was just simply trying to remain unobtrusive and capturing the moments I felt were important, such as photographing him with various members of New Orleans R&B royalty who would drop into the studio."

McCartney clearly had a genuinely high regard for New Orleans' local musicians, and the likes of Earl King was a regular visitor during recording sessions. Smith recalls taking photos of King with Wings between sessions at Sea Saint as they gathered in front of the camera. It was clearly an incredible experience for Smith to fraternise with and photograph one of his heroes. "Paul used to love him [Earl] visiting. Paul and the group loved him," claims Toussaint. "Earl was a magical writer and performer as well, and he was a very innovative guy."

King was one of the city's best-loved musical sons, and he had worked with Toussaint two years earlier on the New Orleans album *Street Parade*. "You have to understand that in New Orleans, music is way more than just a part of life. It's a city of music," says Smith. "It's the birthplace of jazz. We are a melting pot of different cultures and musical tastes. Cajun, rock, blues, jazz . . . It's all here. Musicians gravitate from all over the country to live and play in New Orleans. It's a magical city with a magnetic effect on those who come here. McCartney was inspired by New Orleans musicians: Professor Longhair, Ernie K-Doe, James Booker – all these people had been on Paul's radar screen. He, just like musicians from all over the world, are drawn to New Orleans because it *is* so diverse. Many of the British musicians love New Orleans, and the music and musicians that are rooted here."

Following one of the recording sessions for classic Wings single 'Listen To What The Man Said', the group jammed with Toussaint and legendary local musicians Dr. John and Professor Longhair, who were joined by Traffic's Dave Mason. "Dave Mason dropped in at Paul's request. He was playing a gig in New Orleans," Smith, who was absent from the session, recalls. "Paul found out about it and asked me to contact the promoter and ask Dave to drop by."

Not only had Longhair influenced Toussaint but he'd also inspired Mac Rebennack, better known as the legendary Crescent City musician Dr. John. Toussaint enthuses about his musical prowess. "Me and Dr. John started recording in the studio around the same age, as a guitarist and a pianist. He is a wonderful guitarist. He could write, and he could arrange, and he could do all the things that scholars do, you might say, and he did them very well."

Crucially, Dr. John's playing had partly inspired McCartney's quest for a suitably funky electric piano part on Lennon's *Abbey Road* composition, 'Come Together'. "He wanted a piano lick to be very swampy and smoky," recalled Paul in 1984, "and I played it that way and he liked that a lot. I was quite pleased with that." I asked Smith how important Dr. John's role remains in any celebration of New Orleans music. Smith was succinct in his reply. "Dr. John *is* New Orleans music. He is musical royalty here. He's the man."

Once the sessions had begun in earnest and McCartney had settled in New Orleans, he phoned Lennon at his Sutton Place apartment one evening in late January. "We'd like you to meet us here," Paul reminded John. Pang remembers Lennon's clear enthusiasm after taking McCartney's call. Perhaps the tentative prospect of Lennon's arrival ran through McCartney's mind as the sessions wore on: following the phone call to New York, Paul was awaiting the arrival of a man who could help him fulfil a dream, a man who'd challenged him to produce some of the finest moments of musical inspiration in a generation, arguably the greatest songwriting team of all reconvening to create musical magic. As May noted in her book, *Loving John*, what was important to Lennon was how enjoyable it would be for him to watch Paul record.

As February beckoned, Lennon was keen to make plans to reach Louisiana. He had resolved to make the journey to New Orleans a week later, after completing the mastering of the *Rock 'N' Roll* album. Two weeks into McCartney's sessions at Sea Saint, Lennon eventually realised that reuniting with Paul was an invitation he should not forego. In a sense, Lennon would have to decide at this point who (or what) he wanted: Yoko or Paul. In one ear, Lennon heard Pang's loving, supportive voice, urging him to renew his creative alliance with Paul. He also heard a distracting and influential voice, enticing him back home to the Dakota. With the heightened promise of a new songwriting collaboration within reach, just days before Lennon planned to leave New York, a decisive factor occurred to dramatically alter their plans.

When Paul phoned Lennon again at the end of January, John had already left for what he anticipated would be a much-welcomed, evening-long smoking cure session at the Dakota. In reality, it would prove a life-changing weekend of tumult and transition. While McCartney settled into life in New Orleans, Ono had made a number of teasing calls to Lennon during January with news of a curious invitation. She insisted that the stars were now aligned for her estranged spouse to undergo a 'secret treatment', a seemingly potent cure for his age-old nicotine addiction, part of an alternative 'smoking cessation' program. "Yoko called John to say: 'Today was the day. The stars are right. Gotta come today, we've gotta do this cure to get you to quit smoking.'" After recording *Walls And Bridges*, Lennon had felt that he was losing his breath when he was singing. "He couldn't hold his notes in the studio," Pang claims, "and he said it wasn't good for him." Pang strongly intuited that Lennon had already disclosed to Ono his plans for New Orleans. Perhaps a reunion would have spurred Lennon into leaving her for good. Or maybe Ono was afraid that she might lose John forever if, with May's encouragement, he reunited with McCartney? "John had made up his mind to run away from her," Pang insists. "She would telephone him, and in a rage John would say: 'I'm not talking to that woman.' John was rediscovering so many things – his friends, his music, his son."

Nonetheless, Pang had become increasingly apprehensive about the cure proposed by Ono as January had unfolded. She told John she was far from happy about him visiting the Dakota on the evening of January 31.

She attempted to find as many reasons as possible to persuade him not to go. "I just had a very weird feeling. Something didn't feel right. And we got into an argument about it, 'cos I didn't want him to go."

Lennon became annoyed, but saw that Pang had grown upset. He refrained from creating unnecessary friction, and attempted to reassure her there was nothing to worry about. "What's the problem?" Lennon shouted, trying to convince her he would return home later that evening. "Come on, don't worry, I'll be gone for a couple of hours and I'll be back. We'll go wherever you wanna go for dinner, anywhere you want to go."

Not only that, Lennon then insisted they would make their plans later that night to travel together down to New Orleans. "Everything," biographer Albert Goldman enticingly stated, "was in readiness for the long hoped-for reunion." Lennon, meanwhile, had arrived at the Dakota anticipating a powerful treatment for his nicotine addiction before returning to a healthier way of life with his young lover.

Pang's instincts proved to be correct. Just days before May and John had intended to travel to New Orleans, John abruptly returned to life at the Dakota. Despite his mysterious actions, Pang still firmly believed that Lennon loved her. "I always knew in my heart, but his actions proved differently. He went back and nobody knew what the underlying situation was. But *I* knew. How can you prove something that you only know spiritually?" According to Pang, the first week of February had been scheduled for Lennon's historic trip to the Crescent City in lieu of a studio reunion with Paul. "We were supposed to go, because John wanted to write and record with Paul, and we were getting ready to go."

With New Orleans representing a great opportunity for the two men to work together, it would, Pang rightly insists, have been a great gift for all Beatles fans. "But the opportunity to work together again always stemmed from Paul. It never came from John," claims Badman of a temporarily nostalgic Lennon. "Once he was reunited with his wife, nothing else mattered, and that included reuniting with his former songwriting partner." Ono subsequently blocked Pang from contacting John while he recovered from his treatment that Friday night. "The first sign May received that something strange was afoot was when she called the Dakota around 10 o'clock in the evening and asked to speak to John," wrote Geoffrey Guiliano. "She couldn't get through to him. May sat up all night, waiting for John, but he never came home." Following this alleged hypnotism or therapy-based 'smoking cure' session at the start of February,

277

Lennon's mysterious, unplanned return home has always been shrouded in intrigue.

After her attempts to contact him at the Dakota that weekend had proved unsuccessful, May eventually saw John again on Monday morning in the waiting room of their dentist's office. She was shocked and concerned at what she was confronted with. A sleep-deprived, zombie-like Lennon looked strange, dazed and disorientated. He also sounded confused, even incoherent. This was not the John Lennon she had expected to see after he'd undertaken his weekend-long 'smoking cure'.

According to Albert Goldman's lurid account of proceedings, Lennon had alternated inexplicably between being ill and passing out during this tumultuous weekend. He repeatedly lost consciousness before allegedly being given another dose of a powerful herbal brew. He later admitted to Pang that it had resembled something of the Primal Therapy he'd undertaken four years earlier. Ono, meanwhile, insisted John had been poisoned in what must have been a particularly potent potion. Considering he had complained of sickness and an unnatural state of lethargy, Pang suspected that something a little more manipulative had been involved as part of Lennon's treatment.

Meanwhile, journalist Peter Hammill, scheduled to interview Lennon that day, encountered a man who seemed mystified to find himself back in the familiar surroundings of the Dakota. He barely had any recollections of the defining events that had taken place six weeks earlier at the New York Plaza either. His sense of time and place had certainly been better. Hammill poignantly described the former Beatle's demeanour as one of a man recovering from "a serious illness".

Lennon attempted to make light of the situation, describing the turn of events as little more than a mid-morning outing for coffee and papers that somehow became a permanent change of address. Their interview soon proved untenable, and was re-scheduled for a later date. Lennon was left with no other choice but to inform Pang, much to her disappointment and astonishment, that Ono had allowed him to come home. "I was just going over for a visit and it just fell in place again. It was like I'd never left. I realised that this was where I belonged. I think we both knew we'd get back together again sooner or later . . . I just walked in and thought: 'I live here, this is my home. Here is Yoko, and here is me.'" Ono, Pang learned, believed it better for their immigration case if Lennon resided at the Dakota.

Whether by accident or design, Lennon had opted to return home to his wife, leaving Pang unsure of the motives. Lennon explained he still loved her, and had permission to continue seeing her from the safe distance of his luxurious home on Central Park West. It seemed inexplicable that Lennon would return to her after experiencing so much apparent happiness with his younger partner.

This weekend also precipitated a change in attitude about his relationship with McCartney, appearing to undo some of their friendship-restoring efforts. "When he returned," Pang says, "he was a different person about Paul. It wasn't the same. He was saying: 'Oh, you know when Paul and Linda used to visit us? Well I couldn't stand it.' Obviously something had happened on the other side of Central Park. Any thoughts of going to see Paul, or writing with him," insists Pang, "just went out the window. I mean, it wasn't there anymore. It was never encouraged. Yoko told John: 'You don't need to do this [go to New Orleans].' He told me this. He said: 'Yoko told me I don't need to do this.' I *know* John wanted to do it."

As Doggett rightly insists, it was a turn of events which scuppered their short-term hopes of a musical reconciliation. "It was a kind of safety blanket, that Beatles reunion thing," adds writer Keith Badman. "With his life seemingly upside down now, John was nostalgic, but only briefly, I believe. But once Yoko was back on the scene, his interest in rekindling the Fabs disappeared."

The strong probability is that Lennon and McCartney would have worked together once again had John not returned to the Dakota.

The day after McCartney recorded 'My Carnival', his personal ode to the New Orleans festive season, Lennon had been getting re-acquainted with his own Crescent City influences. His recent recording work had harkened back to the rock'n'roll education he'd enjoyed in the late fifties. A nostalgic Lennon happily eulogised about the songwriting finesse of Fats Domino during a lengthy radio discussion with WNEW's Scott Muni on February 13.

Busy enthusing over the work of the New Orleans powerful boogie-woogie and blues piano legend, Lennon had also recorded a Domino classic during the lengthy gestation of his *Rock 'N' Roll* covers album. "He's been cutting big sellers since 1948 or something," John recalled. "He was up before rock'n'roll even." Later responsible for such classics as

'I'm Walking', 'It's You I Love', 'Blueberry Hill' and 'Blue Monday', Domino was one of the first black American artists to be accepted by a mainstream audience.

Domino's nickname provided the title for his huge R&B hit single, 'The Fat Man'. With his Creole-soaked vocal and musical identity, Fats never conceded to current trends. After helping to shape what became the fifties R&B phenomenon, New Orleans became a hotbed for this new form, attracting musicians to the Crescent City who recorded with groups of local players.

With an accomplished musical ability notable even by the city's exceptional standards, the well-regarded, amiable Domino became one of the city's vanguard artists. While not as extravagant as some of his contemporaries, he duly developed into one of America's most cherished performers.

Meanwhile, Lennon also discussed with Muni the subject of Domino's songwriting collaboration with producer and bandleader Dave Bartholomew. A Cuban-flavoured sax riff was first introduced into the early rhythm and blues idiom courtesy of Bartholomew's 1949 'Country Boy' release. This innovation became an essential rhythmic component of what became known as R&B, the progenitor for the first wave of classic late fifties American rock'n'roll. As a pioneering figure in the almost imperceptible shift between R&B and rock'n'roll before featuring in influential musical movies such as *Shake, Rattle & Roll*, Domino would later recall that rock'n'roll was the "same rhythm and blues I'd been playin' down in New Orleans".

Domino and Bartholomew wrote songs, radio host Scott Muni insisted, utilising countless everyday expressions. "I do it myself," Lennon revealed. "If I hear something, the song writes itself." Lennon had also recently re-read Tennessee Williams' classic Crescent City novel A *Streetcar Named Desire*, and had worked on a turn-of-the-year demo simply entitled 'Tennessee', apparently intended for possible inclusion on the successor to *Walls And Bridges*.

With a new creative start in mind, Ray Connolly agrees that the influence of the New Orleans R&B environment might take the two men back to their adolescent musical instincts. "I would imagine that Paul would have been very happy to have had a bit of help, wouldn't you? They would have gone back to being when they were 14 or 15, and it would have been interesting to sit around and talk. 'Let's try this' or 'Have you heard this one?' 'Why don't we do this?' Neither of them ever had it again."

Having met in a suburban Liverpool church field in 1957, a Lennon-McCartney Mark II collaboration in 1975 in the Louisianan delta was not an unthinkable prospect. "I think they needed each other," stresses Ray Connolly, "and the sum of the parts was never equal to the whole. John probably wrote . . . how many good songs after they broke up, maybe half a dozen? I doubt there were many more, maybe 10? And Paul around the same."

As both a creative and songwriting alliance, Lennon and McCartney may well have benefitted from working together amidst the unique musical vibration of New Orleans, a city representing an ideal place to let go of the past and start again. Far removed from Los Angeles and New York, their partnership may have been transformed into a different proposition in the Crescent City. With Lennon eulogising over Domino at this point, it seems obvious that he'd have revelled in such a vibrant setting, from where the first great wave of American rock'n'roll swept across the Atlantic into the musically voracious port of Liverpool. Having Lennon's name on the subsequent sleeve for *Venus And Mars* might well have bolstered sales, too. What's more, McCartney may have played on Lennon's forthcoming album in true *quid pro quo* spirit. "This may have led to them working together again," Clayson insists, "even if not in the previous context."

"I imagine if John and Paul had got together, it would have been on each other's albums. I think they were aware we may be disappointed," Connolly claims, "because it wouldn't be what we'd imagine it would be. I'm sure there were times when John and Paul must have thought, 'I wish I could ring the other one, and ask them to come over. "Listen to this, what do you think? It needs something that I haven't got."' As *Rolling Stone*'s Paul Nelson opined during his review of the album: "Lennon probably had nothing whatsoever to do with *Venus And Mars*, but somehow the ghost of his sincerity not only haunts but also accentuates the cool calculation of the McCartney project."

In Nelson's esteem, "a jarring primal scream or two" may have saved McCartney from making what he considered a bland commercial attempt to become "pop music's Romeo and Juliet". As McCartney biographer Peter Ames Carlin recounted: "Paul would not have submitted these kinds of songs to John without tasting his editorial wrath." In a spirit of renewal, both men may have been keen to write fast, inspired by the dynamic of the Crescent City. Would a then-successful Sea Saint have been a good setting for a Lennon McCartney reunion, I asked New Orlean native Smith? "Oh, of course," he enthused. "That would've been epic!" They may even have sought to rediscover something of their old, one-on-one songwriting approach in the studio.

Following years of collaborative estrangement, some initially awkward moments of mutual musical indecision might inevitably have followed. "On the first day, either John or Paul might have started to boss the other guy around, and the sessions could have ended right there," Doggett guesses. "My gut feeling is that both of them would have erred on the side of not upsetting the other."

The strength of any new material may have come through a sense of musical adventure. After years of unchallenged leadership, McCartney's perfectionist, conservative core might have been breached by Lennon's joyous urgency to seize the moment, conjuring a series of stunning vocals that reprised every voice he'd ever adopted across a suite of contemporary rhythm and blues. Duly challenged and inspired, Paul may also have rediscovered an old lyrical depth in familiar company. McCartney clearly sought inspiration from the city's musical heritage, searching for a soul-deep vocal grandeur in the vein of Beatles standards 'Oh Darling!' or 'Lady Madonna'. 'Oh Darling!''s doo-wop harmony approach, replete with requisite Little Richard-esque vocal echo, had been rehearsed during early morning studio run-throughs while recording *Abbey Road*. "I wanted it to sound as though I'd been performing it onstage all week," Paul later admitted of a song which Lennon admired and he felt better suited to singing. McCartney's vocal attitude became clear when O'Duffy observed something of his intentions during a studio buffet lunch one day.

"Paul would be imitating the local guys, wanting to expand his voice downwards because they have this thing of going [adopts deep, Southern drawl] '*Heeyyyyy maaaan.*' I can't remember the exact phrase, but Paul was trying to practise that, just for fun." 'Lady Madonna' was a song whose vocal had been strongly inspired by the Crescent City maestro Fats Domino. Starkey producer Richard Perry later encouraged Fats to record his own cover version, the final hit of a lengthy career that had included more than 30 chart hits during the fifties and early sixties. (One of George Harrison's earliest musical memories of rock'n'roll had been of hearing Domino's 'I'm In Love Again'.) Meanwhile, Toussaint believes that his and McCartney's duet version of Domino's 'I Want To Walk You Home' proved a perfectly apt contribution to the 2007 *Goin' Home* tribute album to Fats.

With Lennon having enjoyed his fast, spontaneous collaboration with Bowie in mid-January in New York, a relaxed studio, a fresh setting and a familiar face may have been conducive to Lennon's creativity. "I remember there being a rumour about John possibly coming," recalls Smith. "I believe I may have heard the rumour from Alan O'Duffy."

"There was some thought that he was going to join us," the engineer recalls. "John was just up in New York, and they had been talking to each other."

Paul's manager, Alan Crowder, expressed his views in no uncertain terms in front of the engineer. "He hoped John didn't come down," O'Duffy reveals, "as all this sort of organisation we were trying to do would go to pot. He was intimating that John was something of a loose cannon." Yet O'Duffy sensed that McCartney would have embraced Lennon's presence. "I'm sure Paul would have enjoyed it, and he'd have thought it was a great idea. It wouldn't strike me as being at all unusual. It might have turned into: 'Well, let's do that.' It might have gone further, and they'd have decided to do something together."

"I think Alan O'Duffy probably had more of a pulse on the situation. Alan Crowder was probably trying to keep the attention focused on Paul," Sidney Smith insists, aware of Lennon's rumoured visit to the studio. However, Smith claims that Paul never discussed The Beatles in his company in the studio. "McCartney was just another musician renting the studio. At least that's the way it appeared to me, and Toussaint was really in his own world." The producer had remained unaware that McCartney had invited Lennon to visit Sea Saint. "No, not until now," he admits when asked about any prior knowledge of Paul's invitation. "That's really nice to know."

Having settled into his New Orlean recording routine, McCartney would soon enjoy the colourful experience and ambience of Mardi Gras, celebrating its centenary holiday festival. The added attraction of the carnival atmosphere made the trip a more tempting, enticing prospect for Lennon. As a native of the city, Toussaint was well-accustomed to its celebratory feel during its world-renowned party season. Yet a defiant and celebratory character typifies the city, even when the carnival isn't in town, Smith maintains. "The culture is *alive* in New Orleans. We throw a party for everything. There is a festival of some sort almost every weekend."

Mardi Gras remains an all-inclusive festival, despite its salacious reputation. Culminating on Fat (or Shrove) Tuesday, the carnival's festive season features huge parties and masked balls as part of a life-affirming celebration.

Rolling down the city's streets, elaborate, *flambeaux*-led parades are followed by local crews riding legendarily exotic floats that tour the city's heaving streets, bedecked in traditional carnival colours: purple for justice, green for faith and gold for power. Small toys, coloured beads and wooden coins are tossed down to young and old alike amongst the buoyant throngs. McCartney later claimed that it was only upon their arrival in the city that they discovered the annual festivities were in full flow. Booking time off from the studio for two or three days, they dressed as clowns and 'did' Mardi Gras.

Mingling with the crowd while adorned in silk harlequin costumes, necklaces, and heavy face paint, Paul and Linda assumed they would blend seamlessly into the extraordinary street parades. McCartney was clearly surprised at the familiar reception amongst local revellers as he and Linda soaked up the celebratory atmosphere. "I thought, 'No one will recognise us.' But people in the street said, 'Hi Paul!' 'No, I'm a clown . . .' 'Hey, Paul!'"

Unsurprisingly, the McCartneys' public forays didn't last long, and the couple were forced to retreat back to their third floor balcony as they surveyed all manner of drunken revelry around them. Walking around the French Quarter and witnessing the procession of costumes and masks was a unique and thrilling experience. Having entered into the traditional festive spirit, disguising their celebrity would later cause some unexpected embarrassment during the Lundi Gras celebrations on February 10.

With the all-day festival in full swing and the annual Orpheus parade proceeding through the city's streets, the McCartneys had ventured out to St. Bernard's Civic Auditorium to watch Dr. John and The Meters in action at his wild, annual Mambo shindig. Their musical presence gave the evening "the authenticity and energy to turn everybody royally around," reported one local writer, neatly capturing the night's raucous sense of occasion.

"By the time the festivities ground to a halt five hours later, the capacity crowd had been turned every way but loose by the nitty-gritty sounds laid down by the funky Doctor and his second-line pals," wrote one Big Easy scribe. "Filling the dance floor with their incredible costumed presence, the freaked-out, under-30 audience danced, shouted, and generally partied its collective brains out in fulfilment of everybody's wildest public fantasies, and the musicians had as much fun as everybody in the place."

Amidst the *joi de vivre* of the occasion, the McCartneys' impeccable disguise resulted in them being ejected from the room, remaining unrecognised due to the former Beatle's heavy make-up. "Their disguises were *so* good that Dr. John's security people literally threw the McCartneys off the stage," Smith recalls, also present on the night of the concert. "It's a story that Dr. John still recalls to this day." The Crescent City legend clearly remains amused by the incident whenever he is reminded of it.

Regardless of any drunken misunderstandings, Paul and his studio entourage were the toast of the town. "I have photos of the Mardi Gras and it was quite extraordinary. Amazing! Paul, at the time, was the most famous face on the planet," remembers O'Duffy, "and he used to have a great joke. If we were going out together, and needed to get in somewhere, it was: 'Don't you recognise the face?' If you were walking down the street and someone on the other side said: 'Aren't you Paul McCartney?' he would say: 'I wish I had his money!'" Sidney Smith insists the group were in suitably festive mood. "Oh, absolutely. They took to New Orleans like a second home. They tried to participate in everything they could."

Onlookers recall seeing the McCartneys standing on balconies on St. Charles Avenue, blowing bugles, throwing beads and gazing down at the amazing sights below them as wild, colourful processions streamed past on the streets of the Crescent City. "Paul and his entourage were camped out on a balcony of a restaurant where all of the parades were passing," Smith recalls. "Before heading up to be with them on the balcony, I shot several images from the street level as Paul engaged with the crowds below, throwing beads to the masses on the street. Once I joined them on the balcony, I shot a variety of photos of him, Linda, the kids, and others in attendance."

McCartney remained in the midst of recording sessions as the Mardi Gras vibe reached its height. He recorded newly improvised composition 'My Carnival' (initially entitled 'New Orleans' in honour of the city) in front of a local News Scene 8 TV crew around February 12. The song remained unreleased for a number of years, eventually surfacing as a B-side in the mid-eighties. "I remember the media being invited into the studio to film Paul playing that song," Smith recalls. "Most media people at the time were equally as giddy about being around a Beatle. After all, it was 1975 and Paul hadn't toured the US since the break-up of The Beatles. Any opportunity to be around Paul McCartney was a thrill for anyone."

'My Carnival', however, did not make the final track-listing for *Venus And Mars*. 'New Orleans', written in cahoots with Linda, featured lyrics based largely on Linda's recollections of the sights, sounds and aromas they experienced around the city. The original song's lyrics were populated with oysters, bourbon, pralines and the sound of fifties music echoing through the crowded streets. Paul also recorded an impromptu version of 'Babyface' with the city's very own Tuxedo Jazz Band. "It's a backing track of me playing on the piano for a TV video tape. But when we were in New Orleans, I took the track and asked these fellows to overdub, and like, these guys don't know what earphones are. They're a trad band, right? A genuine, New Orleans brass band. They couldn't get the tempo for a while, but then they started to get it."

McCartney also taped a version of Professor Longhair's 'Go See The Mardi Gras', a song about the carnival's revivifying effects on the soul. Paul would often experiment with New Orleans music on piano, such as Professor Longhair's song, but Smith doesn't recall any local Cajun, jazz or blues records playing in the studio. Toussaint and Dr. John were both disciples of Longhair. According to writer Ed Ward's Rock & Roll Hall Of Fame tribute, Toussaint was a main exponent of the local "carnival sound – a raucous, polyrhythmic beat that was solid but complex, like a rhythm-and-blues rhumba crossed with the second-line rhythms of Professor Longhair."

Longhair (aka Henry Byrd) was an R&B stylist whose unorthodox piano-playing combined blues, boogie-woogie and rhumba. Anthemic songs such as 'Tipitina' and 'In The Night' duly became part of a seventies renaissance for a singer whose talents were rediscovered in his home city. "Of all the things I had been mimicking off of the radio, with Professor Longhair, it was like nothing else I had ever heard or anything I could relate it to," Allen told me. "He had lived and breathed what he played. His whole life was there in the moment," he enthused. "It was a new language, and there was nothing debatable about it." A genuinely great pianist residing in a city full of wonderful piano players, Longhair was living on the city's South Rampart Street when he was 'rediscovered' in the seventies.

Just days before leaving Sea Saint, McCartney conducted interviews for TV stations a week after Mardi Gras on February 20. If Paul had taken note while watching the TV in the Sea Saint facility, he'd have been likely to see Lennon's *Rock 'N' Roll* album being given heavy endorsement.

Talk of a prospective Beatles reunion surfaced during a nationwide, multi-station radio link-up the following day as Lennon promoted this rush-released new album. He insisted that the most sensible course of action would involve "going into a studio to get relaxed together and make some music". Whilst nothing was currently in the offing, he insisted, this ideal scenario of Lennon's sounded similar to the opportunity on offer from McCartney down in New Orleans.

Sat in New York's Capitol Records office on Sixth Avenue, Lennon was busy discussing his newly released *Rock 'N' Roll* album with an array of coast-to-coast radio station DJ's. "Before our chat, a buoyant John talked on the telephone to no less than 35 different disc jockeys simultaneously across America," remembers *Melody Maker*'s Chris Charlesworth, who watched while Lennon undertook his radio interviews. "I like 'Stand By Me' and 'Be Bop-A-Lula' is one of my all-time favourites," Lennon announced in response to a question about his teenage music idols, before going on to discuss the problems he had in making the album.

Rolling Stone writer Jon Landau opined in his review of Lennon's return to roots project: "If I didn't know better, I would have guessed that this was the work of just another talented rocker who's stumbled onto a mysterious body of great American music that he truly loves but doesn't really understand. In paying tribute to his musical childhood background, Lennon sounds like he's forgotten he used to perform material like this seven nights a week and that he used to record it several times a year."

Two weeks or so after his return to the Dakota, and having recovered from his hypnotism-based 'smoking cure', Lennon clearly still had intentions of visiting Paul, unaware that the sessions at Sea Saint would soon close. After being thanked by some rather more accommodating journalists for the years of musical joy and inspiration he'd provided as a Beatle and solo artist, Lennon's voice suddenly pipes up through the crackle and buzz of telephone wires one final time. "Say hello to Paul in New Orleans," he politely urges the Big Easy's WTIX radio DJ, Bobby Reno. "Are you gonna try and get back down here?" the same DJ quickly interjects. "I'm gonna try and get there before he finishes," Lennon replies, offering this promising pledge to reach town before ringing off.

287

But time was running out. McCartney would only be at Sea Saint for just a few more days. Paul sent Ringo a postcard on February 24, their last day's work in the Crescent City studio. His missive featured a photo of one of the city's celebrated street-trams on its cover. "*Dear Richard*," the card read: "*Hello from New Orleans. We're moving on tomorrow to LA to finish* [the] *LP or album*." "'Have you heard the new Beatles single?' used to be the most important thing in the world," recalls O'Duffy. "I remember people saying: 'Have you heard Paul's new album?' I remember 'Rock Show' and '. . . Titanium Man'. I haven't listened to the album for a long time, but it was fantastically important."

"I just thought I'd do a new LP," McCartney would later recall. "I had a bunch of songs on my scroll, and I thought it would be better than *Band On The Run*." The resulting work of *Venus And Mars*, critic Peter Ames Carlin insisted, was a "highly polished, deeply assured album that took in styles and ideas ranging from hard rock to piano ballads, to orchestrated forties pop; from comic books to science fiction; from the joys of young love to the ebbing light of senescence. Everything came with a purpose."

The following day, February 25, Harrison turned 32. He was no doubt the lucky recipient of a typically humorous birthday collage from John, busy being photographed by Bob Gruen outside the Dakota as George celebrated back home in England.

CHAPTER TWELVE

When Two Saints Meet

HAVING promisingly reported that he and Paul were firm friends, Lennon and McCartney were clearly communicating on good terms at this point. Perhaps further inspired by a prospective visit to New Orleans, Lennon had set his sights on returning to the studio in late March to begin work on a new album. If Lennon's move back towards rock'n'roll didn't necessarily signify a move closer to The Beatles, it certainly wasn't something he was willing to rule out. "Well, let's just say we're good friends," he told the assembled cast of radio journalists. "At least we're talking, and we're all happy with each other," he admitted as McCartney's sessions drew to a close. "If we got back together, it wouldn't be for one last show, right?"

Softening his attitude towards his musical past and having revealed his increasing willingness to revisit the group's back catalogue, Lennon's change of heart about revisiting classic Beatles material had become clear. Having performed two Beatles compositions in November during his live appearance in New York, Lennon had also happily been involved in a re-recording of one of his underrated, late psychedelic classics in mid-January. Lennon also admitted his enthusiasm about revisiting 'Help!', one of what he considered the few emotionally authentic compositions of his Beatle career.

Lennon later informed Pang that a revised version of the song would have resembled the *Walls And Bridges* track 'Scared'. "I mean it – it's real. The lyric is as good now as it was then," he explained to *Rolling Stone* in 1970. "It's no different, you know, and it makes me feel secure to know that I was that aware of myself then. It was just me singing 'Help', and I meant it." Pang would often be treated to a re-interpreted rendition of this decade-old Lennon favourite. Keen on re-recording it the way he'd heard it in his head, this new version, Pang claims, was beautiful.

"I'd do 'Hey Jude' and the whole damn show," he insisted with no little enthusiasm on February 21 in conversation with Chris Charlesworth. It was a song which had touched Lennon as much as it impressed him, and one which he'd always hold in high regard amongst his partner's great musical creations. As one of love's prime objectives, salvation and healing appeared inherent to the appeal of 'Hey Jude', let love in when you doubt yourself, McCartney's letter-like song of spiritual resolve insisted. For those who needed to heal, 'Hey Jude' aimed to reach the heart and take away the pain. Paul's song of spiritual balm also articulated something of our loving potential to heal others.

Lennon would also praise the longevity of another of McCartney's classic compositions, 'Eleanor Rigby'. During a mid-March interview with the French media on The Beatles' largely timeless body of work, Lennon claimed that much of The Beatles' material would stand up in any period unless music *really* changes, he enthused. "We were always ourselves. It doesn't matter what period or what era, that will go down in 200 years as a great song. When it gets down to the nitty-gritty, it's the song, you know?"

The overwhelming classicism of the Lennon-McCartney songbook had, Lennon claimed, intimidated would-be cover artists in the past, and he sounded positively proud of their work and legacy later that year. "There are so many good singles that The Beatles wrote that were never released," he told *Hit Parader*. "A few people in the past have done Beatle songs. But in general they feel you can't touch them. 'You can't do a Beatle number . . . You can't touch a Lennon song; only Lennon can do it . . .' Why don't people do them? It's good for me, it's good for Paul. It's good for all of us."

Later that year, Lennon admitted he had finally accepted that any new studio work would always be compared to that of his incredible Beatles legacy. But more importantly, he'd also resolved not to let the charts dictate his art. "I do think now in terms of long term. I'm an artist. I have to express myself. I can't be dominated by gold records. The art is more important than the thing, and sometimes I have to remind meself of it."

Having reached Los Angeles in order to bring *Venus And Mars* to fruition, McCartney rented a house in Coldwater Canyon where he put the finishing touches to the new album at Wally Heider Studios. Work included overdubs, backing vocals, string segments and saxophone parts to adorn the suite of contemporary pop, rock, R&B and soul-inflected songs. Paul scooped a brace of Grammy awards for Best Pop Vocal Performance and Best Produced Non-Classical Recording for the acclaimed *Band On The Run* album. "Sometimes an artist is in tune with his times. Paul had enjoyed that experience in the sixties, spectacularly so," claimed biographer Howard Sounes, "and his luck was holding into the seventies."

Clad in an unusually foppish tuxedo, Lennon attended the event in New York and witnessed The Beatles being honoured with a place in the Grammy Hall Of Fame. He also presented the Record Of The Year award for Olivia Newton John's single, 'I Honestly Love You'. Also present were Paul Simon and Art Garfunkel, with Art emerging from the audience to accept the award on Newton John's behalf. The halting dialogue from the podium ran like this:

Lennon: "Hello, I'm John. I used to play with my partner, Paul."

Simon: "I'm Paul. I used to play with my partner Art."

After Garfunkel had walked onstage to collect Newton John's award, Lennon jokingly chided Art for his seriousness during his brief speech. He then began a conversation with Simon.

Lennon: "Are you two [Simon & Garfunkel] getting back together?"

Paul Simon: "Are *you* two [Lennon & McCartney] getting back together?"

Simon may only have been jesting, but later that same night, Lennon confided in Garfunkel about this very dilemma. After sharing the awards podium, Lennon invited Garfunkel to a post-ceremony gathering at his plush Dakota apartment. It had been a memorable evening and would, for his guest, swiftly become an unforgettable night.

Garfunkel would later relate the story of this encounter to film director Seth Swirsky whilst sat on his apartment deck overlooking Central Park, pointing to the Dakota apartments in the distance on Central Park West. Garfunkel was fascinated by Lennon's grounded nature. Captivating and engaging, Art quickly realised that John instinctively knew what to say to put him at ease. "He was connected, human and real," Garfunkel insisted, "and that's what he did with the whole planet earth. He was a hit record – his very being was like a hit." He clearly admired the commercial qualities which had enabled The Beatles' music to entrance the whole world.

Having entered his Dakota apartment, Lennon took the singer into his private bedroom to talk in confidence, away from Ono, Simon and guest David Bowie. Sat on the edge of his bed, Lennon quizzed Artie in incredibly disarming fashion about his recent studio reunion with Paul Simon. "I understand you just recorded together recently in Nashville," the same location McCartney had chosen to take the newly repaired Wings to stretch and develop as a band the previous summer. "Tell me about your work. How did it go?"

Garfunkel and Simon had actually recorded in Muscle Shoals, but the two men had nevertheless reconciled their differences and recorded top ten hit 'My Little Town', their first new material in more than five years. Garfunkel regaled Stuart Grundy with his own detailed account of the sessions. "It's always Paul's impression that my style is not raunchy enough. And so he says: 'Here's a song that I think would be perfectly tailored for you. A song I'm in the middle of writing. I'd like to give it to you as a gift, because I think it's perfect programming for you in terms of balancing out your album.'"

Art then demonstrated that the song's bridge was ideally suited to a two-part harmony. "He sings melody, and I immediately jump to a harmony. Instinctively for a change, I go for the lower harmony, instead of the higher harmony. It gives us a slightly different kind of blend." Suddenly, the two men were singing together again for the first time in almost five years. "So we enjoyed it a lot, and I guess we felt by the time we had run the song down, that it's good for us, and there's no reason *not* to cut it. We simply enjoyed it too much, so we said: 'All right, let's cut it.' He succeeded in showing me some very good players who I'd like to work with again. I remember winter was receding finally, and there was a very nice smell in the air, and we spent three days cutting this track to 'My Little Town'."

Meanwhile, Lennon was just as keen to gauge Garfunkel's feelings about their reunion, curious to understand how it had felt to work with Simon again. Garfunkel summed up their mutual affection with one of Simon's favourite phrases, one which Lennon had previously used to describe his feelings for McCartney: "We have enriched each other's lives."

Garfunkel was later asked if he'd been more appreciative of Simon than his partner had been of him. He agreed, feeling a little aggrieved that he'd not been given due credit for helping to make Simon's songs such classic popular recordings. "I sometimes think we are not too different from The Beatles. In that, first and foremost, is a long-standing friendship that underlies all this stuff. We don't want to take our careers so seriously that we actually blow the old and dear friendships that we have."

Perhaps Lennon should also have canvassed Simon for his advice, after he'd recorded at Sea Saint and worked with Toussaint in early 1973 whilst making his *There Goes Rhymin' Simon* album. Simon also recorded a rendition of 'Take Me To The Mardi Gras', a song attempted by McCartney during his February sessions. Only Harrison's *Living In The Material World* would keep the album off the number one spot. Simon later ranked McCartney as one of music's all-time great composers, placing Lennon in the second most illustrious tier of classic songsmiths. Simon believed in Lennon's evocative and powerful economy as a lyricist. Enigmatic works such as 'Strawberry Fields Forever', 'I Am The Walrus', 'In My Life' and 'Norwegian Wood', Simon insisted, ensured Lennon's enduring appeal as a songwriter.

Back at the Dakota, Lennon shifted in his seat and shared his ongoing creative dilemma with Garfunkel. He revealed that he'd been receiving calls from *his* Paul in New Orleans, asking if he'd like to participate in this latest, Toussaint-based Louisianan project. Lennon and McCartney's friendship, it seemed to Art, was strong enough to warrant such an opportunity.

A true man of instinct, a quality which often drove his creative decisions, Lennon sensed he ought to seize this opportunity to work with Paul once again. For the first time, he now seriously contemplated a reunion. "He wants to know if I'm available for the recording, Art. Paul's interested in doing something with me. He wants to work with me again, and I'm thinking about going to New Orleans to help him with his new album." Lennon then posed to Art a startling, unforgettable question. "What do *you* think I should do?"

Eliciting a similar reaction to that of Pang, the enormity of the question left Garfunkel speechless. "It was a *musical* question. It wasn't a heavy personal question. Imagine John Lennon saying this to me. Can you imagine how it felt? John Lennon asking *me* for my advice!"

"It's fascinating that Art Garfunkel went back to John's house and John asked him for advice," Seth Swirsky later commented. "How many times do you get pulled into John Lennon's bedroom, and asked advice about how to get back with Paul McCartney? We're talking about the greatest songwriting team in history."

Understandably flattered, Art instinctively felt that John was measuring Lennon and McCartney's situation with that of himself and Simon, testing him to ensure his ego was comparable "as a colleague and musical contemporary." But as far as Art was concerned, the Lennon and McCartney songwriting team had always been a little *more* equal than others. Garfunkel gathered his thoughts. He sensed his answer may just be the catalyst for a reunion.

Urging John to do it, Art reminded him about the vitality of his successful musical collaboration with McCartney. With true eloquence, he pointed to the thrilling sound they'd created together. "What I found with my Paul," Garfunkel admitted, "is the harmony and the sound happenings are a full agenda. It's great fun to harmonise. If you've not made that blend that you used to make in a long time, you'll see that it's pleasurable. Just to produce the harmony is such a nice sensation in the ear and in the heart."

Have fun, he enthused. Revisit the shared creative thrill of making music with someone you once created such a successful sound with. Ignore the strands of history, he urged Lennon, and leave any old complications behind. "If you can return to the fun of that sound with your old buddy, it will keep you busy." Keep things on a purely musical level, he insisted, and leave your personalities to one side. If he went with the fun of the musical blend, it would prove a pleasant and enjoyable experience. Lennon looked satisfied and nodded in agreement.

Garfunkel left the Dakota early on March 2, confident that he had done enough to encourage John on the subject of a musical reunion with Paul. It was, as far as he was concerned, a straightforward, uncomplicated matter.

Having been privy to Lennon's thoughts during this confidential discussion, Garfunkel soon revealed a tantalising sense of the conversation he'd had with Lennon in March. "I wouldn't be surprised if some of The Beatles or all of The Beatles do something together," he told Stuart Grundy a little later that year. Despite returning to the supposed security of his marriage, Lennon had now canvassed his partner and fellow musicians on his creative dilemma. He'd eventually conceded this *was* the right opportunity to reunite with McCartney, and would answer his old friend's musical call.

Guided by the need for security, Lennon would later claim that his reconciliation with Ono meant he was too busy enjoying his renewed marriage to join Paul in the Crescent City. It was almost as if this development had suddenly superseded any prospect of creative collaboration. "I was supposed to be going down to join Paul in New Orleans, but my personal life sort of interfered with that. I just never made it to New Orleans, sorry Paul."

After Garfunkel's departure, Lennon conducted a post-Grammy Awards radio interview at around 5 a.m. with Alex Bennett. Ono and house guest Bowie were also included in the broadcasted discussion. Just two weeks after Garfunkel's visit, Lennon welcomed British interviewer Bob Harris to his Dakota apartment in mid-March. Amongst other topics for discussion were Lennon's friendship with McCartney. As the subsequent broadcast proved, the chances of a creative reunion appeared to be back on the agenda. However, Lennon spoke with a little less candor than he had while in Garfunkel's company a fortnight earlier.

Remaining suitably vague as he skirted the subject of new opportunities with speculative optimism, no mention was made of New Orleans in front of the TV cameras. However, Lennon insisted that his fabled bond with McCartney had been largely restored. Unaware of the private plans which had been proposed for New Orleans just weeks earlier, Harris asked Lennon the inevitable question about a long-awaited Beatles reunion. Despite feigning mock surprise, it was a subject Lennon still hadn't ruled out. His amicable comments, partially directed towards McCartney, revealed only part of the truth of their relationship.

Whilst Lennon hadn't worked with Paul after experiencing a more difficult time, he insisted that they were close once again. "Him and me are okay," he emphasised, "so I don't care what they say about that. The only thing that matters is how he and I feel about those things." Having initially enthused about an upstate New York autumn show back in the spring, Lennon's thoughts had subsequently turned to The Beatles prospering as a musical entity on record once again.

"Everybody always envisaged the stage show," he told Harris. "But, to me, if we worked together, [it would be the] studio again," he insisted of his most comfortable musical environment. "The stage show is something else. If we got back together, it wouldn't be for one last show, right?" Lennon had also wanted to record at least one new Beatles track as a prelude to a more formal reunion. "If one [song] comes around and it works, maybe we'll do another," he told Pang. "It was to be behind-the-scenes. 'A quick one off, and let's see from there,'" she enthused.

With his mind no doubt on Paul's recent invitation to join him in New Orleans, Lennon explained more of his feelings and musical instincts about a Beatle reunion. "It was strange, because at one period when they were asking me, I was saying: 'No, never. What the hell. Go back? Not me!' And then it came to the period when I thought, 'Well, why not? If we felt like making a record or doing something.' Now, when I'm keen to do it, I turn the paper and George is saying: 'Not me.' It's never got to the position where each one of us has wanted to do it at the same time. I think over the period of being apart, we've all thought: 'That would be nice. That wouldn't be bad.'"

If all four Beatles wanted to do it, if they got into a studio again and turned each other on musically, and they made something worthwhile for release, *then* it would be worth it, Lennon maintained. The voice of their critics would be irrelevant. In rather *blasé* fashion, he reasoned that if McCartney was eager to pull it together, then despite his busy schedule, he'd be happy to go along with it. Alternatively, if Harrison, Starr and McCartney happened to be in New York, he would happily invite them to play on his forthcoming album. "Then it'd be a Beatle record," he enthused, "if they were around!" Turning to look into the camera, he sings Doris Day's signature refrain: '*We'll meet again, don't know where, don't know when!*' with just enough humour to make his point.

During an interview with French TV the following day, Lennon confirmed his plans to head into the studio in less than two weeks' time. Perhaps he was hoping that, with McCartney now a frequent visitor to New York, his old partner might arrive at some point to play with him during the prospective sessions. Lennon certainly seemed to be the Englishman that fellow musicians who arrived in New York were eager to see, keen to know exactly what was happening and the places to be seen.

As a nod to McCartney's new musical endeavour, disco fan Lennon performs an *ad hoc* piano rendition of contemporary blockbuster 'Lady Marmalade', Patti LaBelle's recent, Toussaint-produced Sea Saint classic. "They [LaBelle] had so much energy and they had an air of theatre as well," Toussaint recalls. "And they were ready all the time, and with their attitude, it was really wonderful. Their energy lifted us from the rate that we normally operate at." Grinning into the camera, Lennon sings a spirited version of its catchy refrain, '*Voulez-vous couchez avec moi, ce soir?*' He was even pictured wearing a T-shirt with this suggestive phrase emblazoned across his chest. "All together now!" he enthuses, clearly enjoying the moment while attempting to recall the subsequent verse of the song.

McCartney then reciprocated Sehorn's earlier gesture by flying dozens of leading New Orleans musicians to LA for his own shindig aboard the *Queen Mary* ocean liner in Long Beach on March 24. McCartney hired 'Fess', as he was affectionately known, to play the *Venus And Mars* end of recording party along with funk band The Meters, an occasion which subsequently produced a live 1978 Longhair album. The party saw musical performances from Lee Dorsey and Ernie K-Doe, and the gathering included appearances from Harrison, Mal Evans and Derek Taylor.

It was the first time that Harrison and McCartney had socialised together since their brief meeting in New York in December, and illustrated that a mood of Beatle *rapprochement* still remained. "When we had a party in the States to celebrate having finished the album, someone came up to us and said: 'Hello Venus, hello Mars.' I thought: 'Oh no.' When I write songs, I'm not necessarily talking about me, although psychoanalysts would say: 'Yes you are, mate.' But as far as I'm concerned, I'm not," McCartney later admitted to Paul Gambaccini.

Following John's pro-Beatle speculations during media and TV interview appearances that spring, McCartney's wife continued to encourage both men to consider reuniting during the summer of 1975. "If ya wanna make me an offer . . . unless we work together again as Linda keeps – how shall I put it – *suggesting*?" Lennon wrote to Derek Taylor in one of his humorous missives about McCartney. "I can't really see it myself."

McCartney, meanwhile, began to consider his lack of contact with Lennon while touring *Venus And Mars* with Wings that year. He admitted to biographer Chris Welch that the odd telegram or follow-up phone call might have helped keep them on musical terms. But by the end of the year, John's contract with Capitol was complete. "He wanted to disappear," Voormann insisted during his *LENNONYC* interview. "'I'm not owned by *you*. I'm *free*.' He was definitely happy when he didn't have to fulfil his contract. I'm sure John stopped listening to the radio for a long time. He just played what he wanted to play."

In the summer of 1975, writer Ray Connolly received a card informing him that not only were the Lennons back together, but that Yoko was pregnant. "I wrote back a reply saying: 'Congratulations,' and John replied saying: 'It's the husband here, how are you?'" "John walked into the office and said: 'Don't tell *any*body, but Yoko's pregnant,'" Cicala remembers Lennon saying during one of his last visits to the Record Plant. "He was like a guy who was having his first baby. His voice was an octave higher, with joy, with his baby. He never said he's not going to come back, but he had to take care of the baby." "I felt it was a relief to see him be happy suddenly," Voormann admitted. "It wasn't easy for him. He was a very, very complicated person. He was very sensitive, and people didn't realise it."

In March, *Melody Maker*'s Chris Charlesworth reported that John's negotiations to remain an American resident would reach a climax within the next three months. Lennon's lawyer, Leon Wildes, had evidence which showed that the Government "deliberately ignored his application, actually locking the relevant document away in a safe. This was because of a memorandum which was circulated by an unknown Government agency to other Government agencies which stated that John and Yoko were to be kept under physical observance at all times because of possible political activities."

The subtle sense of looking forward to a possible new collaboration during this phase of reflection on his Beatle past was even apparent in public. During his salute to Lew Grade in a mid-April TV performance, Lennon's stage band wore surreal, Janus-like face masks on the back of their heads. In his final TV interview appearance on the Tom Snyder TV chat show on April 28, Lennon insisted that the group had been sending out subliminal messages over the years, reporting on their own state whilst ahead of their time in terms of musical expression. Having also argued the case for a musical universe operating on a vast cyclical basis, a hip, forward-looking Lennon was also seen espousing the virtues of reggae and disco in front of the American TV host.

Even in 1976, McCartney was keen to persist in his attempts to reconcile with Lennon. "He visits me every time he's in New York. I just happen to be the one in New York, and I love it. So whenever he's in town I see him. He comes over and we just sit around and get mildly drunk and reminisce." Paul visited John at his Dakota apartment in April, and the two men were sat together one evening in front of the TV when Lorne Michaels, the NBC *Saturday Night Live* show's producer, made an on-camera appearance in which he offered to pay The Beatles $3,000 to reunite on the show. This was in response to a promoter offering the band $50 million to get back together.

Despite the temptation to grab a cab and head over to the studio and appear, completely unannounced, the logistics of the task suddenly seemed too onerous, and they opted to remain in Lennon's apartment. "That was a period when Paul just kept turning up at our door with a guitar. I would let him in, but finally I said: 'Please call before you come over. It's not 1956, and turning up at the door isn't the same any more. You know, just give me a ring.'"

"I realised that I couldn't always ring him up to ask about business," something which McCartney regarded as his main priority at the time.

"So we did that, and I had a lot in common with him because we were having our babies, and I was into a similar sort of mode. So the air cleared, and I was able to speak to him and go and see him."

Lennon would later inform friend Bob Gruen in typically forthright fashion that he felt he had already worked with two of the greatest artists in the world. "He believed that Paul and Yoko were two of the greatest artists to work with, and he felt lucky to work with both of them. I was at the Dakota one time when Paul and Linda visited – it was a few weeks before Christmas in '75. We were sat in his bedroom and the doorbell rang. There was super security at the Dakota. Paul and Linda were singing Christmas carols. They were really happy to see each other. They seemed like old mates and they were on a very friendly basis. Hugging, patting each other on the back . . . like high school buddies who hadn't seen each other in a long time and really liked each other."

After making a film on the life of James Dean, Connolly and director David Puttnam had written to Lennon in 1976 about the production of a documentary on John's life in New York. "I'd been in touch with him. I wrote to him: 'Dear John, why don't we do this? Why don't we do a documentary on you?' And the reply came back. It was something about not having the energy. Something like: 'Not likely! I'm not about to do that!' He'd disappeared in '76, and I didn't know what he was doing. He hadn't emerged," Connolly observes. "What does he do all day? He liked journalism, he liked journalists. He was a good talker, and he could be very interesting. But he just dropped out. We'll never really know, I don't think."

So it was that for the remainder of the seventies Lennon withdrew from the music business, living on the other side of the Atlantic while relatively remote from his former colleagues. Having secured his green card he was able to travel and return to the US without hindrance and though he never returned to the UK, he visited Japan to meet Yoko's family, and in 1980 famously piloted a sloop to Bermuda.

Later that same year he made his final album, the Jack Douglas co-produced *Double Fantasy* at the Hit Factory in New York and it was evident that Lennon clearly never lost his love for his former group and colleagues. Connolly, a fan of 'Woman' and 'God Bless Our Love' amongst the final additions to Lennon's body of work, wasn't surprised to hear this. "He knew they [The Beatles years] were the best days of his life, and he knew it was his best work. He was nostalgic for the companionship."

Jim Keltner believes that the musically accommodating, commercially appealing *Double Fantasy* would have heralded a starting point for some incredible subsequent work during the early eighties. "They peaked. John got right where he wanted to be. Musically, that record would have been a spin-off for some amazing stuff to come, and that's what was so frustrating. It made sense and they were accepted."

Keltner's mood lifted when I recounted Douglas' story about John's enthusiasm for the group's music during the *Double Fantasy* sessions. "If they played a Beatle song, everyone had to stop, you *had* to stop. And then he'd get up close to the radio, and he would narrate the song for you," he told the *LENNONYC* team. "Which was when you realised, and which he was not afraid to admit, that he *loved* that band, and that it was *his* band, and that he absolutely loved it. He loved the guys, and he would talk about how much he loved them, and what an amazing experience that was."

Douglas, too, was happy to hear this. "Once The Beatles had broken up," Keltner reflects, "John was gone within nine, ten years. He was gone in 1980. 19-*80!*" An incredulous Keltner's voice relates a sobering fact that he still finds hard to fathom. "He was . . . almost only *beginning*. That's just astonishing to me. It's just unbelievable. He hadn't had a chance to get over anything, or make the changes in his life you normally do. John didn't stick around long enough – he was only in my life for around a decade.

"And probably at some point, he would have been willing to talk about stuff. I'm convinced, and I know without a shadow of a doubt, that if John had been here, we would have remained close friends, because we had so many things in common. It would have been a tremendous relationship with John to the end. He would be so fantastic."

Contrary to the conversations Lennon held in Keltner's company in the studio, Douglas admitted that John would often discuss McCartney during the *Double Fantasy* sessions. "I'm so pleased that John was more than willing to share stories about him and Paul," Keltner admits. "Sharing what it was like to be John Lennon. My wife always says: 'Can you imagine what John would be like now? I wonder what John would be doing?'"

By the turn of the decade, Douglas insisted that The Beatles' wound was close to being healed. He also revealed that Lennon, McCartney (and, it was hoped, Harrison) were scheduled to write material for a new Ringo album in 1981. Utilising some of the fresh compositions recorded during and after the *Double Fantasy* sessions, they were subsequently released as the posthumous *Milk And Honey*. However, Lennon's excitement about the project ("It's gonna be the boys! Get ready to do it – it's gonna be the boys!" he'd told Douglas) was soured by the lack of recognition for Lennon's impact on George's life in his recently-published autobiography, *I Me Mine*.

Douglas explained the exciting scenario to Michael Epstein. "The Beatles wound had almost healed, honest to God. It was very close to being healed. My understanding was that Paul was on board with John to do this Ringo record. According to John, that was set. He kept talking about it. They were gonna do the next album. It was going to be a Ringo album, and Paul and John were writing material for it. A lot of it John had already written, and *Milk And Honey* material was slated to be going to Ringo. He talks about which songs are for Richard Starkey - an album backed by The Beatles! I mean, c'mon, this is a blast!

"The only problem was that George wrote *I Me Mine*, and kind of left John out of it, as if he never existed. 'It's my band. I made his career,' he said, getting real angry if he talked about it. But I'm sure George had his reasons. George hadn't signed on for this thing yet, but John was pretty sure George wasn't going to let it go by if he found out they were gonna do Ringo's record. That was in the plans. Nothing to do with John's career, it was a piece of unfinished business that had to be done, *with love*. Because they all loved Ringo, they adored him and they'd do anything for him. How would you do it? You get your three buddies playing for him, and write the songs for you."

Where McCartney was concerned, Keltner agrees that Lennon bore no animosity towards his old partner. "I *know* he didn't. I knew him too well. John just needed time. What I would have loved would have been to see the four of them play. But if John had wanted to do almost anything, I think Ringo, Paul and George would have been along for the ride. If I'd been doing a project with George, and he'd said: 'I'm gonna have the others come in and do something,' that would have been heaven for me." "I think there was a cassette, it was something that John said, that read: '*For Paul*,'" recalls Connolly. "And he said: 'I'll give this to Paul, and see if he has any good ideas.' And there were songs which he had that he didn't finish before he died."

Shortly after Lennon's death, in 1981 Harrison's idol Carl Perkins played McCartney a song entitled 'My Old Friend' that he was sure had been a psychic gift from John during the making of McCartney's *Tug Of*

War LP. Perkins 'received' a song that summed up his warm feelings about the visit to Monserrat. An unusually strong song, Perkins had no need to even notate its melody or lyrics. When Carl sang the song for Paul and Linda, he came to the lines: *'if we never meet again this side of life, in a little while, over yonder, where there's peace and quiet my old friend, won't you think about me every now and then?'*

Tears streamed down Paul's face, and it helped him to connect with his grief over John's death. The last time Paul spoke to John, Lennon had urged Paul to "think of me every now and then, my old friend". McCartney would swiftly pen his own ode to his former partner, 'Here Today'. *'You were always there with a smile/I really loved you, and was glad you came along.'* Lennon was there, in this emotional song, once again. As Walter Everett wrote, 'Here Today' was one of McCartney's most inspired, personal and unaffected works, "a haunting tribute to the partnership which began in the fields behind St. Peters' Woolton Parish Church, Liverpool".

Lennon loved McCartney, and one wonders how much Paul realised this fact. Revealing the unabashed affection he had always retained for his partner, if anyone doubted the sincerity of McCartney's love for Lennon, then Paul's candid portrayal of their relationship can be heard in this letter-style song written to John with love. It would not be until Lennon's demo recordings of 'Free As A Bird' and 'Real Love' were released to McCartney by Ono in the early nineties that Paul fulfilled his ambition of collaborating on new (albeit posthumous) Lennon material with Harrison and Starr.

Harrison, of course, remained convinced that Lennon had not really died in a spiritual sense. But then his relationship with Lennon had often been rooted in the cosmic realm. They might have enjoyed little personal contact in the decade before Lennon's death, but in Harrison's eyes the bond could not be broken. Harrison had initially been angry that Lennon had been denied the opportunity to leave of his own accord. "John realised and understood that we are not just in the material world. He saw beyond death, that this life is just a little play that is going on. And he understood that. If you can't feel the spirit of some friend who's been that close, then what chance have you got to feel the spirit of Christ or whatever else you may be interested in? *'If your memory serves you well, we're going to meet again.'* I believe that. I should hope that he's in a good place. He had the understanding, though, that each soul reincarnates until it becomes completely pure, and that each soul finds its own level, designated by reactions to its actions in this and previous lives."

As far as Lennon's widow was concerned, there was still much to be revealed about Lennon's spirit and his true identity. "I mean, there are many mysteries and shaded corners in his beautiful persona that have not been revealed. Or shaded corners of his life that could be revealed at some point. I would say this much. When John made that Jesus Christ remark, the whole world thought it was very tacky and all that. Now the world is wiser and it can see that John wasn't particularly being disrespectful. In other words, many things are not being revealed yet, only because people are not yet ready for it. And I think when we all get wise, then we'll start to see what he was saying was right. I think there's a lot people are going to discover about John, about John's spirit. Not even just hidden things – it's right in their faces, and they can't recognise it. Things will have to unfold naturally, that is the best way – otherwise it's a waste of time. At the same time, all things will unfold one day: it's up to us how much wiser we get."

It's 1989, and May Pang meets the McCartneys at a private rehearsal for Paul's forthcoming world tour. Pang was pleased that, after many years of waiting, she finally had the opportunity of proving something important to Paul. "I said: 'I just want you to know that John really loved you,' and he said: 'Oh, yeah, sure. I knew that . . .' I'd wanted to [tell him] for ages," she insisted during a 1997 interview in New York, "but never had the chance."

"They loved each other," Linda affirmed of the Lennon-McCartney relationship years later. "They were friends, and carried on being friends. It was deeper than any of us will ever know."

Paul had been his partner during such a considerable and prodigious period that he might well have relished the chance to thank him for the love he gave people in his songs and The Beatles' music. Lennon loved him dearly, but was privately concerned that he didn't realise this. "There were a couple of opportunities to get back together, and I would have liked it," McCartney had claimed in 1984. "I liked working with John, and I certainly miss not having someone like that around."

Pang confirmed to Paul that she and John *were* going to travel down to see Paul and Linda in New Orleans whilst working on the *Venus And Mars* album. Pang also told Linda that John genuinely wanted to write with Paul again. Linda then urged Pang to disclose this news to Paul. "I said: 'Can't you tell him?' She said: 'No, I want it to be you.' Having beckoned Paul over she said: 'May wants to tell you something that John said to her.' I said to Paul: 'John really wanted to start writing with you again.' Paul looked at me and said: 'Oh yeah . . . that would be *great*.' He looked very pleased to hear that. I'm not sure if he thought I was just trying to make him feel good. I could tell by his tone of voice that he thought I was just being nice, polite. I mean, it was a long time . . . I could have said anything."

The following year Pang was invited, along with her husband, the legendary and one-time McCartney producer Tony Visconti, to Paul's Buddy Holly birthday party bash in New York. McCartney had some exciting news to share. "I went over to Linda, and she didn't recognise me. I said: 'It's May, remember John and May?' She [Linda] threw her arms around me and hugged me. She said: 'I've always wondered what happened to you. I always liked you so much!'" Linda had read Pang's book, *Loving John*, and said: "I know it's true what you wrote, I know what you've been going through. I support you, and I'm so glad you've married Tony."

Having burst through the door, McCartney rushed over to speak to Pang, who was in the midst of conversation with his wife. "Did she tell you?" he yelled ecstatically as he approached May. "I haven't told her yet," Linda replied. "Paul said: 'You know [Beatles' PR] Derek Taylor, how he always sells his memorabilia stuff?' And I said, 'Yes . . .?'" "'One of Derek's postcards from John fell into our hands,' McCartney said. 'John had written, "*Thinking of visiting the Macs down in New Orleans.*"'"

An avid letter writer and postcard scribe, as editor Hunter Davies' recent tome *The John Lennon Letters* makes clear, what he'd actually written (in typically punned fashion) in his letter to Taylor was '*possibly down to New Orleons* [sic] *to see the McCartknees.*' For Pang, who had no knowledge of the postcard's existence, it was similar to finding a deeply buried needle in a Louisiana haystack. For a disbelieving Paul, who'd harboured doubts about Pang's sincerity, it corroborated May's revelation the previous year.

Paul saw hand-written evidence of John's ambition to visit New Orleans for himself, proof that Lennon really had entertained thoughts of reviving arguably the greatest songwriting partnership of the century. "I don't think Paul ever talked about it, probably because he didn't realise at the time how close Lennon came to turning up," Peter Doggett maintains on the subject of a New Orleans collaboration. "We only know about Lennon's view of the idea from a letter to Derek Taylor and from May Pang's account in *Loving John* and her suggestions that Yoko put paid to the whole idea."

When the three remaining Beatles decided to meet each other again in 1993–94 to record Lennon's unreleased songs, Paul and Ringo's enthusiasm to record this material was balanced by Harrison, who was unsure about the viability of the idea. Having needed to be persuaded, he later realised their work focused people's minds on what they had sang of back in the sixties. The new music, including 'Free As A Bird', was a gift from John which seemed to say: 'Let's spread our wings and see who we really are.' There is so much that we can achieve, and there is so much that we are unaware of. A bird can fly and take wing, so why can't we?'

I asked Keltner to share a studio highlight or two from the incredible years he enjoyed with either former Beatle. "There were so many wonderful times spent in the studio with George, so many songs and so many magical musical moments. I remember many late nights spent listening to 'Stuck Inside A Cloud'." It's a song that regularly proves an emotional experience for Keltner, and is a song that's evocative of a special time and place.

"That's always been one of my favourite songs. It has a magical, mystical quality, and it's so English. That's one of his older ones that he used to play for me all the time. But that one, for me, does it to me. I don't know why. We would be sitting in the studio late at night, and I'd say: 'Hey, George, play ". . . Cloud' for me," and he would put it on and sing along with it. When I hear it now, I can almost smell the air surrounding the studio at Friar Park."

Keltner clearly feels blessed to have spent so much time with both John and George in his life for the best part of 30 years. "I treasure the fact that they were in my life, and my family and my kids got to know John and George intimately. When John died, George, Paul and Ringo lost their big brother. But they did what you always do, carry on with your loved one in your heart. But George was just an amazing guy. I was very fortunate to have both John and George in my life like that. I think that if John had lived, George would have had a different view on a lot of things. I think that's how strong John was in George's life.

"George has been gone a long time, and had he still been here after all

305

this time, there would have been a lot of changes." Over time, Harrison became something of a wonderful brother to Keltner. Jim and his wife Cynthia visited George shortly before his passing at a friend's beach house location where they spent the day together.

Having invited the Keltners to stay for dinner, George did something which intrigued his long-time friend. "He did the most extraordinary thing, later that night. Just before we left, he put on a Beatle tape. He played some old Beatle stuff which was very unusual for him. He was enjoying watching the film, as we all were. That was the last time that we saw him up and walking and talking, and he did actually seem okay."

Keltner never gave up hope, even four days before Harrison's passing. "When we left him that day, we were walking three feet off the ground as we got to the car," he recalled in a musician's magazine interview. "We had been talking and laughing with him a little bit, and he seemed to have rallied and had his strength, and it was just so wonderful. God, it was just fantastic: '*Hi, Jimmy*.' It was just such a great gift. That's what I'm holding onto."

Keltner was candid enough to admit his surprise at the eulogies which followed George's passing. Unsurprisingly, the drummer never considered Harrison (or Lennon) as icons in the classic sense of the word. "He was an extraordinary guy. To me he was just George, my beautiful friend, who I kind of took for granted over the years. He wasn't like most of your friends. I know it sounds trite: 'Well, he *was* a Beatle, so *of course* he was an extraordinary guy.' But it's so much more than that."

"George just had a way of handling everything so beautifully," Keltner told one interviewer when asked about Harrison's beliefs. "He was deep with his religion, with his spiritual side, and even though we don't share the same religion, I believe that God must be blessing him immensely right now. And he never changed, he never wavered. He was always talking about how great one of these days it's going to be to get out of these old bodies."

The Beatles' influence on their generation and on their musical contemporaries had been immense. "I had a great and deep love for George," said Art Garfunkel. "I loved him a lot. I was deeply saddened by his going."

"It just hurts so bad," Keltner confides about his friendship with Harrison. "I want to hear that beautiful, soft accent. Forget his singing, I mean, I used to just love to listen to him *talk*. And all the funny stories about him being the quiet Beatle – he was the most talkative person I know. He didn't stop talking. But the thing that was beautiful about George was that he always had something to say. I used to see people get their feelings hurt being around him."

Keltner's respect and sympathy for his former Beatle friends remain undiminished. "I felt so bad for Ringo when George died. He'd lost his two dear friends. You've seen that [Martin Scorsese's detailed biopic, *Living In The Material World*, in which Keltner appears] where he breaks up at the end. Ringo is a sweet, dear guy, and one of my closest, beautiful friends. He and Paul are in great shape and touring all over the world, making people happy just to be able to see them, let alone hear the music."

Starr and McCartney also appeared at the Harrison tribute *Concert For George* in 2002, alongside band leader Eric Clapton. "It was a very emotional night. People told me it was both powerful and intimate. Eric [Clapton] put together the band based upon people who were close to George and who had a history with him over the years."

This included the likes of Harrison's son, Dhani, Ravi and Anoushka Shankar, Tom Scott, Jim Horn, Billy Preston, Jeff Lynne, Joe Brown, Klaus Voormann, Gary Brooker, Jim Capaldi and Tom Petty amongst others. I asked Keltner if it was possible to encapsulate the time he spent with Lennon and Harrison, to convey its meaning to him as a fan turned colleague and friend.

"As clichéd as it sounds, it was like something that I *dreamt*," he insists. "It was not something that could ever have possibly happened to me. I can guarantee you that back then, it was a *very* heavy experience. I'm just very grateful that it did."

Having affectionately described George as his "baby brother" in his on-camera tribute in 2001, McCartney made a surprise return to Keltner's life on this special occasion. "At one of the rehearsals, I remember standing on the corner of the stage talking with someone, and I felt this hand on my shoulder, and I turned around and it was Paul. He gave me a big hug, and as he talked to me, I started crying. I just completely welled up. It had actually been 30 years since I'd spoken with him and been in his presence. His voice, that soft Liverpool voice, it just was too much. It just hit me so hard, that he was a brother, he was one of the four."

In 2008, Sir Paul revealed that he wanted to reunite with Ringo. "Yeah, I would love to [work with him]. We do things from time to time together, but it doesn't always come up." He confessed that getting his schedule to work with Starr's is the most difficult hurdle to overcome. "Sometimes he'll be on tour when I'm not," he said. "But we don't rule it out, it'd be great. He's a great drummer and we're used to each other.

"If John and George were still here, it's highly likely we would've had a Beatles reunion," Paul admitted on the release of Scorsese's documentary of George's life in the autumn of 2011. "I think we would've mellowed to the point where we would've said: 'Come on, let's do it.' The thing was, whenever we got together, no matter if we were arguing, we played great. We knew each other so well; we read each other. So if Ringo would speed up a little bit, we were like [fingers] in a glove . . . It would've been great," he stated.

McCartney would be spotted, almost 40 years on from his fruitful sessions in the Crescent City, riding a street tram in New Orleans in 2013, singing Beatle songs for astounded fellow passengers, before performing there in concert in October 2014. He remains happy to perform with Starkey again onstage, as their celebrated Grammy appearance earlier that year demonstrated.

But most importantly, McCartney admitted to seeking some form of approval for work-in-progress compositions for the *Memory Almost Full* and *New* albums from Lennon during spirited 'visits' from his former partner. These silent yet satisfying acts of songwriting communion with Lennon have always proved cathartic and reassuring for Paul. "'Would John have let me write that line or is it just too soppy?' Sometimes I just think, 'Too bad, it's my song . . .' But I'm *always* cross-checking with him."

ABOUT THE AUTHOR

RICHARD WHITE is the author of *Young Soul Rebels*, a biography of Dexy's Midnight Runners, published by Omnibus Press in 2005. He has also written books on the Stone Roses and Stevie Wonder. He lives in Northampton.